Beside N

'This story would be important, and emblematic of our time, even without the celebrity arts buzz that emanates from it, and the beautifully felt-out insights of one of Britain's best actors ... This is also a human, funny, nakedly direct memoir, beautifully written, warm and thoughtful about famous people – with lots of theatre anecdotes and insights – and family ... If you want to know what it means to use every grief and rejection in the service of your art; if you want a tender thoughtful optimistic insider-view of the British theatre scene of the last 25 years: read this.' *Financial Times*

'Different, better and more interesting than any other thespian memoirist.' *Literary Review*

'Few autobiographies are so self-questioning ... Sher's writing, frequently chatty, often moving, never loses its sincerity and dignity.' *Scotsman* (Read of the Week)

'Enthralling reading' *Spectator*

'The engrossing story of the leading actor's life and times, from his upbringing in South Africa to his climb to the top at the RSC. A witty, self-mocking, cleverly structured book.' *Hampstead and Highgate Express*

'Delightful, insightful, entertaining and illuminating' *Manchester Evening News*

BESIDE MYSELF

An Autobiography

Antony Sher

ARROW

Published by Arrow Books in 2002

3 5 7 9 10 8 6 4 2

First published in the United Kingdom in 2001 by Hutchinson

Arrow Books
The Random House Group Limited
20 Vauxhall Bridge Road, London SW1V 2SA

Random House Australia (Pty) Limited
20 Alfred Street, Milsons Point, Sydney
New South Wales 2061, Australia

Random House New Zealand Limited
18 Poland Road, Glenfield
Auckland 10, New Zealand

Random House (Pty) Limited
Endulini, 5a Jubilee Road,
Parktown 2193, South Africa

The Random House Group Limited Reg. No. 954009

www.randomhouse.co.uk

A CIP catalogue record for this book is available from the British Library

Papers used by Random House
are natural, recyclable products made from wood grown in
sustainable forests. The manufacturing processes conform to
the environmental regulations of the country of origin

Typeset in Goudy by MATS, Southend-on-Sea, Essex
Printed and bound in Great Britain by
Bookmarque Ltd, Croydon, Surrey

ISBN 0 09 941653 0

For my family:
My mother Margery, my late father Mannie,
My brothers Randall and Joel,
My sister Verne

CONTENTS

ILLUSTRATIONS

John, Paul, Ringo, George and Bert, Cloud Nine, and *Prayer for my Daughter* (John Haynes)

The History Man © BBC Enterprises

Goose-pimples (John Haynes)

Shylock in *The Merchant of Venice*, and *Singer* (Ivan Kyncl)

Holocaust Memorial, With Jacovas Bunka, In Plunge (Mark Douet)

Hello and Goodbye (Ivan Kyncl)

Alive and Kicking (Christine Parry © Film Four)

Training for *Tamburlaine* (Ivan Kyncl)

Tamburlaine and *Stanley* (Donald Cooper)

Greg Directing (Jonathan Docker-Drysdale)

Titus Andronicus (Henrietta Butler)

Cyrano de Bergerac (Zuleika Henry)

The Winter's Tale and *Macbeth* (Jonathan Dockar-Drysdale)

Knighted by the Queen (BCA Film)

All drawings and paintings by the author

Every effort has been made to seek copyright permission. The author and the publishers apologise for any inadvertent breach.

ACKNOWLEDGEMENTS

I would like to thank my excellent editor at Hutchinson, Paul Sidey, and the fine group of theatre photographers whose work appears on the photo insert pages: Henrietta Butler, Donald Cooper, Mark Douet, Jonathan Dockar-Drysdale, John Haynes, Zuleika Henry, and Ivan Kyncl.

PART I

....

Now

I

THE BOY

MY FIRST MEMORIES are of shit and love. In that order.

I'm aged about two in the first. It's night-time. I mess my bed. It fascinates me. I cup an especially shapely turd in my hands and start towards my parents room. My sister, Verne, aged five, intercepts me. She's horrified. The object in my hands instantly transforms itself. A moment ago it was marvellous – now it's foul. I have produced something foul. The shock of this never leaves me. It will recur again and again in my life: me bearing forth some seemingly splendid thing, only to bump into a critic.

I'm aged four-and-a-half in the second. I'm sure about that because, as a June baby, I've started kindergarten six months early. Another boy in the class is smaller than me, with soft brown eyes and hair. His openness and vulnerability draw me. His maleness too – I'm certain this is part of it. I'm a dark and unlovely shape, I sense this already, while he is completely beautiful. I fall in love. It's exactly like the adult experience, a drug. In his presence I feel my blood changing and an exquisite substance pumping round my veins. He fills my mind. I carry ecstatic images of him to sleep each night and wake with them each morning. Everything is joyful, everything. I remember us holding one another and wheeling about on the playground. Then something happens, I don't know what – it's to do with shame again – something's wrong, something's bad and we're separated. The moment of this is very clear. We're both getting into our parents' cars. My view is low down, only four-and-a-half years' growth above the

3

pavement. There he goes, climbing into the car. I have no further recollection of him. Not of him – though I'll certainly see his likeness again.

This is where I grew up, at number three, and where Mom still lives. She has fetched us from the airport. I lean my head against the car window, frowning, as she drives past the house to the hotel at the top of the road. I knew this would feel strange.

Because this visit is brief and we need some holiday time to ourselves, Greg and I aren't staying with Mom or Verne as we usually do, but have opted instead for the President Hotel. We have a suite on the fifth floor. Hurrying to the balcony, I find it has a bird's-eye view of Alexander Road.

The houses are big, square and double-storeyed, built in 1927. Coming up from Beach Road, the first three roofs – a condominium of flats – are a faded charcoal colour, then there's a silvery aluminium roof and then ours, a terracotta tile, quite a darkish red, clearly showing a white track of seagull droppings along the crest.

Montagu House. The Sher family home.

Mom has a cup of coffee with us in the hotel, then leaves. We're going to unpack before strolling down. I stand on the balcony watching her drive to the house. From within the car she presses a remote control and the security gates open. My gaze drifts to the house. All the blinds are drawn and the windows shut. Partly to keep out the heat, which Mom can't abide in her old age, partly to keep out intruders. Cape Town is becoming as dangerous as Joburg, the whites say. There were several bombs recently, while murder, rape and muggings are commonplace. A few months ago a black man tore a gold chain from round Mom's neck as she took her morning constitutional along the beach front. And a year or so before Dad died, he was attacked by two Coloured youths in town. They were after his wallet, he tried to resist, they ended up knocking him over and splitting his scalp on the pavement. Fourteen stitches but otherwise he got off lightly. Well – physically. The incident unsettled him deeply. He was a successful businessman, now retired, a family man, a loyal citizen, a pillar of the community, throughout his life respected by all his staff and servants, *die ou baas* (the old boss). What had gone wrong? It was as though South Africa itself, and not just two of its lawless children, had reached up and yanked him to the ground. He stopped going on walks, stopped going out much at all. He spent all day on the patio in front of the house, pacing around or sitting and sleeping; an old zoo animal yearning for the Africa it once knew. I can see this patio from the hotel balcony as Mom goes inside – or half see it. The security wall round the house is high and the foliage from her cherished garden grows tall. What with all this shade and the heavy sun awnings over its closed windows, the place has a hunched, secretive look.

I feel like a spy, perfectly positioned up here to observe that particular building. What clues can I pick up about my past life? As the week progresses it continues to disquiet and move me. I roll over in bed first thing in the morning and there it is. Like a waking dream. I did so much dreaming in that house down there; now it's like I've become a dream myself, suspended above real life, a dream or a ghost. The shadowy atmosphere of Montagu House adds to these sensations: it looks like a house where everyone has died, a house that's been shut up and sealed, a house I can no longer enter.

We moved there in 1959, when I was ten and known as Ant, which I deplored. I remember us all sitting on boxes and cases in the hallway that first evening – sunset and sea visible through the open door – eating sandwiches and drinking pop, surrounded by the smell of fresh paint and new carpets. I remember Mom commenting *yet again* on the lucky coincidence of this house's name – she was born and brought up in Montagu, a pretty spa town 120 miles north-east of Cape Town – it was surely a sign that we were meant to live here, and live happily. I remember feeling very safe. I was in a strange place, yes, but Mom and Dad were here too, and my siblings, Randall (sixteen), Verne (thirteen), and Joel (four), and our trusty cook, Katie, and our current maid, Elizabeth. I would be looked after. My meals would be provided, my cases would be unpacked, my bed would be made, I didn't have to do anything, make any decisions, explore this unfamiliar territory on my own. I wasn't to know it then, but the next time I would change addresses, going into the army after school, and to England after that, the experiences would be so alarming that I'd be left with a permanent fear of moving. Now all journeys unsettle me, even small ones like between the homes that Greg and I keep in London and Stratford. 'Is it the Wandering Jew in me?' I ask Greg solemnly.

'Maybe,' he answers. 'Or just your way of getting me to do all the packing.'

On that beautiful evening in 1959 I suppose it would've been our servants, Katie and Elizabeth, who hauled the cases upstairs and emptied the contents into drawers and cupboards. Supervised by Mom. Dad would've done nothing. He was probably pouring the second or third massive Scotch in the side room off the lounge, the room he was to claim as his den and bar. Maybe some of his drinking pals were round that night. These tended to be family, mostly uncles: Uncle Nicky and Uncle Arthur, Dad's brothers – both very gentle men, the first large and calm, the second short and nervy (shell-shock from the war) – or Uncle Jack, married to Mom's sister Rona: a charismatic man with large ears, big belly, a rolling walk, a twinkle in his eye.

At first I was in a big bedroom at the front of Montagu House, sharing with Joel. I remember standing at the window one day, soon after we moved in. The view was of the Queen's Hotel, a marvellous colonial establishment, all rolling gardens and shaded verandas (later knocked down to build the President, where we're currently staying), but what actually caught my eye that day was the sight of Dad hurrying along Alexander Road, heading up towards the roundabout, and Marlborough Mansions. His mother lived in the ground-floor flat. A huge East European woman with a faint moustache and the musty smell of old age, suddenly flapping her hands to alleviate her rheumatism, she terrified me. Dad was always popping up the road to see her, but there was something different today, something about his walk, his face. He didn't look like Dad at all, but young and lost. That evening, Mom explained to us that his mother had died. I'm afraid I was rather relieved.

A few years later the big bedroom was split down the middle with a hardboard partition. I was delighted to get the half with the wall safe, which I prized. The division had been created to allow Joel and myself some privacy. Shortly afterwards I managed, I don't know how, to get our Coloured garden boy, William, to give me foot and even bum massages. He stopped this after a bit and tried to explain why: 'It's not healthy, Master Ant.' I felt disappointed. Still pre-pubescent, I was genuinely innocent of the fact that these pleasurable sensations were connected to something called sex. William was Cape Coloured and I've always found his people very attractive, with their long, lean muscles, the dance to their walk, their elastic-band accents stretching and snapping at words.

I was about fifteen when I started masturbating – in the bed in my partitioned room. I clearly remember the first smell of sperm (*vaguely like some stuff Katie uses in the backyard, a kind of soap, or is it bleach?*) and an overwhelming sense of relief; I'd been a late developer physically. Now I became very proud of the manly features appearing on my small body. One afternoon I brazenly changed out of my swimming trunks in front of a window which looked on to the upstairs *stoep*, while Margaret – our new current maid – was ironing there. She gave a sly smile and touched her head, the tight black curls there, commenting on what was sprouting in my groin. I took this as a sign of encouragement and a few nights later went into her room – the 'maid's room' in the backyard – to show her my hard-on. Like William, she tried to find a way of explaining – '*Haai* no, this isn't OK, Master Ant!' I had made no clear plans for this particular hard-on – what I wanted her to do with it – and when she rejected me, I just assumed it was because she worked for us: she could get into trouble for initiating one of the young masters of the house. I knew nothing about the Immorality Act, forbidding sex across the race barrier.

I knew very little about the apartheid laws at all. I wasn't aware that blacks were forced to carry passes, and to live separately, in townships. (This didn't apply to Coloureds at first and when I was growing up their beloved District Six was still intact, in the middle of Cape Town.) Even though I was aged eleven in 1960, when the Sharpeville massacre occurred, I have no recollection of it. It wasn't just that the government was ferociously efficient at censorship; no, ours was the most apolitical of households. The whole family voted for the Nationalists, in an automatic, non-thinking, but quite affectionate way, calling them the Nats. Mishearing at first, I thought this was a real name, another uncle perhaps – Uncle Nat. Neither of my parents read books much. Dad liked his morning and evening newspapers, the *Cape Times* and the *Cape Argus*, and Mom favoured glossy magazines from abroad, about fashion or Hollywood. No word of criticism about apartheid ever made it into Montagu House and, as far as I could see, all of us – the masters and servants living there – were perfectly happy.

In time I would come to understand that apartheid had a damage effect on us, the whites, the fat cats, as well as its obvious victims, known then as 'non-whites'. You can't grow up in a crazy world – a world that judges people on the colour of their skin – without going a little crazy yourself and my family have an impressive record (not untypical among South African whites) of drink problems, drug abuse, eating disorders and other cases of friendly fire. But during the fifties and sixties we thought we were happy. No, that's putting it mildly – we thought we were in paradise. We'd made a pact with the devil for this paradise, but it was a tame one; it didn't call for any violence or cruelty on our part.

'This South African sunshine is nice and bright, hey?' Uncle Nat said to us. 'Just bask in it. Just close your eyes. Leave the rest to us.'

Whenever I talk about this, I hear myself sounding like the citizens of the towns of Dachau or Auschwitz – 'We didn't know, we didn't know!' In fact, I'm saying something worse – not that we didn't know, but that we didn't see. Robben Island was there, right there, clearly visible from the pretty white beaches of Sea Point, yet we didn't see it. We closed our eyes and basked. Prisoners were on that island because their skin was the wrong colour, and there we were, fooling around with our own, trying for darker and darker tones, in our pitch-black sunglasses, not *seeing*.

If I really think hard I can summon a vague sense that something was wrong, just on the corner of my vision. The drunkenness of the Coloureds, for example. A vicious, despairing kind of drunkenness, with women fighting and men urinating in the gutter – these sights glimpsed from our air-conditioned limousines as we cruised past District Six en route for the bioscopes and department stores in town. There wasn't a big black population in Cape Town, so their misery was even less apparent. But then one morning the *Cape Times* gave the inhabitants of Montagu House quite a fright, even the children. The paper felt duty bound to tell us about an evil plot, which had been uncovered and foiled by the police – just in time! Thousands of black people from the townships of Langa and Guguletu were planning to march on Cape Town and seize it. The newspaper published maps allegedly collected during the police raids, showing key points for the takeover of the city. One was at the top of our road, at the roundabout, just across from Marlborough Mansions: the Greek café on the corner, Tony's Café. This was to have been one of the headquarters of the black army.

I felt more puzzled than scared. For the first time I heard the grown-ups use the phrase 'They'll murder us in our beds', but I didn't understand it. Why should these non-whites feel so vengeful? And ungrateful. We treated them well, we the Sher family, we were good to our servants and to the staff at Cape Produce Export Company, Dad's firm which sold raw skins and hides overseas. Yes, the non-whites were an inferior form of life – Uncle Nat's State and Church taught us this – but why should this make them miserable? Were dogs and cats, horses and donkeys, all going around harbouring terrible grudges? All awaiting their chance to turn on us? (I read *Animal Farm* round about this time, and decided yes, they probably were.) Anyway, the *Cape Times* was very reassuring. It said that the wicked ringleaders of the plot, a few Commies, liberals and other low life *skollies*, had all been caught and imprisoned. Our heroic police force and our army were the mightiest in all Africa. Nothing of this kind could ever happen again.

The other major event that shook us in Montagu House during my youth has come to symbolise the surreal world of apartheid South Africa for me. Prime Minister Verwoerd's assassination in 1966. It was very dramatic. Shortly after 2 p.m. on Tuesday, 6 September, as the afternoon session got under way in the House of Assembly in Cape Town, one of the parliamentary messengers, Demitrios Tsafendas, crossed to Verwoerd, drew a long knife from under his jacket and stabbed him to death. (By now I'd read *Julius Caesar*, and again literature and life came crashing together.) I listened to Verwoerd's state funeral on the radio – Uncle Nat didn't permit TV till 1976, long after I'd gone – and was very taken with the eloquence and emotion of the broadcaster. This was historic. This was our Kennedy killing. Well . . . with a crucial difference, South African style. Both were enigmatic murder mysteries. But while the plot behind *The Dallas Gun* was endlessly subjected to public investigation and debate, our version, *A Dagger In Parliament*, became an eerily closed book.

Years later, when I got to know Helen Suzman, she told me about being in parliament that day – she was the only Progressive Party MP, the *only* official opposition to apartheid. After the stabbing was over, a goggle-eyed, finger-wagging P. W. Botha, later to be State President himself, charged across to her and yelled, 'It's you who did this – you liberals – now we'll get you!' Though wildly wrong in his accusation, Botha wasn't alone in assuming this to be a political act. Verwoerd was known as the Architect of Apartheid and his assassin was of mixed blood. This *must* be political. But no, our papers quickly assured us, paradise was safe, there was no plot, no unrest, *nothing political was going on*. Demitrios Tsafendas was simply a lone madman – a madman who claimed that a giant tapeworm lived in his guts, urging him to do the deed. Next we heard there'd be no trial; the judge at the hearing said he couldn't judge Tsafendas 'any more than I can judge a dog' – our beloved Prime Minister had been killed by a madman with a devilish case of indigestion, nothing more to it. Yet there'd be no cushy asylum for this particular madman. Oh no, no, he'd be locked in prison and the key thrown away. And that was it; the matter was closed as securely as the door to Tsafendas's cell. No trial, no evidence, no public examination of the facts, just a bizarre sentence. It was Kafkaesque (even down to the presence of the giant insect), yet nobody I knew found it strange. Until recently I didn't find it strange myself. Then I read Henk van Woerden's excellent biography of Tsafendas, A Mouthful of Glass, and was amazed. Here's the story of a man born to a Greek father and a black mother in Mozambique, savagely rejected by his own family, humiliated at boarding school in the Transvaal, kicked from country to country like a piece of junk, now a sailor, touring the world on the weirdest of odysseys, searching, searching for home, the ultimate displaced person and all because he's a baster, a half-breed. This same man ends up killing the Architect of Apartheid. And the act isn't political? Naturally the government preferred this interpretation and had the perfect excuse. The man was mad. But are we born mad or do we have madness thrust upon us? What about national madness, state madness? These were not questions our betters wanted us to ask. Otherwise we might have scrutinised the two men fastened over that dagger – a victim of racism and its high priest – and said to ourselves, 'Well there's clearly a lunatic here but which one is it?'

In 1995, when I was researching my novel Cheap Lives, set on Pretoria's Death Row, I was helped by Andries Nel of LHR (Lawyers for Human Rights) and he revealed a surprising twist to the story. The prison where they incarcerated Tsafendas was Pretoria Maximum Security and the section was in fact Death Row. Unable to hang him, Uncle Nat had devised the most fiendish punishment imaginable: life on Death Row. In a cell directly under the gallows, so that he could listen to the machinery and noises of death for the rest of his days. Since no one else was visiting him, members of LHR did, and were shocked by his condition. The warders regularly pissed in his food. A man living in hell, Tsafendas had found only one way of defending himself: he'd gone deaf. That way at least he wouldn't hear the gallows any more. Finally, after the fall of apartheid, someone found the key to his cell and the old man was transferred to Sterkfontein psychiatric hospital, where he remained till his death in 1999.

By the time of Verwoerd's assasination in '66, I'd changed bedrooms in Montagu House. Randall had married and left home, so I moved into his room at the back of the house. This was a smaller, darker room – the walls were painted a gloomy charcoal colour – suiting the new phase I'd plunged into. The journey from childhood to adolescence had been across an invisible bridge, yet one built of concrete; I picture the toll gate being in a safe, sunny, golden land (the fifties) and the exit in a weird and unstable one (the sixties); then it turns to air again, so I can never go back.

Thump thump . . . a tennis ball hitting the dark walls . . . *thump thump* . . the family complain, but it's my way of cramming for exams, pacing around, throwing the ball . . . *thump thump*.

I'm not alone in the room. I have a constant companion: my dog, Tickey. She'd been found as a stray – a ratty little black mongrel, very anxious, probably beaten a lot. Despite her new life of luxury in Montagu House, she's still prone to fits of shivering and panting. Any loud bang will induce these and she becomes quite inconsolable. I love her. She's runtish, dark, ugly, scared – she's me in animal form.

I don't fit in. I don't fit in at Sea Point Boys' High, where the general obsession is sport while mine is art. I don't fit into South Africa, for ditto reason and I don't fit into the world. My growing instincts are all towards my own sex and surely no one else in the world is as sick. I must be from another planet.

My parents had started subscribing to *Life* magazine. In one edition there was an article on a flood somewhere in the Far East. A lean young man was pictured struggling out of the water, just wearing white underpants, wet through. I carried this magazine into my darkly walled bedroom, put the usual sign on the door – *Tape recorder on*, DO NOT ENTER!!! – and fell to, hunched over the image of this screaming, half-drowned man. 'Ugghh,' I groaned as I finished – how disgusting I was.

Thump thump went the tennis ball . . . *thump thump* went my fist . . . *thump thump* went adolescence.

Today Cape Town is one of the gay capitals of the world – a fact I still find hard to believe. On the first evening of this trip in January 2000, Greg and I visit Howard Sacks. He lives in one of the mansions halfway up the mountain; millionaires' mansions, incredible modern palaces clinging to the flanks of Lion's Head. From Howard's sundeck you get a vast view of the Atlantic Ocean and beach-front suburbs: the whole of Bantry Bay and Sea Point, including Alexander Road and, yes, you can just make it out, the seagull-stained terracotta roof of Montagu House. If before I felt I was hovering above my old home like some dream figure – bird, ghost or spy – now I'm in complete fantasy land. Life at Howard's is like a Hollywood movie about Hollywood, except all the gorgeous bronzed bodies are male. Quite apart from Howard's partner, Chris, or 'Cuddles', a handsome Afrikaner giant, there seems to be an endless procession of pin-up guys in swimming costumes wandering on to the deck. Some are neighbours, some are visitors from abroad, some are youths who came to one of Howard's famous parties and never went away. Howard is very generous; born in Joburg, a trim, dashing figure in very black sunglasses: a gentleman playboy, elegant, modest, self-satirising. When one of this evening's guests complains about the wind in his garden, Howard immediately slips into expat tones: 'We can't even keep our sun umbrellas down, chaps – life is certainly hell here in darkest Africa.'

The talk is of all Cape Town's gay spots. I listen, shaking my head. Can this really be the place I grew up in?

They discuss the recent bomb in a gay club – it killed several people. There was also a bomb in a (straight) pizza bar in Camps Bay. The campaign seems designed to cripple the soaring tourist industry of the New South Africa and was relatively successful: although Cape Town was set to be one of the main millennium holiday spots, the hotels here were only half full. No one has claimed responsibilty. Possible suspects are either PAGAD, the bizarre organisation which began as vigilantes and turned into a terrorist group, or else some right-wing force, possibly in the police.

To the whites on Howard's sundeck, the New South Africa is as dangerous and crazy a place as the Old one was during the last two decades of apartheid. Violence is constantly in the air, making quite fantastical shapes. Someone tells us about a new security device that's being tested to combat the muggings at traffic lights: you press a button in your car and flames shoot from the door, incinerating your attacker.

'How's *Macbeth*?' Howard suddenly asks. A passionate theatre lover and former trustee of Joburg's famous Market Theatre, Howard was very supportive when Greg and I did *Titus Andronicus* there in 1995: our first collaboration as director–actor. *Macbeth* is our fourth.

Greg answers: 'Yes, it's going very well, can't get a ticket.' Turning to me for support, he adds, 'I think it's regarded as a bit of a hit, isn't it?' I nod in agreement, slowly, feeling dazed.

Macbeth?

I'm currently playing Macbeth.

In England, in Stratford, for the Royal Shakespeare Company.

I'm an actor, a classical actor, in British establishment theatre.

I met the Queen for the first time recently, at Prince Charles's fiftieth birthday bash at Buckingham Palace. I was invited because he's President of the RSC. Its Chairman, Sir Geoffrey Cass, introduced me to HM as 'one of our leading actors, ma'am'. She frowned – she didn't recognise me, so how could I deserve Sir Geoffrey's evaluation? – and paused for what seemed like a very long time, before finally saying, 'Oh, are you?'

I felt like replying, 'No, of course not, Your Majesty, you've seen through me and I give up – I'm just a little gay Yid from somewhere called Sea Point on the other side of the world – I shouldn't be here. I don't know why I am; I'm a trespasser, I'm an impostor, I'm . . . well, as Sir Geoffrey said, I'm an *actor*.'

3

ESTHER AND MAC

ESTHER HAS DIED.

The timing of this trip is really very odd. As well as Mom's birthday and Dad's funeral, I'm arriving in Cape Town just three days after Esther's death.

We heard about it as soon as it happened – Mom phoned us in Stratford – but it didn't really hit me till I saw it in print last night, in the complimentary edition of the *Cape Argus* they gave us on South African Airways. As I found the page with death listings, my eyes filled. There was a whole column: Caplan . . . Caplan . . . Caplan. One of the tributes was mine: *Esther, a remarkable teacher – to whom I owe my career.*

Esther Caplan was known as Auntie Esther to all her pupils, though I had a special claim to this name, for my brother Randall had married her daughter Yvette. Esther was officially a teacher of Elocution. This word was more respectable than Acting and more comprehensible to any parents sending their little darlings for tutelage. To learn to speak nicely made sense; to learn to act made none. Why would anyone in Sea Point become an actor? There was CAPAB, which did occasional shows at the Hofmeyr, and there was Maynardville, which did an annual Shakespeare in its leafy open-air auditorium, but there was little other theatre, no film industry whatsover and television didn't yet exist. There was some radio work, yes. In other words employment for about five and a half actors in Cape Town; not a career worth considering for the wealthy residents of Sea Point.

It certainly wasn't a career for *me*.

This had been made blindingly clear during my youth. I can date the moment precisely: June 1962. When I turned thirteen. And had my bar mitzvah.

God knows I don't want to sound racist, but I think there's a slightly cruel streak in the Jewish religion – in a bracing, Old Testament kind of way. I'm not even going to talk about circumcision, but bar mitzvahs – bar mitzvahs! – imagine the minds that cooked up this as an initiation test: our boys will *sing* their way into manhood.

I'm tone-deaf, seriously tone-deaf. During my theatre career I've been surprised how often songs crop up in straight plays. And each time the musical director has said to me, 'There's no such thing as tone-deaf – *I'll* teach you to sing!' And then a few weeks later, usually just after the dress rehearsal, they say, 'Perhaps you were right – would you mind terribly if we cut your number?'

So when, aged twelve, I commenced a year's training for my bar mitzvah, which included learning to sing a portion of the Torah, I found myself enduring one of the worst experiences of my childhood. You had to practise singing in front of a class of other boys. They clasped their hands over their ears or mimed fainting with pain as my thin, shivery voice slid around in the air, hopelessly seeking and missing note after note. These torture sessions were conducted by the short, heavy, ginger-haired figure of Mr Bitnun: one of those men who have never been children themselves, but always dead-eyed, hunched behind a desk, sour with boredom and impatience.

On the weekend before my bar mitzvah this squat and gloomy toad visited Montagu House. He had bad news for my parents. There was no way I could sing my portion next Saturday morning. He'd tried to teach me – God knows he'd tried – but it was impossible. I'd have to *speak* the portion. This was virtually unheard of, reserved only for the most disabled of boys. I remember the meeting taking place on the downstairs *stoep*. I was sitting, the three grown-ups standing, rather formally. Dad went inside – to pour himself a massive Scotch – while Mom dealt with it. Taking a deep breath, calming herself, she told Bitnun a story which I'd often heard her tell people before, and which always made me cringe – (she still tells it, I still cringe): 'When Antony was born he had a cowl round his head, a thin membrane. You might know what that means, Mr Bitnun, I presume there's some reference in the Bible. Our doctor – Jack Prisman – he came running over to me. He said, "Margery, you've just given birth to a great man." So. D'you see what I'm saying?'

Bitnun frowned. He was used to the mothers of Sea Point being ambitious for their son's bar mitzvah, wanting it to be the best *ever*, but this woman was moving on to quite another sphere – she was taking off into orbit.

Mom continued, her tone still deadly calm: 'What I'm saying, Mr Bitnun, is that there's no way that Antony will speak the portion next Saturday. He will sing, Mr Bitnun, he *will* sing!'

Bitnun was not a man to be easily frightened – you have to be more awake to be frightened – and proceeded to fight his case, explaining in ever grislier detail what it was like to hear me sing.

The synagogue will fall down, I decided as I listened to him, my shivery little voice will bring down the whole building like the walls of Jericho.

I sat there, wide-eyed, pygmy-sized, as these towering giant forces, the Jewish Mother and the Bar mitzvah Teacher, slugged it out between them.

She won, of course. No contest, really. Next Saturday morning I *would* sing.

During the week, my body came to my rescue. I developed flu, severe flu. Jack Prisman – the man who presided at my birth, playing both doctor and soothsayer – said he'd never known flu like this. On the big day I managed to stagger on to the *bima* and croak my way through the service. Everyone said I did very well, considering.

That night, as I went to sleep, I made a promise. Never again would I stand up in front of people and open my mouth.

There was no need to. My talent lay elsewhere.

Since the age of four, shortly after my tragic love affair in kindergarten, perhaps because of it, I've been proficient at drawing. Alone for hours, lying on my tummy on the floors of my various bedrooms – in our Marais Road home and then Montagu House – drawing faces, bodies, people; it's always people. I can't do landscapes. Which is strange because I love them, and enjoy describing them in travel writing and fiction – yet can't put them on to sketch pad or canvas. It's people that obsess me. And from my earliest scribbles, they are people in bizarre or dramatic situations. ('Oh,

Ant, why are your pictures so *morbid*?' aunts and uncles would ask long before I understood the word.) My great sources of inspiration were *Mad* magazine – especially the movie caricaturist, Mort Drucker – and Michelangelo. I copied the latter shamelessly. When my drawing of *The Deluge* was printed on our Rosh Hashana card in 1963, I experienced a brief surge of fame and liked it very much. At school, too, my drawing skills helped compensate for my inadequacy elsewhere, winning me prizes and praise. Eventually it was to secure an even greater reward: exemption from PT.

I'd tried the sporting life – as a short-distance sprinter and rugby wing – but it wasn't for me. I was very short for my age and slight of build. Aged thirteen I started wearing specs. Aged fourteen there was *that* incident in the school showers . . . !

It's all Leon Dreyfuss's fault. I've told this to various therapists over the years, dubbing it the Dreyfuss Affair.

We'd just done PT. We were in the showers. Leon Dreyfuss arrived next to me. He took one look and said, 'My little brother's is bigger than that.'

It was like an earthquake – the shock wave that passed through me and my young life. A moment earlier I was innocent – our family word for penis was 'birdie', a sweet little thing – I was unselfconscious; I was aware of being short of stature, short little Ant, nothing worse than that. Now I was a freak.

Now I could never shower next to Leon Dreyfuss or any of the other boys again. Which meant never doing PT again. But how on earth would I manage that? The PT instructor was Basie. The Afrikaans word '*baas*' means boss, and '*basie*' is the diminutive. Meant ironically in this particular case. Basie was a six-foot-six, broken-nosed, brick shithouse of a man crammed into white shirt and shorts, their buttons popping and seams ripping as he moved. He personified the South African male for me, a sort of caveman. Not a creature to beg mercy from. Not a teacher you go to and say, 'Sir, apparently my genitals are developing a bit slower than Leon Dreyfuss's little brother. Could I be excused PT till they've caught up?'

Perhaps Mac could come to the rescue.

Mac – John McCabe – a hefty, bushy-eyed man, quite jokey-aggressive, but far less intimidating than the rest of the staff. For three reasons: 1. He was a Scot – hence British not South African; 2. He was the art master at Sea Point Boys' High, hence art not sport; 3. He liked me.

From the day I arrived in his class I was singled out as a favoured pupil and I basked in the spotlight. Here at last I had the upper hand. The other boys – the ones who excelled at rugby and whose little brothers were hung like horses – they felt uncomfortable in art class. They couldn't draw or even do lettering (Mac was teaching commercial art for the same reason that Esther taught elocution rather than acting – no one in Sea Point was going to become an oil painter) and they were easily unnerved by Mac's strange Scottish humour – 'Och, lad, yer Pepsi Cola poster's nae gonna sell so much as the Pep!' Meanwhile I, the sensitive one, could do no wrong: 'Dinnae bother with this poster crap, Sher, you just draw figures, faces, whatever yer fancy, I just want you to draw, draw, draw.'

There was encouragement and affection coming from Mac, which I hadn't known from any other teacher. They tended to be in the Bitnun mould: cold-eyed men sleepwalking through their jobs. I put this down to the fact that Mac was blessed with a British soul, steeped in tradition and culture and all things wise. Actually, in retrospect, I suspect he was probably as conservative as most South Africans. I remember him reporting on a visit home to Scotland in the sixties and his revulsion at seeing men with long hair. 'From behind you couldnae tell who was bloody who!' On a similar theme, he sat me down after my *Deluge* picture was finished and pointed – with long, horny, paint-stained fingernails – to the semi-naked figures swarming on to islands in the flood: 'No, no, Sher, you've gone and put a man's chest on that woman. Your male and female anatomy is a complete bloody shambles, lad. Can you not inform yer precocious wee fingers that the lines of the female need to be rounded, while the male's are squared-off?' I wanted to mention that my hero Michelangelo observed no such rule, but this would've been impertinent, so I promised to rectify the problem in future.

I've never done any teaching myself, so I don't fully understand the investment made in a cherished pupil, but during high school I became aware that Mac was becoming more and more ambitious for me. For the first time I heard the phrase, 'training overseas'. My parents were talking about it, too. (When I say my parents I really only mean Mom; Dad was either at work, or in his den-bar with the uncles.) Art school in Italy was mentioned. Why Italy? Michelangelo, I suppose. How would I understand my tutors? It wasn't important. Montagu House was a place of dreams.

'CAPE BOY OF 14 IS WONDER ARTIST!' shrieked a newspaper headline.

Together with two other boys, I held an exhibition in an unoccupied shop on Sea Point Main Road and actually sold some pictures ('A watercolour went for 15/6d!' I boast in my 1963 diary). At the annual school art exhibition I was the star. Oh, I liked that.

So, after the horrifying Dreyfuss Affair, I approached Mac with a carefully rehearsed speech: 'Sir, the big figure compositions take so long – isn't there some way I could do extra art classes, sir? Like during PT, say. I'm not good at it, never will be "sporty". There isn't some way you could have a word with Basie, sir – is there?'

And that was it. Permanent exemption from PT. Never again would I have to strip naked and go under the showers with others of my sex. Not until after school, anyway – in the army, by which time it was starting to carry a hint of painful pleasure, and then in the furtive gay saunas of seventies London, when it turned into a positive addiction. For now I was safe, saved by art.

But . . .

My shyness. It wasn't just over my slow-developing genitals. It was everything. I had been born in the wrong country, possibly on the wrong planet. I was happiest lying on my bedroom floor, devising big, epic pencil drawings of teeming nude figures fleeing some cataclysmic event. *The Deluge* was followed by *The Four Horsemen of the Apocalypse*; the men now baring the chiselled chest of Gordon Scott, currently Tarzan at the Saturday-afternoon bioscope, and the women adorned with the voluptuously rounded boobs of Diana Dors.

I've always been a loner, but with one crucial factor: there has to be someone else at my side. I'm Geminian and I must have my twin. In adult life my two major partners have in fact been real twins – first Jim then Greg – but even in childhood and youth, I sought and found soulmates for a series of all-consuming friendships. One would have to finish before the other could begin. I never had friends, only *a* friend. During the crossing of that strange bridge from childhood to adolescence my constant companion was Cecil Bloch. Short, plumpish, very brainy, a bright-eyed hamster of a boy, Cecil shared an interest in drawing and painting – the art exhibition in the Sea Point shop featured his work too – and it gradually developed into a fascination with theatrical make-up. This was inspired by a book in the school library about Alec Guinness. (God knows how it got there, on shelves heaving with burly, thick-backed tomes in praise of rugby scrums and Voortrekker wars.) It showed step-by-step photos of the actor's transformations into Fagin, the family of roles in *Kind Hearts and Coronets* and so on. Cecil and I set up what we called the Stroud Make-up Studio (named after the hero of *The Birdman of Alcatraz*, a film which fascinated us with its story of mental escape from your physical surrounds) and we created elaborate putty-and-greasepaint disguises on one another's faces, photographing the results: I still have snaps of myself as An Old Man, an Arab, Genghis Khan and others. Then some tiff occurred, I can't remember what, but our make-up sticks were solemnly divided and I found a new best friend. Tony Fagin.

Our partnership was much more intense and inward-looking; even our names, Ant and Tony, fitted together to make one. At break time we were to be seen pacing round the playground, hands behind backs, two bespectacled figures, one tall, the other not, earnestly debating themes like 'Life and Literature' or 'The Art of the Motion Picture'. We dubbed ourselves 'geniuses'. We didn't know what we were geniuses at, but, never mind, we'd find something. The other boys laughed at us and we despised them. In our last school year we were both made prefects. One of the teachers mentioned there'd been some hesitation about my nomination, with several of the staff wondering if I'd have enough authority to control the mob. When I heard this, I compensated wildly and became a horrid little Hitler, screeching 'Silence!' across the quad or sentencing people to DT without mercy. Of course, public mockery of Tony and me became more discreet, now, and the cries of *moffies* and bunnies somewhat quieter. (Surprisingly cute words these, gentler than queer or cocksucker.) Anyway, the boys were quite wrong about the nature of our friendship – sex was a completely taboo subject.

There was Tickey too. Constantly at my side.

And Mom. In keeping with my new loftiness I retitled her Mater, abbreviated to Mate. 'Can we go to the Chinese Restaurant in Mouille Point again, Mate, just the two of us – can we?' Boy, was I in a classic relationship there.

But Mate was getting worried about me. Whether alone in my room, playing with my tape recorder (!), or going on long walks with Tony Fagin and Tickey, I was becoming more and more withdrawn. Something had to be done. A couple of years earlier I'd taken some classes with my older cousin, Audrey Gootman, teacher of drama at Herzlia School, and these served, briefly, to prise me out of my shell. Maybe something like this would help again . . .

And so to Auntie Esther and Elocution.

We actually did some of it at first – elocution – trying to iron out those ugly South African vowels, and I remember her encouraging me to say *ektewelly* instead of *akchilly*. But we quickly moved on to her main passion. Drama.

Esther had been an actress herself, during her youth in Joburg, and even worked with the most famous Jewish South African actor there's ever been, Solly Cohen (later known as Sid James, the lovable Cockney of *Carry On* fame), but now she was a teacher: this had become her Great Role. She was an outrageously theatrical figure, perhaps a type you'd only find in the colonies. She was Sybil Thorndike with a touch of Ethel Merman thrown in. Tall, proud, big-bosomed, with a crash helmet of lacquered blond hair, skin darkly tanned and quite leathery, splashed with turquoise eyeshadow and bright-pink lipstick. She didn't talk, she boomed and trilled. She didn't walk, she strode. She didn't gesture, she carved the air – thumb arched, forefinger splayed from the rest. Ballet dancers use their hands like this to compensate for not being allowed to speak. Esther was sometimes lost for words too, but only after emptying the dictionary: 'Oh, my darling, that monologue was so outstandingly, brilliantly marvellous that . . . it was so superbly, fantastically, unbelievably amazing that . . . oh, my darling, I *ektewelly* don't know what to say!'

She called everyone 'my darling' – everyone, family, pupils, servants. She was the warmest of warm springs; she bubbled, she gushed, she overflowed.

Given her style, the surprising thing is that she was fascinated by modern drama. By improvisation, by the Method School in New York, by the new plays coming from England by Osborne, Pinter and Wesker. So my first lessons in acting were not what one might expect from a grande dame elocution teacher in some former corner of the empire – not in Rattigan, Coward or even Shakespeare – but something altogether more contemporary.

I quickly developed an appetite for my weekly visit to Auntie Esther's studio: a bare room above some Main Road shops. The bar mitzvah fright was forgotten. That was about singing – I couldn't sing, full stop – this was about something more mysterious and attractive. Disguise. I'd briefly tasted its joys while encased in the putty-and-greasepaint masks devised with Cecil Bloch, but this went a lot further and deeper. I ceased to be little Ant, hopeless at sport, mocked in the showers. Instead I became anyone I wanted to be.

At first the work was very private – just me and Auntie Esther – but I soon grew greedy for the next phase: a public audience.

Every year there was a local Eisteddfod in Cape Town's City Hall. Along with Esther's other pupils – Tony Fagin now among them – I entered several categories, Monologues, Duologues, and my favourite, Improvisation. You'd be given a subject, five minutes to think about it and then you were on. I used to cheat. I'd prepare situations, speeches and characters, usually based on favourite film performances – Oskar Werner in *Ship of Fools*, Harry Andrews in *The Hill* – and somehow adapt these to whatever subject I'd been landed with. No one seemed particularly fazed by the arrival of world-weary Viennese doctor or sadistic British RSM into a scene entitled 'A quarrel on Clifton Beach' and I did well; I won prizes. Not top prizes. I was not as good a child actor as I was a child artist, but from my point of view acting was gaining on art. It was one thing to hide away in a bedroom, devising epic images of human catastrophe (I was currently doing *The Holocaust Drawings*), but acting offered an amazing new alternative – you could hide away in public! Later I would have to spend years unlearning this notion – acting isn't about hiding, it's the exact opposite – but for now the difference between the two hideaways, art and acting, thrilled me. There you were, completely guarded and safe – your performance as protective a capsule as four bedroom walls – and yet your refuge was somehow crowded with people, and clamorous with the noise of celebration. You heard clapping and cheers – unlike an art exhibition where people drift past your pictures silently – and you heard laughter. Warm laughter.

In my penultimate year at school the English teacher, Quinn, mounted a production of the Whitehall farce *Simple Spymen*. Tony Fagin and I got the two leads, me in the Brian Rix role, the dupe, the clown. The gales of laughter that night were overwhelming; a storm of approval from the same people who'd scoffed at us in the playground. I was hooked.

The drug of laughter, the megalomaniac thrill of the cheering crowd . . .

As I hear the tinny echo of cliché drift into the story, it strikes me that I'm not being altogether fair to myself. The attraction in acting is more deep-seated. I recall one late afternoon, finishing a game of Cowboys and Indians in the garden of the old house in Marais Road – me aged about ten or eleven – and my sister Verne unwittingly playing the critic again. She said, 'You're going to have to stop this soon, y'know, it's puerile.' I had no idea what the second half of her statement meant, but the first was unequivocal. *You're going to have to stop this soon.* I remember staring at the churned black soil under a hedge where I'd been hiding and thinking how beautiful that place looked – a dark and dreamy place of make-believe – and how I didn't want to leave it. Ever. Was there really no way to cheat fate: this inevitable business of growing up, of becoming sensible, of stepping politely on the earth instead of rolling in it? Was there no way of playing on?

Well, yes, there was, I discovered during the performance of *Simple Spymen*; yes, there were people – adult people – who did this for a living.

These thoughts happened to coincide with the irresistible rise of a rival in art class. A boy called Bishop. At the end of Standard Nine he won the art prize. And at that year's school exhibition he sold more pictures than me. Aged sixteen, I was a has-been.

I broke the news to my parents (i.e. Mate) first. 'Maybe I should go to drama school in London, not art school in Italy.' Mate was immediately supportive. I'd been born with a cowl over my head, Dr Prisman had made his prophecy; whichever direction I took I would fulfil my destiny.

Although I still don't remember Dad being part of any decision making, the rest of the family all chipped in – my sister, my brothers, the uncles, the aunts, the host of cousins, the whole extended Jewish kaboodle; our servants, too; probably even Tickey – they all had something to say on the subject and it tended to be the same thing: '*Drama school*? But Ant did that marvellous Rosh Hashana card, with all those naked people drowning. Ant's acting is, with all respect, OK, but his artwork – that's damn fantastic, man. Ant can't go to *drama school*!'

Mac minced his words even less when he heard. The crude, rough side of his character, the side which the other boys feared, the side I'd always been safe from, this was unleashed. He chuckled as he spoke: 'But actors are sissies, Sher, actors are stupid, their craft is interpretative, not creative, it's second-rate. No, no, Sher, you're just making one great big bloody balls-up of a mistake!'

When it became apparent that I really meant it he stopped chuckling.

He stopped talking to me altogether. For the last few months of art classes I ceased to exist. If he looked in my direction, his gaze skimmed the top of my head. He gave me an A in my Matric art exam (my only A; my aggregate was C), but the art prize went to Bishop again. On the day I left Sea Point Boys' High I went up to the art room – a big, long sunny room at the back of the school – to say goodbye to him. He wasn't there. I went to the staff room. Someone said he'd gone home early.

I felt frightened. He might be right. This could be a mistake, a great big bloody balls-up of a mistake.

Meanwhile Esther swelled her great bosom, gestured with balletic poise and boomed assurances: 'You're going to make it, my darling, I know you will, I promise you will. And in England, in London – the very heart of world theatre! Oh, it's so incredibly, marvellously, fantastically exciting that . . . oh, my darling, I *ektewelly* don't what to say!'

We started making enquiries about London drama schools and working on audition speeches.

But first there was a minor hurdle to overcome.

The South African army.

4

RIFLEMAN NO. 65833329

'IF BLACKS DON'T exist we just have to invent them.'
This was one of the sayings in the SADF – South African Defence Force – an all-white affair back in 1967, when I was conscripted for nine months' training. The first three months – Basic Training – was at Oudtshoorn, a flat, dry town in the Cape Province, famous for its ostrich feather trade, and the remaining time was in Walvis Bay, then part of South West Africa, now Namibia.

Walvis is surrounded by the Namib Desert: vast orange dunes with a shading of black on the rims of the deep craters. The small port is a desolate place, a sandy, salty, rusty place. As I think of it there's a feeling of grit between my teeth and under my eyelids, a sense of tiny grains in my food and in the fabric of my bath towel. When the east wind blew the Namib moved into town. At other times mist drifted in from the ocean and then all the edges blurred; you couldn't tell what was sky, what was sea, what was sand. The locals said: 'When the Good Lord made Walvis He was so ashamed He's been trying to cover it up ever since.' It was a place of fish factories, Lutheran churches and a large South African military base.

A crucial strategic base. As the sunny fifties turned into the weird sixties, Uncle Nat grew increasingly paranoid. The rest of Africa was perched ominously on his shoulders, a great ungainly weight of Commies and kaffirs. But with Walvis he held a vital port on the western coast of the Dark Continent and if the worst ever happened he'd be ready; if push came to shove, he'd certainly be able to shove. He had the strongest army in Africa.

And then I went into it.

I wasn't built for army life: short, weedy, bespectacled, spoilt, artistic and, although I didn't fully know it yet, gay. From the very start the army bore a close resemblence to my worst nightmare. At the medical inspection they made you strip naked, then they grabbed your balls and told you to cough. This was ostensibly to check for hernias, but I knew what was really going on. This was a test of my manhood that made the Dreyfuss Affair look like a rave review. 'Let's see the balls on you, *boykie*, let's see 'em and feel 'em, let's see if you've got what it takes to be a big, boozing, rutting, rugger-mad South African MALE!'

I didn't stand a chance. Right from the day I reported to the Castle in Cape Town and was herded on to a troop train, and throughout the three months in Oudtshoorn, the endless drill and PT, barked and snarled at by NCOs who had clearly been specially bred for the job in the burrows and swamps of wildest Africa, I was in a state of shock. It was beyond fear. It was a kind of sadness. My childhood really was over. This was the world and I didn't belong in it. I'd always suspected as much, but I was cushioned before, at school, always able to retreat to art class, to elocution, to Montagu House with all its comforts and luxuries. Now there was no escape. Here I was among a vast cross-section of my fellow citizens – we were called the Citizen Force – fellow seventeen-year-old boys from every corner of (white) South Africa: city boys, farm boys, English, Afrikaner, poor white – and I found little in common with any of them. (There were a few I knew from Sea Point Boys' High, but not the one I wanted – Tony Fagin had gone to varsity, and was allowed to do a different form of episodic military training called Commandos.) It was as I feared: I was a Martian landed on earth.

But if Oudtshoorn was tough, it was a holiday camp compared with Walvis. On the day we arrived, we were marched through the gates and across the vast parade ground to the barracks. All along the way the inhabitants of the camp, the recruits already there, now in the last three months of their training, lined the route and jeered at us. We were like prisoners being led into Rome. The noise was deafening, a baying, mocking noise, strangely elated – listen to the audience on the *Jerry Springer Show*, it sounded like that – and the impression was of arriving in hell. Surely hell is just a place where human beings fail to recognise one another? Why were we, the newcomers at Walvis, so automatically despicable to the ones already there?

Simple. They were *oumanne* (old men), we were *blougatte* (blue bums). Only three months separated us – training not age – yet they were veterans and we were rookies. In case you couldn't tell yourself from them, they all wore moustaches, which we weren't allowed to grow. They were hairy, sunburnt and *woestyn mal* (desert mad); they'd lived in this godforsaken camp for twelve weeks; they'd seen it all, they knew it all. We knew nothing.

So they enslaved us. Each of them took one of us as his personal *blougat*, his pet, his apprentice, his servant – 'If blacks don't exist we just have to invent them' – to be used in whatever way he chose, to fetch and carry, clean gear for inspection, or just to while away the time. Anyone who's been through the English public school will know about the fag system and initiation games. We had them, SADF style. There was 'Press-ups' – you do these with an *ouman*'s foot on your spine. There was '*Maak Styf*' – you stiffen your stomach muscles so that they can punch it, harder and harder. There was the 'Gas Chamber' – you're put in a kit cupboard, the door locked and cigarette smoke blown through the keyhole. There was 'Midnight Call' – you're woken, chased out of the barracks, either into the desert for dune running, or into the bath-house, to strip and lie on your back under cold showers, legs open ('Let's see the fokkin *balletjies* on you, let's see if you've got what it takes to be a fokkin fighting man, a fokkin killer, a fokkin Boer!'). And there were others, which luckily I never experienced personally, like 'Gun Inspection' ('Unzip – get it out – get it up – compare and contrast!') or 'Double Vodka' (several *oumanne* spitting into a glass, which you then down).

A strict hierarchy existed. Rugby was never South Africa's national sport – racism was. Since there was only white skin to play with in Walvis, the order went:

> Afrikaans-speaking Christians
> English-speaking Christians
> Jews
> Poor whites

I had a poor white as my master, my *ouman*, a wiry little chap called Erasmus. Apart from the times when there were group attacks, and a kind of feeding frenzy overcame whole packs of them, he treated me fairly decently on a one-to-one basis. I was at first shocked by being routinely referred to as that fokkin *Jood* – the word is uncomfortably close to the German and these blunt-featured Afrikaners with close-cropped blond hair conjured up further associations – but you quickly learn to stop hearing it. Otherwise Erasmus's worst abuse was to give me rambling lectures on the wine, women and song that made for a good life.

The thoroughbred Boer hates his poor relations, the poor whites – a group created during the Depression, when rural Afrikaners abandoned their farms to try their luck in the cities – he hates seeing his blessed *volk* living like kaffirs. As an *ouman*, Erasmus was in a privileged position, but there was another poor white among us *blougatte*: a gentle, nervy guy with puffy eyes and darkish skin; some Portuguese blood, presumably, from his name – Alfonso. He was treated differently from the rest of us. The stomach punching and other humiliations were done without humour and relentlessly. Eventually Alfonso had a nervous breakdown, went walk-about in the desert, was found, briefly hospitalised and discharged from the army. The *oumanne* laughed about it for weeks.

I met him on a bus a few years later in Cape Town – he was the conductor. We recognised one another immediately. He smiled warmly and thanked me – apparently I'd shown him kindness, though I don't remember this – then he gave me a free ride: 'Agh, have it on the City Tramways, Sher.' As we made small talk, I sat there apprehensively. What if an inspector got on? The army had left me with a permanent fear of uniformed figures. Which one of us, Alfonso or me, would be doing press-ups on the bus floor with the man's foot on our back?

Desperate to escape the physical rigours of army life, the drilling and PT, I tried many ploys. Beginning with my feet. They're very flat. On arrival at Oudtshoorn I hurried to the doctor, the MO, and showed him. He was impressed – 'Those really *are* flat, hey!' – and came quite close to sending me home. But not close enough. Perhaps I could become a cook, he suggested, or a driver. I could neither cook nor drive, but imagined the second would be easier to learn. I was wrong. Three-ton trucks are ridiculously difficult to control, what with all that double-declutching, and

I'm the least mechanically-minded of men. Also, there was just something about the sheer bloody size of the thing that intimidated me. Anyway, the army went through the motions of teaching me to drive these monsters and, even though I made no progress whatsoever, they then went through the motions of a driving test. I failed, of course, and instantly – as I set off I crashed straight into the truck parked in front of me – and was banned from ever again approaching any vehicle belonging to the SADF. Yet, absurdly, I was still in the Driving Corps. That's what the paperwork said and that's where I had to stay. I wasn't happy about this. Without anything to drive, I had to do drill and PT again, and during rest hours things were even worse. The drivers at Walvis were the roughest *oumanne* in camp, the most *woestyn mal*; I was in a barracks full of big, fat, oil-stained, man-beast mutants; or, to put it another way, long-distance lorry drivers. I had to get out.

I went to the Walvis MO and showed him my feet. He was even more impressed than his Oudtshoorn predecessor – 'Now that's what I really call flat!' – and arranged a move to Clerks and Storemen.

There was still a hitch. By that stage all the clerical and storemen positions in camp were taken. Whereas before I'd been a driver without a vehicle, now I was a clerk or storeman with neither office nor warehouse. Then one of the officers had a bright idea. There was an unoccupied office at the very edge of camp, near the main entrance – nobody used it, nobody needed it. I could be clerk there. It made no sense, except on the paperwork: I was a clerk and this was an office. That would do. The fact that I'd be clerk of The Empty Office, clerk of The Office With No Name, this was irrelevant.

So one morning I found myself being led across camp to a building on the far side. I went up a few steps, the door was unlocked and I was ushered into a dusty, darkish room with one desk, one chair, one shelf of old files and one window overlooking the parade ground. Then the key was handed over to me and that was it. I was left alone. For the rest of my time in Walvis. Another five months.

I couldn't believe my luck. I was permitted, officially permitted, to spend all day, every day, here in this little hideaway. I was my own boss, with absolutely no duties, free to do anything I wanted. During the worst of the initiation games with the *oumanne* I'd often had cause to question whether God existed and the answer was always a resounding NO. Now I changed my mind.

Each morning I'd leave the Clerks and Storemen barracks, a much more civilised place than the Drivers' lair and with a much better class of *oumanne* (studious, polite, quite timid types), and I'd carry a little canister of coffee across camp to my office – The Office At The Edge Of The World, The Office That Time Forgot – and there I'd sit all day, reading, sketching, practising audition speeches, or peering out of the window as squads of recruits were chased and bullied round the parade ground. I'd pop back to the canteen for lunch, able to schedule this so I was there first, before the rush, and, having eaten my full, return to my refuge. At the end of the afternoon, I'd toddle back to the barracks. 'How was work today?' people would be asking one another. When the question came my way, I'd reply, 'Believe me, you don't want to know.'

Occasionally some of the officers and NCOs, Walvis's Permanent Force guys, would visit my office – now that it was reopened it provided a new place for them to skive off – and one or two noticed that I had drawing skills. They commissioned portraits of themselves. Then one asked me to do an illustration of weaponry for a lecture he had to give. Then another said that he wasn't crazy about the battalion flag, and could I possibly design a different one.

I cringe to acknowledge this, but in the years that followed my stay at Walvis, when the camp became a bridgehead for the real thing – the war in Angola, South Africa's Vietnam – one battalion of the SADF went into combat under a flag designed by me.

But back in 1966, army life simply became cushier and cushier. When the halfway period was up, the first three months, one of my new officer chums – especially flattered by my portrait of him – suggested I should be promoted. What if a new resident here at camp, a lowly *blougat*, were assigned to me to serve as under-clerk in The Nowhere Office? I'd need to have higher rank. I thought he was joking, but, no, I duly received a stripe and became Lance Corporal Sher. This carried some privileges, like extra passes into town (to visit Maichatz's Tearoom or the Flamingo Bioscope) and extra respect from all unranked inhabitants of the Clerks and Storemen barracks.

Promotion of a different kind was bestowed on all my contemporaries with the arrival of the new intake. We were the *oumanne* now. We could grow our first moustache and take possession of a slave, a pet, a punchbag, a kaffir, a *blougat*.

Surely we wouldn't, though. We wouldn't claim these rights. We had suffered so much in our first few weeks in camp, crying ourselves to sleep at night, fearing we'd crack up and, in some cases (Alfonso wasn't the only one), actually doing so. Surely we wouldn't inflict this on anyone else?

How naïve I was. It all started up again: the '*Maak Styf*', the 'Gas Chamber' and so on; the spectacle of *oumanne* encircling a terrified *blougat* and interrogating him about everything from his family to his foreskin, baying with mockery at every answer he gave.

I didn't join in. There's nothing heroic about this statement. In the same way that I couldn't grow a moustache – physically I was still a late developer – so a kind of timidity, a kind of squeamishness stopped me. I'm absolutely fascinated by human suffering – where would Drama be without it? – but I don't like causing it. Also, genuine bafflement sets in. Surely the equation should go: if I punch him in the stomach, it'll hurt – I didn't like it, he won't like it, therefore I won't do it. This seems logical. But, as I say, I'm being naïve. Logic isn't always what controls us. The equation can also go: someone hurt me, therefore I'll hurt someone else.

It was my first experience of something that would come to obsess me: the syndrome of the persecuted turning into the persecutor. It's in *Middlepost*, my first novel, and it's in many of the characters I've played: the disabled man who becomes a murderous tyrant in *Richard III*, the spat-upon Jew who becomes an avenging monster in *The Merchant of Venice*, the concentration camp survivor who becomes a Rachmanesque slum landlord in *Singer*.

The Jewish example is particularly powerful for me. After I'd left the army, after I'd travelled to London, after I'd been exposed to an uncensored picture of apartheid and heard it described as an atrocity, I went into a state of shock. Atrocity? That was a word I knew well. It featured in my reading on the Holocaust. Yet now it was being used about white South Africans. But – hang on a moment – that included my family. Impossible! The Shers and Abramowitzes fled Eastern Europe at the turn of the century because of the 'atrocity' then, the pogroms: part of a major Jewish exodus. A second wave arrived in South Africa during the thirties and forties, fleeing the Nazis. I'd been brought up with my people talking about themselves as the victims of 'atrocity', not the perpetrators. This British media, the newspapers and TV, they might be very sophisticated, but they were surely wrong, or maybe lying. We'd been warned about this

– in the *Cape Times* and *Argus* – how the rest of the world misrepresented us. I felt upset and trapped. Back at home it was so normal – *blacks were an inferior form of life* – this was as true and simple as your ABC or two-times table, and taught in the same way, as part of your basic education. It couldn't be an 'atrocity'. Could it? We, the persecuted, becoming the persecutor? No – unthinkable. Evil beyond belief.

Or – just completely normal behaviour? I've suffered, now I'm safe. Life has been hard, now it's comfortable. The sun is bright and glorious – I'll bask, I'll close my eyes.

Of course, there's another way, taken by a small but honourable roll-call of South African Jews – Albie Sachs, Jo Slovo, Ruth First, Helen Suzman, to name just a few – the ones who made the obvious connection, the ones who said, 'We *cannot* be racist', the ones who helped to bring down Uncle Nat.

But of course he was a victim too – Uncle Nat – he was also one of the persecuted. Forced out of the Cape by the British – forced on to the Great Trek. Thrashed in the Boer War, again by the British, the inventors of the concentration camp, where thousands of Afrikaner women and children died from starvation and disease. Those Boers who fought on after the ceasefire were known as the bitter-enders. It seems like an apt name. They lost the Cape, they lost the war and, more recently, they lost South Africa. There is truly something bitter in their history.

In 1967, one of Uncle Nat's least heroic sons, Lance Corporal Sher – clerk of The Office that Never Was – began to look around him with renewed interest. Freed from the terrors of army life, and indeed from all its duties, he found himself drawn to two things: nature and sex.

Nature came in the form of the Namib Desert, which I now began to explore. To walk in the Namib is to take a stroll through a form of abstract art: its strange orange spaces, apparently blank yet weighty, complex, restless, these only half remind you of the world you know, they amaze and unsettle without you being able to say why. Near the camp was the lagoon, an inlet from the sea, its long curving beach made not of sand but spongy, mauve-brown mud that oozed through your toes. A dead seal or two was often to be found along the way. Pelicans and storks flew overhead. But most fascinating of all were the vast flocks of flamingo grazing on this huge, quiet expanse of water. Yes, I did do it. I did jump and yell – to see them take off. Years later it provided a crucial sequence in *Cheap Lives* where Yusuf, the Coloured drifter (later to be an inmate on Death Row) suffocates a young Jewish man in the sand of a dune in the Namib:

> Something in his face got torn in the struggle. Eardrums or his tongue or a nosebleed, don't ask me, but suddenly the orange sand got richer. Then it was orange again. Sand is running all the time. It's not surprising they use sand for clocks. At the end I heard a noise. I watched the edge of the dune. A seagull came over. It seemed like it was fleeing something. The edge of all dunes is razor sharp and blurred at the same time. Always a little wind. Beyond the sky was sky blue. Then it bled. I didn't know what was going on. I wondered if some of the guy's blood was in my eyes. It took a few seconds to realise it was flamingos. A hundred thousand flamingos coming over the edge of the dune to see what I had done. Already we were slipping, me and the Jewboy. Everything was strange. The earth was watery. The sky was bleeding. We fell.

Nature came also in the form of the Etosha Pan Game Reserve. On one memorable weekend pass, a business associate of my father, Paul Szabo, a Woody Allen lookalike who lived in Walvis, took me and two companions through the park in his battered little VW Beetle. It was my first glimpse of wild Africa – its game, savannas and skies – and the beginning of an addiction, a pure addiction, the only completely healthy one in my life. I can't visit the wild enough – Kenya, the private reserves in the Transvaal, the game parks of Nepal and India – I can't watch enough editions of *The Natural World* or *Wildlife on One*, I simply can't get enough.

Sex was a growing addiction too, but here it wasn't a case of not getting enough, but of not daring to get any at all. It must've been going on at Walvis, I suppose, somewhere, somehow, between braver souls than me. I was torn between trying to deny my burgeoning sexuality and finding myself in what you could call a gay fantasy: an army full of tanned and fit seventeen-year-olds.

Shower time. Less of a torture than at school, or at any rate torture of a different kind. I remember one late afternoon back in Oudtshoorn. There'd been a power cut in the camp. The showers were in a circular wooden building with a thatched roof, a *rondawel*. Inside, the only light came from high windows – the rays of a flaming Karoo sunset falling into the dark hut, catching the curving sprays of water and the gleaming necks and shoulders of the naked young men crowded inside. From their chests down everything was in darkness, pitch darkness, a hot and thrilling darkness for me – bodies brushing against yours, confusion, laughter.

Later, in Walvis, the entire population of the camp moved out into the desert for a week, on manoeuvres, even the Clerks and Storemen. But not me. I had no job, no duties, and even the army saw the absurdity of transferring me from The Nowhere Office to The Nowhere Tent. So I stayed put, with half a dozen others. You saw them now and then: tiny lone figures crossing the immense landscape of the parade ground or eating at the other end of the hangar-sized canteen. And, once, in the bath-house . . .

He stood at the far end of the tiled corridor, showering in the corner, half turned into it, glancing over his shoulder as I arrived. His features were dark, a bit sly, and I couldn't help noticing – when he slightly rotated his hips – that he was either very well hung or half aroused. A pounding started in my ears. I became aware of the echoing space all around us, the deserted bath-house, the deserted camp. No witnesses, no terrible consequences. Unless I was wrong about this boy. Unless he was just well hung and innocently taking a shower . . .

At times like this I'd simply turn and flee, racing the first ticking pulses of my own stretching flesh.

It was shameful yet exhilarating, it both frightened and thrilled. I couldn't resolve these contradictions, didn't know what on earth was going on.

And then one day there was something beyond sex. Among the new intake, the new *blougatte*, one youth took my eye. Why did he look so familiar? The soft brown hair and eyes . . . vulnerability, radiance, a kind of grace . . . so much gentler than me, who was dark and scowling, encased in layer after layer of caution, the outsider's armour. It took me a while to work it out – the sense of déjà vu – then it hit me like a blow. It was the boy from kindergarten, my first love affair. I'd last seen him being bustled into his parents' car, after some incident, some shame – now here he was again, grown into a man. To see him in the showers was to be winded. He had a swimmer's build, broad shoulders and chest, long muscular limbs;

smooth-skinned except for a vibrantly dark patch of hair above his cock. I hardly dared look down at it – or up into those innocent, long-lashed eyes. The combination of these two features – the one powerful, almost dangerous, the other full of beauty and tenderness – this was overwhelming. I became obsessed. And for the first time in my life (and possibly the last) I lusted and longed from a position of power. I was an *ouman*, he was a *blougat*. I could claim him, own him, do anything I wanted. The temptation was huge, but of course, mister timidity, little Ant, resisted it. I never even spoke to him, never learned if he really was the boy from kindergarten. The chances were nil, of course. Later I would read Jean Cocteau describing the same syndrome: a classmate, Dargelos, infatuates him, then turns into the 'type' which most attracts, and then into the famous flat-nosed, square-jawed profile that recurs throughout his drawings: the Cocteauesque face. His fantasy has become his signature. Knowing nothing about this at the time, the youth's presence in Walvis was just strangely unsettling. And then my memory blurs. I have the impression of him disappearing – exactly like the kindergarten boy – of something happening and of him leaving the army early.

It wasn't because of the Six Day War in Israel (my furtive glances in the showers were enough to establish he wasn't Jewish), although this was to curtail the Walvis experience for some of my fellow recruits, the fervent Zionists. They sought and were granted permission to be released from South African conscription so they could go and fight for Israel. A shock went through the rest of us. Armies were not just indolent, self-abusing institutions like ours. Armies fought wars. Armies killed.

I don't know what happened to the guys who left Walvis for Tel Aviv, but Israel's victory against Egypt that year was widely reported and celebrated in the South African papers. It was, after all, the victory of a tough, militaristic, white-skinned race, small in numbers, yet able to thrash vast hordes of tawny heathens. It was an Old Testament victory and the Dutch Reformed Church cherished that book. The South Africa of my youth was brimming with paradoxes, but this was one of the most intriguing: in spite of the routine cry of '*Jood, fokkin Jood!*' following me through army life, the Afrikaner has always held a curious respect for the Jew. In previous centuries, as the Boers fought and fled their way across the sun-baked expanses of British South Africa, they virtually saw themselves as a tribe of Israelites: they, too, had a covenant with the Lord; they, too, had a promised land. And when they'd finally claimed it, in the latter half of the twentieth century, and were increasingly ostracised by the rest of the world, one of their only allies to remain loyal was Israel.

Before it began I would've done anything to gain exemption from military service, and even while it was happening I kept trying to get out – at the mere sight of any MO I'd start undoing my boots like some mad foot flasher – and I half succeeded, whiling away my days in The Neverland Office, The Office of Oz. But looking back now, I wouldn't have missed it for the world. It was a kind of research trip. Apart from anything else, I learned how to *play* a soldier and I've done quite a few since: Macbeth, Richard III, Titus, Tamburlaine, Cyrano. It's been endlessly satisfying to assume the brutal macho swagger of those NCOs in Oudtshoorn and Walvis; a kind of revenge, perhaps. And with soldiers under increasing stress, like Macbeth and Titus, it's good to let them occasionally snap back into professional mode – *atten*SHUN – and to know that you're doing it properly.

The last few months in Walvis passed slowly; we counted the hours. Then eventually the big day dawned and we were on a troop train again, called Louie, don't know why, and we were skirting the Namib dunes, crossing the dry plains of South West, entering the Republic again, much lusher landscapes, and the guitarists among us were strumming melodies like 'Sloop John B', and, more passionately, 'The Green Green Grass of Home', and all of us were throwing back our heads to join in, even me, tone-deaf me, and then, seventy-two hours after leaving Walvis, suddenly we were hanging out the windows, beating our hands against the carriages, chanting in time to the wheels, 'Go Louie, go Louie, go – go – go!' – and there it was: Cape Town station. It was all over.

October, summer starting. I'd missed the beginning of term at London's drama schools in September – their autumn (how strange) – so a long wait lay ahead before my next big journey.

Everyone's life is full of these and the army was my first. I invariably approach each with more dread than excitement and they're never as bad as I fear. But although my life has teemed with these big journeys, I'm not really built for travel or change. Something in me always aches for home. Even now, aged fifty and no longer able to say reliably where it is, I ache for home.

5

MOM'S BIRTHDAY

Home.

At this point in time I have at least three. The house in Welcombe Road, Stratford-upon-Avon, which Greg and I rent each time we do an RSC show. The house in Islington, London, where we live permanently. And the house that I gaze down at from our suite at the President Hotel: the old, shadowy family home, Montagu House.

On the first morning of our January 2000 visit we unpack our suitcases and then stroll down Alexander Road. A hazy, sunny saltiness hangs in the air. It smells of kelp. It smells of Sea Point. I gulp at it till I'm giddy with memories. At Montagu House we stop in front of the security gates which protect the small driveway. Flimsy aluminium affairs, I doubt whether they'd withstand the push of a determined child, never mind an intruder. We press the bell. The gates open and Mom appears at the front door. Greg goes towards the patio. In a moment he'll compliment Mom on her beloved flowerpots; he always remembers to do this. I watch the gates as they float closed, shuddering feebly.

'Mom, shouldn't you get a better security system?'

'Hmn?' she murmurs in reply (hard of hearing or resisting the discussion?). 'The others are always saying the same thing and I'll tell you what I tell them. It's fine, it's *absolutely* fine.'

She's very sure about things, Mom. I'm a natural doubter, but she's sure, *absolutely* sure. It's a profound difference between us and always has been, even back in 1967 when I was still calling her Mate. Aged forty-seven then, she cut a dynamic figure: her mousy hair dyed auburn and worn in a glossy beehive, her broadish face reshaped with vivid applications of make-up, her fingernails scarlet, her neck and wrists laden with jewellery – you heard her coming before you saw her – and her posture distinctly tall. Although Dad was shorter, no concessions were made; she wore high heels and the shining beehive added a few more inches. She dressed in fashionable outfits acquired during their trips to London and Paris. She swam, she played tennis, she and Dad made a nifty pair on the ballroom dance floor.

Now, on the eve of her eightieth birthday, she's extremely healthy and alert, albeit a slightly frailer and shorter version of her younger self. She still sports a big hairdo, now coloured a blondish grey; she still wears the make-up, the long red nails and the jewellery – but she treads more carefully in the high heels, sometimes does or doesn't hear you and her speech can slur when she's tired. More surprisingly, she's grown cautious, slightly fearful, unadventurous. Travel, once her great passion, is an endurance test now. When she comes to visit us in London she complains, 'What's there to do here?' We're amazed. The shops and theatre, which used to occupy her from morning to midnight, these suddenly hold less attraction. She's intimidated by the West End crowds, the transport; everything's an obstacle. Understandable, perhaps, in an eighty-year-old, but somehow untypical of her. Really very untypical. A mystery.

'The garden's looking great, Marge,' says Greg.

Mom beams, then demurs: 'It's a miracle, actually, because we've had the most terrible south-easters this year – oh, it's been impossible!'

We go inside. Montagu House no longer resembles my childhood home. It was extensively converted in 1977. One half – with our old dining room, kitchen and both my bedrooms – was separated and sold. In the remaining half the ground floor was turned into one big lounge/dinette.

The walls are covered with posters of my shows, drawings I did as a kid, shelves with my books, videos of my film and TV work, and photos of me everywhere. The rest of Mom's children, grandchildren and other family members hardly get a look in. Who am I to question the motives of a Jewish mother, but I do anyway. 'I see the others all the time,' she answers crisply. 'You I only see once a year.' I say nothing. I go through to the backyard to greet Katie. Katie Roberts. She still works for Mom – half a century on – she's seventy-seven herself, but she still travels in from the

Coloured township of Bonteheuwel three times a week to cook and clean. A fit, upright figure, a radiant face, a sweet smile, a gold tooth showing. I embrace and kiss her. She's a bit awkward with this – it's not what she was brought up to do – though she's as pleased by the reunion as I am. We talk about this and that, but conversation doesn't flow – it's not what we were brought up to do. The only one she really enjoyed chatting to was Dad; both from rural areas, both with Afrikaans as their first language. I go upstairs, to his old room. This has been converted into an extension of the Antony Sher exhibition: more photos, posters and drawings. The windows are closed tight in here, too, and despite Katie's constant cleaning there'a a dusty, stuffy feel. It's like a museum, a shrine. I hurry back to the patio.

Cars are pulling up outside Montagu House. More and more of them. Handsome tanned men and women in sunglasses clamber out, their manner noisy and jokey. The Sher clan is gathering – it's like the opening sequence of *The Godfather*, but in miniature – there's about twenty of us, all adults except for Beth, nine-year-old daughter of Joel, my younger brother, and his wife Eileen.

Now a photographer arrives. He's here to do a series of portraits: Mom and her children, Mom and her grandchildren, and so on. The idea is to present her with the results, silver-framed, at the birthday party in a few days' time. He begins with the big group shot: Mom sitting on a chair, everyone else standing around her – children, grandchildren and all partners. The photographer finds it difficult to compose the picture. He tries different groupings, according to height, age or even the colour of our clothes, but no luck. Eventually in desperation, he says, 'Maybe we'd better just go boy–girl, boy–girl.'

We all start to laugh. He's baffled – unaware that myself, my sister and my niece are all in same-sex relationships. The more he frowns the more we laugh. 'Boy–girl, boy–girl,' he says again. 'Wouldn't that be simplest?'

'Maybe,' someone replies. 'But in this family it doesn't work like that.'

By now Mom is laughing so hard she's bent over, legs crossed, specs in one hand, tears ruining her make-up.

I love her for this. The unconventional side of her family isn't just accepted, it's positively celebrated. The not-belonging, the being-on-the-outside, she's known these things herself. Today she's the grand matriarch of the Sher clan and a decade or so earlier she was one of Sea Point's glamorous society hostesses, but life started by casting her in an altogether different role, as a shy and rather plain country girl.

Her parents, Harry Abramowitz and Annie Horwitz, were both born in a small *shtetl* called Plunge – or Plungyan in Yiddish – on the banks of the Babrungas river in north-western Lithuania. They joined the Jewish exodus at the turn of the century. The pogroms were spreading like wild-fire through Russia and Poland, and although they never actually reached Lithuania, the smoke and stink were in the air, and large numbers packed their bags. America was everyone's first choice of destination, the New World for a new life, but the immigration quotas soon filled up and people had to settle for Britain or her colonies, Australia and South Africa.

Harry and Annie hadn't known one another back in Plunge, but eventually married and ended up in Montagu, a pretty valley town with hot-water springs and orchards. He ran the general store, she ran the home: a spacious one-storeyed house on Main Street, with a large *stoep* stretching round two sides, a farmyard to one side with poultry runs and vegetable patches, and a garden behind, with a tyre swing hanging from the big guava tree.

I remember Granny feeding the chickens; I remember playing on the lawn with my cousins, Mark 'n' Neal, 'the twins', and thinking that I feel like a twin too but where's the other half of me?; I remember Montagu's little whitewashed bioscope and the Cowboys 'n' Indian serials on Saturday mornings; I remember a rather surreal image of a man in the street with his pet on a leash and this being a three-legged lion; and I remember Grandpa's store, with rocking chairs and farm equipment hanging from the ceiling, while a row of square open tins stood on the floor below, fragrant with heaps of coffee, grain and spices.

I have a vague mental picture of Grandpa himself – medium build, crinkly salt-and-pepper hair, a squarish face – but only one clear memory. He's bent over a basin, washing his face. It's early morning. He makes a shivery sound in his cheeks – 'Br-r-r-r-r!' – and although I know that Montagu's water can be quite a shock first thing, it strikes me that he isn't from here, he's from somewhere really cold.

I remember Granny much better. She lived till 1985 and is the only grandparent I knew as an adult: a remarkably fit and happy old lady, full of curiosity, which her offspring sometimes called nosiness.

Mom was the eldest of four. She was aged twenty-one in 1941 when her youngest brother Ralph went on a school camping holiday to Clanwilliam in the Western Cape. Granny had a particular fear of water and made Ralph promise not to swim while there. Would a twelve-year-old have kept such a promise? I don't know, but the story goes that he saw a friend in trouble in the river, jumped in to help and that's how he drowned. He was just six weeks away from his bar mitzvah.

The tragedy shook the family so deeply that some never recovered. For the rest of her life Granny couldn't speak Ralph's name out loud. Mom dealt with it in a different way. Spiritualism became her faith. Ralph hadn't really died: he'd simply moved to a different plane of existence; he was there to be contacted whenever she chose. Grief need never hurt so much again.

It intrigues me, spiritualism. As a belief system or cult, I rather like its premise – the air crowded with all the people who've ever lived – but I'm less convinced by its priests. Why do the dead only contact us through a certain 'type'? And why, when I see and hear them, do my actor's instincts alert me to the scent of a related species, the amateur performer?

After Dad died, Mom reported that she'd been to a spiritualist meeting and that he had 'come through'. When Greg and I were next in South Africa, she played us the tape; recording facilities were provided by the medium. This man had an English accent, camp and Northern; Greg identified it as end-of-the-pier Blackpool, but of course the ladies of Sea Point wouldn't recognise the characteristics. He used a particular feature of British speech, the statement/enquiry – 'I think you lost your husband recently, didn't you luv?' – to encourage the sitter to nod or shake their head, and then he proceeded: 'I think it was in September . . . no, October . . . no, Novem . . . yes, it was November, yes!'

I was disappointed. I wanted Dad to have 'come through'. But then again, during his life he had an extremely cynical attitude to these matters, as well as a sharp sense of humour, and even if in death the proof was in the pudding, he probably wouldn't have given Mom the satisfaction of this long-distance call.

They had a combative relationship, my parents, Mannie and Marge. Probably rather sexy to start with. She's told me how, when they met in Dungarven Boarding House in Green Point, there was much tiptoeing from room to room. She was shy and awkward then, the country girl from Montagu, here to attend technical college, quickly becoming excited by the big city. He was much rougher, from rougher countryside – the isolated settlement of Middlepost on the baking plains of the Karoo – moving to Cape Town to join an uncle's business, Weinrich & Sher, and really living it up: a lean-built, hard-drinking, poker-playing, womanising young blade. It's odd to think of them both having promiscuous and wild natures then. Hers quietened with marriage. His didn't. Particularly not the drinking. 'The boozing' – this is how I heard it referred to in my childhood, with a despairing sneer in her voice – 'the boozing'.

Was my father just a heavy drinker or was he an alcoholic? It's a fine line among some white South Africans who drink spirits very freely. Dad never touched the stuff before or during work, but once this was over he hit the whisky bottle with real commitment. Whisky, always whisky. Massive shots of it. Before supper. On an empty stomach. Little interest in wine as a follow-up. Little interest in anything once he'd had those whiskies: silent, morose, sitting at one end of the dining table, a rather threatening figure.

Sometimes the evening whiskies weren't taken at home, but at one of the uncles', or other pals', his *chavers*. Sometimes he'd be late for supper. And that's when the fights started. Over 'the boozing'.

Non-physical fights, often even non-verbal, but very hostile. Both combatants were tireless. They fought the match, round after round, for the full fifty-two years of their marriage, neither giving in.

It wasn't just 'the boozing'. After the initial sexual buzz faded, they struggled to find other points of contact. 'Your mother' is how he started referring to her when talking to us; 'your father', she'd say. As if they could only identify one another through us. They had little in common. He was a typical white South African male – 'I work hard and I play hard' was his favourite motto, meaning a continuous cocktail of business, whisky and rugby viewing – and she was a typical female, the white 'madam', with lots of time for leisure interests. Her love of the arts left him cold.

The theatre put him to sleep, literally. It was as though he and the house lights were connected to the same dimmer switch. As they went down, his head fell forward and as they came up so did he. In between was nothing but oblivion and it made absolutely no difference if his son was in the play. I remember when they came to see *Richard III*; it was a terrific show that day, culminating in a standing ovation. How proud I was that my parents should be present. As I took my bow I glanced at them in the front row, and there he was, the only one still sitting – fast asleep. The house lights hadn't come on yet.

During these annual trips to visit me more fights ensued – over their itineraries. She wanted to shop, shop, shop and see two shows daily, matinée and evening. He wanted to do business (as director of an export company, he had an agent here) and to sit in English pubs. She won of course – she always won – but the fight was essential, bracing even; it was part of it, part of the holiday, part of their whole life together.

Maybe that solves the mystery of her new disinterest in London – her uncharacteristic fear of West End crowds and transport. When I was telling my siblings about it, I even used the word – 'She seems to have lost her *fight*.' Well, yes, she's lost her sparring partner.

The thing they shared most was laughter. Dad had what Mom called a sense of humour when she was being affectionate or a streak of sarcasm when she wasn't. At any rate the warmer version of this reduced them both to tears. He'd begin to tell a story, one of the family classics, like of his aged mother and aunt sitting on the *stoep* at Marlborough Mansions. His mother has arthritis, the aunt Parkinson's. A hawker arrives below – 'Does the *ou medems* want some nice fresh vegetables today?' One woman is apparently beckoning with flapping hands, the other shaking her head emphatically. The man doesn't know whether he's coming or going. Halfway through this account, Dad would be overcome with a kind of hysteria – his voice lifting into a helpless falsetto, his eyes watering – and Mom would catch it. Then, as his glasses came off, so did hers. It's my favourite image of them: all defences down – her formidable strength, his dark gloom – both just helpless with laughter, wiping away tears.

He's not here today, on this sunny Saturday morning, to join the laughter over the boy–girl, boy–girl joke – though then again, Mom might argue that he *is*.

The photographs are duly developed, the best ones blown up, framed and wrapped in golden paper for the big event.

This takes place in an upstairs room at Europa, an informal restaurant on Main Road, Sea Point. There are about forty guests ranged across four tables; there are toasts and speeches – including one by nine-year-old Beth –

there are presentations of flowers and the framed photographs. Mom is radiant with happiness.

My siblings are at the main table. Older brother Randall: fifty-six, heavy-faced, stout-bellied, he runs a small takeaway restaurant in the centre of town; a kind-hearted man, very much at peace with himself these days, having fought and won a battle with alcoholism. Older sister Verne: fifty-three, round-faced, short-haired; after twenty-seven years of marriage and three grown-up children, she came out as gay and now lives with her partner Joan – they run a shop selling kids' clothes. Younger brother, Joel: forty-four, owner of a factory which makes aluminium ladders and chairs; a keen body-builder, tall, mountainous, black hair, black beard, a sort of Jewish Schwarzenegger.

We start talking about the recent millennium celebrations. Joel says: 'The rest of the world got incredible spectacles and shows, whole new buildings constructed, amazing displays lighting up the night sky, and what did we get? – an old man visiting his old prison cell!'

Greg and I exchange a look, open-mouthed. Just over a week ago, in Stratford-upon-Avon, we sat with Greg's parents, watching TV, watching the millennium cross the globe like a midnight sun, igniting the fireworks on Sydney Bridge, the Eiffel Tower, the Thames, and nothing moved us more than Nelson Mandela lighting a candle in his Robben Island cell.

I want to walk out of the party. I want to hit Joel.

It's funny. When I left South Africa in 1968 he was twelve: a plump, big-eared, bespectacled kid, a kind of Piggy figure. I adored him and during those early months in London missed him most. But now, whether bad-mouthing or wisecracking (he's the grim joker in the family pack), he's become a rather aggressive character, and a lot of it seems directed at me. When I question him about this he has a different picture of our childhood: he hated the fuss always being made over me.

That's funny, too, since I envied *him*. He was Dad's favourite. They shared an interest in cars, vintage cars – at last one of us had found something in common with our father! – and today Joel still owns a beautiful yellow-and-black 1930 Ford and a bright-red 1960 Chev Impala. Joel was most liked by Dad and is now most like Dad. He's a businessman, he has a taste for whisky, he works hard and he plays hard. The equation is simple: his labour buys him and his family comfort. He doesn't want politics to interfere with his life. Maybe that's true for most citizens of most countries, but unfortunately South Africans haven't got much choice. Joel resents this. Resents paying for the sins of his forefathers, as he puts it. Throughout his adult life South Africa has been in turmoil. The troubled seventies and eighties with the country constantly on the brink of civil war or a terrible bloodbath, and then the unpredictable nineties, with the New South Africa celebrated by the outside world and its own black population, but derided and feared by whites like Joel. It's a dangerous place, he reckons – dangerous economically if you're running a business, dangerous personally if you're raising a family – it's a dangerous mess, just like it always was. Joel has grown angry and impatient, and isn't afraid to say so. He's blazingly frank, uncompromising, funny, alarming. An unreconstructed white maybe, but he'll be the first to tell you this. I can't help admiring his honesty, his lack of bullshit.

Our millennium discussion is interrupted by the unexpected arrival of Europa's kitchen staff filing into the room to sing traditional songs in praise of Mom's birthday: big black mamas clapping, swaying, their voices soaring. The new hordes of tourists flooding South Africa enjoy these impromptu floor shows, but here's a roomful of slightly more cynical locals. The Sher family sit politely, if a little stiffly, through the performance. It ends with the black mamas going Hip-hip-hooray. Several of our number grimace at this. When Greg and I ask why, we're told that Judiasm doesn't approve of hip-hip-hooray. Why, we ask again. Nobody knows for sure, but someone thinks it might stem from a particular noise made by Nazis as they threw babies into the air for target practice. Meanwhile the black mamas have filed back to the kitchen. My sister Verne hurries out to thank and tip them. This inspires them to return for an encore. Joel rolls his eyes.

I slip away on to the neighbouring table. Here sit my first cousins and their spouses: the Shers, Gootmans and Reiffs. I ask them about a special place. Faces light up round the table. Quite a few of them grew up there and still make a pilgrimage every second year or so. I beg for Greg and me to be included on the next visit, my heart prickling with nostalgia even as I say the word: 'Middlepost'.

6

MIDDLEPOST

WE WENT TO Montagu for some school holidays, but more regularly, and excitingly, we went to Middlepost. In Montagu's little whitewashed bioscope I thrilled to the Wild West serials, but Middlepost did one better – Middlepost *was* the Wild West.

A fleet of limousines, Chevrolets, Fords and Pontiacs, would leave Cape Town before dawn, loaded with family, maids, pets and luggage. All of us Shers and all of the Hesselbergs: Uncle Jack, Auntie Rona, and 'the twins', Mark 'n' Neal. Never in the history of family outings have children asked 'How much further?' with more justification. At least half the 250 mile journey was across semi-desert: hot, bumpy and boring.

'Keep that window closed!' commanded Mom as dust from the convoy swirled into our car.

'But Tickey's feeling sick,' I protested, trying to push her tiny snuffling nose towards some fresh air.

'Close it!' Mom repeated, quieter now, more ominously. 'Or your father will stop the car and let both of you out!' That did it – instant obedience. With its vast flat floor of low thornbush and small stones, the Karoo might resemble the American prairies, but I could imagine nothing more alarming than being abandoned there.

When we did stop, for pee breaks and refreshments, the stillness was uncanny, ticking to a pulse of insects and heat. The women opened plastic containers with boiled eggs, sandwiches and fruit, while complaining about the men and how 'the boozing' had already started: big *dops* of whisky or brandy added to coffee from the flasks.

Hours later, the cars began to climb what seemed like a vertical wall – Ganaga Pass – and then suddenly you were a million miles higher than before, the air fresher and cooler, and the view astonishing: surely that was all the way back to Sea Point you could see in one look? Soon afterwards, Middlepost appeared, looking no bigger than a farm, the late afternoon sun stretching the shadows of its skinny windmills and bluegum trees, or catching on its corrugated-iron roofs.

There was a small Coloured settlement on the outskirts, with some cooking fires already alight for the evening meal. The inhabitants came out of their shanty huts to stare, sometimes wave, as our long fancy cars cruised into town and we slowly clambered out, stamping the dust from our shoes and stretching our limbs.

Dad's two brothers, Uncles Nicky and Arthur, had stayed on in Middle-post after he left, to run the shop, the petrol station, the bar and the motel: a haven for long-distance travelling salesmen, South Africa's Willy Lomans, who criss-crossed the immense spaces with wares packed in the boots of their cars. There wasn't much else in Middlepost: a few homes, a blacksmith, a tiny primary school (whites only) and a police station – well, a policeman's house. The amiable Sergeant Pretorius conducted his duties from a desk in his spare room, while in his backyard there were two cells (one for whites, one for Coloureds) where the occasional drunk sobered up overnight.

It was a little one-horse *dorp*, a typical Afrikaner settlement. In a way, I had an Afrikaner for a father. Dad was a *boerejood* – an Afrikaans-speaking Jew – the affectionate term for his kind in Middlepost.

We stayed for weeks, often timing our holidays to coincide with Jewish festivals. There was no *shul* in Middlepost, no place of worship for miles around, but this didn't really matter. Officially we were Orthodox Jews, but this was more in name than deed. Back in Sea Point we went to *shul* only when absolutely necessary and observed some of the rituals, like *shabbas* supper on Friday night, more as a chance for another all-talking, all-eating family gathering than out of any great sense of devotion. We practised Judaism rather like we voted for Uncle Nat, in a cheerfully casual way.

I remember us holding the festival feasts in the dining room at Middlepost, the motel dining room. I remember the lighting of candles, the breaking of matzos and, to denote one of the plagues of Egypt, the spotting of red wine on the tablecloth. I remember those men who could speak Hebrew, like Uncle Jack, reading portions from the Bible. At other times, we made a *braai* (barbecue) out in the veld, grilling chops and *boerewors*, or held filmshows and dances in the Hall across from the motel – except that the projector kept getting tangled and the gramophone dragged as Middlepost's electricity ebbed or flowed to the mood of its temperamental generator. The men would booze in the bar, the women would moan at them for not coming in to supper – afterwards both sides would join up to play poker, the men boozing more, the women smoking. Sometimes they'd take us, the children, for a walk in the dead of night, to view the veld lit with stars. We'd never seen anything like this in Cape Town: the heavens awash with milky drifts, the earth bright and clear below. This is when I first heard that all human beings have a 'star sign' and that mine was Gemini, the Twins. I knew it! Glancing enviously at Mark 'n' Neal, I thought: but where's the other half of me? Dad told how in his youth he'd driven his car in these parts without headlamps, just by moonlight – but now he'd take us for rides with the lights on, to see the startled, luminous holes of animal eyes suddenly piercing the dark.

During the days, my cousin Leonard and I would go on hunting safaris, leading a group of Coloured boys from the settlement . . . well, no, actually they were leading us. They knew the terrain much better, they knew where to find the game – rabbits and *dassies* (rock hyraxes) – and how to catch them. I watched, appalled and fascinated, as a length of wire, cork-screwed at the end, was inserted into a burrow, and rotated, twisting into the hide of the creature inside. Then it was hauled out, grasped by the feet, swung through the air and its brains dashed against the nearest rock. Leonard and I carried the carcass back into Middlepost, as triumphant as the big white hunters of East Africa.

My first sight of violent blood. I'm squeamish but it mesmerised me.

I watched the slaughtering of sheep in the big yard behind the kitchen. A bleating, gasping animal was pinioned between the knees of Ou April, the headman at Middlepost, and its head stretched back. The knife flashed and a new, vibrant red-and-white mouth opened halfway down its throat.

Once I also watched a bull meet its end. It was tripped up – with ropes round its legs – before Ou April could bend to his task. The lake of blood which spilled from its neck covered half the big yard and turned gold in the sunset. This shocked me and caused nightmares – the sheer volume of blood – and I never watched cattle being butchered again. Not until seeing the bullfight in Spain, when the drama of it began to mesmerise me all over again.

What else? We swam in the dams – large, circular mud-brick tanks alongside each windmill – we played tennis on the cracked old courts beyond the vegetable gardens, we read, we talked, we whiled away the time, with servants attending to our every whim. We were characters from Chekhov, but wearing flip-flops and sunglasses.

On the other side of the world, not that far from where *Uncle Vanya* and *Three Sisters* are set, there's another rural hamlet which holds great significance for my family: the town of Plunge (the *shtetl* Plungyan) in Lithuania. It wasn't only both of Mom's parents who were born here, but also Dad's father, Joel. (I suppose the coincidence is less than it seems; arriving in their new homeland, members of the old community must have sought one another out.) This Joel left home in 1897, aged twenty, to travel to South Africa.

What must that journey have been like? I tried to imagine it in my novel, *Middlepost*, which follows the framework of his story if none of its details: the long sea voyage, the slow change of hemisphere and climate, of light, of smells, of sounds, of everything familiar, your own clothes starting to itch, to feel wrong, your language too, your habits, your *thoughts* – until the entire universe becomes an utterly different, upside-down place. Nowadays we know what everywhere else on earth looks like, but my grandfather Joel was semi-illiterate; he would never even have read about South Africa, never mind seen any pictorial images of it. Here's the moment in the book when, waking late on the big day and finding the ship already docked in Table Bay, he sees his new homeland for the first time:

He broke into a run and turned the corner. The wind was powerful, a wild shadow raced across the deck making him jump back, while at the other end a sheet of tarpaulin, big as a mansion, reared up in the air. *Crack* it went, then collapsed, revealing a sight which took away his breath. A mountain filled the sky. The Table Rock, which the ship people had been telling them about throughout the voyage. There it was: a giant mass sliced perfectly flat along the top, as if half of it was missing, as if there might be even more somewhere else! The town was miniature by comparison, a white strip gleaming along the base, its buildings joined by the glare of the sun and then broken here and there by dark vegetation pouring down the slopes. Church bells rang out from a dozen different directions. He listened, smiling with fear, as the alien music looped over and under the roar of the wind.

Speaking only Yiddish and with hardly any money, Joel somehow made his way into the interior and began to work as a pedlar, trekking on foot from one isolated farm to the next, selling buttons and thread, trinkets and toys. This was the time of the Boer War when the Afrikaners saw themselves as a persecuted race, a holy tribe robbed of their promised land, so they identified with these lone Jewish strangers turning up on their doorsteps and welcomed them. One family story relates how a particular farmer, having no space in his house, invited Joel to sleep overnight in the stable and afterwards felt strangely blessed by the visit.

Eventually Joel reached Middlepost. The settlement was then owned by a man called Nightingale, a lone Englishman among an increasingly hostile community of Boers. There was a skirmish nearby – the Battle of Middlepost! – and the English lost. (Today there's still a mass grave next to the motel, commemorating the fallen officers and men of the 11th Imperial Yeomenry, and an empty, whitewashed ammunition dump which looks like a big eggshell tossed on one hillside.) Nightingale fled. The Boers, then the second-class citizens of South Africa, were unable to claim Middlepost, so Joel bought the whole place for a song.

Having already been mistaken by one farmer as the Second Coming, Joel now turned into a kind of Solomon-the-Wise figure, sitting in judgement of local disputes at Middlepost. This is bizarre because he never learned more than a few words of Afrikaans or English, and wouldn't have had a clue what was going on. (I picture him as a kind of Holy Fool character, a figure who crops up both in Russian and Yiddish literature.) It was arranged that he marry Mary Weinrich, born in the Latvian capital Riga. She was from much posher stock. The story goes that at her first glimpse of the barren stone and thornbush landscape which was to become home, she started weeping, couldn't stop and almost cured the district's notorious drought. She spoke a totally different Yiddish dialect from Joel, so they couldn't communicate. In the same way that Joel was never able to speak the languages of his adopted country, nor could he speak the language of his marriage. The predicament of these two people, locked together yet isolated, perhaps explains that strain of morose intensity which sometimes haunted my father's personality.

When I was researching the fictional *Middlepost* it astonished me how little Dad and his siblings could tell me about their history. No one could even point to Plunge on the map, and they didn't have any curiosity to locate it for themselves. At the time of writing the book, in 1987, Lithuania was still locked away in the Soviet half of Cold War Europe, so I couldn't visit it. But I found Mr Rostis Baublys, who ran a splendid little Lithuanian library from the front room of his west London home, and he provided much information. All my discoveries came as news to the family. Joel had never told them, for example, about the fabulous Orginski Palace on the outskirts of his home town. This was the summer retreat for a family of White Russians. Each year, exactly like the Coloured people of Middlepost watching the Shers' convoy arrive, Joel must've experienced something similar. Yet he never spoke about it. Nor did he mention the crippling taxes which the Russians imposed on the Jews, nor the pass laws, the vicious bullying, the grotesque accusations about Jewish hygiene. Immigrants usually take their stories with them. Why not this time? All that Joel's children knew was that he'd made an heroic journey across the world, a journey which transformed the fate of the family: from poor pedlars to rich businessmen and landowners, from underdog to ruling class.

A piece of the puzzle was falling into place for me. My family couldn't make the connection between Jewish and black oppression because they were largely ignorant of their own history. Joel didn't sail into Cape Town harbour as a colourful immigrant with a samovar under one arm and a folksong on his lips. He was a refugee from persecution determined to bury his previous life.

And the new one was wonderful. All he had to do was bask in the sun and close his eyes.

He died in 1951, when I was three. I have no recollection of him. Mary turned into that huge old lady sitting on the *stoep* at Marlborough Mansions, confusing hawkers with her flapping wrists and frightening us, her grandchildren, with her faint moustache and her strange stale smell; not just an old lady smell, something else, something foreign. And then there was that day in 1959, shortly after we moved to Montagu House, when I saw Dad hurrying up the road looking strange – young and lost – and later found out that she'd died. I remember nothing else about her.

But Middlepost . . . Middlepost I remember with a tremendous flooding of sensations . . . the smell of milk and blood and woodsmoke in the yard . . . the creaking of windmills, like big empty tins rolling down the road . . the brown *brak* bathwater, in which it was difficult to lather soap . . . the candlelight at night (when the generator had failed *yet again*) melting the sharp angles of the thick walls in the motel, making the passageways lurch and straighten, making you feel you were on that ship again, sailing from one life to the next . . .

The RSC took our production of *Macbeth* on tour to Bath recently. As I sat making up each evening, there was a noise in the corridor that kept catching my attention, making me hesitate, my senses tingling. It took me a few days to work it out. The self-closing springs on the fire doors – they needed oiling. Each gave a small mournful squeak as people came and went. Sounding exactly like the screen doors on a farmhouse – those outer doors kept closed when everything else is thrown open in the hottest weather – a farmhouse, or a motel in the middle of nowhere.

I blinked. I was in Bath, England, in the Theatre Royal, about to play Shakespeare's Scottish king. How odd it was. I caught my eye in the mirror, smiled, whispered the magic word – 'Middlepost' – and resumed my make-up.

7

DAD'S BURIAL

On the first Sunday of our January 2000 visit to Cape Town we finally buried Dad.

Or tried to. Again.

Six years and three months after his death, in November 1993.

A few weeks earlier he and Mom had come over to stay with us, on their annual visit. It was later than usual so that they could see my marathon RSC season, *Tamburlaine* and *Travesties*. In fact, it was touch and go whether he'd be able to come at all this year. Aged eighty-one, his health was failing, his spirits too – after the mugging which split his scalp so bloodily – and he was spending all day, every day, behind the security walls at Montagu House, slowly pacing round the patio or dozing in a chair. But his doctor finally gave a thumbs-up, they arrived and he revived instantly, becoming more alert and active. He and Mom had their usual fights about how much she wanted to visit the shops and theatres, and how much he was boozing, but all in a livelier, better-natured way than usual. They came to my shows; she loved them, he fell asleep; all was normal, all was well. Then they got a gift from the gods. A visit to Buckingham Palace. As President of the RSC, Prince Charles was hosting a fund-raising event for potential sponsors; a group of RSC actors past and present, including Gielgud, Dench and Jacobi, were doing a short entertainment, and I was asked to contribute 'Now is the winter' from *Richard III*. We weren't allowed guests. Greg, not yet a director with the company, couldn't come.

But in exchange for a few of my limbs and part of my soul, the RSC agreed to sneak in Mom and Dad.

Their excitement was tremendous. 'Who would've thought it, hey?' Dad kept saying. 'Me, this little *plaasjapie* from Middlepost, who'd've thought I'd ever be going to Buckingham Palace?' We took him to Moss Bros to hire a DJ and Mom arranged for her favourite black-and-gold necklace to be transported with friends on the next flight from Cape Town.

The big night came and went in a flurry of nerves and thrills for me, especially when I was doing my party piece, and realised Mom and Dad were sitting directly behind the royal party, and that Dad wasn't asleep! At the end of the evening, back in Islington, we took snaps of one another in our finery and regaled Greg with all the stories. Dad went downstairs to change. When he reappeared he was wearing dressing gown, vest and slippers – and the Moss Bros bow tie. He couldn't undo it. Grabbing the camera I caught the moment Mom turned and saw him. She exploded with laughter – that loving laughter they shared – while he stood there grinning, clown-like, in bow tie and underwear. That photo turned out to be the last ever taken of him.

A few days later shocking news arrived from Israel, where Rona Hesselberg – Mom's sister – had emigrated with her family. Her son, Mark, had suddenly collapsed with a heart attack and died. Mark of Mark 'n' Neal, 'the twins'.

I'd never seen Mom like she looked after taking the call. Sitting at the phone in my study, hand across her mouth, eyes closed. I went with her into the guest bedroom to tell Dad. He was still in bed, wearing his South African 'shortie' pyjamas, and was without his glasses, those heavy, black-rimmed, dark-tinted glasses which could act like a small barrier or fence across his eyes. When the glasses were off, like now, they left two red, raw-looking dents on either side of his nose and a particular look on his face – gentler, blanker – a myopic look somewhere between thoughtfulness and bafflement. The news stunned him into silence. As an ailing eighty-one-year-old, death was often in his mind, but Mark was forty-six; that was no age to die.

They arranged to fly to Israel that night. They'd stay a few days, then come back here for their final week, before the big return home – which Dad was dreading. The New South Africa scared him; there was nothing more to it.

During the late afternoon I was writing in my study, when he knocked and came in, a funny smile on his face which I recognised: half sheepish, half wicked. Could I please help him to a vodka, a large vodka, he asked, sounding a little like one of the beggars in London's streets, and could I please do this without *her* knowing. (Vodka was a new boozing ploy – it didn't have whisky's giveaway smell.) I was happy to oblige. He and I had developed a better relationship in recent years, based on my growing professional success to some extent. As a businessman, he'd always been puzzled by the arts and my participation in them. But if I was doing well – and to him the Buckingham Palace visit was proof of it – then it was all right, it was kosher. So a kind of warmth, absent in my childhood, grew between us, especially manifesting itself in a secret guerilla war against *her* and that never-ending campaign against 'the boozing'. I was developing my own dependency by this stage, on something a bit harder than booze – cocaine – which neither of them knew about.

I drove them to Heathrow. At the departure gate I said goodbye in the usual way, hugging her, shaking his hand. Then they vanished among the crowds, him looking very small, wearing his blue sailor cap, his walk slightly uncertain, slightly babyish, searching for the ground with each step.

Mom rang from the hotel in Herzlia the next afternoon. They'd just got back from Ra'anana, where Rona, Neal and the rest of the Hesselbergs live. It was terrible, she said, the grief was terrible. Mom's voice was shaking. I felt sorry for her. Long ago – after the drowning of her, and Rona's, young brother – she decided that grief would never hurt again. She'd spent years toughening herself against it, through spiritualism, but it was no good – grief was hurting again. She and Dad had come back to the hotel for a rest – Dad was napping beside her – and would have a quiet evening, returning to Ra'anana in the morning.

Greg and I held our own little wake for Mark and were quite drunk when the phone rang again at about 9 p.m. Greg answered it, then quickly handed the receiver to me. I heard Mom's voice, low and dry, say my name, and then, 'Dad has died.'

He'd carried on napping, quite restlessly. She watched a Woody Allen film on the movie channel, then went for a bath. Returning, she noticed his lips were bluish. Tried to wake him, couldn't. Reception sent up a security man, who tried artificial respiration. A doctor arrived, tried various things . . .

Now both Mom and I had dreadful tasks. She had to phone the Hesselbergs and add to their grief and ask for their help. I had to phone South Africa and break the news to my siblings.

I never thought it would be this way round. Ever since I left South Africa, I've dreaded the day when the phone would ring and one of them would deliver this news.

When tonight's calls were over, I didn't seek comfort from Greg, but rather my mate Charlie. I had some in the house, took it into my study, closing the door in Greg's face – he hated the growing habit but was helpless to stop it – and stayed up through the night, snorting line after line. Grief – stay away, grief – don't hurt, grief.

It didn't catch up with me till we were on the plane to Tel Aviv the next morning (Greg had made all arrangements while I was locked in the study) and it was the image of the hotel security man trying artificial respiration that did it. He kissed Dad, this stranger *kissed* him. I never did. We never touched, except to shake hands. Like two nights ago, when we said goodbye at Heathrow, our final goodbye as it turned out: we ended our relationship as we'd always conducted it, at arm's length. Dear God, heterosexuals are so fucking queer. How can you have a son and not want to hold him, hug him, kiss him? But of course it wasn't just his fault. I remember once, at Cape Town airport, as we were departing from our annual holiday, Greg suddenly said, 'Oh, Mannie, come here and give me a hug' and Dad did, fastening his frail hands behind Greg's back to return the friendly squeeze. I watched, eyes filling. It was that easy. Yet I couldn't do it.

Reaching Tel Aviv, we went by taxi to Herzlia, to the Sharon Hotel. Mom was standing behind the glass doors, very still, very planted, as though she'd been waiting a long time. She was watching out for us, but now, as we climbed out of the car, she didn't seem to see us. Perhaps something to do with the reflection of the glass. I stood right in front of her and she didn't see me. Maybe she had died, maybe she was the ghost. I went through a side door. She said, 'There you are.' I hugged her and began to cry. She was calm. More than calm. Up in the room, a different one from where he'd died, she told us about his last, restless nap. He'd changed into his shortie pyjamas, she said: 'He didn't usually wear pyjamas for an afternoon *shloff*, but anyway this time he did, and there he was, snoozing away, muttering and garbling all sorts of nonsense.' As she spoke – with the faint disgust of someone who'd endured this kind of thing for many years – it gradually dawned on me that his death was a relief. To her and to him. In a way it was death-to-order. As though he'd said, 'At the age of eighty-one I'll fly away from South Africa, which is frightening me, I'll go see my son, I'll do something I never dreamed of doing – visiting Buckingham Palace – I'll pop over to Israel too, say hello the family there, then I'll change into my shortie pyjamas and have a little lie-down.'

We spent the weekend in Israel, a strange weekend, some of it surprisingly enjoyable. On Saturday Mom wanted time with Rona, just the two of them, so Greg and I hired a taxi for the day and went to Jerusalem. Greg, who'd never visited before, would later say, 'Mannie was always a very generous man and Jerusalem was his last gift to me.' Our driver was an amateur tour guide. 'Just one question,' he said when we asked him to devise the day's sightseeing. 'What religion are you?'

Greg replied, 'One lapsed Catholic and one lapsed Jew.'

'But the lapsed Jew has seen Jerusalem,' I added. 'So show it to the lapsed Catholic.'

As protection against the sun, I'd brought along Dad's blue sailor cap. I felt a bit funny when Mom suggested this and, when no one was looking, sniffed it apprehensively, but there was no trace of him. A few hours later, when I'd been sweating, I sniffed it again, wondering if the heat from me would've released a scent from him, like with old costumes worn by other actors, but there was still nothing.

During the course of the day we managed (unintentionally) to offend both an Arab and a Jew; the first, a souk trader, by asking him where the nearest bar was, and the second, the warder at the Wailing Wall, by trying to take a photo of it. As this ferocious bearded man rushed at us, yelling and clapping his hands, and as we fled, our camera fell and opened. When we had the film developed only this one shot was spoilt. Greg saw it as a sort of miracle. I was less impressed. If God is so busy ruining tourist snapshots, does that explain why He hasn't time for some other matters that need His intervention?

I hadn't seen the Hesselbergs for twelve years. They'd endured a lot – Uncle Jack died shortly after they arrived in Israel – but always found comfort in their faith; they're devout Orthodox Jews. Now they were sitting *shiva* for Mark: staying in the house all day, perched on low benches and stools, saying prayers, clothes deliberately torn, all mirrors covered. People constantly visiting, bringing food, joining the prayers. All of these visitors were South African – no natural-born Israelis – it turns out that Ra'anana is a home from home. Rona had aged – maybe just in the last few days – and bore a curious resemblance to Granny. Neal, the surviving twin, looked shattered with grief: a hunched posture, his eyes hollow and black, hardly any whites showing, his chin unshaven, the flaps of his torn shirt held together with a safety pin.

In the evening, *Kaddish* was said, the Prayer for the Dead. All the women had to leave the room, even Rona, even Karen, Mark's widow. Greg and I, having no yarmulkas, put handkerchiefs on our heads. Oddly enough, I was able to chant this particular Hebrew text: I'd recently learned it for the TV film, *Genghis Cohen*, in which I played the title role, a concentration camp victim who returns from the dead to haunt the camp's commandant.

Afterwards we had supper with the Hesselbergs and their South African friends. The atmosphere became surprisingly ordinary, social, unmournful. People were interested in my career – Mom was full of Buckingham Palace stories of course – and I was interested in their experiences during the recent Gulf War. Neal showed us his air-raid shelter, now a laundry room. Another man, a neighbour, started relating stories about the Falashas, the Ethiopian Jews in Israel: they were confused by the air-raid instructions, unable to comprehend either Hebrew or English. One family stayed in their shelter for days, failing to recognise the all-clear, and one old man suffocated to death in his gas mask. These anecdotes were told humorously. I don't know why I should've been surprised by this – South African whites laughing at the stupidity of kaffirs – but I was. Were Jewish kaffirs no better, then? Was it really just about skin pigmentation, then, just skin deep, nothing more?

Greg had to return to London on Sunday morning, for work, and now my strange Israeli weekend became a lot stranger. Mom and I were due to fly out later that evening, to South Africa, but we'd be going without Dad, or 'the body' as everyone suddenly started calling him. We'd hit a bureaucratic nightmare. The Israeli sabbath is Saturday, the South African one is Sunday, so nobody could do the paperwork. Yet the funeral was scheduled for Monday. Could we hold the funeral without him – it – the body – Dad?

Well, it would just have to be a kind of memorial service and then, when the coffin arrived, we could do something else for the actual cremation.

The cremation. Ah. Another problem. I know little about Jewish law, so I didn't spot this one coming. After lunch Neal asked me to take a stroll with him.

At 4 p.m. in the afternoon, Ra'anana looks vaguely like a South African country town, vaguely like both Middlepost and Montagu: the single-storeyed houses have practical, unlovely gardens with chicken coops and vegetable patches, here and there are orchards, the sprinklers on the go all the time, with a kind of frenzy, the water burning away as it falls. Yet there's also something that's unmistakably Israeli: a rushed, half-finished look everywhere – as though building work is forever being interrupted by a new emergency or war – doorways don't quite fit the walls, sandbags hold down a tin roof, pavements disappear halfway along and turn into a piece of wasteland, this into reclaimed desert and this into the real thing. It gives me the shivers, I'm not sure why. There's something stark and merciless here, a no-nonsense battle for survival, to the death if need be, which makes South Africa seem like a school playground. The macho swagger in South Africa has a sort of absurdity to it and those guys sort of see the joke. Here there's no joke. Israel is the most *masculine* society on earth; hard-muscled, grim-faced, combat-clad – and that's just the women. I think it's why I always feel uncomfortable here. I need the feminine in things. And there's something else that troubles me. Here it is again – the persecuted-persecutor syndrome – except I truly can't tell who's who any more. Some of the South African Jews who moved here came out of despair – 'We want a future for our children!' (They came *here* for a safe future?) Others came because they're fervent Zionists. Neal is somewhere between the two.

Today, looking even more haunted than before, eyes even blacker, stubble thicker, he wasted no time: 'I've got something to say. Please hear me out. Forgive me if you don't like this. My mom asked me not to talk to you about it. But I have to. I have to get it off my chest.'

He explained that it was a crime against Judaism to have Dad cremated. The law forbids mutilating the body in any way. (Even autopsies are rare.) He implored me to talk to Randall and Joel, and convince them to cancel the cremation. Why didn't he suggest I also talk to Mom and Verne? Because Jewish law is sexist. And of course homophobic. Not long previously, the chief rabbi in Britain, Jakobovits, proposed a plan that would not have shamed Dr Mengele, suggesting that gays be genetically identified and eliminated before birth.

I felt a strange anger bubbling up, but remained polite, reassuring Neal that I didn't mind him mentioning this and that I'd discuss it with the family. Then I changed the subject. I told him how we'd had all the old home movies put on to video. The films were unsteady and overexposed, but wonderful – they look like memories feel – showing childhood as one long hazy summer's day. All those holidays in Middlepost and Montagu, with lots of footage of them, Mark 'n' Neal . . .

As I said this phrase – Mark 'n' Neal – this catchphrase from the past, I suddenly broke down. He embraced me, saying, 'Go on, it's OK, I tell you, man, I've cried buckets this week, go on, yes, it shows you *are* a Jew, like Uncle Mannie was a Jew! Yes, it's OK, it's OK.'

I reeled out of his embrace, his evangelical embrace, wanting to shout, I'm not crying because I'm a Jew – I'm crying for my father, for your brother, for us, for the old times!

But I didn't, of course. We went back to the house for evening *Kaddish*. I watched numbly as Mark's mother and wife were banished from the room again so that a lot of strangers, but *male* strangers, could say prayers for him. Neal pushed the Jewish Book of Mourning into my hand, urgently pointing to the section on cremation. I discreetly put it aside. Then, as Mom and I were leaving for the airport, he put a yarmulka on to my head and suggested I keep it on. It would make getting through Customs easier, he said. I took it off as soon as we were in the taxi. But Neal was right. To go through Israeli Customs is to be grilled for a crime you haven't committed. I was subjected to all sorts of odd questions, like why I'd stopped learning Hebrew as a child. (*Did they really want the story of my bar mitzvah?*)

Finally we were on the plane. The video screen had a feature I hadn't seen before: a map of your journey with a little plane gradually inching its way along, with accompanying data about speed, altitude, et cetera. It was the kind of thing that interested Dad. 'What's the population of Stratford?' he'd ask, as though I knew or cared. But it fascinated me tonight: this picture of Israel, England, Africa and our little plane . . .

So we were flying home without him – it – the body – Dad.

When transportation was finally arranged, three days later, the cost was obscene: £4000. Joel, joking grimly as always, said, 'People spend fortunes to be buried in Israel – trust Dad to do it the other way round.'

Joel was the first to rush forward as Mom and I walked into the Arrivals area at Cape Town airport – not waiting for us to reach the barrier, where a great crowd of smiling people stood, here to meet holidaying family or friends. As he hugged Mom, I heard her sob for the first time. Now Verne was at my side and we embraced. Now Randall. We stood there, hugging and changing partners as in some strange slow dance. Meanwhile other passengers were struggling to squeeze past and the whole spectacle was being watched by the smiling audience behind the barrier. We presented a long tragi-comic scene, played in silence, except for our quiet weeping.

Katie, on the other hand, was howling – back at Montagu House – howling with grief. She'd always said, 'Madam and Master is like parents to me' – apartheid trained her well – and now, half addressing Mom, half praying to her own departed mother, she cried, 'Ooh Mommie, Mommie, ooh God, the poor master, poor Master Mannie, what's going to happen now, what's going to happen to me?' In her passion she was perhaps revealing more than she realised. Dad was her ally at Montagu House, her pal – I used to wake up each morning to hear them in the backyard, chatting away in Afrikaans – whereas Mom was her boss, her critic; they had rows and bust-ups, Katie packing and leaving, coming back. But this morning Mom took her in her arms and rocked her: 'Katie, Katie, it's all right, the master went peacefully, it's all right, nothing's going to happen to you, there's a place for you here, there'll always be a place for you here.'

We wanted her to come along to the memorial service, but she refused. She didn't have her Sunday best here, her church clothes, and it was unthinkable to go to Master Mannie's service dressed in her maid's uniform. We all implored her, Joel becoming quite aggressive – 'Katie you *have* to come, we can't do this without you!' Someone found her a raincoat and she relented.

Meanwhile I had a similar problem: nothing suitable to wear. Mom suggested I look in Dad's wardrobe. I went upstairs. His room was shadowy and airless. I pulled open the blinds and windows, muttering, 'Let in some fucking light!' I found a jacket, shirt and trousers that vaguely fitted. The trousers were too short, but I could just get away with it, wearing them low on the bum like he did. It was odd, I felt I was climbing into a costume;

preparing to play Dad. Later, going for a pee, I experienced an even stranger sensation: reaching for myself through his flies.

The service was held in the Reform Synagogue in Green Point. The others had decided on this because Dad didn't really belong to our old *shul* any more, the Orthodox one in Marais Road, and anyway the unusual circumstances – Dad missing his own funeral – required a liberal attitude.

The big chamber was only half full. I tried not to notice. (Poor Dad – a small house for his final show.) We sat in the front row, me wishing Greg were here. Katie was in a corner right at the back, the only 'non-white' in the congregation and the only one weeping throughout. The rabbi was a tall, bearded, youngish man, an American. Why an American? I wondered, and concluded that all the South African rabbis must have got the hell out of here. This man had never met Dad, mispronounced our surname, saying Sheeeer or something, and trotted out a few all-purpose platitudes, which were rather like the clothes I was wearing, only half fitting. Basically he bluffed his way through. Not all that different from the spiritualist medium who would later convince Mom he knew which month Dad died. Both men struck me as not very good actors. Both bring out the professional in me: sorry but I don't *believe* this, could you try and put some conviction into it, please? I glanced along the row to the family. They looked rapt in a glazed kind of way. Not with emotion but with the instant boredom that hits whenever priests open their mouths. Religion is a pretty irreligious thing, really: it gets in the way of you and your feelings. It anaesthetises and oversimplifies, it numbs and dumbs down. The service ended with the tall American coming down from his platform, his stage, and instructing us, Dad's four children, to say *Kaddish* for him – Verne was allowed to join in, this being the Reform *shul*. 'One, two, three,' went the rabbi, and started. I was the only one who vaguely knew the Hebrew, from *Genghis Cohen*, so the others just had to pretend, and mumbled their way through, embarrassment now getting in the way of their grief. What a thoroughly pointless exercise. How I envy those societies where mourners gather at gravesides, throw back their heads and just wail.

I slept in Dad's bed that night. Sniffing the pillow before I got in. The linen was fresh. Of course it was. Katie would've changed the sheets the morning they left for London.

*

On Wednesday an El Al plane flew into Cape Town with a coffin in its hold, finally bringing him – it – the body – Dad – back home. I assumed we'd all go to the airport to see it in and to accompany the hearse to the crematorium (I'd relayed Neal's point about the sin of cremation, but no one felt it relevant to the Shers' own DIY form of Judaism), and then at last we'd hold our own ritual of grief. To my amazement, nobody wanted to go. Mom said, 'There's no point, no need, it's not *him* arriving.' I expected this of her, but my siblings' response was more a surprise. Joel spoke for them all, and with characteristic clarity: 'What, and see him thrown off the plane like cargo? No, thank you!'

'But not if we're *there*,' I argued. 'They won't do that if we're *there*.'

There was no winning them round; the undertakers would meet the plane on their own. I couldn't believe it. This phrase, 'the body', was just bullshit. Of course it was *him*, of course our flesh and bones are part of us too! After all the fuss and expense of bringing *him* back, we weren't going to meet *him*, weren't going to travel with *him* on *his* last journey.

This was my first reaction. My second came after Randall and Verne offered to drive me to the airport – they wouldn't come in themselves, but were happy to take me – and I heard myself answer tetchily, 'No, no, it's fine, I won't go either!' In truth, I felt relief. I wasn't looking forward to seeing the coffin arrive. I was dreading it. Stuck in my mind was a comparison between the first voyage that the Lithuanian Joel Sher made to South Africa and this, his son's last. The immense loneliness of both journeys and of both figures: the one standing on a ship deck as the world slowly changed around him for ever, the other packed into a box.

That night I flew back to London, back 'home'.

A few days later Mom rang to report that they'd been to the crematorium and collected the ashes. She said these came in a cardboard container – 'sort of like a shoebox but smaller' – and that the family had divided them into various portions. To be planted in their different gardens – she planned a rose bush for her allocation – and one would be scattered at Middlepost when my cousins went on their next pilgrimage. Would I like one too? Yes, I said. I'd heard about Derek Jarman mixing a friend's ashes into the paint for a portrait of him and I wanted to do the same with Dad.

When I got my share – a heap of gritty red, grey and white particles in a squat plastic tub – I put it in the back corner of my art materials cupboard, unable to summon the courage to go through with the plan.

As the years passed, I felt haunted by Dad – haunted by the image of him making that last lonely journey home, packed in a coffin – haunted so vividly sometimes that it was as if Mom's faith, the truth in spiritualism, had been revealed to me and ghosts really did exist. Except it wasn't comforting, this ghost, it didn't 'come through' like those Blackpool mediums claim, with vague little prophecies about all being well in your future; it came through as a painful thing, a thing of conscience, a sense of wrong, of misjudgement.

If only I'd gone to the airport to meet him, if only, if only . . .

Last year the haunting suddenly got worse, a mixture of guilt and grief, a real mess of it. With my fiftieth birthday fast approaching, I was troubled by Beckett's grim phrase about us needing to leave a stain on the silence. What stain had Dad left? In a hundred, two hundred years' time, when some nerdish Sher wanted to construct a history of the family, where would he go to seek out Mannie? I asked my siblings if they'd like to join me in creating a little memorial to him, somewhere that *I* at least could visit on trips to South Africa. I still had that plastic tub of his ashes in the back of my art materials cupboard and it was still three-quarters full. I'd eventually done a painting of him as planned – in fact, of him, his father and myself in a composition called *The Male Line* – but even though this was executed during a long, urgent, cocaine-fuelled session, I'd grown squeamish about the Derek Jarman idea and mixed only a small amount of ashes with the oils. Now my idea was to bury the rest somewhere in Cape Town and plant a small memorial plaque above them.

At the time of Dad's death my siblings surpised me by refusing to go to the airport – now, six years later, they amazed me by revealing that they all felt the same way. Dad was unburied somehow – his death an unresolved issue for each of them.

Excellent. I began to conjure up the scene in my mind. The four of us, just us four, standing round his resting place, saying goodbye at last, forgiving him for being the rather distant father he was, or coming to terms with it, or whatever. We'd stand there, hugging, each telling a story about him, we'd laugh, we'd cry and that would be it: Dad would be buried.

*

On Sunday morning, 9 January 2000, we drive out to the Jewish cemetery at Pinelands. It's a rather bleak place, on a flat landscape, the soil sandy, its perimeters marked by plain fencing. As you enter there's a sign advising you not to visit graves unaccompanied: report to the building and someone will come with you. This is a South African cemetery and there have been muggings.

Mom has come along – to my surprise – as have all the family, all my nieces and nephews, all my cousins, everyone. And a rabbi has been found to bless the memorial plaque; he's fitting us in between a whole series of marriages today. 'Four weddings and a funeral,' quips someone. Nothing is as I envisaged it. I'm carrying a plastic bag, and in it the tub with his ashes, but there's no possibility of burying these. That part of the plan was forgotten and the plaque is already cemented in place, straddling the resting places of his parents, Joel and Mary. Their gravestones are impressive black marble slabs. How odd – I've never seen these before. Did Dad never visit them? Probably not. Probably preferred to leave death alone too. Pity. I wish he'd brought us here and said, 'This is where my folks are buried, let me tell you some stories about them.' Aren't heteros queer? They expend so much passion and ambition, wealth and worry on this 'generation' thing, and then often forget to cherish it.

The rabbi arrives. Oh, no. The tall American from before. No, no, no. He didn't know anything about Dad then and doesn't now. It all starts again. Him busking his way through a little service, squinting at the gravestones for names and dates while spouting all-purpose platitudes, mistakenly addressing most of these to Mom (I'm scared she'll suddenly snap back, 'Stop talking to me – I don't even believe in you!') and, at one point, Greg.

No, no. I don't want this. A stranger intruding on our privacy again; an unengaged actor speaking the lines, feeling nothing.

I struggle to concentrate on Dad, lifting my face into the sunshine, but it's difficult. Except when he sings, quite sweetly, the rabbi keeps getting in the way of my thoughts.

And then it's the *Kaddish* again. But *Genghis Cohen* was six years ago now, so I can't say the Hebrew any better than the others and have just to mumble into my beard, blushing, feeling stupid.

He goes. People say, 'What a lovely service – didn't he speak beautifully?' I blink at them in amazement. They drift away. My siblings and I hang back. As Neal explained, cremation is forbidden by Jewish law, and even in these informal circumstances, we have to do the next bit secretly. Between us we shake out the contents of the plastic tub. A breeze instantly starts spreading it around. 'Oich,' goes Joel – 'My hayfever!'

As we leave, Randall takes me across the road to the other half of the cemetery. Esther was buried here just three days ago. Her consecration (laying the stone) won't happen for a while, so it's just a freshly closed grave for now, with a tag stuck in: MRS E. CAPLAN, 6/1/00. After all the palaver over at Dad's stone, the atmosphere here is much more peaceful. I silently say goodbye to her and thanks. Now, remembering something, I break into a smile. I've done this before – said my farewells before – but to her in person, over the telephone, trying not to let my voice betray my emotion. It was last spring. She was dying then, the doctor said, it was only a matter of days. Her son Ashley, who lives in America, climbed on to a plane, as did a beloved niece in Australia. Hearing there was to be a family reunion, Esther struggled up in bed and had her hair done. By the time her relatives reached her side, she had revived magnificently. Eventually they had to go home again and she lived for another six months. She'd caught the scent of a party, a public performance, and so snatched another half-year of life. How perfectly *Esther* that was.

Back in our hotel room I sit staring at the plastic tub. I'll have to throw it away now, though this feels strange. Some remnants are left inside and a few grains fall from the lid, dusting the table. I collect these on one finger. It reminds me of that final wipe across the surface after a coke binge. I think about tasting them, these tiny specks of Dad, but don't. I carry the tub to the balcony and tip it over the view beyond: Alexander Road and the old house, Montagu House, hunched and shadowy, looking closed, sealed, as though everyone inside has died.

8

LEAVING

'ANTONY . . . ANTONY.'
  'Ja?'
  'Just come out here, just come look at this.'
  I walk on to the *stoep*, Tickey scampering after. Dad is standing there with a tumbler of whisky, pointing across the sea to the setting sun. It's beautiful but familiar: a daily spectacle of fire and water. I'm taken aback nevertheless – it's not like Dad to notice sunsets. I feel uncomfortable. Everyone else is out; he and I are alone for the evening.
  (I'm aged eighteen. Filling in the long months between the army and the big move overseas. The dialogue's from my diary – where I'd started meticulously transcribing conversations. It's Thursday, 4 January 1968.)
  'It's terrific,' I say.
  'You see that cloud?' he says. 'Looks like a tank.'
  'A –?'
  'Tank. You know?'
  I don't, but remain silent. Dad's not an articulate man, but tonight for some reason he's trying to make contact.
  'You know what I mean?' he checks again.
  'A tank.'
  'Ja, a, a shooting tank, a –'
  'Ah.'
  We stand in silence. Tickey trots down to the end of the *stoep*, lifts her

small black face into the evening sunshine, scents the sea breeze, glances back hopefully – any chance? – nope – and trots back.

'That cloud there,' I say to Dad. 'The . . . sort of . . . the last one.'

'Ja.'

'Reminds me of a flamingo – we saw them up in Walvis – flamingos.'

'Didn't you see tanks too?'

'Hmn? Yes, of course.'

Later. We're at supper in the dinette, the informal eating room off the kitchen. You can hear Katie moving around next door, clearing up, coming to the end of her day. At the table there are long stretches of silence, both of us staring at our plates as we eat. We continue to do so – no eye contact – when Dad suddenly says: 'So, you're going to London – make a career out of that?'

'Yup.'

'You don't think I should've been . . . or you should've . . . what I thought of the set-up?'

'Pardon?'

He doesn't answer. He's had several more whiskies since our talk on the *stoep* and there's a familiar pattern to any conversation – it starts and stops, it loops round – and a familiar look to his heavy face: dull, dark anger; his moist grey eyes hard and sad behind the thick black glasses.

'I didn't discuss it with anyone,' I say after a while, lying. 'I decided for myself.'

'Haah?'

This isn't really a note of enquiry, more a little bludgeoning grunt; it closes rather than opens doors. Another long pause. The conversation could be over. Then he says: 'After all, I am your father too. If there's a problem in his business, he comes running so fast it isn't true, and he –'

'Who's "he"?'

'Randall, that's who's "he". He says, Dad the position is such and such, I say, Randall, I can either help you or I can't, and that's the end of the story.'

'Well, if I was thinking of going into business, you'd be the first person I'd . . . but it's not like a business.'

'Why – you not planning to make money?'

'Yes, of course. Eventually. I hope. But . . .'

He's staring at my talking face. I could be reciting verse.

'Too proud, hey?' he says. 'Too proud.'

'Pride doesn't come –'

'All right now let me ask you a question, a silly question y'understand, they say I'm sarcastic . . .'

He eats. I wait. Eventually he resumes: 'What if I'm not in a position to support you – haah?'

I don't, can't, answer.

'C'mon – jokes aside – you think you'd still want to go to London and –'

'Yes.'

'Haah?'

'Yes. I'd work.'

He gives a small, private laugh, then becomes morose again: 'After all, you could just come into the lounge for five minutes, you could sit down with me, you could just be honest, you could say, look you big bloody sucker I'm not interested in your bloody opinion about –'

'It's not that at all.'

'– You could just say, It means nothing to me and that's the end of the story.'

'No, I'd very much like to know what you . . . to hear your opinion of . . .'

'I'm sorry. I'm sor-r-ry! Ask me *now*. I must be a sucker. No, my boy, you can just forget about it. Sor-r-ry. Just forget it!'

We hold one another's gaze for a moment, dumbly, then stare at our plates again. I'm wondering how all this started. Had he planned this discussion, waiting for an evening when we'd be alone? Did he intend it to be gentle, loving, father-to-son? Is that what the business on the *stoep* was – with clouds and sunsets – an attempt to talk my language? I take a mouthful of food. It's gone cold.

Katie looks through the door: '*Kan ek ma' wegvat*, Master?' (Can I clear, Master?)

' *Dankie, ja.*' (Thanks, yes.)

I watch Katie's hands as she collects the dishes: the thick fingers, slightly bent by hard work, the yellowish-brown nails. Once at junior school they showed us a film about hygiene with huge, animated close-ups of germs and how they spread. I became obsessed by this and convinced that, since Katie was Coloured, 'non-white', there was an aura of dirtiness surrounding her and then I took to wiping any cutlery she'd lay down for me. She was terribly hurt by this. She'd worked for the family since before

I was born, she'd helped raise me, she'd cooked every meal I'd ever eaten.

Nowadays, like everyone else, she's just puzzled by me: '*Haai*, Master Antony, you're going to kill yourself with all your kind of talking,' she said the other morning. 'An ordinary person can't carry on like that. It's like a lawyer talking.'

Tonight, once the table is cleared, I excuse myself, hurry upstairs to my room, Tickey scurrying after, and lunge for my diary.

I like the old joke:

> My *mother made me a homosexual*.
> *If I give her the wool will she make me one too?*

I don't know why I'm gay, whether it's design or detour, genetic or learned behaviour. I suspect, prefer, the former, but if it's the other I've always felt it's less to do with her than him. She was Mate, a soulmate, almost more. When I read our letters from the army days, I blush – they're like love letters – but I'm also moved to find her revealing a side which few others saw. Her role in life was of commander-in-chief and that often meant battle conditions: she ran the house, ran the family, tried to supervise four strong-minded kids, a temperamental cook, a succession of inebriated maids and a hostile husband. She yearned for a quiet life, not only to indulge in the pursuits of other Sea Point madams – the hairstyling, manicures and massages – but to seek inner peace. It's not just spiritualism that draws her, but also the spiritual in earthly life, in nature, in art. In the letters she writes of long solitary walks, of gazing at views. She tries to describe these, becomes embarrassed by her purple prose, apologises. She says she's bought Durrell's *Alexandrian Quartet* for me, started to read them herself and is swept away by his poetic vision. There's a dreamer in her, a loner, an outsider too – the country girl, rather plain, then, and self-conscious – once fantasising about a more stimulating, more enriching, more creative life and eventually finding that potential in her third child. I gloried in her love, yet resisted it too. It carried a proviso, a sub-clause – her belief in Dr Prisman's prophecy at my birth – and to me this felt like a kind of threat. Little Ant will be a GREAT MAN. When she said this it sounded like it was carved in stone, in letters bigger than the title of *Ben Hur*. Would I ever be able to live up to it? Would she ever be satisfied?

Would I? We'd done *Macbeth* for matric, so I knew a little about the illness that attends ambition. The play is about a powerful female force (Lady Macbeth plus the witches) saying to the hero, 'You can have everything you want, just don't read the small print.' Shakespeare must've had a Jewish mother.

I had her love, but it was his I craved. Yet he frightened me. Why didn't he seem impressed by my artwork, when Mate and all the other Shers went apeshit over it? Why didn't he seem to notice me at all? He was absent all the time – either away at work or sulking at supper – absent yet menacing. He never hit us, but often threatened to. He'd been a boxer in his youth, he claimed – bare-knuckled bouts at Middlepost, I assumed – and his punch was so hard he was reluctant to use it. But he would, if pushed. I was convinced that it would be *me* – I'd somehow be the one who pushed – I'd be on the receiving end of his violence one day. He glared at me with such non-comprehending anger. Like I wasn't *his*. (Yet I knew I was – we were so alike – with our scowling sad faces.) I lived in fear of the day when he'd finally raise his fist, his boxer's fist, and rush at me.

The only time I actually saw him hitting someone was in the back garden of our first house in Marais Road. I watched him chasing Golie down the path to the maid's room, slapping as he went, both men losing their balance. Golie was Katie's husband, a black factory worker, always drunk. Later, in old age, after he quit the booze, they became a devoted couple, but he caused Katie a lot of misery during the early years, so I suppose Dad was 'teaching him a lesson' that day. The image sticks in my mind of them tumbling down the path together. It's funny if you think about it – one drunk punishing another.

Dad's surprise interrogation about my intended career couldn't have come at a worse time. I'd returned from the army no longer sure that I wanted to be an actor. It seemed like a long time since I'd attended Auntie Esther's elocution classes and performed little improvisations at the Cape Town Eisteddfod. These struck me as childish things now. And Mac's words rang in my ears: acting is interpretative, not creative, it's second-rate. I'd definitely turned my back on drawing and painting, but what about writing? My diary was becoming a new best friend and a new creative outlet.

I kept silent about my doubts. It had been so difficult deciding whether to be artist or actor I couldn't introduce a new idea – author. So plans were proceeding on the London drama school front. The playwright Ronald Harwood (formerly Horwitz) is my mother's first cousin and was acting as adviser. RADA was still good, he reckoned, but Central was currently the best. Then that was it, Mom said, Ant would go there. Ronnie warned that competition was fierce. Mom replied that the problem was non-applicable: few other canditates were likely to have been born with a cowl. She asked Ronnie to make enquiries about bedsitters near the school – an area of London called, curiously, Swiss Cottage – and she booked our air tickets. On Tuesday, 16 July 1968, we'd be leaving for overseas.

Overseas. That mythical word. Over seas. Just how many did you have to cross? And what would you find at the other end? *Overseas*. A mythical place. Mom and Dad went there every few years and returned with theatre programmes featuring Olivier, Gielgud, Richardson, Guinness, Edith Evans, Sybil Thorndike. Names so famous I couldn't think of them as living, breathing mortals. Well, they weren't, obviously – they inhabited this place called Overseas.

My theatregoing in Cape Town was extremely limited, mostly confined to CAPAB at the Hofmeyer, where, apart from one striking actress, Yvonne Bryceland, the work was what I'd later learn to call reppy. The plays were imports from the West End and Broadway, like *The Corn is Green* and *Barefoot in the Park*, pretty tame fare. What with the cultural boycott – playwrights like Pinter and Wesker refusing to let their work be performed under apartheid – and our own dear Censorship Board – 'Agh, man, there must be no disgusting, liberal, Commie filth performed on our stages!' – there wasn't a lot left. Anti-government theatre like the Space in Cape Town and especially the Market in Joburg were yet to come. But I did have one memorable theatre experience before leaving South Africa. At the Little Theatre near the Gardens in town. It was a new play by a South African author, an unknown author – this went without saying; how could a South African author be anything but unknown? – and he was appearing in the show as well. What an unusual piece it was. About poor whites, for God's sake. You avoided them in the street – or army – and yet here you were watching a piece of drama about their lives. A brother and sister, he a recluse, she a prostitute. They have a reunion, talk, row, eventually fight and part again. And that, as Dad would say, was the end of the story. It was titled *Hello and Goodbye* and the unknown, strangely named author was Athol Fugard. I'd never seen anything like this on stage – the play's rawness, pain and humour. It was like a blow to the face. The dialogue sounded *real* – the male character, Johnnie (brilliantly played by Fugard) spoke exactly like Alphonso in the Walvis camp. So plays weren't just about unfamiliar figures – reserved English governesses or kooky American couples – plays could be about *us*. What did we, the Shers, a comfortably off Sea Point Jewish family, have in common with the pair in *Hello and Goodbye*? Their strange ugly accent, with its flat vowels and barbed consonants, that stone and thornbush accent, it wasn't too different from our own. They called their dead mother Mommie and – setting aside all nonsense about Mate – Mommie was what we, and Katie, and every other South African I knew, called out in the dark. There's a moment in *Hello and Goodbye* which hit me powerfully that night and still seems one of the best in modern drama. The sister, Hester, who's searching through old suitcases filled with family belongings, suddenly finds a dress and says: 'My God, Johnnie! Smell! It's her. Mommie. Smell, man. It's Mommie's smell.' This made me cry and I'd never cried in a theatre before. Mom was sitting next to me – her own smell, the perfume she wore, a powerful, comforting drug that still stops my heart when strangers carry it past in the street – and although she didn't cry, she nevertheless agreed, when we discussed it later, that the play carried quite a punch.

The bioscope was making an impact on me too – or the cinema, as Tony Fagin and I preferred to say. We were compulsive cinema-goers, at the Van Riebeeck or Metro in town or the artier ones, the Broadway on the Foreshore or the Alvin in Camps Bay, walking all the way back to Sea Point afterwards, locked in lofty discussions about the Art of the Motion Picture.

If Uncle Nat's Censorship Board guarded us from liberal, Commie filth on stage it was as nothing to his vigilence in the bioscope. All offensive material – i.e. sex, blasphemy or racial equality – was heavily and clumsily cut. Sequences would be chopped halfway through their course and jump to elsewhere in the story with no attempt made to ease the transition. It's like the censor *wanted* us to know he was at work. He was having to watch the most unspeakable excrement from Overseas, day in day out, and he wanted us to know the sacrifice he was making – the corruption of his own soul for the good of ours. I pictured him as a gaunt, bearded Afrikaner, an old-style Boer, incessantly muttering prayers, leaping at the spools of film not with a pair of scissors, but a bayonet or his own teeth.

Yet some got through, amazingly, the subtler ones, like John Schlesinger's *Darling*, where the decadence is just below the surface. The mad Voortrekker at the Censorship Board couldn't see that far; issues were just skin deep for him, either black or white. I watched *Darling* in a strange state of shock. So this is what goes on in London – this is Overseas – you don't just get theatre there, starring any legend you care to name, you get *this*. There was a gay character, played by Roland Curram, and when he and Julie Christie take a Mediterranean holiday, he exchanges a funny look with the handsome waiter over breakfast one morning – a look I'd never seen before – and then later the waiter comes to collect him on a scooter, and they drive off into the night. They're going to have sex. You don't see it, but you know it – well, not the mad Voortrekker, or he wouldn't have left it in (he probably thought the waiter was taking Roland Curram to his parents for tea and prayers), but I knew it.

Is this what gave me the idea? I don't know, but I started going for walks at night along the beach front, above Graaf's Pool. This was a men-only nude sunbathing enclosure. Mainly a meeting place for fat old Jewish men who'd sit gossiping all day long, each fingering his balls aimlessly, like Greeks do with worry beads, flipping and rolling them in the hand. But there was another presence here too: younger men with a look in their eyes – a look I could now identify as the *Darling* look – a look that gave me an unsettled feeling, a feeling of quite profound threat, a rather nice feeling.

So without any clear notion of what I wanted, yet with a kind of sixth sense, an animal's sense that nourishment is near, I took to strolling along this stretch of promenade at night.

Eventually it happened. A figure was sitting in the wooden weather shelter above Milton Pool Beach, deep in shadow. I sat at the other end. After a moment or two he shifted closer. I smelled him before seeing clearly: a perfumed man. Coloured. About thirty, with soft round features. He touched my leg. I half touched his. He whispered, 'Let's go down to the beach.' I shook my head, but indicated we could find somewhere else. Not this beach, it was too far from home. I was about to take a momentous step, I needed to be nearer safety.

We walked all the way back to the beach at the bottom of Alexander Road, called, oh dear, Queen's Beach. We went down the steps, crossed the sand to the rocks on the left. There, in the deep shadow of the wall, he sucked me off. I can't remember if I touched him in return.

Bill Clinton might disagree, but this was the loss of my virginity. Well, the first of several times: later, properly, with a man, later with a woman, later with a man again but adding the ingredient of love. For now, however, it shook me to my core. It wasn't just that I'd had sex with a man; I knew about the Immorality Act by now – I'd had sex across the race barrier. I'd broken so many taboos in those few moments I was probably eligible for Death Row. We climbed back to the street and parted. Convinced that he was watching and would try and seek me out again, I pretended to go into a nearby block of flats, then snuck round the corner to Montagu House. Locking myself in the bathroom, I took off every stitch of clothes and shoved them in the laundry basket, mingling them among items already there, fearful that Katie or our current maid, Lena, would empty it in the morning and *know*, by the smell – his of perfume, mine of sperm – and then I showered for a long, long time.

February, March. During my last few months in South Africa I acted professionally for the first time, at Maynardville, the open-air Shakespeare theatre. The play was *Richard II*. The British actor Bernard Brown was an excellent Richard and the production was by the distinguished South African and later Israeli director, Leonard Schach. I carried spears, I brought messages, I emoted passionately just out of the spotlight. During rehearsals I was given lifts to and from Maynardville by two of the actors who lived in Bantry Bay, next door to Sea Point. I remember the shock of seeing their small flat on the first morning and realising there was only one big, unmade bed.

These two weren't engaged in some fast, furtive act of immorality on a beach at night. These two were living together openly. It was brave of them. I mean, I could've reported them to the police.

April, May. Winter coming to Cape Town. Mists, drizzle, the foghorn keening away down at Moullie Point, the incredible, cannon-like thump of Atlantic breakers along the beach front. Tony Fagin and I walk for miles, along the woodland trails of Signal Hill and Lion's Head, or on the beautiful, long, white curve of Noordhoek Beach; we walk and talk and dream of great things, Tickey always trotting after, my runtish little black mongrel, myself in animal form.

My passport arrives – my first passport. I look at my photograph. This is worrying – this isn't what *actors* look like. My black specs make me vaguely resemble that Buddy Holly person who died, except I'm even plainer. My hair is worn in a timid Beatles fringe (they've been banned in South Africa recently because of something Lennon said about Christ) and the rest of my features are just rather smooth and bland, the nose a bit too big, the chin a bit too small.

In just two months' time, Mom and Dad will fly with me to London, wait while I audition at Central (a mere formality; the competition weren't born with a cowl), help me move into the Swiss Cottage bedsit and then leave.

How will I survive? I who've never shopped, cooked or thought for myself? I who can't easily talk to strangers or make friends? I, alone in London: massive, teeming London, currently Swinging London (I can't *swing* – I'm the least swingiest person I know!), London of hippies and *Darling* and decadence, London so far away from home, London the capital of Overseas.

This is a mistake, a terrible mistake, a great big bloody balls-up of a mistake.

June. On the 14th I turn nineteen. My last birthday in South Africa? It isn't just a question of training in England – I sort of know that I won't be coming back; everyone sort of knows it. Like other white businessmen, Dad had been sneaking money out of South Africa for some time, into bank accounts in Switzerland and the Channel Islands. He called these funds 'nest eggs'. Things hadn't even started to go wrong for the whites of South Africa yet, so maybe it was a Jewish thing: one day we might have to pack those old bags again. The family liked the idea that one of us was moving Overseas, creating not just an egg, but a whole nest elsewhere. My 1968 diary tells me that Granny and the Hesselbergs came round for the birthday supper that night, even the twins Mark 'n' Neal. They're twenty-one, commercial accountants both, well past family suppers, but it's a Friday, it's *shabbas*, and they're devout. Their father, Uncle Jack, he of the big-bellied rolling walk and warm, twinkling spirit, says to me, 'May you have lots of joy out of yourself.'

July. Just before I leave, one incident brings me face to face with apartheid South Africa in a way that I haven't known before.

My attempts to learn to drive in the army were so ludicrous and unsuccessful that I've used these spare months to try again, in a car rather than a three-ton truck. To my surprise I master the skills fairly quickly and pass first time.

One night as I'm driving home from Tony Fagin's, turning down Arthurs Road, a drunk black man suddenly staggers in front of my car and I hit him. I can't be going more than ten miles per hour but it's enough to send him thumping over the bonnet and on to the road. Leaping from the car, I find him lying on his back, very still, a trickle of blood coming from one corner of his mouth. I've seen enough Hollywood films to know what this means. It's serious. For him and for me. I'm meant to fly away to London in about a week. The accident has happened outside the staff entrance of a block of flats and people are gathering, Coloured and black people.

'Get the police,' I say to them.

No one moves. Odd. Then one woman, still dressed in her maid's uniform, says, 'The police will be your friends.'

'Don't be silly,' I reply, thinking she means literally, 'I haven't got any friends in the police. We must send for them.'

The atmosphere is strange. Why aren't these people obeying me, these men and women whom, even at the age of nineteen, I'm used to ordering about? Instead, they come closer, gathering round the car, bringing a strong smell of booze with them. They look hurt and angry, as though I've deliberately knocked over the man.

Suddenly a voice shouts to me from above and I see white faces leaning over a balcony. The police are on the way, they say.

Within seconds the familiar grey van arrives, separating the crowd. The first constable to climb out takes one look at me and says, 'Hey, Sher – now what've you been up to, man?'

I blink, staring at him. His name's Potgieter. He was at school with me. I remember him because he was poorer than the rest of us and often picked on. One day, during break, a mob attacked him, tore off his trousers and lifted him into the air, showing all. I watched from a window. I was a prefect by then, and knew I should do something. Instead I decided, wisely I think, to cower under the sill. I had no idea what happened to him after school, I certainly didn't know he'd become a policeman.

'So howzit going, Sher?' he asks, shaking my hand.

The crowd looks as surprised as I am – except for the woman in the maid's uniform. She's not surprised at all. She's smiling grimly.

'Ja – no, it's fine, thanks,' I answer.

'Don't worry about this,' he says, nodding to the man on the ground. 'We'll sort it out. You go on home.'

'Right – OK – thanks.' I leap into my car, steer round the body and flee.

Later Mom phones to make enquiries. The police say the victim isn't seriously injured and there's nothing more we need do.

Is this true? What injuries would a drunken black man have to sustain before these policemen would describe it as serious? They can do the paperwork with their eyes closed.

I go to sleep that night feeling a strange mixture of guilt and power. Who doesn't long to be let off after a motor accident? And it's more than that. I'm a citizen beyond suspicion, beyond the law, beyond even my own instincts about right and wrong.

It's a good thing I'm leaving this country – I could get to like it here.

Tuesday, 16 July 1968 is a cool grey day, trying to rain.

The atmosphere in Montagu House this morning is unusually quiet. The two occupants who seem most anxious are the two who understand least what's happening, yet sense it deeply: Tickey, my dog, who retreats to corners to watch all the packing and carrying, very flat-eared, very tense; and twelve-year-old brother Joel, plump, big-eared, bespectacled, Piggy-like, who keeps sighing loudly and saying, 'What a business, what a business.'

The farewells begin. Lena first, our current maid. We shake hands. She's prepared a little speech, but can't remember it for a moment. She keeps hold of my hand, eyes closed, lips moving, then it comes out suddenly: 'May you have a prosperous journey, Master Antony, may you have good health and happiness.'

Katie next. She's nowhere to be seen. I go into the backyard calling her name. She comes to the door of her room, eyes wet and red. I've often treated her badly, rudely, but none of this matters. Her respect and affection for the Shers is unconditional and boundless. She was working for us when I was born and now I'm going. She too has prepared a little speech, but can't get out a single word. My throat is full too. We shake hands limply; we can't hug, it's against the law. I go into the kitchen and start crying. This is no good – tears aren't something the Shers do. I get myself together and move into the hall. At which point Mom bustles past, muttering angrily, 'Katie is weeping copiously, she's upset me terribly!'

Everyone else is coming to the airport, so there's only Tickey left. She's crouching before me, head very tight, body shivering slightly. Not like when there's a bang; this is more controlled, more conscious. She knows something terrible is about to happen, but not what it is. I give her the briefest of pats and head for the door. Joel has watched, open-mouthed. 'That wasn't a decent goodbye,' he says.

'I want it to be short,' I explain, and then, louder, for Mom's benefit: 'or I'll start weeping copiously too!'

Joel is baffled, but follows to the car. Dad starts the engine, reverses down the drive. I say, 'Hang on a moment.'

I run back into the house and kneel next to Tickey. I stroke her tight, confused face carefully, let her lick my hand, then hurry out again.

There's quite a little crowd at the airport: immediate and extended family, and Auntie Esther, of course, straight-backed, proud-bosomed, beaming and gushing: 'Oh, my darling, I don't know what to say, it's all going to go so well, so outstandingly, marvellously, brilliantly well that I'm simply lost for words, I just wish you everything, *everything* you wish yourself, go well, my darling, go well and do well, make us all proud, give us lots of *nachas*, I know you will, oh fly, my darling, fly!'

Tony Fagin's here too. He's without his specs – he broke them last night, he says – and suddenly looks like Dad can, much softer, less certain, frowning all the time. We shake hands; we can't hug, it's against the law. Two other former schoolmates – Deon Irish and Malcolm Sandler – have come all this way to say goodbye too. I'm surprised and touched.

But I mustn't cry. I've feared that I'll cry at the airport and I'm determined I mustn't. It's only when, having said all the goodbyes and I'm heading for the gate – I remember it seemed a particularly *sharp* gate – Joel runs after me, his face blotched with light and dark patches, and whispers his own pre-planned speech: 'Good luck, Ant.'

There's a large group of heart surgeons on the plane. It's only a few months ago, in December 1967, that Christiaan Barnard performed his pioneering heart-swap surgery and there's been conference after conference in Cape Town.

The distinguished company makes Mom glow with pleasure. 'Won't it be wonderful,' she says dreamily, 'if in ten years' time you're as famous as them?'

Famous? I'll be lucky if I'm still alive.

I feel no excitement as we taxi to the runway, only terror. I've never flown before so there's that too. As the plane goes into its astonishing final acceleration, I write in my diary, shakily:

16/7/68 There's absolutely nothing I can do to stop what's happening now. It'd be like trying to press against the huge forward, forward charge of this machine. It's unbelievable but it's happening. Help.

PART II

....

Then

9

ARRIVING

MY FIRST MEMORIES are of television and snow. In that order.

Walking into the hotel room – the Pastoria, off Leicester Square – my hand was actually trembling as I reached out to switch on a TV for the first time. It was like opening a window. That square of glass held a new view – an immense view – a view of the world which Uncle Nat preferred us not to see. Hence his government newspapers, his government radio, his government church, his book bannings, his Beatle bannings, and his mad Voortrekker gnawing at spools of film. Here in Britain life was different. Here freedom of speech was cherished – available via any hotel TV set – here was something that made me feel safer than I ever had before.

I'd never seen snow either. That came later: long after my parents had left to go home. I was lonely that first winter and cowed by everything again. London was a huge, baffling spaghetti bowl of a city – witnessed by its *A-Z* with that twisting jumble of streets, some so small you couldn't read their names – and it was dark, grimly dark. The sun didn't rise till past eight o'clock – some days it didn't rise at all – and then it was night again by about four. But one morning I awoke to an astonishing show of light and radiance. Thick snow had fallen during the night. London suddenly looked beautiful, friendly, simplified again. I walked for hours, amazed. I touched the stuff, I tasted it, I washed my face in its whiteness.

But I'm jumping ahead . . .

*

We were met at Heathrow Airport by the Blakes. Peter was the London agent (now retired) for Dad's business and Aileen his wife: he a German Jew by birth, fleeing in the thirties, she an English rose. They were more than business associates of my parents, they were friends. And they've been more than friends to me; they've been guardians.

As Peter drove us into Piccadilly Circus I felt puzzled, vaguely disappointed. It wasn't round. Surely a circus was round? It looked round in photographs and films. But it wasn't. It was a funny jagged shape, with tall narrow corners leaning into the centre, every surface a confusing collage of adverts and neon.

Peter steered the car into St Martin's Street where the Pastoria stands. As we were climbing out, a man walked through the hotel entrance. I caught my breath. Milo O'Shea. Star of the recent film of Joyce's *Ulysses*, which had been shown in South Africa with, of course, a frenzy of jump cuts during Molly's soliloquy. I'd only been in London for five minutes and I'd seen a famous actor. My ancestors came to South Africa expecting to find gold and diamonds lying in the street. I came to London expecting to find stars everywhere – theatre stars, film stars, pop stars – and I'd already been luckier than my grandparents ever were.

That night we went to see Scofield in Osborne's *Hotel in Amsterdam* at the Royal Court. It wasn't very good, but who cared? Scofield, Osborne, the Royal Court – these were mythic names. On the first weekend, Mom and I travelled up to Stratford to see *King Lear*, directed by Trevor Nunn, with Eric Porter as Lear and Michael Williams as the Fool. This did seem good. And the Royal Shakespeare Theatre, Stratford-upon-Avon, the Warwickshire countryside – mythic places.

But I wasn't here just to gawp and worship – I was supposed to enter this world of Royal Courts and Royal Shakespeare Theatres, enter it and make it mine. We had an audition booked for Central and a bedsit booked in Swiss Cottage.

Though I suspected it wouldn't be quite so simple.

My fears were confirmed when we went to visit Ronnie Harwood in his Kensington home. He and I hadn't met before. Seeing me, he was surprised and couldn't disguise it. I saw an expression in his eyes which I'd seen in my own, in the mirror. This isn't what an actor *looks* like – this short, slight, shy creature in black specs – an accountant, maybe, or in modern terms, a computer nerd or trainspotter – but an actor, no. Ronnie himself

1. A SOUTH AFRICAN BOY; aged 9; growing up in the sports-mad world of fifties South Africa, I felt sure I'd been born in the wrong country, and possibly the wrong planet.

2. IMMIGRANTS.
Top: the immigrant
arriving; an illustration
from *Middlepost*.
Bottom: my father's
parents at a family
wedding, 1912; my
mother's parents at her
wedding, 1941, with
Ralph, the youngest son,
who drowned tragically
nine months later.

3. MIDDLEPOST. *Top*: my father's mother with him (centre) and his brothers Arthur and Nicky at Middlepost in 1916; the sign says, 'Joel Sher licensed to sell wine, malt, spiritous liquors by retail.' *Bottom*: Greg, Dad and self on the outskirts of Middlepost (and that's the whole of it!) in 1993.

4. Teachers.
Top: Mac and self (aged 13); Esther directing Tony Fagin and self (aged 16) in *The Bespoke Overcoat*.
Bottom: my childhood drawing *The Deluge* (shamelessly imitating Michelangelo) on our 1961 Rosh Hashana card.

5. LEAVING AND ARRIVING. *Top*: Katie Roberts in the backyard at Montagu House; self in the army, 1967. *Bottom*: Newly arrived in Leicester Square, London, in 1968, with parents.

6. OUT AND ABOUT. *Top*: Jim Hooper when we met in 1975. *Bottom*: the gay 'scene' in my painting *Only Connect* (1985); this image, of people crowded together, everyone searching yet looking in different directions, is based on a photo of ostriches.

7. THE LAST PICTURE OF DAD: with Mom, after their visit to
Buckingham Palace on 28th October 1993, a week before he died.

8. Woza S.A.! Greg and self (with white-bleached hair) together with cast and friends during the run of *Titus Andronicus* at Joburg's Market Theatre in 1995.

used to be an actor, with Wolfit's company (the source for his acclaimed play, *The Dresser*), and fitted the bill far better. A handsome and gregarious man, full of entertaining theatre stories and impressions, this was how an actor should be.

Leaving my parents chatting to his wife Natasha, Ronnie took me into his study to hear my audition speeches. My modern piece was Mick from *The Caretaker*. Ronnie mentioned that he knew Pinter well; they'd been in Wolfit's company together and had remained great friends, often playing cricket together. I went white. Pinter was another mythic figure. You could tell by his photograph on the back of the Methuen play texts: dark, grainy, vaguely blurred, a snapshot of someone not quite of this world. Yet Ronnie played cricket with him! Learn this and then try doing a Pinter speech.

Ronnie watched and listened politely as I struggled through it, in my unique Sea Point Cockney accent. 'Good, good,' he said thoughtfully. I knew something was wrong; 'good' wasn't a Ronnie word; I'd only just met him but sensed that superlatives were more his style. 'And your classical?'

'Wolsey.'

'Wolsey?'

'From *Henry VIII*.'

Ronnie frowned. It wasn't just that *Henry VIII* is one of Shakespeare's least known and liked plays, if indeed it is his entirely; it was also the choice of role. Was I best suited to this? Wolsey, the 'butcher of Ipswich', a huge gross man, a crushing steamroller of a politician, an all-powerful cardinal and a – let's not mince words – a Christian. He was as Christian a Christian as you get. He was so Christian he was a kosher Christian. Was Wolsey really the best vehicle to show off my talents? Might Shylock not have been a better choice with, say, Johnnie from *Hello and Goodbye* as my modern piece? Maybe. I've no idea how Esther and I settled on the Wolsey speech ('Had I but serv'd my God with half the zeal I serv'd my king'); it was probably to do with the recent film of *A Man for All Seasons*. I'd loved Orson Welles as Wolsey, loved his bloated indolent power. And I was versatile, after all, people were always saying so, I was a character actor . . .

'Wolsey,' said Ronnie thoughtfully. 'Right, Wolsey it is, then.'

He sat very still, frozen almost, as, before him, this short, bespectacled boy began to waddle round his study, arms hanging wide of the body – meant to indicate great girth, but perhaps more reminiscent of the

Frankenstein monster – while speaking in low, wheezing tones tinged with a slight American accent.

'That's good, good,' Ronnie managed to say at the end, his ebullient voice strangely hushed. 'Right, well, I don't think there's much I can add to that. Good luck for Tuesday.'

At 10.30 on Tuesday morning, 23 July 1968, with Mom excitedly working the cine camera, catching the moment for HISTORY, and with Dad absent, on a business meeting with Peter Blake in the City, I bounded up the front steps of the Central School of Speech and Drama in Swiss Cottage to do my audition.

The plan was for us to visit the bedsit afterwards, to view where I'd live.

The audition was extremely swift, over in about ten minutes. I remember nothing about it at all. Next thing, the Registrar popped her head round the corner of the lobby, where I and the others sat, and sang out: 'Sorry – none of you today.'

Was that it? Could it really be that fast, that cursory, that conclusive?

Yes, yes, yes it could.

Mom was lifting the cine camera back to her eye as she saw me reappear on the steps, then hesitated, noticing my expression.

After I told her, we stood for a while in silence. It was a bright English summer day, but London suddenly looked ugly, hostile, alien.

'Don't suppose you want to view the bedsitter just for now?' Mom said after a while.

'No thanks, Mate, not just for now.'

Travelling back to the hotel, trying to work out what had happened, I decided there must have been some kind of mistake. It simply couldn't be true. I'd travelled halfway across the world, I'd packed all my things, I'd left home. There'd been a mistake. I'd get back to the hotel and find a message from Central: We didn't mean *you*. When we said 'none of you today' we didn't mean *you*. We just didn't want to make it worse for the others, but YOU – of course we want *you*!

There was no message. Dad came back from his business meeting and heard the news. I saw the look in his face. Not 'I told you so', but something worse, a look of real anxiety. He was a businessman, he didn't understand the arts and didn't pretend to, but he knew about taking calculated risks, gambling on an investment which could pay off in the future. The women, Mom and Esther, the ones who knew about these things, had assured him that I had real talent, to put it mildly: Ant was 'outstanding' at acting – not Ronnie's cautious 'good, good' – but 'outstanding', 'brilliant', 'unbelievable'. For the first time Dad, like all of us that day, wondered if this was what it sounded, a load of bullshit.

Mom rang Ronnie. I sat listening to her side of the conversation: 'But why Ronnie, *why* – you saw him the other day, you saw how outstanding his work is – the little Cockney character and the fat old priest – what more could they want? Why did they turn him down, *why*? One doesn't even get given a reason, an explanation – how is a person supposed to proceed without knowing what went wrong? Can't you do something, please?'

I felt I was aged twelve and three-quarters again, about to be bar mitzvahed, and Mr Bitnun has come round to the house to tell the folks that I wasn't up to it. And Mom refuses to hear him. My Ant *will* sing.

My Ant *will* act.

No, that's not fair. She wasn't her usual fighting self. She was shaken. Her belief in me and my destiny was profound, she wasn't going to swerve from it, but she was nevertheless shaken by what happened at Central today, quite deeply shaken.

The important thing, Ronnie urged, was to move on. I was still in time for auditions at RADA, choice number two on his list. Meanwhile he'd try to find out what happened at Central, where he'd done some teaching. I don't recall him reporting back on this, so I don't know if he failed to speak to them, or was simply too embarrassed to relay what they'd said.

The RADA audition was a week or so later. Again, I remember little about it – did I do the same pieces, or did Ronnie tactfully suggest new ones? – don't know, but the experience was very swift again, just in–out. The difference was they didn't tell you the result straight away – they posted it to you.

The news duly arrived. A rejection, as I feared, but tougher than before. The wording suggested that there were several versions of this letter and of rejection. It said: Not only have you failed this audition, and not only are we unable to contemplate auditioning you again, but we strongly urge you to seek a different career.

It was meant kindly, I believe. They had seen someone who wasn't meant to be an actor – I saw it myself every time I looked in the mirror – and it was their duty to prevent this person from ruining his life.

My looks were one thing and the fashion was about to change – early on in London, a man in the street asked, 'Aren't you the actor from that new film, *The Graduate*?' – but what about talent? Was I really that execrable in those two auditions? Well, yes, quite possibly. My terror, my confusion, my choice of pieces and the general stupidity of auditions – lifting a speech out of context and speaking it to the middle distance or a chair – all of this could've made me fairly execrable, I think.

Dazed, I started to play the role of tourist.

We stayed in London during August, with some expeditions beyond. Curious to see more of this new land – a land where I might not be settling after all – I went with Dad and Peter Blake on their business trips: down to Yeovil in Somerset, where I glimpsed *Goodbye Mr Chips* being filmed at the railway station, and up to Peebles in Scotland. There was a shortage of rooms in the hotel here, so Dad and I had to share a double bed. This was impossible for me – a terrible Freudian nightmare – so I got up in the early hours and tried sleeping on a sofa in the foyer. As soon as it was light, I went for a long walk, marvelling at the countryside – gentle patchworks of meadows and hedges – exactly the kind of British landscape I'd seen in films, falling in love from afar. Returning to the hotel for breakfast, I found Dad in a bad state – white-faced and shaking. Not with anger, but fear. He'd woken, been unable to find me, panicked and sounded the alarm. I was amazed. I never knew he cared that much.

There was a trip across the Channel too. My parents wanted to show me Europe – all of it – so we did one of those crazy coach tours, seeing ten countries in about a week. My only memory is of getting on to the coach in Paris – then everything speeds up and blurs. But climbing on to the coach sticks in my mind. Mainly because there were fourteen Pakistanis on board, a family called Patel. We climbed straight off again. We went into head office. Could we change tours? No we couldn't. We got on to the coach again. We sat down next to one of the Patels – you couldn't *not* sit next to one of the Patels – and then it started: the first conversation and the inevitable first question, where are you from? I watched Dad's face. A strange expression – a kind of shame. Back at home, if ever the subject of politics came up, and mostly it didn't, the men in the family would all go into chest-beating mode, fists bunched, heads held high – the rest of the world didn't understand us, look at the mess in the rest of Africa, or the Southern states of America, or Notting Hill in London – we were right, and everyone else was wrong! Yet now, on this coach in Paris, Dad looked rather different and spoke the two words – the name of his homeland – very quietly. To his and my surprise, Mr Patel just nodded cheerfully and said, 'Ah, we're neighbours, then.' He was from Uganda. In a few years' time, Idi Amin would expel Mr Patel from his birthplace and all the other Patels around us, and indeed every single Ugandan Asian. I think Mr Patel understood something about the complexities of racism, and that's why he smiled so warmly at Dad, and continued to treat us with civility and friendliness, almost sympathy.

The coach started and we were off. Maybe it wasn't just that we went too fast – was that Vienna or Venice, Munich or Milan? – maybe I wasn't concentrating properly on Europe. I had something far more important on my mind.

Ronnie was trying to find out about other drama schools, but there was something dispiriting even in the search. He'd always said Central and RADA were *the* ones; in my mind they were synonymous with training in London. And I'd failed both. I was still trying to absorb the shock.

It's Wednesday, 4 September 1968.

We're travelling by taxi to the west London Heathrow Terminal on Cromwell Road. It's a supermarket or something now, but in those days, you and your luggage could be transported to the airport in white-and-blue buses with the red BEA logo.

The time has come for Mom and Dad to leave. They're going home via a spa in Italy, at Abano. A bedsitter has been found for me – not in Swiss Cottage! – in West Kensington, in a flat owned by an elderly Hungarian woman, Mrs Forbat.

When we say goodbye at the Heathrow bus terminal Mom suddenly starts crying. Uncontrollably. I'm shocked. I've never seen her cry at all, never mind like this. She probably hasn't since the death of her young brother, Ralph. Dad and I shake hands. He says, 'All the best, hey?' – then repeats it in Afrikaans: '*Alles van die beste, hoor?*'

They get on to the bus and move to the seat in the back window. As they leave, I photograph them waving goodbye – Mom still mopping tears – and later stick the snap in my diary.

I trail back to Mrs Forbat's at West Kensington Court. I have a room and balcony of my own. The rest we share.

I go out on to the balcony. The weather's getting cool – my first British autumn is coming and my first winter. I stare at the big road alongside the flats: West Cromwell Road. It's the airport road. This hasn't really registered before. I'm living on the airport road. I'm in London, but not quite. I've arrived, but not altogether. I could go back at any moment. Just by stepping out of the front door.

The afternoon and evening drag by slowly. I spend much of the time gazing up at the sky, watching different planes pass overhead. One of these must hold Mom and Dad.

Later she rings to say they've arrived safely at the spa. She confesses that she continued to cry all the way, she cried non-stop for about four hours. I remember the story of Dad's mother seeing Middlepost for the first time and crying so much she almost cured the drought.

As I put down the phone it hits me. They've gone. They really have gone. I'm alone in London. I know the Blakes, I know the Harwoods, but no one else. And there's no drama course in place, not even other auditions at the moment.

I feel sick. I bend over, holding my middle. Not to vomit. It's a worse, different kind of nausea – more like a feeling of panic. A panic that doesn't end. Loneliness. I've never known anything like it. What I've sampled before – like in the army – wasn't the real thing. This is. This is the grown-up brand. This is where everything is down to you.

THE RED AND GOLD
SICKNESS

SOME TWENTY-FIVE YEARS later, in the autumn of 1996, I was playing Disraeli in the film *Mrs Brown* and arrived at Middle Temple on the Embankment, where the sets had been built for us to shoot the Parliament scenes. Most of the people called that day were extras, to play the MPs, but there was one who had some words to speak – two words, to be precise: 'Order, order!' – the Leader of the House. We got chatting. His name was George Hall. This sounded vaguely familiar. Oh, of course. Head of Acting at Central. He'd held the post for many years, including 1968 when I auditioned. He must've been sitting out there, in the dark of the auditorium, when I did my pieces. I didn't mention this, but was filled with strange emotion that day. Here I was, playing one of the main roles in the film, and here he was, retired from teaching, filling in time doing a bit part. I felt no relish from the situation, more a kind of anger. How quickly, how easily he'd dismissed me back in 1968, what a fright he gave me, Mom and Dad that day as we sat in our hotel room, trying to work out what to do next and for many months afterwards. How many other actors were turned down as swiftly and just gave up straight away? I was lucky. I had Mom – Mom and her certainty. It's been oppressive sometimes, her certainty about my future, yet without it I'm not sure I would've survived that first shocking rejection.

Again and again, as we filmed the Parliament scenes, my anger came and went, quite privately, a funny mess of complicated feelings. After all, George Hall had only been doing his job back in 1968. His response to my audition was, as I've already said, probably justified – I was a bag of nerves, doing all the wrong speeches and no doubt completely dire. I've always believed that talent and non-talent sit quite closely together, like very good ideas and very bad ones, the brainwave in the middle of the night. This thing we later carry forth proudly into the light – is it art or shit? Everyone's felt a prejudice about this or that actor. I may rate his work, but something about him jars badly for you. Which of us is right?

Talent? Skill? Luck? Destiny? If you make it in this business, this strange gamble of a business, you never know why, you never find out. You're just aware of a myriad set of circumstances that could have made things go a very different way: external forces and internal demons.

The timing of my encounter with George Hall was especially odd, because I was just starting all over again. The filming of *Mrs Brown* was my first time back at work after several weeks in a clinic for cocaine dependency. George Hall may have been the first man to step on my dreams, but more recently the only person doing that was myself. My work schedule – playing marathon theatre roles while writing and illustrating books at the same time – was often described as punishing, but the truly punishing part was my idea of recreation, with a glamorous recreational pal called Charlie: the long, long, high-speed binges, the thudding depressions afterwards, equally long, but with time creeping now, sometimes standing still.

Well, I was clean now, sober too – I had to stay off alcohol for the foreseeable future – I was 'in Recovery' and I was coming back to work. Work. My first, my main addiction, the one I share with Dad, the one that probably saved us both from total wipe-out. We're workaholics first, boozers and cokeheads second. But work was strange now, everything was strange. Recovery is a world of mirrors and echoes. You see yourself, hear yourself, all the time. The clarity is startling, not very pleasant, not great for an actor – this playback you keep getting of your every move, every sound – it was going to take some getting used to. It was unbearable to start with.

How did I get to this point? I'd been asking myself this question over the last few weeks, sitting in room 318 at Charter Nightingale Hospital. The view from the window was uncomfortably reminiscent of my first few months in England, in a bedsit overlooking the roofs and streets of west London. There were times when it felt so similar, when *I* felt so similar – inexperienced, powerless, failed – that I whimpered with fear. Maybe none of it ever happened. Maybe I just stayed in a small, gloomy room, peering out nervously at a city I couldn't enter. And if it *did* happen, the whole career, not just as an actor but writer and artist too, everything I wanted, then how the fuck did I get back here, to this place, this lonely room again?

It's something I'm still trying to figure out, even here, on these pages. Though God knows this is a fairly strange place to do it.

When a friend heard I was writing this book, he said, 'And will you tell the truth?'

'The truth?' I said. 'But this is autobiography.'

I've done enough psychotherapy over the years to know that autobiography is a kind of fiction and I've written enough fiction to know that this is embarrassingly autobiographical. Novels are like dreams. The landscape looks crowded with other people, but really there's only you present. Only you making it up. The actor is his own material – he's the one in front of the audience, it's inescapable – but it's true of all art, whether painting, music or movies: however much he might coyly deny this, the creator's personality is overwhelmingly present. And I think the reverse is equally true: we're endlessly creative with our own lives. Second by second, minute by minute, we're interpreting it, editing it, starting to reinvent it. 'You'll never believe what's just happened to me,' we tell one another daily, determined that ours should never be a dull story. We needn't worry. Life is a fantastically bizarre journey which only needs faithful recording, no embellishment. The film maker Fellini gets it most right for me. The parade, the circus, the way everyone else seems to be grotesque, looming into frame, while we, the viewers, the Normal Ones, gasp at the spectacle, comforting ourselves with its nostalgic, tinny tunes. Is experience built on memory or fantasy? Fellini asks, and then consigns both to the same glorious heap, rotting together, regenerating together; life becoming its own myth.

Double-checking the information in this book, I've been constantly surprised. For instance. Three of my grandparents came from the same little Lithuanian *shtetl*, Plungyan. This has always been one of the family facts, one of the *only* facts about our history. And it has a nice, warm, special feel to it, a knot almost perfectly tied; three out of four – we just missed the full house. But it's not true, my research suddenly reveals, they weren't all from Plungyan. A relative assures me that my mother's father, Harry Abramowitz, was born in Kaunas, in central Lithuania. 'That's funny,' says Mom, when I tell her. 'I always thought it was Plungyan.' Now I don't know whether to go back and change the references earlier in the text. I decide to leave it. For as long as I can remember we believed that three of our grandparents came from the same tiny place, never knew one another, travelled across the world and then came together to create the Sher family. Was this a mistake, a lie, or just evidence of the general fog that surrounds our former life in Eastern Europe? Don't know, but there's something important about leaving the original story in this book.

More important than the truth?

The truth? But this is autobiography.

The London I was peering at in 1968 turned out to be crawling with drama schools. There are careful strictures now, but at that stage all sorts of establishments were operating, trying to exploit the worldwide appetite for learning acting in London and becoming the next Albert Finney or Tom Courtenay, Julie Christie or Vanessa Redgrave. *Anyone* could call themselves a drama school. I auditioned at three more.

One was very small, the De Leon in Richmond, run by an old lady who auditioned me in her front room. The next was slightly bigger, Mountview – it's since become very good – where they auditioned me in a back garage. And the third was well established, among the top five, in fact, the Webber-Douglas Academy, where you auditioned in their theatre, the Chanticleer.

I was accepted at all three. My luck had suddenly changed – or was it my audition speeches? – I can't recall, but naturally I chose Webber-Douglas. Unlike Central and RADA, who only had a September intake, Webber-D. had three a year, so I was in time for the next. I would start training to be an actor on Monday, 6 January 1969.

Huge relief all round. Much told-you-so-ing from Mom, a thoughtful '*Mazeltov*' from Dad – this gamble might still turn into a decent investment – and a sigh of relief from the Blakes who, while generously providing meals and theatre trips, had also started, very tactfully, to speak the unspeakable: 'Maybe returning to South Africa wouldn't be the worst thing in the world.'

Oh yes, it would. I couldn't have explained why to them, or even to myself. But I had my own sense of destiny, and it wasn't so much to do with fame and fortune – though of course these would be nice – as to do with identity. There are people born as men yet profoundly convinced that they're women. I had a similar sense, though about my passport rather than my gender. I believed I'd been born in the wrong country. It wasn't South Africa's politics that made me feel uncomfortable – not yet, I was still as politically naïve as can be – but the swagger, noise and *certainty* of its people. Life was simple to them, all in black and white. They had an answer for everything. Here in England, which was, after all, a much older, wiser society, people seemed to prefer questions to answers. I liked this. The population was cautious, discreet and courteous. I slipped quietly among their ranks.

With about three months to fill before I began at Webber-D. I spent my days exploring my new city, and my nights either in front of the TV or at one of the theatres.

Theatre. British theatre.

It even *smelled* different from theatre back home.

If you sat near the front, as I liked to, there was an aroma released as the curtain rose, a kind of breeze that went over you momentarily, distinctly cool in temperature. To the nostrils the scent was both musty and bright. Later I'd work out that it's the glue called size in every set, it's the fireproofing, it's the freshly laundered costumes, it's the oily, powdery scent of make-up, it's from the actors too, their breath flavoured by a dozen different throat sprays, gargles and lozenges; but at the time I would've sworn that the musty-bright smell was of age, of experience – centuries and centuries of practising this art – and of ghosts, thousands of ghosts, a long, winding parade of them, where you could glimpse Irving, Kean, Garrick, Burbage, Shakespeare himself . . .

I'd always feel slightly unwell on my theatre visits, giddy and sweaty – the sensation is rather like flu, some pleasant strain of it – unable to think properly or see straight. I was catching what Cocteau calls the red and gold sickness; I was falling in love with theatre. (Up until then I'd just been in love with acting.) I had spent so many years poring over the West End programmes which Mom and Dad brought back from their trips, or the copies of *Plays & Players* which were delivered monthly, I'd spent so much time fantasising about London theatre back in South Africa (*South Africa – where was that? – 'overseas'*), now I couldn't fit the experience into a compartment entitled 'Reality'.

But these flu-like symptoms, these vaguely ecstatic illnesses, were as nothing when I finally saw *him*.

Olivier.

Live. On stage. At the National.

The Blakes had introduced me to the National's system of mailing-list booking. I'd tried for *Dance of Death*, requesting a seat in the middle of the front row, please. To my amazement, this duly arrived by post at Mrs Forbat's flat in West Kensington Court: the very ticket I'd asked for. But how could this be? Back at home I'd read about *Dance of Death* in *Plays & Players*; they said it was already one of Olivier's great performances: the remarkable ugliness he achieved with the make-up, the backward stagger on the heart attack, literally death-defying. How could it be that some little *nebbish* just turns up from South Africa and gets a seat in the front row?

Travelling to Waterloo that evening, I felt the usual onset of pleasurable flu, as well as something more, a strange sensation, a kind of fear. This was it. I was about to see acting as good as it gets, a career as high as they climb.

What was Olivier like that night? Impossible to say. By the time I took my precious seat – AI8 – my flu had turned into fever, the blood was banging in my head and a tiny shiver worried my flesh. The exquisite musty-bright aroma coming off the edge of the Old Vic stage seemed stronger than in any other theatre in London, and of course there was an extra ingredient tonight, the scent of *him*. Olivier. Laurence Olivier. The actor I most wanted to see in the world and here I was, at his feet. The evening started to feel rather like that coach tour of Europe; it passed in such a blur that by the time Olivier got to the famous backward-tumbling fall, this looked like perfectly normal locomotion. Finally it was the curtain call. He strode to the front of the stage, right to the edge. He began his bow and kept coming, it seemed – his nose was surely going to brush mine! – and those amazing hooded eyes examined me for a millisecond – an eagle swooping down to look at a mouse – and then, in a rush of air, thunderous with applause, he was lifting, turning, gone. And I breathed again.

Even though he wasn't remotely aware of it, he'd looked at me. Me, Antony Sher, from Montagu House, Alexander Road, Sea Point. Laurence Olivier had looked at me. We *were* on the same planet.

I was eventually to work at the National myself, in its new home on the South Bank, and when I was doing *Uncle Vanya* in 1992, playing Astrov to Ian McKellen's Vanya, he and I became friends. During a conversation about Olivier over dinner one night, Ian suddenly said gloomily, 'We can't match him – none of us can – ever.' I looked at him in surprise. Ian was and is something of a hero to me – for his political as well as his theatre work – and by then I'd come to regard him as a better actor than Olivier, more truthful, more dangerous. Ian's psychological studies of Shakespeare's dark characters – Iago, Richard III and Macbeth – are remarkable; they fill me with admiration and envy. We sat in silence for a moment, then Ian shrugged, quite aggressively, refusing to say more, and we changed the subject. But I suddenly understood what he meant. It wasn't a question of playing a few Shakespeare roles well and a critic or two saying it put them in mind of Olivier. The man had lived his life on a different scale. I was wrong that night at *Dance of Death* – he and I weren't on the same planet; or at any rate he was in orbit above it most of the time, a genuine star. I can identify with only one tiny part of his life: the beginning. An adoring mother, a cold father. But any similarity ends quickly: his mother dies when he's very young, abandoning him to the stern rule of the clergyman father. In Anthony Holden's excellent 1988 biography, *Olivier*, he shows how this badly bruises the boy's self-image, the healthy form of self-love, while at the same time fuelling his ambitions. Holden's portrait is of a restless soul forever howling 'I'll show you!' to the world, succeeding beyond all expectations, yet somehow never at peace.

I'm fascinated by Olivier's beauty – that radiant, matinée idol beauty he's blessed with as a young man and then spends the rest of his life trying to cover up: with nose putty and funny teeth, with wigs and moustaches, and with acting. ACTING. The accusation that he's all technique and charisma, but no heart, isn't strictly true. His heart lay in his very attempts to disguise it, protect it, bury it ever deeper in that mighty fortress he's constructing, the fortress called OLIVIER. His determination never to be vulnerable is itself moving. Because he doesn't, can't, succeed. It shows in his eyes. It's why they're so powerful. Tynan describes them as 'lion eyes searching for solace' and that's exactly right; they have exactly that cold-hot look, flame behind glass. He is a lion, a king of the beasts, yet one who's searching for solace. For me it keeps coming back to the image of a young man, a beautiful young man, who hates himself. Nothing can ever cure this hatred, so he builds himself up bigger and bigger. In the end it's phenomenal. The combination of beauty and self-hatred, and, of course, talent, colossal talent and imagination – his characters remind me of Michelangelo's monumental portraits; they have an almost marble feel, awesome yet quite cool – these add up to one of those unique giant lives. God knows what special membranes coated his features at birth, or what soothsayers were present. I mean, come on, he's the actor with a cheer sewn into the very fabric of his name: Olivi-yaay!

If I'm completely honest, along with the excitement of the *Dance of Death* evening, there was also vague disappointment; Olivier was already ill by this time and the backward tumble was only marked through. Scofield in a much poorer play, *Hotel in Amsterdam*, had already moved me more and would continue to do so, in *Vanya* and *The Captain of Kopernick*, with that strange, bruised look (his brow is like a boxer's) and that tone of hurt in his drawling, ringing voice. Olivier's own contemporaries, Gielgud and Richardson, would also stir my emotions in *Home* and *No Man's Land*, their souls clearly on display in both pieces: Gielgud's elegant and lonely, Richardson's a marvellous, batty, broken kind of thing. But it's Olivier I'm always drawn back to. I saw his last major performances – Shylock, Tyrone in *Long Day's Journey* – and although they continued to frustrate (*why isn't he contacting me more?*), I couldn't get enough, and saw them again and again. Ian McKellen is right – it's hopeless trying to measure up to him. Olivier is the lion king, the dominant male in the pride of twentieth-century actors and, as a father figure, he's not dissimilar to my own: uninterested in us, his descendants; frustrated, selfish and competitive. I don't altogether like him, yet I can't take my eyes off him.

When I become a professional actor myself, I dream of meeting him, but this stays just out of reach. Instead, I have a series of strange, close encounters.

In 1978, attending a charity do at the Royal Court, I'm in the loo. He comes in. Here we are, no longer divided by stage and stalls, orbit and earth, here we are on the same floor level at least – and in a gentlemen's toilet, for God's sake. I pee on my shoe. Will he come to the urinal alongside? No – he goes into the stall.

In 1982 I'm at the opening of the Barbican with my then partner Jim Hooper, also Adrian Noble and Joyce Nettles. I get drunk on all the free champagne. Pushing through the crowds, I crash into an old man, mutter 'Sorry' and move on. The rest of the group cry, 'Do you realise who that was?' Spinning round, I recognise Joan Plowright first.

In 1985 I'm nominated for the Olivier Best Actor award for *Richard III* and *Torch Song Trilogy*. He's in a box to the left of the stage. When they introduce him, I feel sick – that flu-like sick – and watch, dazed, as he stands to take the applause, doing his distinctive wave, cupping palmfuls of air. We get to Best Actor. I win. As I receive the statuette, I contemplate saying, 'An Olivier award for Richard III, will it bite back?' – but dare not and instead say, 'I'm delighted to be the first actor getting an award for playing both a king and a queen.'

In 1987 I'm part of the entertainment for his eightieth birthday at the National. It's a light-hearted romp through the history of British theatre, with a roll-call of actors from Burbage to Himself. I've been cast as Henry Irving, a role I'm no more suited to than Cardinal Wolsey, especially since I'm currently big-bearded and big-haired for Shylock at Stratford. At the supper afterwards, the director Sean Mathias guides me over to the head table and introduces me as 'one of our young leading actors'. The great man is ill with Alzheimer's by now, and struggling to keep up with the evening, busking his way through endless meetings with familiar and unfamiliar faces. He gently cuffs my face and says, 'What a fine beaver.' Is this slang for beard or have I heard wrong? Then, finally, we shake hands. But I know he's as unaware of me now as on that first encounter, the one he knew even less about, when he bowed at the end of *Dance of Death* and his gaze happened to land on one shaking figure in the middle of the front row.

Exploring London during those months before drama school, the place amazed me as much as my early visits to its theatres. The grassy plains of Regent's Park, the woody hills of Hampstead Heath, the plasticky neon façades of the West End, the long, grim traffic routes of West Kensington – this was less a city than a country, with different landscapes and towns, and with an extensive railway system allowing travel from one region to another, the tracks now above ground, now below it. It needed its own map, this railway – an odd, childlike map drawn in primary colours – and the place itself, London, this needed an atlas. You didn't need an atlas to find your way round Cape Town – a little fold-out leaflet perhaps, but not a book, a whole book. No, London wasn't just a country, it was the world. With one part that's Caribbean, others that are Indian and Greek, and here's Little Turkey, Chinatown, Kangaroo Valley.

Where's South Africa? It isn't here. Just a tall, heavy, fortress-like building in Trafalgar Square with the familiar orange-white-blue flag snapping in the English breeze. I sense that Londoners don't like this location, don't like South Africans – white South Africans – and therefore might not like me.

I lose my accent, even before drama school, I learn to hit the 'y' at the end of words lightly, more 'i' than 'ee' – 'veri' say the English, 'veree' the South Africans.

It fools people. When they ask where I'm from and I say here, London, they believe me. But then the problems start.

'Where did you go to school?'

'Um – Hampstead.'

'Really, which one?'

I blush, I get confused, I shut up. From now on I do anything to avoid a certain question – the one that awoke a strange shame in Dad when Mr Patel asked it – where are you from? I'm learning about South Africa, about apartheid, and I'm not liking what I learn. Can it be that we, the Shers, were part of what people here are calling an abomination, a crime against humanity? But we never hurt anyone, oppressed anyone. Katie *likes* working for us.

She and I write to one another. After a few letters I ask her to stop addressing me as Master Antony. She doesn't reply. Then, during a phone call home, Mom asks, 'What have you said to Katie? She thinks you're angry with her.' I'm stumped. Apartheid has done a good job. On us both, really. I'm trying to deny being what I am – a white South African – but what am I otherwise? It's a good thing I shall turn into an actor soon, turn into other characters, because I haven't a fucking clue who Antony Sher is any more.

One night, about a month before drama school, travelling home by bus after a theatre visit, I'm whiling away the journey glancing at an attractive, black-haired young man when he suddenly glances back. We reach his stop. Now he looks at me very directly. I get off with him. We go back to his room, in a student house in Shepherd's Bush. The sex is awkward; it takes a long time. At last we talk. I ask what he's studying. Theology, he replies. Noting my expression, he adds, 'Jesus said we should love all men.' Still naked, he accompanies me to the front door. Outside, turning back, I see him through the frosted glass: the flesh of his torso, the badge of pubic hair. It's the most erotic moment of the evening.

Well, good, I tell myself as I tramp back to West Kensington, you didn't enjoy that any more than the first time, so you're obviously not queer.

WEBBER-D.

WHEN GRANNY HEARD I was going to marry my girlfriend she became ill. Literally. She took to her bed. The family spent weeks calming her down. It wasn't the sex of my intended spouse (dear God, how would she have reacted if I were pairing off with a guy?) but the religion. A non-Jewish girl, a *shiksa*. I'd told her the happy news first because Mom and Dad were away on one of their trips, and I needed to tell someone. I felt so proud. I was engaged – I was going to wed – I was *normal.*

The relationship with Maggie, as I will call her here, a glamorous blonde New Yorker in my class at Webber-D., started after the first term, during the holidays. We went hitch-hiking in Europe, eventually ending up on the Greek island of Hydra, which was specially beautiful at Easter time. I played out *Zorba the Greek* fantasies. At night we slept on a beach, never touching. But then, on the overnight ferry back to Brindisi in Italy, we tried it. No good – equipment not working.

Back in London, after term started again, we went to see the film *The Killing of Sister George* and I finally confessed: 'I think I'm like them.'

'Lesbian?'

'You know what I mean.'

'I do, honey, and I don't buy it!'

That night I lost my virginity for the second – or was it third? – time, and soon after we moved into a small third-floor flat in Clanricarde

Gardens in Notting Hill. Later to a bigger, basement one in Courtfield Gardens in South Kensington, nearer the school. We lived together, happily, for two years. Then, as the time approached for Maggie to go home, we got engaged. And then I told Granny . . .

Hers wasn't the only negative reaction. Maggie's parents had always been kind to me, but they weren't overjoyed by this news. Her father was one of the editors of a top magazine. They were American aristocracy; I was from a small business family in Cape Town. I think they had more ambitious plans for their daughter.

A few months after returning to the States, Maggie stopped answering my letters. Later I heard she was married. It broke my heart. Then I lost my virginity again – making love while being in love – with a man. I finally knew that I was definitely gay, even if not yet glad to be. Although I'd continue to deny my true nature for a while and even enter into a brief marriage, I simply wasn't meant to be straight. Between them, and without necessarily intending it, Granny and Maggie's parents had pointed me in the right direction.

Drama school was tricky for me at first. Mainly because I had a previously unknown but crippling disability.

A wobble.

We dubbed it this, the 'wobble', me and the speech teachers.

Whenever I got up to speak in class, to read or recite a piece, a shiver of tension crept into my voice, already straining to sustain its false English accent, and slowly hijacked the exercise. Eventually I'd have to give up and sit again, blushing scarlet, trying not to hear the suppressed giggles of the others.

Come to think of it, this wasn't a completely new experience. I'd known it before: in bar mitzvah classes, under the sour, dead-eyed gaze of Mr Bitnun.

That was singing – I couldn't sing, I knew I couldn't, I accepted it – but this was *speaking*. This was a basic tool of the trade. How could I be the actor who didn't speak? Or could I make a career just playing very jittery characters?

I had sleepless nights for most of the first term. It had been so difficult getting into drama school. Now I was here, yet somehow sabotaging myself. And hanging over us, at all times, was the threat of expulsion, or what they called weeding out. The audition system wasn't over. At the end of each term certain students were told they'd made the wrong career choice and advised to leave. This made me rather nervous. Which made the wobble worse. But then something happened . . . a gradual thing . . . student life, moving in with Maggie, growing up . . . my attention shifted off the wobble, and then, like hiccups, it just vanished.

One of the speech teachers had always been less worried about it than I: Sheila Moriarty, a short, grey-haired, smoky-voiced powerhouse of warmth and good sense, one of the veterans of the school. She was on my side from the start. Which is just as well, since it wasn't just the wobble holding me back, but support-breathing too. This involves filling the lungs fully, but low down, no raising of chest or shoulders, keeping the ribs extended while using the diaphragm to empty the breath – and then, at the last moment, exploiting the reserve supply held in those outstretched ribs. *What?* It's easier playing rugby, believe me. The battle to separate my breath into different compartments more often resulted in a burp, fart or swoon rather than well-modulated speech. Only me, though. The other students mastered the technique effortlessly.

I'm a slow learner. Whether it's driving three-ton trucks in the army, or new methods of breathing at drama school, or the various sword fights, dances and other skills I've had to acquire during my career (the *Tamburlaine* rope climb – *oich!*), it just takes me for ever. Then I reach a point of getting pissed off, the oh-fuck-it point, of realising I can't do this and don't care – and then it falls into place. Odd. Obviously I need to start rather than end with the oh-fuck-it point, but that's not in my nature. I'm the swot, the goody-goody, the one eager to please.

Webber-D. taught no rigid philosophy of acting. Thank goodness. I've come to realise that the only rule is that there isn't one. Flexibility and openness are the key. Whenever I've devised a 'method' for myself it ceases to apply to the next role. I did a vast amount of research for *Richard III*, virtually none for *Torch Song Trilogy*. For the first I was seeking inspiration – trying to picture it as a new play, trying to imagine Olivier hadn't put his stamp on it – while the second simply requires you to play from the heart. The actor is a portrait painter – of others and of himself. The job should keep growing and changing as you do. So I was lucky to go to a drama school whose main emphasis was on the practical. We had regular classes in voice, movement, dance and fencing; also singing (from which I was instantly banned), and make-up (which I relished). We did 'Speaking Shakespeare' with the actor Nick Amer, from whom I first learned two basic principles: you have to paraphrase every single word in every single speech, *translate* them into contemporary English, and then, when you've understood everything, get it back up to speed, like normal speech. We talk very fast, very deftly, and Shakespeare is easier to understand at this pace than when it's overemphasised. All the same, I never imagined a classical career for myself – the Bard was somehow the preserve of the honey-voiced, middle-class English students among us – and my favourite classes involved physical acting. Mime and Improvisation.

These were taken by two dynamic performers themselves: Ben Bennison and Steven Berkoff. The first was a witty rubber band of a man, a Yorkshireman; the second was from London's East End, a much darker character. Strutting, snarling, grinning, half human, half creature, he charmed and frightened us. Luckily I was one of his favourites. He devised a version of *A Midsummer Night's Dream* for my term: a violent, funny, sexy version, in which I played a demonic Puck. That production was revelatory to me. I discovered I could tap into a strange energy for the character and express myself forcefully through the same small body that seemed so inadequate back on the playing fields of Sea Point Boys' High. Even though this was Shakespeare, I felt I had some advantage over those students who could only speak the verse beautifully; they looked a bit awkward in Berkoff mode, whereas I felt released. There was something strikingly un-English about the *Dream*'s director, something I could identify with. We share the same ancestry – East European Jewish – but there was even something African here. The Cape Coloured people who fascinated me back home with their dancing walk and razor-sharp gestures, even the street fighting and wild drunkenness of some – Berkoff was urging us to use our bodies with the same electric muscularity. He demonstrated it himself all the time: some bolt of power seemed to be coming up through the ground, charging his limbs, glowing in the air around him. I liked this. I wanted it. And it seemed feasible; it was somehow accessible to me. Though strange. An earth power in little Ant?

But he was changing too, of course, little Ant. He was living with a glamorous New York girl, he was gregarious, with a whole circle of friends, not just one soulmate, and he was enjoying student life. He liked the parties, he'd started to smoke, to drink.

Until that point alcohol had been anathema to me. It was 'the boozing' – the sharp edge on Dad's breath, the whisky sting – and it was the cloying sweetness of the blood-red Pesach wine with which we dotted the tablecloth at Middlepost. But now it was necessary to put aside my squeamishness for research purposes. I was playing Archie Rice in a scene from *The Entertainer*, and he's drunk in it. What's it like to be drunk? My first experience of alcohol was extra strong cider in a pub down the road from Webber-D. I enjoyed it; not the taste, but the sensation of getting pissed. Drink was like acting – it allowed me not to be me. Later, cocaine would provide a much better option. For now, the only drug I sampled was marijuana and it just made me sleepy.

I suppose it could be said that I dipped my toes into the sixties. Right at their end: 1969. Given our backgrounds – me from the most culturally constipated place on earth, Maggie from American high society – neither of us was ever going to be relaxed enough to turn into serious hippies, but we bought shaggy waistcoats and cheesecloth Indian shirts at Portobello Market, we played Simon and Garfunkel in our Notting Hill flat, we grew our hair. Mine, being curly, spreads outwards not down. Instead of wearing it in a big frizzy halo, fashionable at the time, some streak of South African conservatism inspired me to brush it. The results were bizarre: strange shelves of hair emanating from the deep parting I'd somehow managed to excavate; all leading to a massive, tangled clump sticking out at the back. My report card from Webber-D. at the end of the first year mentions nothing else: *Do something about that hair!*

I have snapshots of Maggie and myself in Hyde Park during our first summer. The air is soft and bright, permeated by a slight haze from the exhaust fumes and heat of the big city, as well as a million joints and joss sticks alight that Sunday afternoon. We are the straightest of sixties people (and now, thank God, I'm the straightest of men too), yet we look dreamily high on it all: Swinging London.

We stayed up through the night of 21 July 1969 to watch the first moon landing. I felt moved by the idea that, for those few hours, the whole world was doing the same thing – except South Africa, who couldn't. They still weren't allowed TV.

My South African accent was further eradicated at Webber-D. and whenever possible I'd still tell strangers I was British. It wasn't just that I was ashamed of apartheid, I was also ashamed of coming from a cultural wasteland. How could you become a famous actor if you were a white South African? (There was Janet Suzman, but she was from a family famously opposed to apartheid – her aunt *was* the Opposition in SA – so she didn't count.) Also, how could you become a famous actor if you were Jewish? (There were David Kossoff and Alfie Bass, but I didn't fancy a career playing cuddly old *kvetchers*.) And how could you become a famous actor if you were homosexual? (There was some story about Gielgud being caught cottaging once – a terrible disgrace.) No, I couldn't be any of these things, so each was set aside and locked away. Later my life would resound to the squeak, whoosh and bang of closet doors swinging open, but for now I denied everything I was.

It surfaced though – home – at unexpected moments.

One day I received a letter from Mom. She thought I should know that Tickey had been knocked down, just outside the house. Katie found her in the gutter, injured but conscious, and nursed her for many hours. It was no good, though – she died later that evening. Maggie was away in New York when I got this letter. Alone in our flat, I started to cry. For a dog? How soppy – but I think I was crying for myself as well: the other runtish little mongrel in Montagu House. Anyway, I sat on the floor of our London flat, put back my head and howled for hours.

For the final-year shows, Webber-D. tried to cast you in a lead role at least once, a vehicle geared to your specific skills, aimed at helping you secure an agent or work, or both. I was given *The Love of Four Colonels* by Peter Ustinov. He'd written it for himself, creating a series of cameos in send-ups of Shakespeare, Chekhov and gangster movies, via a role called something like the Dark Fairy (or am I just describing myself at the time?). Maggie played the other one, the Good Fairy. The show went well and I remember experiencing the intoxicating injection of laughter shots again, like at my high school show, *Simple Spymen*.

But I wasn't the leading light of my year, not by any means. That honour was shared by Charlotte Cornwall and Brian Deacon. In fact, Brian went straight from Webber-D. to play a starring role with Glenda Jackson and Oliver Reed in the film *Triple Echo*. An unimaginable achievement. The rest of us were sick with envy.

Webber's principal, Raphael Jago, made two predictions about me

during his final assessment. One, that I'd have a career rather like Lionel
Jeffries; two, that I wouldn't come into my own till I was in my thirties. He
was perhaps wrong about the first, but – although it came as depressing
news to a twenty-two-year-old – absolutely right about the second. Just
after I turned thirty in 1979, two exceptional projects came my way, one
on television, one on stage, and both helped hoist me up the ladder.

I'm never quite sure whether drama schools are worthwhile. Can you *learn*
to act? Probably yes and no. On the one hand you can learn technique (I've
always regretted not going to art school simply to learn the craft, the artisan
side of being an artist); on the other there are fine examples of actors who
never trained. McKellen and Gambon, for instance, who possess two of the
best voices in the profession. But if, like me, you're not blessed with a strong
voice to start with and have two left feet, and don't easily pick up new skills,
then it's no bad thing to spend a couple of years making a fool of yourself in
a relatively protected environment rather than the much rougher world of
professional theatre. I suppose the most persuasive argument for drama
schools – though this could be achieved through other means, like travel –
is the chance, the time, for students to do some growing up. At Webber-D.,
even though I'd been through the army and lived alone in London, I was
still completely confused about my identity and so my notions about acting
were all awry, all about disguise rather than revelation.

The casual dress of flesh.

The visible soul.

These two phrases are from Anthony Burgess's inspired translation of
Rostand's *Cyrano de Bergerac*, which I would later play and, although they
refer to the play's conflict between beauty and ugliness, between our outer
and inner beings, they also strike me as perfect descriptions of opposing
acting styles. At the start of my career, inspired by Olivier and his putty
noses, Guinness in the Ealing films and Peter Sellers in practically
everything, I was obsessed by my characters' casual dress of flesh, whereas
I'm now more interested in their visible souls. But this is difficult when
you're nineteen or twenty. What do you know about the terrible parting
between Masha and Vershinin in *Three Sisters*? This isn't what I'd
experienced at Cape Town airport; this is two hardbitten people coming
to the end of a tacky affair, which nevertheless seemed like a last ever
chance of glory. How do you capture the silence and anger in Pinter's

characters? This isn't childhood sulking; this is stuff soaked in the disappointment and duplicity of adult life. How do you play Shakespeare? I'm *still* not mature enough to play Shakespeare. He writes people and language in such complexity it's like the real thing. A mass of contradictions and layers. Every time I do one of the big roles I begin by becoming baffled by its inconsistencies and then, if I'm lucky, I learn to embrace these seemingly loose ends. Not by attempting to tie them up, just by holding on fast.

Before learning to act there's learning to live. How can you start pretending to be other people before you've become one yourself?

I left Webber-D. with no prospects. Others had secured agents and jobs, but not me. Maggie went back to America. I had to move out of our large basement flat in Courtfield Gardens and into a bedsitter again, a miserable one in Lexington Gardens: an Edwardian house whose big rooms had each been sawn into three. I was in a corner of the first floor, with a sliver of a window. All my friends from Webber-D drifted away to places outside London, either to the reps or their homes. I felt very lost again and had an alarming sense of déjà vu – one that would continue to haunt me – here I was, alone in London, in a bedsit, whiling away the days, the weeks, the months. It was as though I'd only just arrived. I still couldn't start my new life. The Blakes, ever kindly and hospitable, ever providing meals and theatre trips, began to say it again: 'Maybe going back to South Africa wouldn't be the worst thing in the world . . ?'

Oh, but it would! Now more than ever. I had cauterised all South Africanness from my identity. Returning wouldn't have been just a failure – it would've been a kind of death.

Then one day Mr Jago phoned from Webber-D. A colleague of his, John Scarborough, was running a one-year post-graduate course at the Stables Theatre in Manchester. It was apparently a lively if somewhat hybrid arrangement, shared between the University Drama Department, the Polytechnic School of Theatre and Granada Television. The latter were offering bursaries for the course. Jago could guarantee me one. Was I interested?

I packed my bags, moved out of that small, dreadful slice of a room and travelled north. It was a journey that would lead quite quickly to one of the most exciting theatres in the country, the Liverpool Everyman.

Liverpool, Manchester and Frinton-on-Sea

'Your watch flew off during the speech.'
'Yes,' I mutter.
'You ignored it.'
'Yes,' I say more confidently.
'You shouldn't've.'
I hesitate now. 'But I didn't want it to throw me.'
'Why not? It happened. It *was* throwing. It threw me – it should've thrown you – you should've *used* it. Things don't always go according to plan on stage. They shouldn't. That's dead theatre, man, that's fucking dead theatre.'
'Yes,' I say, biting my lip. 'Sorry.'
He stares at me with tired, puffy eyes, he scratches his beard, he pushes his fingers through unkempt, probably unwashed, reddish-blond hair, then suddenly he gives a surprisingly gentle smile: 'But it was good. We'll let you know soon.'
'Right,' I say. 'Thanks.'
I think it's gone quite well. I might get a job. Here. At the Liverpool Everyman. That's Alan Dossor retreating up the aisle as I pick up my watch and gaze at the broken strap (what Berkoffian energy caused it to snap

during the speech?) – he's running one of the most original and exciting reps in the country; he's a fine director but a difficult character, so people say, he doesn't suffer fools gladly; he's something of a visionary, a passionate socialist. The Everyman is as it sounds: theatre for the people. The people of Liverpool. Most of the shows are performed in Scouse accents, whether modern plays or Brecht – Brecht is especially popular here! – and Shakespeare is done in a modern, anarchic way, borrowing the circus style from Brooke's recent *Dream*, while adding the Everyman's own distinctive brand of showmanship.

I came over from Manchester a few nights ago and saw an example of their work: *Canterbury Tales*. Not the cosy West End version, but their own. It was amazing, unlike anything I've seen, more like a riot than a play, or a carnival maybe; the entertainment ferociously charged. The cast all seemed to be supermen, super-performers; all able to clown, sing, dance, do backflips and eat fire. One started a striptease in the middle of his soliloquy – you could tell he was improvising, he hadn't done this before – and the audience went berserk. He rode the waves of laughter like a champion surfer, in control, going on his journey, despite their greater, wilder power. It went on for several minutes, with round after round of applause. I sat there open-mouthed.

I mentioned this to Alan Dossor at today's audition. He chuckled: 'Yeah, he's pretty good, that guy – Jonathan Pryce.'

This was clearly a theatre where, if your watch strap broke, you *used* it.

The audition over, I went outside. It was a bright June morning. The Everyman is positioned on the rise of a hill and Liverpool was sparkling below, smelling of the sea, a bit like home. And maybe destined to be home too? But as I strolled down to Lime Street Station and caught the train back to Manchester, I grew more thoughtful. If an offer came through, would I survive the Everyman? My acting was all detail and structure, carefully rehearsed, not particularly spontaneous, nothing like what this Jonathan Pryce was doing. Would I be able to change, to grow? I wanted to. I suspected that acting needed to be a constantly developing craft, but was the Everyman the right place? The atmosphere was very macho, very hetero. Dossor was famously set against camp theatre, in every sense. From this point of view the timing wasn't great for me. I was just coming round to the idea of being gay again . . .

*

During the post-graduate course at the Stables in Manchester I'd had two more affairs with women and one was rather more than an affair – I got married. To the splendidly named, splendidly spirited Jo Jelly. Was this my last attempt to be straight, to have that 'normal' life which everything in my upbringing pointed to? I don't know; I was very confused. The marriage didn't last long – though my friendship with Jo has – and I was soon involved in the first proper gay relationship of my life, with a fellow student, a fine, kind chap whom here I'll call Carl.

The Stables course was run like a sort of rep, with shows every few weeks – *Macrune's Guevara, A Collier's Friday Night, The Real Inspector Hound* – as well as classes; Jo Jelly was the movement and dance tutor. Two of my fellow actor-students went on to greater things, though in different fields. Bernard Hill, already a terrific presence, very funny in comedy, very powerful in serious roles, was eventually to be Yosser in *Boys from the Blackstuff*; while Jane Edwardes was to change course as drastically as any actor can and became a critic. I was delighted when I heard. This surely guaranteed good reviews for evermore in *Time Out*, where she settled. Not at all. She's always regarded my work with a faintly disapproving, faintly suspicious eye. Maybe it was something I said in Manchester.

The year was a happy one. And at its end, although the post-grad course awarded no degree, I have a sense of winning a glittering prize: travelling over to Liverpool on that bright June morning and auditioning at the Everyman. A letter duly arrived from Dossor. Its tone was brisk and practical, yet read like poetry: We are offering you a job at £18 per week for next season starting rehearsals on the 28th August. Keep us informed of your changes of address when you leave Manchester and also reply to this letter confirming your acceptance of the job.

I like to tell people I started my career at the Everyman, I like the sound of that pedigree, but it isn't completely true. With time to fill before the 28th of August, I was lucky enough to get another job, a job which actually secured my Equity membership. So my career really started at Joan Shore's summer theatre at Frinton-on-Sea. That year, 1972, it expanded to Southwold as well, with the company commuting back and forth between the towns. Both had quaint little theatres, more like village halls, and I think we were even lit by footlights.

Two-weekly rep. Four plays in eight weeks: Agatha Christie, William

Douglas-Home, others of that ilk. Acting ASM, which means playing roles plus stage management duties. How did we find the time – to learn lines, to make props, to rehearse one play while performing another and party too, late into the night? I haven't a clue, I couldn't do it now.

My strongest memory of Frinton, however, is nothing to do with the theatre.

I was walking along the front on Saturday morning, a clear, perfect day, when a middle-aged woman in a wet bathing costume suddenly clambered up from the rocks below. Could I help? – she'd been swimming with her husband and he'd got into trouble. Looking out to sea, I couldn't spot him. Another passer-by ran for the police while I stayed with the woman.

'I'm sure he'll be all right,' I said to her. 'Just stay calm.'

'I'm completely calm,' she replied in a strangely steady voice, 'but we must do something very, *very* soon.'

A policeman arrived, a tall, old-school bobby, who immediately led along to the right, following the drift of the tide. His step quickened and broke into a run as we reached the next beach, then, tearing off his trousers, shoes and socks, he went into the water. I still couldn't see what he had. But a few moments later he returned to shore dragging a figure with him: weirdly loose and grey-skinned. The policeman tried artificial respiration for a long while, then gave up and apologised to the woman. She dropped on to all fours and vomited.

The shock of this has never left me. It was my first (and, in fact, only) sight of a dead body, and my first glimpse of the here-one-minute-gone-the-next trick in the magic of existence. I'm still haunted by images of the couple planning their holiday, arriving at Frinton, waking in the hotel room that morning and saying, 'What a perfect day for a swim.'

My family have a long history of hellos and goodbyes. I'm very jumpy about the latter – ever since that incident in Frinton – and about all partings, however brief. When he commutes between London and Stratford, Greg is under strict instructions to call me as soon as he reaches the other end. But of course when the moment comes you still miss it. 'Bye, Dad,' I said at Heathrow on the evening they flew to Israel. 'See you next week.'

And so to Liverpool – when the 28th of August finally came – Liverpool and the Everyman.

My first show here was, untypically for them, a completely

straightforward production of *King Lear*. An Australian actor, Brian Young, played Lear, Jonathan Pryce was Edgar and I was the Fool. My first go. Ten years later I'd start my RSC career playing it again, this time to Michael Gambon's Lear.

I struggled with the part both times. Yes it's poignant, yes it's absurd – an early incarnation of Sam Beckett arising in Shakespeare's soul – but it's always seemed important that he be *funny* too. It's his job, as Fool: he's hired to make people laugh. Try that with Shakespeare's gags, though. They ain't a barrel of. It could be done, however: I'd seen Michael Williams play the part in my first ever visit to Stratford; his face held in a wide, bleak grin, a strange mask of comedy; he was both funny and troubling. At the Everyman production my solution was to give the character a slight underbite, creating an unintentionally goonish sound to everything he said. It seemed appropriate to the cruelty in the play.

Two Everyman lessons were learned immediately. The first when I introduced 'my character' – a little shuffling figure with the underbite – to rehearsals one morning. 'Yeah, that could work,' said Dossor, then immediately turned to Brian Young: 'What do you think – would you have this guy as *your* Fool?' This was a revelation to me. Creating a character isn't just your own business. Since the Fool is like an appendage to Lear, a kind of pet, it's only right that the actor playing Lear should be involved in delineating the role. Actors playing married couples need to negotiate along similar lines.

The second lesson came with a kick.

We were on stage, in performance, doing one of the storm scenes, when Jonathan Pryce's foot suddenly contacted my arse quite forcibly. I'd been flattered to hear, via Kate Fahy, then his girlfriend, now wife, that he was going out front to watch my first scene, and she'd never known him do this before – but the kick was less flattering. It said, 'Wake up!' It said, 'You're on automatic, you're just doing what you've done before.' It was a rough lesson, but a good one. It's essential to reinvent, remint each moment in a play, again and again, night after night. It's perfectly possible to treat stage acting like driving a car – your body goes through the motions while your head thinks about the shopping – but this doesn't make for the best theatre. I learned a lot from Jonathan Pryce. About danger on stage. There are certain scenes – of crisis, of emergency – when real danger is required. Something you can't fake. The actor has to send a frightening jolt through the air, surprising the audience, surprising the other actors, surprising *himself*. Jonathan could do this naturally. I couldn't. So I watched, I learned, I changed.

As a city, I liked Liverpool more than Manchester. They're only fifty miles apart, but while Manchester struck me as rather flat and characterless, rather Northern grim (this was in the early seventies – it's livened up since), Liverpool is built on hills and water, all up and down, two of its crests topped with cathedrals – the old, dark nineteenth-century Anglican one and the weird, modern, Catholic 'wigwam' – and, being an international port, it's filled with all sorts of characters from heaven knows where, to say nothing of all the Irish popping over for a weekend or a lifetime. Actors joining the Everyman had to learn the Scouse accent straight away, almost as an initiation test, and this was like a key to the place itself. It's salty and impolite; you create it somewhere towards the back of your throat, you half gargle it, half spew it out of one corner of your mouth; it suits the throwaway, wisecracking style of the locals; their humour has a glancing, unexpected spin to it, with that Irish twist too, a bit frisky, a bit dark, very fast.

'Yer a'right dere, la?' (Are you all right there, lad?)

My first year at the Everyman was exhilarating. Not only Jonathan Pryce in the company, but Bernard Hill (also joining from the Stables), Pete Postlethwaite, Alison Steadman and Julie Walters. Aside from Dossor directing, there was also Richard Eyre. The writers were Willy Russell, Alan Bleasdale and John McGrath. It was one of those golden ages which blesses some theatres from time to time. I would've gone to any rep that would've hired me, so it was pure good fortune that landed me at the Everyman.

I played young Yorry in McGrath's *Fish in the Sea* – J. Pryce in terrific form as the other male lead, a Glaswegian wreck – I played Buckingham in a very anarchic, very Everyman, circus cage *Richard III* – J. Pryce in terrific form as Richard – and I played Enoch Powell in Chris Bond's eccentric but vibrant play about him, *Tarzan's Last Stand* – J. Pryce in more modest form as Macmillan. I managed to achieve quite a likeness as Powell. Something about the man was available. Not just his vocal and physical mannerisms (endlessly studied from film and tape) and the three-hour make-up (like doing a small oil painting each evening), but something about his dry and angry soul too. I knew about racists. I could summon up a special prickle of commitment for his most famous speech: '. . . And like the Roman, I seem to see the River Tiber foaming with *much blood*.' During our run, the May Day parade was held in Liverpool, ending at the docks. As a publicity stunt, I was spirited along in full make-up and costume, and slipped on to the platform in between two of the speakers. Below me were several thousand of the city's work force, very vocal, very Scouse and very angry – this was 1973, the Tories were in power, Heath was Prime Minister. As I began to address them, their initial shock and fury was as rewarding as the laughter when they caught on. I think I can honestly say it was the most bracing performance of my life.

The Everyman was one of the few places where, as a twenty-four-year-old, I could get to play leading parts. And there's no amount of drama school training that equals learning on your feet, especially if the play is resting on your shoulders. You're in touch with the rhythm of the whole evening, you feel when it works, when it drags, when the laughs fail or come in the wrong places. You take responsibility. Not just for your role but the whole show.

'What do you want to *say* as an actor?'

This question was Dossor's best advice to me – uttered when we were both a bit pissed late one night, down in The Bistro under the theatre, a marvellously smoky cavern where actors grazed and watered after the shows. I didn't understand him at first. What did I want to *say*? But actors didn't *say* anything. Acting was interpretative not creative, it was second-rate – Mac's words still rang in my ears like a curse – writers and directors were the only ones who did any *saying*. 'Bollocks,' retorted Dossor. 'You won't become a really good actor till you put yourself on the line, till the job's vital – *which* plays you do, *why* you do them, *how* you do them – it's got to mean something to you, man, before it's going to mean anything to the audience. Otherwise just go be a plumber – y'know, if it's only a craft, a skill – just go ride a bike. If it's only talent you're offering, don't bother us with it – there's plenty in this country – only bother us if you've got something to say!'

Good God. I reeled away down Hope Street that night (isn't it wonderful, a theatre called Everyman on a street called Hope?), my head awash with booze and excitement. Actors are taught to be passive, to be grateful for any work, to do as they're told, to not think for themselves, to leave everything to daddy director; they're the second-class citizens, the kaffirs, in the great state of Theatre. But for me, things would never be quite like that again . . .

I'm not in favour of the old actor-manager system. The people who still practise this bore me, their egos bore me. I like having a director, but I prefer to work with not under him. I ask to be a part of all the early decisions. If it's a new play and the writer is open to further drafts, I ask to be involved in those discussions. If it's a Shakespeare, I ask to know how we'll cut it, when and where we'll set it. Most of all, I ask to be in on the initial design meetings. There is a type of production where the designer brings drawings of all the play's characters to the first day of rehearsal. So he knows how I'll dress or brush my hair before I do? How dare he!

I must have been feeling quite angry with my parents by the time they arrived in Liverpool at the end of my first season, judging from this diary entry:

27/6/73. St George's Hotel, Liverpool. I choose a number, knock on a door, and there, squashed into a box-like room miles above the ground, I find my mother and father. Wearing her wig and make-up, she looks exactly like she did five years ago, except her body is thinner, bonier. He will be a dwarf on his deathbed. Less air in his cheeks and chest than I remember, but the heavy, furrowed face is as strong as ever, now with thick white sideboards creeping across the cheekbones to those black glasses that resemble a tinted, bullet-proof barrier. He shakes my hand politely. She hugs and kisses. Later I jump when she places her hand, all knuckles, rings and red nails, on my thigh.

Sex, that's what it was all about – sex.

During that year in Liverpool, my lover Carl was only able to visit occasionally, so I topped up my sex life by cottaging in the Gents loo at Lime Street Station. Coming out had become doubly difficult because of the Everyman. It was even more macho than I had first suspected – the place was like a bloody rugby club. And I'd heard that Dossor wasn't just anti-camp, he was anti-gay. As a young actor in Bristol he was very pretty, much sought after and pestered – so the story went – and now when senior

Everyman actors were asked to do auditions with him, they were briefed that if they spotted any poofters it was automatically no. So the story went.

When Dossor invited me to stay in the company for a second year, something snapped. He liked my acting, but not my kind. I made a promise to myself – no more hiding. Dossor would either have to accept me for what I was or I'd leave. Pacing round my flat in Huskisson Street, I rehearsed a speech: 'You normal people! I'm sick and tired of hearing about you. Who are you, where are you? Why weren't you my parents, my teachers? Why aren't you here at the Everyman – or elsewhere in Liverpool – or anywhere I've ever been? Why have I never met you? I've *never* met you. You normal people!'

It sounded great. Unfortunately I didn't have the courage to say it to Dossor (or anyone other than my diary).

One of the actresses, Angela Phillips, volunteered to break the news on my behalf. I held my breath. A day or two later she reported back: 'He was very laid-back about it. Said he'd known for ages. Said it didn't matter in the least.'

So much for rumour.

But the big one still lay ahead: telling the folks.

I was joining them for a summer holiday in Europe. After seeing one of the last performances of the season, Adrian Mitchell's *Mind Your Head*, they went back to London to wait for me.

When the last night was over, I headed south too.

10/7/73. Royal Angus Hotel, Leicester Square, London. The curtains are half drawn in Mom and Dad's room, the bed rumpled. Every afternoon at this time they have a lie-down. But today she's here on her own – Dad's away on a business meeting with Peter Blake – she's reclining on the bed wearing a kaftan. Her wig lies on the table among a gory field of make-up. Her own hair is shapeless and dull-coloured.

I will tell her today.

Scanning the *Evening Standard*, she suddenly laughs.

'What?' I say.

'Have you seen your horoscope?'

'No. Let's hear.'

'"Things which go awry can soon be put right so don't panic, don't indulge in gambling or speculation. Keep an open mind; further developments will make things clear."'

She has read this as if every word is staggeringly apt and now looks up with a knowing smile. I frown back, wondering why the people who write this stuff – it's like musak in print – and the people who read it, don't just call one another's bluff.

'Oh dear,' she says. 'I don't like the sound of mine.'

'Why?'

'Let me just finish . . . oi-yoi-yoi! . . . oh, well.'

'What?'

'"You will be getting wind of matters which have been kept under cover. Take note of—"'

I can't stop from laughing out loud. I may have been wrong about horoscopes!

'What is it?' she asks. I shake my head. She gives a calm smile. 'Why – have things been kept under cover?'

'They certainly have.'

'Well, get it off your chest then.' She's smiling, but not looking at me; casually leafing through the paper. I hesitate. She adds, 'It's all right, I'm too old to be shocked.'

As I speak, I hear that old enemy – the 'wobble' – slip back between the vocal cords; 'Well, you know how in my letters I've mentioned being a bit unhappy this past year?'

'Mm?'

'Well, it's all down to one fact . . . coming to terms with . . . something I've known a long time, but have never . . . the fact that I'm homosexual.'

Silence. No reaction. Either I'm not looking at her or she's not looking at me. How formal that word sounded!

'Pardon?'

'What?'

'That you're what?'

God, to repeat it.

'Homosexual.'

This time it sounded loud, defiant.

And it's all over. She's relaxed. Says: 'Y'know, I frighten myself sometimes. I really do. I *knew*. I've always known.'

'You knew?'

'That's why I was so relieved when you and Maggie were together.'

'Yes, well, so was I.'

'And then Jo – the marriage!'

'Well, yes.'

'But Antony, this started in Sea Point.'

I gulp. She can't know about my first time – with the perfumed Coloured man – on Queen's Beach.

'Which of your friends was it? What was his name? Never mind, but I remember his mother phoning to say she'd caught the two of you together.'

'How old was I?' I demand. I want to hear it's in kindergarten. Oh, I so want to hear this.

'I don't know. About eight or nine.'

I look away, hiding my disappointment. 'Well, that's hardly . . . I mean, all kids of that age . . .'

'I know. But it's always stuck in my mind.'

We continue to talk for a hour or so. As I leave I say, 'Thank you for understanding.'

She says, 'Just one thing – we can never tell Dad.'

'Ah.'

2/8/73. Malaga, Spain. I grow fonder and fonder of my parents. They're spending so much of this holiday unselfishly, trying to make me happy, to give me a good time. We're growing brown and healthy-looking under the sun. Mom and I talk often and freely about my homosexuality. I told her there were treatments and cures, and she was puzzled why I don't want to take these. Dad still doesn't know. He's a strange man. Full of fears. All sorts of fears. Of anything unknown, unfamiliar. When suddenly asked to taste the wine by an authoritative waiter, his hands shake as he lifts the glass, and his grey eyes behind the heavy black specs look helpless and afraid. He's suddenly the *plaasjaapie* from Middlepost, quite out of his depth.

8/8/73. Due Torri Spa Hotel, Abano, Italy. I'm having a sort of *Darling* experience. There's a waiter here. Doesn't look Italian. A dark blondness. His brow has a touch of the fox, or some sly charming dog. At mealtimes he notices me staring and smiles. People with great beauty don't mean their smiles to be so unsettling. They smile because they're confident; they've smiled like this since they were ten. That's the problem. It's the smile of a virgin boy from the face of a very experienced man. As I leave the dining room, he always seems near the door – or do I delay my exit till he's in position? – and then he smiles at me again, and says goodbye in Italian, his eyes shining from under the shadow of that sly forehead. Trouble is, he smiles the same way to the old ladies here. I'm afraid this is a *Darling* experience without the scooter ride into the sunset. I feel very randy every night, irritable with it, prowling the dark gardens and deserted swimming pool like a criminal looking for a crime. Then I go to sleep in pain. Early this evening, as I was scanning for talent from my balcony, a striking male figure appeared below, though not quite the kind I was seeking. Dad. Looking round for me. Dressed in black, there was something about him, his short, dark heaviness, the powerful head dominating the body, almost too big for it, pulling it forward, something reminded me of the *corrida* bulls we saw in Spain: at half-mast, when the fight's half done. Earlier today, at lunchtime, we argued fiercely about South Africa and I hated him, hated his prejudice, his ignorance, his conditioning. But that's over now. I go downstairs and have a drink with him. He's quiet and relaxed. Perhaps less full of his stories than usual – obscure anecdotes that you're left to piece together yourself – but surprisingly easy company. After dinner he goes for a stroll while Mom and I sit down to finish our game of Scrabble. But as soon as he's out of hearing she says: 'You'll be interested to know I've told him everything. He mentioned that he thought something was worrying you, so I grabbed my chance.'

'And how did he react?' She just shrugs. 'What – nothing?' I ask.

She shrugs again, then says: 'He didn't understand why you don't want to take the treatments so I told him your reasons. And he wondered why you'd bothered with the relationships with Maggie and Jo. So I explained that too.'

'Nothing else?' I ask, amazed.

'Nope.' She gives a final shrug.

'Does he know what it *is*?' I ask, reflecting on the small population of Middlepost. 'I mean, exactly.'

'Of course!'

When he comes back from his walk, we spend the evening together, the three of us, a good evening. I sense an uncharacteristic gentleness in him tonight, which confounds all expectations. But is this compassion or bewilderment? Is Mom right about him comprehending fully, or is it again like being asked to comment on some fancy wine and simply not knowing what you're expected to say?

My second season at the Everyman wasn't as exciting as the first. Not sure why, although the syndrome is familiar, somehow. There's a terrific blaze that goes through my life now and then, sometimes creatively, sometimes destructively, hot stuff either way, difficult to rekindle. The highlight of that second year was, unexpectedly, a painting. A giant painting. The company did Chris Bond's version of *The Country Wife* and, since I wasn't in it, someone suggested I create a backcloth for the set. I stayed up through the night for about a week, working on stage while it wasn't being used, slowly improvising the composition: a strange, joyful, grotesque image of a massive Earth Mother figure surrounded by a clutch of contemporary figures – Powell, Heath, Longford, Nixon – as well as some weirder, half-human, half-fish creatures. I've always wondered what happened to the canvas afterwards.

Willy Russell wrote the last show I did there, a play about the Beatles: *John, Paul, George, Ringo and Bert* – Bert being a fan who narrates their story. George Costigan played him, Bernard Hill was John, Trevor Eve was Paul, Philip Joseph was George and I was Ringo. Dossor directed. A show about the Beatles – in Liverpool? Well, exactly. We only risked miming one early number – 'She Loves You' – and left the rest to a remarkable female singer-pianist whom Willy discovered in a downtown folk club. She was plump, bespectacled and Scottish, performing with her face lost within an untidy mane of red-brown hair, nose just inches above the keys. But if the rest of her body was chronically shy, her voice was spared the affliction; it just climbed out of her and flew – a clear, ringing sound that seem to rise from the earth, lightly brush your spine and head straight for heaven. This was the theatre debut of Barbara Dickson.

We were a hit. Not only among local audiences, whose great folk myth was being retold in a way they recognised – 'Da coulda bin *me* dere, la, *I* coulda bin a contender!' – but also by the national press. London producers started flying in and, before we knew it, Robert Stigwood and Michael Codron had joined forces to bring us down to the Lyric Theatre, Shaftesbury Avenue.

Aged twenty-five, I was suddenly headed for the West End.

JOHN, PAUL, GEORGE, RINGO, BERT AND JIM

THE FAMILY FLEW OVER for the opening night: Mom, Dad, Randall, his wife Yvette and her mother – my former Elocution teacher – Auntie Esther.

'Oh, darling, my darling, I told you you'd make it, and here you are already, a leading role on Shaftesbury Avenue, a star of the West End, about to take London by storm – this is London, darling, London, the heart of world theatre! – oh, my darling, this is so incredibly, unbelievably, fantastically thrilling that . . . well, I *ektewelly* don't know what to say!'

In her own way Esther was only putting into words what we all felt – all of us in the show – we were in a sort of fantasy. Not only playing the West End, but playing the Beatles. During one of the previews a large party of Japanese tourists came to the show and, unable to read the programme, mistook the premise of the evening: not a fictional reunion of the Fab Four, but the real thing. When we mimed to 'She Loves You', they began to scream, this somehow spread through the rest of the audience and the noise grew until it felt like the Lyric was shuddering, ready for take-off. It was a taste, just a taste, of what the Beatles themselves must have known. For the press night party Stigwood had us all bussed out to his country mansion and here again, as we cavorted through the night, in the grand rooms, the vast grounds, the swimming pool, was a sample of life as a star; not a West End star, but several echelons up, a pop star. Not a career I'd ever contemplated for myself. My lack of musical skills had made it hard learning even the rudiments of Ringo's drumming technique – not, apparently, the most sophisticated in musical history – just so I could *mime* to that one number. One of the musicians in the show, Terry Canning, had volunteered to teach me, but eventually, like all my music teachers before and after, he gave way to despair: 'Oh, just flop your head from side to side and hope no one's watching your hands!'

My flopping head was adorned with a Beatles wig, I had a false nose (created by a film prosthetics expert) and the rest – Ringo's drooping eyes and thick lips – was done with greasepaint. The whole make-up took about two hours each evening. The family filmed the process with the cine camera, and filmed me going around backstage, and filmed themselves outside the Lyric, beaming with pride, pointing to the front-of-house photos, the press quotes, the poster (which I'd designed), and filmed the audience too, the ushers, buskers on the pavement, pigeons coming in to land, everything and anything connected to this glorious moment in London during the summer of 1974. Their excitement was wonderful; it moved me. To them this really was 'making it'; they didn't need more. I was less satisfied, though. Ever since the show opened, I'd been harbouring an unhappy secret. I knew my performance wasn't very good.

Ringo Starr isn't Enoch Powell.

This ought to go without saying, but nevertheless here lay the problem. I had yet to learn the golden rule about acting – there isn't one. No blueprint. No single technique. The method I'd used to capture a verisimilitude of Powell in *Tarzan's Last Stand* had been so successful I tried it again with Ringo. Hours were spent studying film footage and audio recordings, endless sketches were made of movements and mannerisms, phonetic jottings were done about accent and speech patterns. All this work had yielded results before because it exactly suited Powell. A very structured character – the polished-up Midlands tones, the dart-like gestures, the clenched shoulders, the flashing eyes. I mapped out a series of clues about him and then, like those drawings where you join up the dots, put them together and hey presto, there he was, Enoch Powell, walking and talking. Ringo, however, resisted this method. The real man is quirky, relaxed, spontaneous, a one-off personality, difficult to pin down, difficult to copy. The more effort I exerted the less I succeeded. There's nothing effortful about Ringo at all.

One night, driving home from the theatre, I heard the man himself being interviewed on the radio. Had he seen the Beatles show in the West End, they asked. 'I haven't, no,' replied the familiar Scouse voice, with its deep drawling tones. 'But I hear I'm not very good in it.'

I had to pull over to the side of the road. He was right. I knew he was. He'd simply said exactly what I felt. It was a shock all the same. To hear your character answer back. To hear him say, 'You're not very good as me.'

I was still upset and angry by the time I went into the theatre the following night. This proved to be the best possible thing. I'd reached the oh-fuck-it point. I stopped pushing the performance and it immediately worked better.

The only Beatle who actually came to see for himself was George Harrison. We peeked through the set and some thought they could see him. How would the audience concentrate, I wondered, with their necks twisted round, watching him not us. Backstage the excitement grew. Would he come round afterwards? Would he encourage the others to visit the show? Would we get to meet the one who was hero to us all – Lennon? No, no, no. Harrison left during the interval. He had to, he explained in an interview later, or he'd have started throwing things.

Disappointing again, yet understandable. What must it be like to see a play of your own life? Imagine actors playing Mom, Dad, Katie, or Little Ant. It would all be so wrong.

Meanwhile audiences flocked to the Lyric. We played the show for a full year, eight times a week. After the initial excitement of opening, a long run can become something of an endurance test. Round about the halfway mark, we all started forgetting the lines, despite knowing them inside out. That was the problem, actually – we no longer knew them in a way that made sense. We were on automatic pilot, thinking about the shopping, thinking about anything other than this endlessly looping story that had entrapped us like a recurring dream.

Luckily I found a second job, a day job, during the Beatles run. Gay Sweatshop.

The previous year Ed Berman's community theatre, Inter-Action, had helped to form a women's group and now planned a gay one. A committee was formed consisting of Drew Griffiths, Gerald Chapman, Roger Baker and Allan Wakeman, and they organised a series of one-act lunchtime shows at Berman's Almost-Free Theatre (so-called because audiences paid whatever they could afford), a small fringe venue in Rupert Street, just across from the Lyric. This was Gay Sweatshop's first season and I was in it.

Despite my time at the Everyman, I wasn't completely at ease with the notion of political theatre. Preaching to the converted can lead to very dull drama. But here was a case where the converted were worth preaching to. You might be gay, but were you glad to be? Homosexuality had only been legalised here in 1967, a year before I arrived, so freedom was almost as new to the British as it was to me. There were discussion groups after each show, counselling and literature available. One slender booklet, *With Downcast Gays*, became my own bible for a while. I was learning about myself by participating in both the plays and the discussions. It was a relief to be in a totally gay milieu at last, and sexy too.

The play I did that first season was *Thinking Straight*, by Laurence Collinson. Later I also did *The Fork* by Ian Brown at the Edinburgh Festival, and later still a play which Edward Bond wrote for Sweatshop, *Stone*, which I performed with Kevin Elyot (himself destined to script the famous gay play, *My Night with Reg*).

A note in Sweatshop's programmes said that although everyone working on the shows was committed to the basic principles of liberation, they weren't necessarily gay themselves. This was a vital disclaimer for the straight actors in the season and a useful one for people like myself. Although 'out' to my parents and close friends, I was still reluctant to go public. I feared it would affect my career. This was nonsense, but it would take me another fourteen years before I was ready to stand up and be named. By then, I was simply tired of flannelling in interviews, or having to disguise my true pride in shows like *Torch Song*; and I was impressed and humbled by what other gay actors, like Ian McKellen and Simon Callow, were doing for the cause. Perhaps, most important, I was about to publish the book of my paintings and drawings, *Characters*, and I refused to lie about the relationships and interests portrayed on those pages. It was one thing to be dishonest as an actor – that job fools around with the truth all the time – but somehow quite unacceptable as an artist. When I did come out that year, 1989, via an interview about the book in *The Times*, there was no fuss. In fact, rather disappointingly after all the time I'd spent agonising, it made no impact whatsoever. If I'd been a movie or TV star it might've been different, but theatre actors aren't news. Never mind – one person noticed. That Sunday the phone rang in our Stratford house and a voice said, 'Hullo, Ian McKellen here, we don't really know one another – hope you don't mind, I got your number from the stage door – but I just wanted to say one thing. Thank you.'

There was another name I mentioned a moment ago.

Simon Callow.

Ouch.

'How jealous are you?' Greg asked the company on the first day of rehearsals for *A Winter's Tale*, when we came to do it in 1999. He invited us to fill in a *Cosmopolitan*-type questionnaire, along the lines of: If you came home and found your partner in bed with someone else would you – A. shoot yourself; B. shoot them; C. join them? I didn't score very high. Apparently not a particularly jealous person (I think Greg was rather miffed), but of course the exercise was about sexual jealousy. That's the type in the play. Had the questionnaire been about professional jealousy my results might have registered on the Richter scale. I wrote an article in the *Guardian* about preparations for *Winter's Tale* and when the playwright David Edgar came to the first night, he said – with a characteristic dry twinkle – 'How marvellous to tell the British public that your interpretation of one of Shakespeare's major characters is based on feelings about Simon Callow.'

The moment I saw Simon – he was in the first Sweatshop season too, in Martin Sherman's *Passing By* – I felt a curious sense of gazing into a looking-glass. Short, stocky, dark, with a certain oomph to the work. Hmm. Bob Hooper, playing Brian Epstein in the Beatles show, knew Simon and provided more information to fuel my disquiet. He was Geminian, born the day after me, on 15 June 1949. Born here, but brought up in South Africa, in the Cape. And yes, in case I was confused by that disclaimer in the Sweatshop programmes, yes he was gay. In fact, Bob now revealed that he himself was having a ding-dong with Simon. That's quite a lot of coincidences, I thought, since I'd just had a ding-dong with Bob.

Is rivalry inevitable in the arts, possibly even healthy? Maybe. It can be bracing, it can be humbling and it can drive you completely fucking nuts.

For the first decade or so in the profession I felt I needn't bother, since Simon was having my career for me. In *Plays & Players* he was named Most Promising Newcomer – *shouldn't that be me?* – then he gave an acclaimed performance as Arturo Ui at the Half Moon – *my part, surely?* – then he went to the National to star in a hit play about Mozart – *well, I'm sorry, but I could've played him* – then he began to write books – *hang on, I was going to do that* – and on and on it went. Me going up for the same part as him, members of the public coming up to congratulate me on performances he'd given. I avoided meeting him. Once I had to flee a theatre because I'd spotted him in the foyer. But sometimes he'd get by without my noticing and then I'd suddenly hear his laugh during the show – it's a distinctively hearty laugh – and realise I was trapped in the same auditorium. And then that laugh would come again and again. *That laugh.* I was playing Salieri to his Mozart, except this was in real life.

At the same time I felt puzzled by generous things he was writing about both my acting and my books. It didn't seem like his blood was running with the same poison as mine.

Finally, in 1999, after the *Guardian* article on Leontes, I suddenly received a long, warm letter from him. He said he'd been amused to read my 'coming-out' about jealousy and should we meet?

During a great, four-hour-long lunch at the Caprice – we had a lot of catching up to do – the discussion turned to a beautiful young actor with whom we'd both worked. Although the guy was straight, well ninety per cent straight, I'd had a brief affair with him.

'It's the only thing I've truly envied you,' said Simon.

I sat back, amazed. Could this be true? I still envy you so much, I thought; I envy the creative flood you're enjoying at the moment (he was doing the screenplay of his Peggy Ramsay book while I was suffering writer's block), I envy the CBE you received on your fiftieth birthday (I turned fifty the day before without any gift from the Palace), I even envy the fact that you're not envious! Yes, that's it: most of all, I envy your happiness. This was the most surprising thing about finally meeting Simon. I was expecting the brilliant mind, the skill as a raconteur and I'd had some foretaste of his generous spirit. But I wasn't prepared for the sheer joyfulness of the man, apparently quite at peace with the world. Damn him! A most unexpected friendship has flourished since. 'Isn't it time for another supper?' Simon wrote recently. 'With just the four of us – y'know, you and me.' Yes, we often refer to our Geminian selves, though I'm no longer sure we're quite as twinlike as I thought.

It was during the run of the Beatles show that Bob Hooper introduced me to his brother, Jim, born ten minutes after him. Real twins. Though not identical.

Seeing Jim for the first time, I caught my breath. Here he was again: the beautiful, soft-eyed male I'd first fallen in love with at kindergarten. Jim's looks as a twenty-five-year-old were exceptional and radiant; as much to do with a light inside him as his delicate features; as much his visible soul as the casual dress of flesh. The gift of grace – it's supposed to be a female quality, but it's especially wonderful in a man. It can be a fragile thing, though. Jim had almost died at birth – they were triplets; a tiny girl didn't survive – and something of that extreme vulnerability haunts his personality still, almost to a fault. We found we had several things in common. We'd both been sensitive children, interested in the arts, growing up in what felt like the wrong place – Jim was from working-class Wolverhampton – and we'd both become actors. On the other hand Jim, as the second, the younger twin, was naturally accommodating, patient, content to follow, whereas I was selfish, wilful, driven. We fitted together perfectly. Within a few weeks of meeting, we began living together, first renting a small flat in Belgrave Gardens, St John's Wood and then, six years later, with Dad's help, we bought a house in Islington.

This was a neglected old property when we first saw it (Georgian, dating from 1824, in a terrace of artisans' homes): no bathroom, no inside loo, its WWII Anderson shelter still rusting at the end of the garden. But as we visited again and again, there was something immensely attractive here, something about the way its smallish rooms and stairwells filled with sunlight, at the back in the morning, at the front in the afternoons. We gutted and restored it . . . well, I say we, but Jim was far more imaginative in this area than I was, and in the long patch of ground at the back he created a lovely tumbling garden. We extended the rear basement into a conservatory, serving as my study-studio-gym. This became a treasured Room of my Own, and the building became home. *Home.* Even if in the broad sense I'm still not sure where home is, the Islington house is certainly the safest place I know on earth.

My 'education' at Gay Sweatshop had taught that gay couples didn't need to ape straight marriages. We had the option of recreational rather than reproductive sex (AIDS was not yet a threat). Sex could be separated from love, too, if we wanted; it could just be treated as an appetite or body function, to be sated, relieved, exercised whenever the need arose. This is a very male thing of course, based on our instinct to rut, rut, rut. Lesbian society has the same choice available, yet has never embraced the promiscuous scene with the same fervour.

Right from the start, while sharing an intense emotional and physical relationship, Jim and I also gave ourselves licence to enjoy the scene. There were only two rules: we were free to have sex with other people but not to fall in love, and we would tell one another *everything*. We mostly visited the scene together – whether London's gay saunas or Mykonos island – then we'd separate, have casual sex, and join up again to go home and cuddle in bed. At times it seemed like the ideal life – a loving partnership, domestic security, plus oodles of nooky – at other times less so. Jim was strikingly attractive; I wasn't. He scored effortlessly; I didn't. In this kind of situation – the meat market – looks are everything. You don't talk. No chance for me to say, 'I may not be throbbingly handsome but I'm quite interesting when you get to know me. I'm an actor, doing quite well' – no time for any of that. You get one glance, one quick assessment – face, body, packet – and that's it, you're either on or you're not. On Mykonos the young beauties of Europe, dishy beyond belief, practised a small head toss to mark their disinterest – 'cutting' you like Restoration fops – a brisk yet thorough dismissal, which could leave you quite winded. I'm the Elephant Man, you'd think, in a *Playgirl* calender. I sometimes spent hours being rejected, sometimes whole days, yet kept coming back for more. A curious addiction. I couldn't figure it out, until a few years later when I first went to a psychotherapist and he observed: 'Maybe it was the rejection that you liked. It's what you knew best, what you grew up with – a man whose affection you wanted and who kept ignoring you.'

In February 1976 Jim and I flew to South Africa for a three-week stay.

We said the main purpose of the trip was for him to meet the family, but this wasn't entirely true. It was my first time home. My first return to South Africa after eight years away. A journey so important I had to underplay it, had to give it a different rationale, a different name. I was terribly nervous. In fact I couldn't have gone back on my own. I needed my twin with me, someone who'd understand, understand completely, all the feelings churning round inside me, however crazy they seemed. I had this peculiar fear that as soon as I stepped back off the plane some gigantic South African force – the army, perhaps, or just my old life – would clamp closed around me, reclaim me and make escape impossible. Ego played a part too. I had always vowed I wouldn't return until I was successful. Was I successful now? I'd played a title role in the West End (a cheat this; there were five title roles in the show), I'd gone straight on to a new David Hare play at the Royal Court, *Teeth 'n' Smiles*, and then to the Royal Lyceum, Edinburgh, playing the lead in Bill Gaskill's production of *The Government Inspector*. My prospects were good. But were they good enough? Did they warrant the big return home as a hero? That was the fantasy. Photographers at the airport, a brass band perhaps, a red carpet.

Instead, there was just the Sher family. Did I say 'just'? A great crowd of Shers – Jim couldn't believe how many we numbered – the immediate family, with four new nieces and nephews, and Granny, the Hesselbergs, Esther, other aunts, uncles, and cousins: *everyone* had come to greet the plane. To them it was very simple: yes all right, I was returning with some glory maybe – maybe, schmaybe – more important I was returning as a son, brother, uncle, grandchild and so on. I felt all sorts of emotions. There were so many intense sensations – triggered by smells, sounds, the fall of light on this or that – and they were so familiar, so lovely. Why had I turned my back on all of this? I hated South Africa – I said this repeatedly back in England – I was appalled by its system of apartheid, ashamed of its cultural poverty, keen to be a 'British' actor – again and again I said it: I hate South Africa! Yet this didn't feel like hate. This was more like the opposite. And something else, something even stronger. This was home. That word again.

Home. Love. Hate. A triangle, a difficult equation, it's always there for me in South Africa.

I'd made the homecoming conditional – Jim and I had to be given a double bed in the spare room at Montagu House. My parents complied readily. Ever since I came out to them, they'd grown more and more at ease with the fact. There was no more talk of treatments or cures. I'd always expected Mom to be comfortable with my sexual identity, but Dad's acceptance, his warmth towards Jim at the airport that morning we arrived and throughout our stay, this continued to amaze me. Where in his life – in either the macho Afrikaner farming communities of Middlepost or the Jewish business circles of Cape Town – where had he ever learned to be tolerant towards gay people? I don't know. Jim's folks had also confounded expectations with the warmth they showed me. It's good when parents surprise us. We think we know them so well, especially their prejudices.

My brothers, Randall and Joel, knew the truth too and were fine. My sister Verne and her husband Ronnie didn't, and Mom said we shouldn't tell them. They were rather homophobic as a family, she said, following an upset at their son's school, when one of the teachers was suspected of fancying him. The irony is that, a few years later, Verne ended her marriage and settled down with a new partner, Joan. Verne and I, who shared little in childhood, have since become exceptionally close. It's good when siblings surprise you too.

Katie, the Shers' long-serving cook, was now also doubling as maid in the house, so she'd be making up the double bed in the spare room each morning. She'd see the sheets where Jim and I had lain and loved during the night. What did she think? '*Hulle is net soos broers*', (They're just like brothers) I heard her say to Dad in the backyard one morning. Katie is a deeply pious Christian; this was the only way she could comfortably interpret the situation.

And Granny? Granny, who'd become ill when she heard I was going to marry Maggie, a *shiksa*. Ageing now, but still fiercely independent (everyone warned me about 'the elbow', her response if you tried to help her up a step), she was forever popping into Montagu House, full of that twinkling curiosity which her offspring sometimes called nosiness. But she maintained her innocence too, rather like Katie, by inventing yet another version of our relationship: 'Antony's here with a nice friend from England, a bachelor like himself. Who knows, maybe they're going to play the field while they're here!'

And what of Randall's young daughters, Monique and Heidi, or Verne's small son and daughter, Wayne and Kim? They had no problem with who or what we were. They were simply delighted by the arrival of not one but two new uncles from 'overseas' and there was no question which was favourite: the handsome English one. Jim has a natural touch with children. Home movies show us with them on the beach; the film *Jaws* had opened recently and Jim is pretending to be a shark, one elbow held at a fin-like angle above the water as he swims towards the ecstatic, shrieking kids.

Jim himself was in a perpetual state of wonder throughout the visit. It was all so different from his own upbringing in Wolverhampton. 'There are marble pillars in your hallway!' he'd observe in hushed tones, or, 'You're having steak and eggs for breakfast!' Something else intrigued him too. 'What's going on at mealtimes?' he asked. 'Why are your family always rowing?'

'They're not rowing,' I explained. 'They're just being Jewish.'

It was illuminating to view life here, and my childhood in a way, through Jim's eyes. Yes, my family *did* communicate in quite a dramatic way – 'Oh I could murder her,' they'd say casually; 'I could just tear out her throat' – and yes, maybe this alarmed sensitive little Ant when he was growing up, sending him fleeing back to his bedroom, and the drawings of catastrophe and apocalypse spread over the floor.

One day I invited Mac round to tea. I wanted Jim to meet him. And anyway there was unfinished business between us, Mac and me; we'd never said goodbye when I left school. He was angry about my choice of career then, but surely now that I'd had some success as an actor, surely he'd see that I made the right decision?

He was a more subdued character than I remembered. The bushy eyebrows, the long, paint-stained fingernails, the beer belly, these were still distinctive features, but he looked greyer, smaller. We first encounter teachers like we do parents, looking up at them in every way. Later it's strange meeting them face to face.

As I tried to tell him about *John, Paul, George, Ringo and Bert*, I mentioned that I'd designed the poster. He interrupted, with a surprised laugh – 'The poster?' At school he'd exempted me from commercial art; he'd encouraged me to more creative work.

'You doing any figurative drawing?' he asked. 'Any painting?'

'Now and then,' I replied, lying. I'd put art aside for now.

'Now and then,' he repeated, with an odd, grim smile, then changed the subject.

I was relieved when he made an excuse and left early.

The holiday held one or two other awkward moments. After the initial pleasure in our reunion, the family and I weren't always totally enamoured with one another. Now the loud, combative style of conversation at mealtimes wasn't just us being Jewish; now we *were* rowing. Invariably about apartheid. It's evil, I'd say, just pure evil. Look at the mess in the rest of Africa, they'd reply, look at Britain and the support for that bloke you played, that Powell bloke, look at all the race trouble in America. But how can you support it as Jews? – I'd ask. How can you live in luxury while most people here are being persecuted; how can you be comfortable earning your money like that? How can *you* be comfortable, they'd retort, using this same money to go to drama school? Trapped, I'd get more insulting. Fuelled with pre-supper whiskies, Dad hit back, supported by Uncle Jack. Others joined in – one of the twins, Mark or Neal, challenging me: 'How can you say we're not good Jews?' – Mom declaring, 'Thank you very much, the conversation is over!' – Yvette protesting, 'But no, Antony's right. It's completely bloody gross what's happening in this country!' – while Jim sat cowed in the middle, wishing he were back in England. Then Katie would come in to clear the dishes and we'd all go silent in a way that I remembered from childhood, suddenly halting a conversation because *they* had entered a room. It was curiously respectful of us, or, more curiously, a sign of conscience, of shame.

Licking my wounds after these scraps, talking it through with Jim, I realised I had to be very cautious about claiming the moral high ground. Even just *visiting* South Africa you had to make your own little pact with devilish Uncle Nat, for the place was endlessly seductive. Family fights aside, the holiday was glorious – sun, sea and feasting – and when we reached its end we were nicely browned and fattened, lazy and peaceful, no longer that inclined to challenge the local way of life.

Katie asked us the time of our return flight. Her husband Golie (he whom Dad had once beaten in the garden at Marais Road; now a sobered-up and devout husband) wanted to watch the plane pass over their township, Bonteheuwel, near the airport. It was the beginning of a little ritual. Everytime I visited South Africa afterwards, and until his death in 1995, they'd find out the flight time and Katie would say, 'Golie will be watching.' This was their way of blessing my safe return to the place called Overseas.

Everything changed after that holiday in February 1976. When I look at the snaps or home movies of it, I imagine I can actually see this. A yellowish glow that isn't just the bleaching of time, but the aura of a lost world.

Montagu House was split into two shortly afterwards and completely converted. I'd never again see those rooms where I grew up.

Mac died unexpectedly just a few months after we saw him. Oddly enough, I started painting and drawing again then, and eventually published the results in *Characters*. I wished he'd lived to see that.

The Hesselbergs began moving to Israel in 1977; first the older twin, Mark, then the other, Neal, then Uncle Jack and Auntie Rona. Jack died shortly after arriving. It was the beginning of a series of tragedies for them, culminating in the sudden death of Mark and, strangely linked, the death of Dad.

The Hesselbergs had left South Africa because it was changing – for the worse, in their opinion. And the decisive change dates from just after our February 1976 holiday. Apartheid would never again be as it looked on that trip: completely intact, seemingly invincible, supported by a powerful fusion of one-party government and the strongest army in Africa.

The change began four months after we left, in June 1976, and came from the most unexpected source: the children of Soweto. They said no to learning Afrikaans at school – it was the language of the Boers, their oppressors – they said no and when it wasn't heard, they started fighting, with stones, bottles, knives. No match for the military might of the Nationalist government – a famous press photograph shows the corpse of thirteen-year-old Hector Petersen being carried from the carnage – and yet, despite all the odds, in the end they would win, the children would win.

to play the main house of the Royal Shakespeare Company in Stratford and again at the Market Theatre in Joburg (who'd've thought a South African stage could hold that power?), but the first time I knew it was stepping on to the stage at the Royal Court.

This is where Modern Theatre was born . . . this is where Look Back in Anger *was first performed . . . this is where Olivier did* The Entertainer *(he must have done the front-cloth routines right here, on this stretch of stage) . . . this is where Bond's* Saved *shocked London . . . this is where I saw Scofield on my first ever night in England . . . this is where I'm acting now.*

'Are we nearly . . . ?'

My opening line in *Teeth 'n' Smiles* – playing a character who never finishes his sentences: Anson, a shy Cambridge student with the unenviable task of supervising a visiting rock band. David Hare proved to be a fine, surprisingly objective director of his own writing, Helen Mirren and Jack Shepherd both became role models – real risk takers, always keeping it alive – and the show was a sexy success. But it was the Court itself that excited me most. I wandered around in a happy daze, touching the shabby walls, lingering on the worn, winding stairways. Even the front of the building fascinated me. Here, in the middle of fashionable Sloane Square, Chelsea, here was this tall, frail, brick façade; an elderly party trying to stand straight – more Chelsea pensioner than Sloane Ranger. How strange – the home of Modern Theatre looked past it.

It's difficult for theatres which house a revolution, which provide more than entertainment or even great drama, but actually change the way people think. The Market, Joburg, was again to inspire similar feelings. An affectionate sadness, a warm sensation, the afterglow of a roaring fire. . . if only I'd been here at the time! It's difficult for these theatres ever to ignite the blaze again: to live up to their reputations. The Court had been through a very low period when we came to do *Teeth 'n' Smiles* in 1975, and a new artistic directorate – of Nicky Wright and Bob Kidd – had just been appointed. By the time I returned after another spell in repertory theatre (including an especially good year in Richard Eyre's Nottingham company), it had changed again, and now Stuart Burge was in charge. I worked there from 1977 to 1979, doing three shows with the man who was himself to become the next Artistic Director, Max Stafford-Clark.

Actors sometimes develop a kinetic relationship with a particular director. I've experienced this several times: with Alan Dossor (the

Everyman shows), with Bill Alexander (*Richard III, Merchant of Venice*), with Terry Hands (*Singer, Tamburlaine*), with Greg, of course (*Titus Andronicus, Cyrano, Winter's Tale, Macbeth*) and with Max. He's easily among the best I've known. Which simply means that his methods make sense to *me*, to my understanding of human nature – or no, rather they increase that understanding and so take me further on as an actor. I'm not drawn to directors whose skills lie primarily in staging the play, however brilliant their eye might be. I'm not a stand-up-and-do-it actor – it takes me a long time to build up the courage – so I don't respond to stand-up-and-do-it directors. My on-stage energy, learned from Berkoff, is high, so it needs to be built on strong foundations, or else it just becomes over the top, as my worst work clearly demonstrates. Each time I do a show I'm hoping for a gradual process, a growing, learning process – learning about the kind of writing we're doing (whether Shakespeare or Stoppard, how to *speak* the language?), learning about the themes and topics in the play (if you're playing Macbeth, what is it actually like to murder someone?) and, most of all, learning how and why the characters behave as they do. I want rehearsals to be slow, thorough, even cautious. I want us all to make mistakes, to acknowledge that you can't always tell if it's art or shit you're holding up to the light. I want the director to have a method but not a restrictive one (anyone planning to hold lessons in metronomic verse speaking, no thank you) and to possess an open, enquiring mind. Yes, there'll be times when the child in me will want him to be daddy director too, but I want him to be a good daddy: not those who know all the answers, just those who know which questions to ask.

It came as no surprise to discover that Max's own father, David Stafford-Clark, was a renowned psychiatrist. Max's style as a man – quiet and patient, wise eyes, frisky smile – and his style in rehearsals – the meticulous, surprisingly enjoyable head-banging sessions – can sometimes make you feel that you or your character, or both, are in therapy. He even keeps jotting down notes: neat little books with tiny handwriting that's difficult to read upside down.

I'm very taken with one of his favourite methods, the Status Game. He begins by handing out playing cards, ace to ten (no Jacks, Queens or Kings), and then the actors circulate round the room greeting one another with just the word 'Hello' (not 'Hi', not 'How are you?' just 'Hello'), this to the power of their card. Ace is low, ten is high. Then you line up, trying to work out

where you are in the pecking order. Once the company have become practised at the skill, there are endless developments. Max's companies spend
hours playing these games – they're extremely entertaining, low status
being particularly funny for some reason – and then gradually develop it
into a vocabulary for working on the text. It's acting by numbers if you want
to be rude, though I find it an intriguing revelation of human behaviour.
Animals do it naturally – the dominant male, the dominant female, followed by a complicated queue – yet we don't think of ourselves as obeying
the same laws. We do, though. Once alert to it, you start to see many things
in relation to status. It's certainly helped me understand why I can suddenly
behave so foolishly in certain circumstances, tongue-tied and red-faced,
while in others I'm noisy and opinionated. Max uses it to unravel power
structures within relationships, whether domestic or public. An obvious
illustration is that of royalty. The actors playing them can't, needn't, play
royal status. Whenever I've met the RSC President, Prince Charles, he's
chatty and humorous, playing a middling five. But *we* – anyone talking to
him – *we* play his ten status, *we* imbue him with power.

My first role in a Max Stafford-Clark production was a man with status
ten. Ritsaart, the mad pseudo-scientist in Snoo Wilson's exhilarating take
on the Bermuda Triangle, *The Glad Hand* – the character is commanding
a ship of fools through that stretch of sea. I had a terrific time in the part
(my personal status reduced only by the fact that it was first offered to
Simon Callow). Ritsaart is South African. It was my first South African
role. How strange, how dangerous to speak in that accent again and on a
British stage. How apt it should be the Royal Court. It was the first of a
series of parts in which I'd play Dad – later van Tonder in Michael
Picardie's *Shades of Brown* at the King's Head, and later again the title role
in our South African *Titus Andronicus* – and they've all been similar, using
Dad's coarse Middlepost-Afrikaans tones as well as his distinctive heavy
presence, his menace, his humour: a dark joker.

My next Max project was the American play, *A Prayer for My Daughter*,
by Thomas Babe, a former crime reporter. It's a haunting, unexpectedly
tender account of four characters getting through the night in a New York
police station. Two cops, two criminals. I was one of the cops, the Italian
American, Dellasante. The other, the Irish cop, was played by the late,
great Donal McCann, and the criminals were played by Kevin McNally
and John Dicks. My character's status was clearly another ten, though he'd

sometimes drop it during interrogation sessions. Not just as a trick. Dellasante is a heroin addict and shoots up while questioning the men who also enjoy chasing the dragon.

Max invited a heroin addict, a raw-boned but articulate woman, to visit rehearsals, bringing along her paraphernalia – just the equipment, no actual substances – and asked her to demonstrate the rituals of preparing a hit. She talked us through the sensations of the rush, too, and each stage after it. For the show itself we created tiny false patches of skin on our arms, which the needle could seem to pierce. The syringe was false too, with a hidden supply of blood springing into view as the plunger was pulled back. All this in the close proximity of the Theatre Upstairs – people fainted nightly. There was full-frontal nudity as well and crackling sexual tension. We were a small sensation. One of my heroes came to see it: John Schlesinger. He was shooting *Yanks* at the time and gave me a brief part in one of Richard Gere's scenes. (It took me several more years of getting to know John, and doing *True West* at the National with him, before I confessed how important he'd been in my adolescence: how the elegant decadence of *Darling* beckoned me towards England; and how I learned about a certain look through that film – the *Darling* look.)

If *Prayer for My Daughter* worked well, I think it's because we delivered it with some authenticity. We were playing cops 'n' robbers, yet Max wouldn't tolerate any of the usual clichés. He's passionate about research (hence the masterclass in shooting up heroin) and this is another of his methods I cherish.

Research is a wake-up call. Drama can be a kind of dream, a kind of sleep, where we imitate art rather than life, believe in fiction's received ideas, fall for Hollywood's view of the world. Look at a street brawl: it's messy, the blows mostly miss, those that land really hurt or stun; it's nothing like what some fight directors encourage actors to do, delivering and taking blows with absurd grace – stylized, macho and pain-free – an insult to the victims of real violence. Look at real grief, too, or real drunkenness – it's not what you generally see on stage. We actors frequently copy previous interpretations of human behaviour rather than the real thing. Research takes you back to the truth. I had used it as a rehearsal technique myself at the Everyman, for Enoch Powell and Ringo Starr, but in an amateurish, hit-and-miss fashion. Max's way was more exact. 'Where can you use this in the play?' he'd ask of some fascinating but irrelevant discovery you'd made. 'Where exactly?' Research is like being a diamond prospector in old Kimberley. Most of what you sift through is dirt, to be thrown away; there's only the occasional gem – but it's worth it. And even the stuff you ditch isn't without value. We're lucky as actors: we're constantly having to investigate new topics that crop up in new shows; we're forced to be curious, to keep our minds open. I'm sure it's why actors go on working to a ripe old age. The Duncan in our current *Macbeth*, Joe O'Conor, is aged eighty-three. Olivier and Ashcroft were playing film parts into their eighties too, and Gielgud till he was ninety-six! I'm lazy when it comes to general knowledge and if I'd gone into a different profession, my scope of interest would have been very limited. I'm not saying acting makes you wise – you only ever graze the skin of any subject you're targeting – but nevertheless I've been forced to look at a whole range of topics that wouldn't necessarily attract me, like sociology (*The History Man*), Saudi Arabia (*Goose-pimples*), Rachman (*Singer*), Disraeli (*Mrs Brown*), sexual jealousy (*The Winter's Tale*) and drug addiction (*Prayer for My Daughter*).

Ah. Yes. It starts as a research project. It ends as a disease.

Unbeknown to Max, another member of the team and I actually scored some heroin during rehearsals and took it to my Belgrave Gardens flat. We told ourselves this was still research, pushing it to the limits. Except we were too squeamish for injections – so we tried snorting the stuff. Not a great idea. We ended up sprawled on the floor, green-faced and nauseous.

But by chance I'd also tried cocaine for the first time just a few months earlier. During the filming of an Adrian Mitchell script about William Blake, *Glad Day*. One of the actors offered me a line of coke in a winnebago parked on location. I remember the sensation being unsensational. The effect was too subtle for my taste, but I loved the glamorous illegality of it. There was such a thrill in this feeling I imagined the buzz from that one little line lasted all day. (In fact, the buzz from a line only lasts about twenty minutes.) I attended an interview that afternoon for a Stephen Frears TV film, *Cold Harbour*, and later when I got the part I thanked the cocaine. The actor who'd given me the line explained that coke cuts out the self-critical part of the brain. Boy, oh boy, was this made for me.

My third Max experience was on a production which would eventually play the Court, but began as a project for Joint Stock, the touring company which he ran with Bill Gaskill.

As with all Joint Stock projects, you start with a three-week workshop. No play exists yet, only a writer and a theme – in this case, Caryl Churchill and Sexual Politics. Seven actors were selected as much for their bedroom tastes as their talent. So we had one heterosexual man, one bisexual man, one heterosexual woman, one bisexual woman, one lesbian and one male homosexual couple: Jim and myself. The group was going to use itself as the primary research material in the workshop; we were our own guinea pigs. With Max and Caryl supervising, we held long sessions – upsetting, funny, sometimes gruelling – when each of us took the hot seat and related our life stories. At other times we did exercises, improvisations and, of course, the Status Game. We had various experts visit the workshop, sexologists and psychiatrists, and, on one memorable occasion, the janitor of the Tower Theatre, Islington, where we were based. A ferocious, hard-faced woman, she'd spent weeks terrorising us. Then one of our number, Julie Covington, suddenly decided to befriend the enemy and invited her to a session. She ventured into the magic circle one afternoon and told us her story. She'd had a rough life and was badly beaten by her first husband. But later she met a different, gentler man and so, eventually, in middle age, experienced her first orgasm. We were all moved when she described it – 'I was on cloud nine' – and a vital part of Caryl's play was to stem from those words.

There's a nerve-racking moment in every Joint Stock project. You've done the workshop and this has been fascinating, but now things go quiet for a while. Twelve weeks, to be precise. Then it arrives: a bound manuscript. *Cloud Nine* by Caryl Churchill. It's a fully fledged play now. With parts. Which is yours? Will you want to do it? Will you like the play?

Cloud Nine is actually a couple of plays, with different settings and periods. I was delighted by the first – a witty, biting farce set in colonial Africa – and by my role: Clive, the district officer, a tight little rule-bound man generally unaware of all the sexual shenanigans going on around him, except when dipping in a toe himself. Victorian hypocrisy and repression were further exposed by a brilliant plan for the casting: Clive's wife would be played by a man (Jim), his son by a woman (Julie Covington) and his black servant by a white (Tony Rohr).

The second half takes place in seventies London. It shows a cross-section of straight, gay and I-don't-know couples, and explores their shifting relationships. My role was Cathy, a five-year-old girl. Although the acting challenge was unique, the writing of Act Two disappointed me. It didn't appear to capture the spirit of the workshop. Our real case histories had been endlessly complex and surprising, whereas these seemed less original, familiar from other plays and films. Altogether *Cloud Nine* didn't strike me as wholly successful. Critics agreed – audiences didn't. The show was tremendously popular. Later, Max revived it at the Court with a new cast, and then Jim and I finally got to see it. A play looks very different from the outside. I was amazed. The first half was deft and clever, yes, like a superior comic strip, but it's the second half that really moves you. As *Torch Song* would also do, it opens its arms wide to an audience, to everyone sitting out there, straight, gay, young, old, and it says we're all in this together. Its humanity was irresistible. I'd been quite wrong about it. It completely caught the spirit of the workshop.

My link with the Court, with Joint Stock and with Max came to an abrupt end after *Cloud Nine*. The next part he offered me wasn't a lead. I said no. This may not have squared with Max's philosophy, but related to an important decision I'd made early on in my career. I believed that if a young actor wants to be a leading man, he has to play leading parts and leading parts only. I was perhaps overzealous on this point because I knew I wasn't natural leading-man material. I didn't have the height, the looks, the accent. I'd have to work extra hard to gain acceptance and here I felt strangely supported by Simon Callow's presence on the theatre scene. We were both untypical leading men; we were both trying to draw a new shape in the air.

15

HOWARD AND MUHAMMAD

'HERE – THIS IS FOR YOU, if you want it.'
 Rob Knights is standing on the steps of 21 Belgrave Gardens, holding a pile of TV scripts topped with a paperback book. It's a sunny Saturday morning, about 9.30. I'm in my dressing gown, just out of the bath. Rob is tall, bespectacled, with strong nose and domed forehead, his style low-key, humorous, very Oxbridge. He directed me as Malvolio at Nottingham and in a TV film, *The Out of Town Boys*.

He says little more this morning, just 'Read the scripts before the novel – the part's Howard', then hands over the stack of paper and leaves. I carry it up to our small second-floor flat. Jim asks me what it is. I shrug, bemused yet tingling. We look at the book: *The History Man* by Malcolm Bradbury. Neither of us knows it. We look at the scripts: a four-part adaptation by Christopher Hampton for the BBC. I leaf through the scripts, just glancing. The character of Howard, which Rob said was mine – if I want it – he's on every single page. This is as leading as leading parts get.

Several hours later, putting down the last of the episodes, I sit back, dazed. The writing is wonderful – complex, witty, provocative – not like TV fare at all. And the part isn't just big, it's fantastic. Howard Kirk is a sociology lecturer at one of the new red-brick universities: an arch manipulator, a ruthless force, bedding staff and students in his stride, a funny, dangerous bastard.

Incredible. No interview, no audition, no call back, no shortlist. Nothing. No warning at all. Completely out of the blue – a major fucking role in a major fucking series!

My excitement was to be short-lived.

That same day, as I began to shout the news from the rooftops, phoning the world and his wife, I spoke to a couple of our friends who also knew Christopher Hampton. They revealed, rather tactlessly, that he wasn't happy with the casting. 'He doesn't think you're sexy enough.'

All my confidence vanished in an instant. Hampton was right, of course, surely he was, the same thing had occurred to me – all those bed scenes, all that sex – you couldn't have some little Sea Point poofter playing that stuff; you needed Robert Powell or Tom Conti or whoever. Oh shit, what to do now?

Later that evening I finally managed to track down Rob Knights in a restaurant. Rob was startled when the head waiter dragged him to the phone, even more so when he heard what I'd discovered. Then he said calmly, 'Well all right, I'd rather you hadn't known about Chris's reservations, but you do, so there we are. My offer still stands. Howard's yours – if you want it.'

There was no way I could or should say no to this. Chris Hampton's opinion had touched on a deep insecurity within myself, about my looks, about my sexual prowess – I was, after all, instantly dismissed on the meat racks of the promiscuous scene – but I'd just have to bluff my way through this one. OK, a side of Howard was the bedroom and party animal, but there was lots more to him. He was Machiavellian, he was a fledgling Richard III. I could play this well – I felt – I hoped.

I actually respond rather well when people tell me I'm not up to the job. I get quite determined.

I threw myself into preparations now. My research trail started at Cardiff University, where I had a friend on the faculty – Michael Picardie, author of *Shades of Brown* – and he set me loose in the Sociology Department; sitting in on lectures and tutorials, interviewing the staff. They all speculated on the identity of Bradbury's model for Howard – a favourite contender being Laurie Taylor, then Head of Sociology at York University. I hot-footed across country. But within moments of meeting

Taylor, he nodded towards a colleague and whispered, 'Don't tell anyone, but there's the real Howard Kirk.' It took years before I finally unmasked the real mystery man. By then I'd started writing fiction myself and, as I've said before, the exercise strikes me as thoroughly autobiograpical. Novels are just coherent dreams. So although Malcolm Bradbury might have appeared to be a wise and genial chap, I'm afraid I must now hereby reveal that he was actually the ruthless sleazeball Howard. And the bumbling, accident-prone Henry Beamish. And the long-suffering Barbara Kirk. And the sexy Flora Beniform. And so on.

We did some pre-studio filming in Bristol and Warwick; the first providing exteriors of the Kirks' home, the second of the campus. Easy stuff – walking down streets, getting in and out of cars – yet nevertheless a chance to flex the character's muscles. Howard's were quite honed by then (I'd been doing overtime in a gym, aware of those bed scenes coming up) and he'd grown a Zapata moustache and long sideboards.

We moved to Birmingham, and Pebble Mill, for the next phase. Each episode was allotted two weeks in the rehearsal room, followed by two days in the studio. Rob and I shared a farmhouse in Moreton-in-Marsh during this period, developing a strong friendship as we commuted to and fro. I was terrified when we recorded episode one, but got better, and quickly. Perhaps thanks to this note from Christopher Hampton: Dear Tony – I know that by bizarre coincidence you happened to discover that I had some reservations about your casting – so I thought I'd write to say that on the evidence of the rushes and the two days in the studio, these reservations have entirely disappeared.

And anyway there are times when an actor's insecurity meets the character's own. In the novel, Bradbury sketches in Howard's background: he's a surprisingly timid soul at first. Purely for reasons of time, Hampton had to omit the History Man's history. But maybe, and quite without intending it, an element of tension in my performance touches it in again: this Howard is a tightly wound spring, an overachiever, clearly compensating for something else.

The show's team was formidable. Our producer was Michael Wearing (later to do *Boys from the Blackstuff* and *Our Friends in the North*) and the cast included Michael Hordern as Howard's prof., and Geraldine James as his wife. His mistress – well, the main one, Flora – was played by Isla Blair. Most of the bed scenes were with her and fortunately we found something in common to help us survive them. We're both bad gigglers. Far from being diffi-cult to do because of the nudity or simulated sex, it just became a question of getting to the end without laughing. Isla held a special threat over me. She'd once laughed so hard during a formal dance at the end of Prospect Theatre's *Twelfth Night* that when they left the stage a figure of eight was neatly outlined on the floor in little glistening droplets. Her character sat astride me for our sex sessions. It was a good incentive to keep a straight face.

Raphael Jago, Webber-D.'s principal, had predicted I wouldn't come into my own till I was in my thirties. And sure enough, I had turned thirty just a few weeks before Rob Knights arrived on my doorstep with that stack of scripts – the best of birthday presents. Yet an even better one was delivered to Belgrave Gardens a few months later: a British passport. I was naturalised on 4 October 1979. I don't think this is quite what Mr Jago meant by coming into my own, yet it seemed like that to me. My former citizenship had felt like an ill-fitting skin and now I was comfortable at last, now I was 'in my own'. I was British. I belonged to a decent democracy, and to one of the most civilised, most tolerant societies on earth. I celebrated by burning my South African passport. Fairly tricky to do, by the way: the passports of the old regime were military green in colour, not that easy to torch.

At the time I honestly believed you could bury your own identity. Absolute bollocks, of course, but that's what I was trying to do. I had little contact with South Africa. The folks visited every year and that was it, really. I never wrote to my siblings and hardly ever phoned. As for friends, my two great soulmates from childhood had travelled overseas as well, but the reunions were disappointingly brief. When I met up again with Tony Fagin in London we were both surprised to find we had little in common any more and drifted apart (reuniting again recently). Cecil Bloch – he of the Stroud Make-up Studio – came over to study astrophysics at Cambridge. We did form a strong new friendship and have maintained it to this day – though mostly via electronic link, for Cecil changed course and countries again, and became a computer software engineer in Silicon Valley, California.

As the eighties dawned I felt that my former ties were cut and I was starting a new life. As an Englishman.

*

The History Man made quite an impact when it was shown in the autumn of 1980: great reviews, a BAFTA nomination (unfortunately up against *Brideshead Revisited*) and questions in Parliament about the sex scenes. Maybe I should've exploited my new-found TV celebrity – it hasn't come my way again – but by the time the series was aired, I'd gone back to the theatre. I always go back to the theatre. In fact, it's rather like South Africa. I try and turn my back on it, but I return again and again. It's home. I love it and hate it. I can't be sentimental about it – it's a real relationship.

The new project was a Mike Leigh play.

He'd seen me at the Everyman – his then wife, Alison Steadman, was in McGrath's *Fish in the Sea* – and had often talked about us working together. Now the call came. He was setting up a play for Hampstead Theatre, intended as a follow-up to *Abigail's Party*, which had been phenomenally successful for all concerned. No, he couldn't tell me what the new one would be about. He didn't know himself, he said; it's how he works – everyone starts with a blank sheet. I wasn't sure I believed him. This continued to be a slight problem: a teensy little suspicion that he always knew more than he claimed.

Embarking on a Mike Leigh project is a unique experience. You meet up on the first day – five actors in this case (Jim Broadbent, Paul Jesson, Marion Bailey, Jill Baker and self) – you go through the normal introductions and then you part, knowing that you won't be seeing one another again for a long time. Our rehearsal period was three months.

Now each of you begins long one-to-one sessions with Mike. He's a small, bearded figure burrowed in a large armchair, with legs wound in a spiral beneath him. Like with Max, a sense of the shrink – except this one has a dark twinkle in big, bloodhound eyes and a rare, unpitying sense of humour. Like Max, a notebook on the lap – except this one fills with untidy jottings and doodles, a kind of graffiti (even harder to read upside down). He asks you to tell him about people you know – people round about your own age but not in the business. Oops. I'd hit my first obstacle straight away. I might be the proud holder of a British passport, but I didn't yet have much experience of British life – not outside the business – so my list was pitifully short. But Mike proved to be flexible. We could concoct a personality, he said, maybe using a bit of so-and-so, some of whatchamacallit, and adding that interesting mannerism from you-know-who.

My primary source characters became Paul Szabo from Walvis Bay – the reclusive Woody Allen lookalike who'd taken me to the Etosha Game Reserve – and another South African, a rich one, in London. Sensing that paradise was closing down, this man had managed to extricate his wealth and was now resident here, whiling away his days, with nothing to do and money to burn.

When you start showing Mike these people – not just describing them, but getting to your feet and improvising – he's insistent that you don't become too demonstrative. There's no need to entertain him – the curse of most improvisation – he's happy to sit quietly in a corner while you slowly inhabit the person. Just *be* him, Mike urges. A man alone in a room does very little. Reads a newspaper, stares into the middle distance, thinks, dozes. Mike allows this nothingness, this absence of action, to go on for a long time, before saying his catchphrase, 'Come out of character.' Then there's a discussion about what he observed and you felt.

His whole method is based on careful layering. He hates seeing actors improvise gobbledegook, busking their way through conversations without knowing the first thing about their characters. Before he'll allow your character to have a conversation – i.e. interact with the other performers – you have to know everything about him, *everything*: who his mother and father are, where he went to school, the nature of his job, all his likes and dislikes, and, yes, what he had for breakfast.

I can't remember why or how my two South Africans turned into an Arab, but gradually, subtly, without any marked turning point, the pair of real-life people merged into a new, single fictional character. He had some of the quirky hermit-like tendencies of Paul Szabo and some of the wealthy, unmotivated laziness of the other – but he was now Saudi Arabian. Nudged that way by Mike, obviously. By this stage he was starting to cook up the notions of a plot, based on private work happening simultaneously with each of the other actors.

Now began my research – or, as I came to call it, my time in exile. An Arab. A Saudi Arabian Arab. Where did he go to school? What are his likes and dislikes? What *does* he have for breakfast?

I couldn't begin to answer any of these. I couldn't reliably tell you a single thing about his diet, hygiene or beliefs. Everything about him was *other*. I'd have to start from scratch. Learn the lot. And the timing couldn't have been worse . . .

The ITV drama-documentary, *Death of a Princess* – showing events leading up to a public beheading in Jeddah – had recently been shown on British TV and deeply offended the Saudis. In fact, it had turned into an international diplomatic incident. The Saudi community in London were particularly incensed and in no mood to help me. Every place I went – whether embassies, bookshops or private addresses – echoed to the sound of doors slamming in my face. You're doing what? – *Slam*. You're an actor? – *Slam*. You want to do a play about us? – *Slam*. Hampstead Theatre considered flying me out to the Middle East, but couldn't find the money in their budget. (I was rather relieved – in Jeddah the slamming sound might've been my head hitting the dust, all on its own.) Instead they sent me to the Isle of Wight. A group of Saudi students were attending a technological course there. I had a strange meeting with them – both sides equally baffled – and learned very little. As I was leaving I went to the toilet in their quarters. No loo paper – just a jug of water in the corner. How did this work? Fingers employed, presumably, but then how do you clean *them*? Dear God, my ignorance about my character didn't just start when he sat down for breakfast . . .

In the meantime, my fellow actors were surely putting the finishing touches to their characters rather than just beginning. No doubt Mike was already bringing them together, in character, and they were starting to improvise the scenes that would comprise the play. I was woefully behind. I'd be left out. There were stories of this happening to other actors in Mike Leigh projects: months and months of work, culminating with a minor role in the final piece. Was this to be my fate?

I saw Mike less and less. Until I had more material, there wasn't a lot to talk about. We'd provisionally called my character Muhammad and decided he was from a family of wholesalers in Jeddah. (The Jewish background which Mike and I share allowed us some insight into this milieu.) Over to me . . .

Then – a potential breakthrough. Someone in Hampstead knew someone who knew someone who'd been to Cambridge with someone from the Saudi royal family. I was to stand by my phone. This man, Prince Someone-or-other, would instruct his people to ring when he was ready to see me. Days passed, a week . . .

Finally – the summons. I went to a mews house off the Edgware Road: smallish, shadowy rooms, curtained at midday, cooled by air-conditioning, sparsely but expensively furnished, white-robed servants and suited aides in

attendance. The prince was a buxom, moustachioed chap in his late twenties, speaking fluent English, a nephew of King Fahd. This isn't quite as grand
as it sounds – the Saudis are polygamous and the big families have scores of
nephews and nieces – but he enjoyed his status (ten and rising); his manner
was charming, yet extremely arrogant. This proved a help. He couldn't quite
follow what I was after – *I* could barely follow what I was after – yet he
detected no serious threat. I wasn't like those *Death of a Princess* people, I
didn't have that kind of TV clout. I was from the theatre, a small theatre,
somewhere in Hampstead. We were 'making up' a play and I wanted to get
my facts straight. Fair enough. He was happy to tell me about life in Saudi
Arabia. His own experience was perhaps a trifle limited – confined to the
luxury palaces of the Saud dynasty – but some things were traditional and
applied equally to the common man. He talked for hours and, as I was leaving, presented me with a handsome stack of gilt-bound coffee-table books
and plastic-wrapped videos, all showing the world of his uncle's kingdom.

Arms full, I rushed back to Mike. At last! I knew what my character had
for breakfast (fruits, cold meats and coffee, coffee, coffee) and although
still a little vague about his toilet habits (I didn't like to ask the prince at
our first meeting), I also possessed street maps of Jeddah, the names of its
schools and colleges, timetables of buses and trains, history books on the
Sauds, others on Mecca, on the *Hajj*, on the faith of Islam. What more did
a nice Jewish boy have to do? Now could we please start? Now could I meet
the other actors and start improvising the bloody play?

From the depths of his armchair Mike stared back in amazement. No,
that's not the right word. When he chooses, those big bloodhound eyes
can suggest unfathomable weariness. 'Start "improvising"?' he echoed, his
slight Salford accent giving that word an extra special proprietorial ring
today. 'But how does Muhammad speak?'

'How does he speak?'

'Yes – does he speak English?'

I faltered. The character we'd been discussing was reclusive, seldom
venturing beyond the perimeters of his family's Jeddah mansion. 'Well, no,
probably not,' I finally answered, with a sinking feeling.

'No,' agreed Mike ruefully. 'No, he'd most likely speak – what?'

'Saudi,' I prompted grimly.

'Saudi,' said Mike, that dark twinkle appearing in the bloodhound eyes.
'And is Saudi different from other Arab languages?'

'Yup,' I answered knowledgeably – as though this mattered – as though I was fluent in any! 'Yup, there's Egyptian Arabic, Jordanian Arabic, et cetera.'

'I see,' Mike murmured into his beard, adding something to the graffiti-like squiggles in his notebook. 'So when Muhammad gets to the point when he meets and, as you say, "improvises" with the other characters, he's going to have to speak to them . . . in some way . . . isn't he?'

'Yup, he is,' I said, now through gritted teeth. 'Back to square one, do not pass Go.'

'Hm?' said Mike innocently.

The next day I went to HMV on Oxford Street, and, using Hampstead Theatre's expense account, bought a Linguaphone set of Modern Standard Arabic. They didn't have a specifically Saudi one and I decided instantly, almost gleefully, to compromise on the meticulous authenticity normally demanded by Mike. My purchase was a fat pack with four tapes and six books. Back at our St John's Wood flat, I started to play the first. It was geared to Western businessmen. Phrases like 'I'm on a flying visit', 'Yes it is very hot' and 'I'm not feeling well'. The language was strange, guttural, difficult. I had no *in* to it. I'd hoped that my tiny knowledge of Hebrew might help, but it didn't sound at all similar. And my only other language, Afrikaans – a smattering of – was even less help.

What on earth was I going to do? I couldn't possibly learn Arabic in the next few weeks, just in order to *start* improvising with the others. We were about a month into the rehearsal period by now and I truly hadn't begun. It was December, Christmas coming up. Things would go even quieter. Just me sitting in this flat – with the Linguaphone.

I got into my car and set out for Hampstead Theatre. I'd talk to David Aukin (currently the artistic director), see what he thought. But we were clearly reaching the point where I might have to resign.

Just before the Swiss Cottage roundabout I saw an odd sight. A long-haired, bearded guy in his late thirties – a guy who'd be called an old hippy – riding a bike, weeping uncontrollably. He almost crashed. He had to stop and climb off the bike. Sitting on the grass verge, he put his head in his hands and carried on sobbing.

This wasn't the aftermath of a domestic row or trouble at work. This was something else. You could feel it in the air. I switched on the radio. The announcer was reading a news report. John Lennon had been murdered in New York.

I slowed the car and pulled to the side myself. We'd spent so long immersing ourselves in the Beatles for the Willy Russell play that we felt we were a tiny part of them. But then the long-haired man crying on the ground probably felt the same thing. And now one of them – arguably the genius, certainly the one we all hero-worshipped – was dead. Murdered. By a fan, they said. What a strange and ugly thing. I turned the car round and drove back home. I had no appetite to talk to David Aukin at the moment. I'd do it tomorrow, or the day after. For now, I was quite content to immerse myself in a long, time-consuming task. I turned on the Linguaphone and started to learn Arabic.

It's three weeks later. We've got another five before our opening night, but I still haven't had a single session with the other actors, or started to work on anything you could call a play.

But tonight I will. Finally. Tonight's the big night.

Mike and I have spent long hours creating Muhammad. The material supplied by the prince, as well as further audiences with him and introductions he's enabled with other Saudis, has allowed us to build up a detailed background for our character, complete with his genealogy, his education and his rather passive role in the family business. Actually, he has a rather passive role in life generally. Bits of costume and set have been provided in one room of the Kilburn house where we're rehearsing – the other rooms probably have bits of costume and set for each of the characters – and so I've been able to practise *being* Muhammad at home in Jeddah; mostly sat outside the front door, against a shaded stretch of wall, watching the world go by, or dozing. He's happiest when asleep, a bit nervy otherwise; the dope, the dunce, the black sheep of the family, constantly bullied by his older brothers. (Mike and I can't simulate these characters; we can only describe them to one another.) The brothers need to visit London on business and are bringing Muhammad along.

As we reach this part of Muhammad's story, my own progress in the Mike Leigh adventure intensifies and becomes more practical. My brown hair is dyed pitch black, my beard and moustache trimmed into the distinctive goatee shape favoured by Saudi men, and special spectacles made, with my prescription but Muhammad's style: a bit flashy, heavily tinted. Like a prisoner in solitary confinement, I suddenly start to catch the scent of fresh air – and other people! – nearby.

I never got very far with learning Muhammad's language, but just by trying I've absorbed some of its sounds and mannerisms, like the way that the word for 'no' ('*la*') turns into a brisk, impatient sound ('*lup!*',), usually with an upward jerk of the hand; also the strange glottal stop in words like 'with' ('*ma-a*'). I can do Muhammad's accent now, if not speak his tongue. Mike and I have decided that he does have some English; only a few basic words ('OK', 'please', 'go', etc.), but by endlessly rearranging their order, he attempts to communicate here in London.

He's arrived now having been sick on the plane – travel sickness is one of his running conditions – and although he's mostly holed up in a high-rise Knightsbridge hotel, peering down at the alien, decadent, Western city below, he's also started making little exploratory trips, at first with the bullying brothers, but more recently on his own, drawn by some of London's forbidden pleasures, especially gambling.

Tonight is one of these solo trips. And Mike wants me to do it for real. The brief is like something out of James Bond:

1 I'm to get dressed as Muhammad at the Kilburn rehearsal rooms. A light, shiny, bluish suit and tie, and black slip-on shoes have been provided by the designer, Caroline Beaver. And in the trouser pocket a big wad of banknotes – real ones provided by Hampstead Theatre.
2 I'm to proceed to the West End, to the Golden Nugget casino on Shaftesbury Avenue.
3 Once inside, I'm to give myself the familiar Mike Leigh directive, 'Get into character.' From then on I'm Muhammad for the evening. I can only communicate with his tiny amount of English or the few Arabic phrases I know. The rest is down to gesture and hand waving.
4 In the Golden Nugget I'm to look out for the actress Marion Bailey. She'll be in character too; a girl called Jackie. In fact, Jackie works at the club as a croupier, Mike has explained, but since Marion can't in real life we'll just have to take that as read. We must also imagine that Muhammad has played the tables this evening and caught Jackie's eye. Now she's clocking off work and they bump into one another . . .

Mike often goes along on these expeditions into the real world. One story tells of a friend discovering him outside a Finchley Road supermarket, his nose pressed intently to the glass. Looking over Mike's shoulder, the friend saw Alison Steadman shopping inside. 'Mike, what's going on?' the friend asked.

'Shush!' came the reply. 'We're rehearsing.'

But he's not coming along tonight to the Golden Nugget casino. For reasons which will become clear later.

I'm inside the club now and inside Muhammad's character . . .

(I should describe the rest of the evening in the third person, the form which Mike favours.)

. . . Muhammad meets up with Jackie, an odd, twitchy girl. She suggests they go somewhere together. He only half comprehends, but nods consent. There's something about her – cheaply dressed, lots of make-up – he's starting to get ideas. They hail a taxi. She gives an address in Kilburn. In the back of the cab she asks, with accompanying mime, if he's got any cash with him? He draws out his wad of banknotes. She's impressed; she's starting to get ideas too. During the journey, he feels ill (travel sickness being a running condition) and tries to communicate this to her. She can't understand. No such problem for the taxi driver. He's been watching this odd couple in his mirror and, having had far too many people throw up in his cab before now, stops immediately. Muhammad staggers to a nearby hedge and stands there, slumped, breathing deeply . . .

(The next day, in Mike's debriefing session, Marion Bailey will reveal that while I was at the hedge, the taxi driver said to her, 'Pworr, you've picked a right one 'ere, luv – why don't I take 'im back down West, dump 'im and you find yerself another punter for the evening?' Although also jumping to the wrong conclusion about Jackie, he was clearly convinced by both our performances. As Mike said, it was our first good review.)

. . . Jackie and Muhammad reach their destination. A house in Kilburn (the rehearsal rooms). Jackie shares a flat here with the bombastic, leering Vernon (J. Broadbent). He has some friends round for the evening, a married couple, Irving and Frankie (P. Jesson and J. Baker). They're just finishing a meal (cooked from scratch by the actors), during which booze has been flowing (real booze). Muhammad is confused. Like Jackie, Frankie is covered in garish jewellery and showing lots of bare flesh – well, it's lots to someone used to seeing women heavily robed and veiled. He thinks he's in some kind of brothel, the men being other clients or pimps maybe. Meanwhile, they're equally bemused by him. He keeps producing a wad of notes and trying to lead the women off into other rooms. Yet he's harmless, easily cowed. He's sport for the evening, and the men's humour becomes increasingly rough and xenophobic. They start spiking his drinks. He's not used to drinking at all; alcohol is forbidden back home . . .

My narrative blurs round about here. First person, third person, who knows, who cares? It's Muhammad's drinks being spiked, but Tony's tummy taking the damage. I remember carrying on longer than I should've. I'm so well trained that I can't stop till I hear the magic command 'Come out of character' from that small bearded figure who's been huddling in various corners and spyholes all evening, rapidly scribbling notes. Then I remember tumbling into the loo, vaguely noticing that a jug with water has been set in one corner, and vomiting violently. My memory gets even fuzzier after that . . . stage management driving me home to Belgrave Gardens . . . carrying me upstairs . . . Jim's horrified face . . . him grabbing the phone: 'Mike, what the fuck's going on?'

At the debriefing session the next morning I'm not the only one nursing a bad hangover. But Mike isn't at all contrite. Quite the opposite. I've never seen the bloodhound eyes twinkle so merrily. Unable to stop chuckling and beaming, he says: 'I think we've got a play.'

Goose-pimples opened at Hampstead in March 1981, played to packed houses for six weeks, then transferred to the West End, the Garrick, and did a further six months. Amazingly, in spite of all the unknown factors and obstacles, Mike had delivered exactly what he promised: a savage comedy in *Abigail's Party* mode, relished by both audiences and critics. Later that year it won the *Evening Standard* Best Comedy award.

Throughout the long improvisation in Jackie/Vernon's flat (if you add the Golden Nugget and the taxi, I was in character for about five hours), Mike was taking copious notes and stage management were operating a tape recorder. Over the next few days the play was 'written' very fast – the best bits transcribed and shaped into scenes; sometimes us doing this as a group, sometimes Mike on his own. Once a scene is constructed it becomes as tightly scripted as if conceived by a playwright. All the broken and looping phrases of real-life speech, every um and ah, is then learned by the actors like any other dialogue and there's no further improvisation in performance. Mike couldn't allow this; it'd be too unpredictable. Although his plays and films shimmer with all the ticks and twitches of human behaviour and the meandering patterns of our lives, they're minutely orchestrated.

I found the run at the Garrick the hardest I've ever done. With a conventional play scripted by an author (I've since done West End runs of Stoppard's *Travesties* and the Burgess *Cyrano*) there's ongoing exploration of the text, but with a play that you've helped to devise yourself, where you know every single thought and motivation in your character's head, there's nothing more to be found. The repetition night after night then starts to feel like a form of Chinese torture.

To be completely honest, I'm a theatre actor who doesn't altogether like theatre acting. Increasingly, now, in the twenty-first century, you're aware that there's video tape to be played, rewound and played again, which is how you feel on matinée days. On the other hand the matinée itself, with its cast of bored actors, will often be a very good show. Theatre acting requires a strange balance between concentration and relaxation. I often act best when tired, ill, hung-over, or preoccupied with a book I'm writing during the day. Suddenly, without planning or trying for it, I achieve that ideal state, that concentration–relaxation balance. It's why first nights are often inferior performances: the actors are concentrating too hard. We try and give definitive interpretations of our roles, when no such thing exists.

Mike has sometimes talked about me doing one of his films. I'd like that. I'd like to create a character in all that detail, experience the exhilaration of first interacting with the other characters, then putting it on celluloid and walking away. That would suit me just fine.

I'm very proud of Muhammad all the same. He won some mentions among the performances of the year, further fulfilling Jago's prophecy about the riches of my thirties. Muhammad's creation involves co-authorship with Mike, of course, but from my side there was a lot of autobiographical stuff: the foreigner, the outsider, struggling to fit in, to communicate, to comprehend. And it was terrific playing a part without speech in a way. His few words – whether 'OK' or '*lup!*' – just became a kind of noise, a kind of grunting, an animal's call, increasingly of distress, yet producing laughter, both from the other characters and the audience.

I borrowed this chap for *Middlepost*. Smous. A Jew now, instead of an Arab, but otherwise pretty similar. The family dunce. A little man who spends his life half asleep back home in Lithuania and then suddenly finds himself in the hostile, alien world of South Africa.

Smous blinked – he was on the other side of the world.

That's the opening sentence of the book. Smous has arrived in Table Bay harbour. He can't speak the language, he can only shrug and nod, and wave his arms in the air. People laugh at him – he's like a silent-film clown – while he feels he's landed on the moon. He is deeply, profoundly lost.

Muhammad and Smous – I know these men well. I love them.

16

STRATFORD-UPON-AVON

MIKE LEIGH was also responsible for introducing me to the RSC. Back in 1974 he was planning one of his projects for the Other Place – it would become *Babies Grow Old* – and, having seen my work at the Everyman, wanted me in it. This meant auditioning for Trevor Nunn. He was about to do *Macbeth* with Nicol Williamson and Helen Mirren, and if I was to join the company I'd have to be in that too.

I remember driving down from Liverpool. An actress friend from the Beatles show, Linda Beckett, came along for moral support. I felt very frightened. I'd spent two years playing leading roles at the Everyman, but that was like junior school. This was the Royal Shakespeare Company.

I remember the last stretch of road into Stratford: the open fields changing into an avenue of woodland, then the first sight of the town, a little country town, a sort of British Montagu, and there, across the river, that big, ugly building, looking like a giant tanker stranded on the shore, flying a tiny yellow flag with letters in black: RSC.

I still experience a shiver of excitement entering Stratford by this road, the Coventry Road, even now thirty years later.

Trevor Nunn auditioned me in the Conference Hall (then the main rehearsal room, now the Swan Theatre). With him was the RSC casting director, Jenny McIntosh (today they run the National Theatre together). I've never been good at auditioning and that day was no exception. I did the Fool from *Lear*, trying to reproduce my Everyman performance, the little shuffling figure with the underbite, but taken out of context – which is the trouble with auditions! – it was a mess. Then I did Buckingham from *Richard III*, again using my performance from the Everyman circus cage production: a cartoon-like smoothie, a Terry-Thomas cad. Trevor was puzzled. He asked me to try it again, but with a Scottish accent. Ah-ha. Alan Dossor had warned me that Trevor might be planning a Scottish *Macbeth* and gave me what was meant to be a helpful tip: 'Trevor's crazy about football – if you get the chance, do your Bill Shankly for him – he'll love it'. My Bill Shankly was from a roadshow we'd been touring round the pubs of Merseyside, in which I did a turn as the legendary Liverpool FC manager. I only had to start with Shankly's characteristic vocal tick – 'Eeeeh' – to get a roar of recognition from the regulars in those pubs and from then on I could do no wrong. Hoping for the same response from Trevor and Jenny, I tried it now. 'Eeeeh.' Nothing. Never mind – keep going: 'Now by the holy mother of our Lord . . . eeeeh . . . the citizens are mum, say not a word . . . eeeeh'. Trevor and Jenny stared back blankly. I struggled on through the speech, determinedly playing my Shankly–Buckingham, but I don't think Alan was right, I don't think Trevor loved it, or even knew what I was doing. 'Thanks,' he called out cheerfully at the end. 'As they say, we'll let you know.'

Mike later reported that Trevor could only offer me spear carrying. (I imagined him and Jenny discussing my audition: 'I suppose we could put him at the back of a crowd and let him go "Eeeeh" to his heart's content.') There was still Mike's project, but that was an unknown quantity. When, a few days later, Codron and Stigwood joined forces to transfer the Beatles show, I decided to stay with that.

A call didn't come from the RSC again until 1982. By then I was more established. Terry Hands, now running the company, had particularly enjoyed Howard Kirk scheming and screwing his way through *The History Man*. 'It was very unEnglish what you did in that,' he said. 'In fact, I wasn't even sure if you were *white*.'

The offer – ironically – was to play the Fool again, in a main-house *Lear*, and a lead at the Other Place: the title role in Bulgakov's *Molière*, a quirky tragi-comedy about the Artist and the State, based not so much on Molière's relationship with Louis XIV as Bulgakov's with Stalin.

We started rehearsing *Lear* in April. Spring was coming to Stratford, buds and blossom everywhere, country smells – livestock going by in a truck – river smells too, the water muddy, a milky brown brew. All peculiarly familiar to me. This place really was like Montagu, but Montagu with Shakespeare.

Lear was being directed by the RSC's new discovery, Adrian Noble. He'd had a string of successes in smaller theatres and now he was being given a go at the big one: the big Stratford stage and the biggest of Shakespeare's plays. Lear was Michael Gambon, recently acclaimed as Galileo at the National, and a powerful cast included Sara Kestelman as Goneril, David Waller as Gloucester, Malcolm Storry as Kent and Pete Postlethwaite as Cornwall.

And there I was – playing the Fool again – and *battling* again. I showed Adrian the little shuffling figure with the underbite. He wasn't convinced. 'The Fool's speeches may seem obscure,' he said, 'but *he* knows what he means. He's the one speaking the truth – he speaks Truth to Power – and I simply can't hear you clearly when you speak like that.'

So back to the drawing board. I tried this, I tried that, I visited the London Zoo one Sunday to study the chimps – later discovering that Gambon was there the same day, gazing at the gorillas – but nothing yielded results. Rehearsals were invigorating nevertheless. Adrian is an inspiring director, brimming with fresh, off-the-wall ideas. We practised the storm scenes on Dover's Hill outside Chipping Campden, Gambon roaring at jets passing from the nearby airbase. I tried to play the Fool in neutral for these sessions, but he kept turning into that little cheeky-chappie jester who appears in traditional productions of Shakespeare comedies, and who makes me throw up. Then one day Adrian said, 'Let's try a series of experiments. Tomorrow play him with a red nose, the next day with a white face, the day after . . .'

We never got past the red nose.

Masks are very liberating – with your face hidden or partly hidden you suddenly have new access to your courage and emotions – and a red nose is simply a miniature mask. Things started to fall into place. My research into court jesters had revealed that they were often cripples or freaks, their disability regarded as funny. I scrunched up the Fool and gave him inward-twisting legs. A wretched figure, but plonk on some clown accoutrements – a battered bowler and elongated shoes as well as the red nose – and the mix becomes interesting. Adrian suggested adding a tiny violin. Ilona Sekacz, our composer, tried to teach me to play. I never learned more than a few basic sawings and pluckings, but it didn't matter. Or that I couldn't sing. For once this was a positive advantage. My tuneless chantings became part of this particular Fool's style, part of his anarchy.

As I'd already learned at the Everyman, the role of the Fool only works in relation to Lear. The Fool is the King's sidekick, his whipping boy, his pet, his shadow. Gambon, himself a superb clown, took to my new character with relish. We began doing our interchanges as little music-hall routines, the tackier the better: me on his knee as a ventriloquist's dummy, or the two of us doing double-act patter, marking the punch lines with a *ta-dah!* gesture to the audience. (Later, Adrian would actually light these like front-cloth scenes with footlights and giant shadows.) Then, with the onset of madness and the arrival of a darker soulmate – Poor Tom – Lear lost interest in his Fool. During the hovel scene he began stabbing a pillow that the Fool was holding – 'Let them anatomise Regan!' – a cloud of feathers arose and Lear never even noticed he'd delivered a mortal blow. This was our solution to a mysterious (or lazy) piece of writing in the play: after that scene the Fool vanishes completely.

Gambon was magnificent at the final run-through. His ability to switch from clowning with his Fool to the terrible rages with his daughters, and then the disintegration into confusion and vulnerability ... this was astonishing. I was able to watch the second half purely as audience, along with Pete Postlethwaite, whose character was also dispatched before the interval. Pete was quite a wild boy then, a hard man, but his boulder-like face was wet with tears when the run-through ended. Mine was too. We had just watched a great Lear. I've never seen it bettered. What is it about Gambon? His scale is gigantic. To stand next to, he's not much taller than me, yet there's something about him, a broadness – something about his features, his bone structure and his soul – which makes his on-stage presence quite colossal. 'It's actually not fair,' Pete said later that evening in the Dirty Duck, as we continued to marvel, 'it's like acting next to a fucking cinema screen!'

This still isn't enough. To explain it. Acting as good as I saw that day. It was my first real exposure to it, in a rehearsal room rather than theatre stalls: a heavyweight actor in a heavyweight role. Great acting. I think it's about contradictions and conflict. Those opposites in our nature, living side by side yet often at war: the adult and the child, the animal and the intellect, the male and the female. The last is most compelling, of course.

The sex thing. Actresses with balls, actors with receptiveness. Brando, Olivier, Scofield . . . they all have a very complicated sexual presence. Take it away and you get John Wayne. And then my head falls forward, like Dad's, as the performance begins. But the good ones . . . Bette Davis, Judi Dench, Fiona Shaw . . . there's nothing simple in their work, but different energies tugging, worrying, enriching one another. The very things that we seek to quell in real life – our appetites, our childishness, our fear – these things make for the best acting, I think. And Gambon illustrated it perfectly as Lear that day. A roaring old lion, yet infantile and frightened; a brutal, blokish man, yet prone to tears, delicacy, compassion; an earth creature, yet touched with grace.

Lear is the Everest of parts. Trying to scale it again and again becomes punishing and ultimately disheartening for the actor. All Lears report this. In performance, Gambon took to larking around, muttering asides to the actors in between his lines. We thoroughly enjoyed this – "Ullo, you little red-nosed cunt,' he'd whisper as I arrived – but I wonder if audiences always saw what we had in the rehearsal room. It's quintessentially Gambon, though. Anarchy. Alongside his very serious talent. Another contradiction.

Meanwhile I became absorbed in rehearsals for the next show, *Molière*, and in the phenomenal social life of that 1982 Stratford company. We'd settle into the Dirty Duck after closing – every evening, it seemed – and drink into the early hours. Alun Armstrong was on guitar, leading rousing choruses. Gambon told jokes. Helen Mirren and Sinead Cusack downed pints like navvies. Derek Jacobi sipped at wine and waved at us from the restaurant, where he was always hunched over a script. (Committed to a marathon season – Prospero, Benedick, Peer Gynt, Cyrano – Derek was the only one who never had any playtime.)

Supervising us was Pam Harris, the Duck's legendary Mistress Quickly figure; a huge, unpredictable character, now ferocious, now fun, with something of Frankie Howerd's huffy vocal style, her tones marinaded in brandy and smoked in Piccadilly untipped. It was often dawn when she started throwing us out – and she could do this literally. Drunk actors fell into the river, others made love on the grassy banks.

It was all going on that summer, sex, drugs, rock 'n' roll, you name it. Slap bang in the middle of this small country town, yet curiously isolated from it. The impression was of being on a university campus, or on holiday:

you were away from home, you were free of responsibility, you could experiment with whatever you wanted. Everyone was having affairs. I was keen to do likewise, and after all, I had permission from Jim . . .

His twin brother, Bob Hooper, wrote a play for the RSC Fringe Festival, *Astonish Me*, a portrait of Cocteau that is as elegant and exact as one of the man's drawings. Playing Cocteau, I felt a strong sense of identification. A man of several abilities – artist, poet, playwright, film maker – unable to choose which to perfect, occasionally more prone to showing off than digging deep, always searching for new ways to *astonish*. (The command, '*Etonne-moi!*' had come from Diaghilev, a figure even more formidable than any Jewish mother.) Cocteau's great love was the brilliant young poet Radiguet, and our director – Pete Postlethwaite again – cast a brilliant young actor called Mark Rylance. Life and art began to blur further. Even as I was learning about the Cocteau Syndrome – successive men all appear to be reincarnations of his schoolboy love, Dargelos – so I was experiencing it myself, for Mark was *him* again: the beautiful boy-man with dark, soft eyes. But no amount of wooing had any effect, nor attempted seduction by chemical substance, nor pining and simpering when all else failed. I became very miserable, and the weather soon followed suit.

British winters fascinated me when I first arrived in this country, but by now had turned into an endurance test: those long months of short days. I was living in Avonside, a crumbling old mansion just beyond Trinity Church ('Hell, we're in a bloody ghost house!' Dad remarked during their summer visit) and this did little to help my growing gloom. I'd been indulging in a bit of coke during the season and accelerated the dosage now. I think I was still identifying with Cocteau; he had his poppy seed and pipe, I my powder and blade. I developed a taste for taking it on my own. Who needs any beautiful boy-men, who needs anyone else at all? Coke is self-love at the end of a McDonald's straw. It's perhaps no accident that a small mirror is also part of the equipment: the ideal surface for chopping your line. As you snort it, you see yourself. You bow to yourself. You and yourself exchange a weird nasal kiss. *Me, me, me.* I used to spend six or seven hours on these private Geminian orgies. The depressions afterwards were gruesome.

Then it happened.

Do our bodies come to our defence at times like these? Mine had before, conjuring up flu for my bar mitzvah. Did it now?

It was November. I was on stage alone, doing the Fool's soliloquy in the storm. Swung into the little dance. Heard a noise – BANG – felt something hit the back of my leg. Thought I'd stepped through one of the floorboards. Fell. Looked round. No hole in the stage. No floorboard sticking up. What made the noise then, what hit my leg?

'Your Achilles' tendon ruptured completely,' explained the surgeon who operated a few days later. 'Shot up the back of your leg like a venetian blind.'

I was back in London, my first Stratford season abruptly curtailed. Six months off work, the surgeon predicted.

Achilles' tendon injuries are a mystery. They happen as frequently to little old ladies stepping off the kerb as to sportsmen in top condition. Also to a surprising number of actors: Judi Dench, Brian Cox, Nick Grace, Sara Kestelman, Graham Turner – all part of the Achilles mythology. There were possible reasons why mine went: lolloping round the stage with feet bent inwards was the likeliest one; the Cocteau Syndrome was my secret explanation to myself.

It turned out that when the surgeon said I'd be off work for six months, he only meant *Lear* – resuming the Fool's twisted position – and not *Molière*. It was crucial to get back into the Bulgakov play because, being an Other Place show, there were no understudies. (Ian Talbot, who now runs Regent's Park Theatre, had taken over as the Fool.) Pete Postlethwaite volunteered to step in as Molière when I left, and had learned and rehearsed it, but just before opening his car hit black ice one night and he ended upside down in a ditch, injured as well. So then *Molière* had to come out of the repertoire altogether. Now, two months after my accident, it was due to go to Newcastle, part of the annual RSC season up there and, although only able to do the part on a stick, I travelled northwards. Rejoining the company, I found that nothing changed. It was all going on as before – only in the bar of the Turk's Head Hotel rather than the Duck – the affairs, the drinking, the drugging. After my last performance I scored a gram of coke and took it with me on the overnight sleeper back to London. I stayed up through the night, wandering naked round the train for some of it. God knows who saw me. By the time I reached home I had a streaming nose and another of those thunderous depressions, cocaine's version of a hangover – I called it a coke-over. 'My soul's been scratched,'

I wrote in my diary. When I told Jim about my night on the train, he said what I already knew: 'You're going to have to do something about this.'

And so to Monty Berman, psychotherapist extraordinaire. Recommended by Richard Wilson, who was later to convert the darker side of his own personality into the glorious Victor Meldrew. Ever since co-starring with Richard on *The Sheik of Pickersgill*, a mid-seventies TV film, we've been inseparable friends – able to share the kind of laughter and frank discussion I've otherwise only known with partners. So as I took this momentous step – seeking out psychotherapy – I was lucky that I had Richard both guiding me and defusing the tension. 'Be warned,' he said, chuckling, 'Monty's very unorthodox.' I couldn't quite see the joke. Not only did I have to overcome my prejudice and fear about seeing a shrink – *did this mean I was mentally ill?* – but I was having to face an unorthodox one too. What on earth did that mean?

Well, it meant that Monty didn't mince his words. 'Bullshit!' he'd retort as you tried to explain away your behaviour. 'You're not allowed to say, "I don't know,"' he'd comment in response to your other main tactic of defence. And he didn't observe the rule about not socialising with patients. Many of his patients were in theatre, which he loved, and he enjoyed meeting them afterwards. In fact, he preferred the word client to patient, and the joke went that Monty, like a top agent, had a great client list: Richard Wilson, Mike Leigh, Roger Allam, Miriam Karlin and now me.

'Well, well, I've heard all about you from Richard,' Monty told me at our first session, 'I always hoped to do some work with you one day.'

I thought he meant because I was such a gifted and fascinating individual. He didn't. He meant because I was such a spoilt and neurotic white South African.

Monty was born and brought up in Joburg. How familiar he was. With his large broad nose, his small heavily bagged eyes, his South African accent – the cry wasn't just 'Bullshit!' it was 'Agh, bullshit, man! – and his occasional use of Yiddish ('Still trying to give Mommie some *nachas*, hey?'), he could've been one of my uncles. Yet he was also profoundly different from them. From one of those highly intellectual, highly politicised South African Jewish families – so unlike my own – Monty had been very active in the struggle against apartheid back home in the fifties.

One of his duties was as driver to Mandela. The law stated that your black servant couldn't sit in front of the car with you and so, under the guise of being the white *baas* carting around his 'boy', Monty transported Mandela from meeting to meeting. In 1960, after the Sharpeville massacre, Monty and his wife Myrtle were arrested and jailed (he claims to have given a notable Lady Bracknell in the prison drama group) and then, while on bail, they fled the country. When I first went to Monty he hadn't seen his homeland for twenty years and wouldn't for another ten. He belonged to the small but vibrant group of South African exiles resident in London and was passionately involved in all anti-apartheid activity here. When he realised how politically naïve I still was, he began to devote part of our sessions to my education. This was again unorthodox, to say the least, but I didn't mind remotely. I was paying him £25 an hour to discuss my childhood, my sex life, my growing drug habit, and it seemed only fit and proper to include the mental state of our mutual birthplace. After all, its craziness was part of my make-up too. In fact, it was tempting to use this as a permanent excuse. Except Monty was far too wily and rigorous to let that one through.

'You'll start by seeing me as a kind of father figure,' he explained at our first session. 'Then as a teacher, a guru; you'll trust me, you'll love me, and then you'll start to fight me, hate me; you'll start seeing me as an enemy, as someone trying to take away your favourite toys – like the coke – and then, finally, hopefully, you'll come to see me just as myself, warts and all, *ordinary*'.

He wasn't right about this. Monty was a very wise man and, as I discovered much later, after his death, a versatile and surprising reinventor of himself, but he wasn't right about this pattern. I never got to see him as ordinary. In fact, I'm not sure I ever got past the father figure, the guru, the hero-worshipping stage.

Every life is made up of a crowd of people, with one or two heads towering above the others. Monty was like that in my life – one of the giants.

I worked hard to get fit enough to play the Fool again. To build up the wasted muscles in my leg, to stretch and soften the new, thickened, sewn-together tendon. Merrily bullied by Charlotte Arnold, my physiotherapist at the Remedial Dance Clinic in Harley Street, and with Monty helping to clean up my act too, this was a period of invisible mending from head to heel. I raced the clock to make the London run of *King Lear*. The RSC had scheduled this to incorporate my recuperation: exactly six months after the accident. I made it. But I was in for a surprise.

Gambon was even more disheartened by climbing the King Lear mountain than when I saw him last. He and Ian Talbot had done less of the music-hall stuff, apparently, and now he didn't want to do any of it. 'It's called *The Tragedy of King Lear*,' he said at our first reunion in a Barbican rehearsal room. 'I'd feel a tit prancing around like fucking Archie Rice.' I couldn't believe my ears. The Archie Rice stuff was what made his Lear unique and more moving than any I'd ever seen. But the original reviews focused so much – too much – on the Fool. One even quoted Wolfit's famous advice to an actor about to play Lear: 'Get a Cordelia you can carry and watch your Fool!' Mike knew our relationship wasn't about upstaging – he'd relished the double act in rehearsals. But those were a long time ago. As I tried to argue for what we'd had before, I broke down and couldn't articulate anything clearly. Mike doesn't like confrontation, or even much discussion over the work. Adrian was young, still relatively inexperienced, confounded by Mike's intransigence and my emotion. The easiest thing was to let it go. We ditched most of the front-cloth stuff. Mike's Lear was now a more traditionally noble figure and my Fool was just a bit frenetic. We showed London a far less interesting version of the play.

You win some, you lose some. Oddly, that production of *Lear* provided both experiences for me.

I moved on to new things. *Tartuffe* in the Pit, as a companion piece to the Bulgakov play about its author (the irreligiosity of *Tartuffe* is what lands Molière in trouble) in a sharply witty translation by Christopher Hampton; he who scripted *History Man* and was now a buddy, and more convinced by my testosterone as an actor. Actually, Tartuffe's sexual presence is so slimy you could cast a garden slug. The object of Tartuffe's desire, Elmire, was played by Alison Steadman. We enjoyed working together so much there were complaints from the audience: could the actors please stop laughing and give us a chance? Nigel Hawthorne played Orgon and I became mesmerised by his subtle comic timing. In my next show, *Maydays* – David Edgar's epic play about the right wing in contemporary Britain – it was Bob Peck's performance as the Russian dissident that fascinated me. Bob himself struck me as enigmatic, quite remote – is he arrogant, is he shy? – a huge, solid tree trunk of a man, quite indestructible. (I write this with the strange knowledge that Bob will die young, in 1999, of cancer.) He wasn't like an actor at all, which is why in some of his performances, like Lermontov in *Maydays* or the title role in Bond's *Lear*, he could move you like no one else.

The Kinnocks come to see *Maydays*. Neil has just taken over as leader of the Labour Party and is impressive to meet: brimming with energy and humour. I'm becoming more alert not only to South African politics, but its British grandparent too. This has always seemed flat and bland to me, its grey debates rather dull after the stark black-and-white drama of apartheid. Until now, that is. Thatcher's more like the guys back home. Her vocal style may be surprisingly incompetent, a droning, mechanical sound (as with priests and mediums, the actor in me wants to shout, 'Sorry I don't believe a word'), but the light in her eye keeps you awake; it's very fearsome, very determined. Like Uncle Nat, she sees life as terribly simple. She has an answer for everything, never a question. Under her tutelage the British character is changing before my eyes. The quiet, wise, enquiring population I first encountered is becoming a nation of know-alls. And what they know is that every issue comes down to me, me, me. Thatcherism is supplying a massive snort of cocaine to the country. *Me, me, me.* Thatcherism is making selfishness respectable.

Kinnock could be a match for her. He can even speak. In fact, when he does, the impression isn't of a politician at all. There's real passion, real humanity. He and Glenys are keen theatregoers, so I get to know them better and better over the years. Her wisdom is very attractive, as is her straightforwardness. 'Oh Tony, why are you always in such depressing plays?' she asks after *Singer*. 'They're like your novels. Why can't you do something just a bit more, y'know, *fun?*'

17

KING, QUEEN, MONK, PEDLAR

'WE WANT THE 1984 Stratford season to introduce a new generation of Shakespeare actors,' is how Terry Hands put it. 'The line-up's to be Kenneth Branagh as Henry V, Roger Rees as Hamlet, Ian McDiarmid as Shylock and you as Richard III.'

So began one of the big adventures of my career. Although I've described this in *Year of the King*, I want to revisit some of it now.

Olivier. It all came down to Olivier. It often does when you're playing Shakespeare. Of the five main ones I've done – Richard, Macbeth, Shylock, Titus, Leontes – he created memorable portraits of four. (He never played Leontes, a loss for the world if a relief to me.) But nowhere does his giant shadow, his defining silhouette, fall more completely than over Richard; so completely that you can barely see the role underneath. This lies in dense shade. Richard's dark soul and the master's black magic have become one. The page-boy haircut, the long nose, the muscular hump, the broken-wing arm, the elegantly lame leg – these things were surely requested by Shakespeare personally, in some lost manuscript (probably shredded and eaten by Olivier). You're left scurrying round the perimeter of this indelible shape, trying to find some break, some little peephole.

'Now is the winter of our discontent.' You don't even like to say it. Don't like to hold it in your mouth. It's been in someone's else. His. You can taste his spit. Feel his bite marks round the edges. His poised, staccato delivery is imprinted on the line: 'Now. Is the wintah. Of our. Discon-tent.'

Once I'd agreed to do the part, an image haunted me: my Richard, still in its infancy, lying there in a cradle, while a huge black figure, fully formed, famously deformed, an infamous child killer, slowly limps towards it.

The RSC invited me to attend the press conference for the new season. Beforehand, I met Ken Branagh for the first time. I confided my fear to him, thinking I'd have a soulmate. After all, his role, Henry V, had the same warning sign hanging over it: *This is the property of Laurence Olivier – trespassers will be prosecuted.* But Branagh just replied cheerfully, 'Oh look, Olivier's performances exist, there's nothing we can do about them, may as well just get on with the job.' *Just get on with the job?* The fearlessness, the folly of youth, I thought, staring at the cherubic face topped with red-gold hair – he'll find out!

Or not. As far as I know Branagh wasn't born with a cowl round his head – he just arrived with a written guarantee in his hand. It was from God and it said, 'You're gonna make it, kid.'

The nonchalance, the certainty with which he'd spoken to me that day were the same qualities which graced his performance as Henry a few weeks later. It was his first time on the Stratford main stage, yet he appeared to be strolling round his backyard. Which proved to be the case, in a way. He left the RSC soon afterwards, formed his own company, did plays, then movies, filmed *Henry*, was nominated for several Oscars and took off into the far blue yonder.

Meanwhile, back on earth, I found myself in a familiar dilemma as I began pre-rehearsal preparations for *Richard III*. How to find a way in? How to see it as a new play? I wanted to picture Shakespeare turning up on my doorstep one day, looking remarkably like Rob Knights and handing over a stack of paper: 'Here – this is for you if you want it.' Research was the answer. Research wakes you up. Right then, let's start with the historical Richard, the real king. No – wrong – dead end. The real king bears no relation to Shakespeare's version, as letters from the Richard III Society will continue to remind me long into the run ('You are yet another actor to ignore truth and integrity in order to launch yourself on an ego-trip enabled by the monstrous lie perpetrated by Shakespeare about a most valiant, honourable and excellent King'). All right, where next? Discussing it with Monty, he reckons that Shakespeare's Richard is probably psychopathic. Let's have a look at these guys, then. The timing's good. The papers are full of a sensational murder trial. The Muswell Hill Monster, Dennis Nilsen. Mad or bad? Sick or evil? No one seems able to say for sure, but there's certainly something about Nilsen that carries a whiff of Richard III. They share intelligence, cunning, and sick humour – Nilsen complains about running out of neckties as the strangulations increase, and when the police find human flesh in his drains he suggests it's Kentucky Fried Chicken. Mind you, I'm wary of playing too funny a Richard III: that seems like the most obvious and least interesting choice. It's called *The Tragedy of King Richard III* (maybe I've got Gambon echoing in my head – 'It is *The Tragedy of King Lear!*') and the man has to possess real danger. Which comes from him being an outsider, the Crookback. With Charlotte Arnold, my merrily bullying physio from the Achilles injury, I visit homes for the disabled. Many of the people I meet, observe and sketch are on crutches. Hey, I remember crutches. I lived on them for about six weeks after the operation. Crutches . . . they're quite interesting . . . like extra limbs . . .

I say it to Charlotte first: 'What about playing him on crutches?'

She laughs. Maybe I am joking. Maybe the idea is ludicrous. But discussing it further, she says that because crutches are designed to take the body weight they would at least be *safe*. Richard III is notorious for crippling the actors who play him. Sustaining a twisted position in this huge role leaves people with bad backs and knees for years to come. (In 1992, Simon Russell Beale played a gloriously poison-toad Richard, but had to leave halfway through with a slipped disc.) Having already encountered these problems as the Fool, I'm determined to find a risk-free solution this time.

'I'm half thinking of playing him on crutches.'

Bill Alexander is on the receiving end of the idea now. We've worked together happily on *Molière* and *Tartuffe*. Something about our different styles fits together well: his patient Englishness alongside my impulsive Jewish Africanness; his perceptive, text-based approach with my more physical, theatrical excesses. We pull in opposite directions, yet stretch rather than hurt one another; we both grow. An attractive, kindly, rather scruffy man, Bill is greatly liked by his companies and that's a help too.

He answers: 'But Richard's a soldier. How would he go into battle on crutches?'

I back off immediately – 'Well, absolutely, what a dumb idea.'

But it won't go away. I decide to test out the crutches privately. Charlotte sends two pairs to the Barbican stage door while *Maydays* is on:

14/2/84. After the show, I'm struggling into the car park with the four crutches when Alison Steadman drives out. She stops in horror. 'Richard III,' I offer in explanation. She nods knowingly. 'Mike Leigh will be proud of you.' Back at home I experiment nervously. The elbow crutches are much better than the armpit variety because you can let go and use your hands. Swinging along on them, stretching like an animal, pawing the ground, rearing up on hind legs, I find they have possibilities.

My fascination with the crutches and Bill's caution about them both become irrelevant when we go into rehearsals. As soon as I get stuck into the text (speaking rather than discussing it), and into the psychology of Richard and into his relationships with the other characters (cooking especially well with Penny Downie's Lady Anne and Mal Storry's Buckingham), the physicality of the character suddenly seems less important. It's a trap for me anyway. There's an element of truth in the jousting between Roger Allam (Clarence) and myself; I call him the Voice Beautiful, he calls me the Body Busy. But then just when I'm ready to ditch the crutches, a curious reversal occurs and Bill starts arguing for them. Actually, it's two Bills by now. Bill Dudley, the designer, has joined the debate. He likes the four-legged idea, reminding us that whenever people curse Richard they use bestial imagery – 'a hell-hound', 'this carnal cur', 'that foul bunch-back'd toad' – and says that by adding long, hanging sleeves to the costume (our setting is medieval) he can even make it six-legged – Queen Margaret's special curse is 'bottled spider!'. We do another test, adding the hump:

30/4/84. Conference Hall. Evening Solus Call. The Bills chat among themselves, pretending not to watch as I begin moving round the room. There's a large mirror at one end so I can observe as well. Charging head on, the massive back rolls heavily like a bison's. Spreading the crutches sideways, I look like some weird bird or giant insect. The wing span (Richard's reach) is enormous and threatening. The range of movement is endless: dancing backward like a spider, sideways like a crab. And you can cover distances very swiftly with a sweeping, scooping action, almost like rowing, the polio-afflicted legs dragging along underneath. We try 'Now is the winter'. For the section about his deformity, I deliberately, slowly exhibit it. Bill A. likes this: 'It becomes a poem of self-hatred, a mannequin parade of the latest deformities.' At the end of the session everyone is smiling. 'Looks promising,' we all say to one another cautiously, but excited. It does seem to contribute to, not hinder, our early work on the text. I drive home to Chipping Campden. It's just gone dark, the sky is still glowing blue, the countryside looks like weird grey cut-outs as the headlamps of the car swing round the narrow lanes. It makes a crazy theatrical effect. I'm trying to contain the excitement, the jubilation. Tchaikovsky's First Piano Concerto is playing on Radio 3. Glorious slush.

But what of Bill's initial point – how does Richard go into battle with crutches? Well, yes, he *is* vulnerable. Play his deformity any way you choose and he *is* vulnerable. He's a disabled man going to war. Our solution is to transfer him from the crutches on to a horse (a huge armour-coated horse-structure which is then carried by his soldiers – like they've carried him on the bier-throne). When this horse is shot from under him in battle, he's definitely in trouble. And Shakespeare has provided the appropriate reaction:

'A horse, a horse, my kingdom for a horse!'

We will certainly earn the right to say that line.

So – the crutches are in. A lot of other early ideas aren't. Like the Quasimodo-type facial prosthetics I've been sketching. Or my resistance to the comedy in the play. Later I will see someone achieve a real heavyweight, non-comic reading of Richard – Ian McKellen in Richard Eyre's revelatory National Theatre production – but for now it seems impossible. For now it seems like an exuberant, even vulgar, young man's play (Shakespeare was about twenty-eight when he wrote it), and I'm an exuberant, even vulgar, youngish actor (aged thirty-five), and though Bill Alexander (thirty-seven) isn't vulgar at all, he oversees this particular union between role and actor with relish.

We're a hit. Beyond wildest dreams. Every time I start a new project my two Geminian halves go to war. One promises disaster, the other fantasy land. For *Richard III* the fantasy was people saying it was the best since Olivier's. Well, they did. Audiences flocked, queued overnight, bartered for black market tickets. Big names travelled to Stratford to see us: Peter Brook, Michael Caine, Donald Sutherland, Charlton Heston. Mom and Dad happened to be at the same matinée as Heston and shared the VIP room at the interval. This made more impact on Dad than the show (through which he'd slept soundly) and he went round for days afterwards shamelessly name-dropping – 'I had tea with Moses.'

To read or not to read? That's often the question. I'm not against theatre criticism. In fact, with some reviewers, the enthusiasts – those who seem to love the job – Billington, Coveney, or the late Jack Tinker – I'm eager to hear their opinion. But only of other people's shows. They're never useful for your own. Whether positive or negative, the printed word makes you self-conscious and it's better to retain your own sense of what you're trying to do; your innocence, in a way. If you've got a long run ahead of you, you simply have to believe in the show one hundred per cent or you're going to be very miserable. That's the theory. But reviews are like cigarettes. They can give you a buzz, they can also make you feel sick – either way, they're not good for you, yet they're addictive. You give them up, you start again, you stop, you tell yourself just one can't hurt. I've gone through various phases: reading, not reading, reading and not reading at the same time (it's done through the fingers, like watching TV when they're showing testicle surgery), but at the time of Richard in 1984 I was adamantly not reading.

When Michael Caine saw the show he said, 'What about those reviews, eh?'

'I don't read them.'

'Don't read 'em? You wrote 'em, din' yer?'

Yes, it was one of those times: you didn't need to read the reviews to know they were good. A few days after we opened, I rang Chatto & Windus, the publishers, and said: 'I think we can proceed.'

Chatto had approached me a year earlier, asking if I'd like to write and illustrate a book about the next part I played. (By sheer chance this was Richard III.) The man with the idea was Antony Harwood. Son of Ronnie.

I hadn't really kept in touch with the Harwoods since those bumpy early days in this country and the last time I saw Antony he was a kid. Now he was a tall and cheerful man (perfectly happy being called Ant), an editor at Chatto. I proceeded cautiously. Yes, I'd be keeping a diary anyway, and yes, I'd do any visual scribblings in a sketchbook rather than on paper napkins, but we'd have to see how it went. What if the production was a flop? You risk this every time you do a great play. Will it be art or shit you lift into the light? The use of crutches in *Richard* perfectly demonstrates the risk. Was this a very good or a very bad idea? Difficult to tell at the time. It just felt dangerous. Anyway, now that the show was a success, there could be a book in it too.

I was entering a new world. I got myself a literary agent. At first, very briefly, for about five minutes, in fact, it was Giles Gordon, but then I discovered he was also a theatre critic – *aargh!* – and had to change instantly. I went with Mic Cheetham – a sinewy, glamorous English lady with a smoky continental aura, a great mind, a great enthusiast, and a great embodiment of Dad's adage about working hard and playing hard – and I've been with her ever since.

As I began working on *Year of the King*, I recorded my initial frustration over the 1984 season: the RSC couldn't find me a second part and, as a workaholic, I feared Richard wouldn't be enough to feed my habit. Well, here I was now, just playing that one part – yet writing about it. Writing. Oh, what a rush this gave, what a high. Acting couldn't compete. You have to leave acting alone at 5.30 when rehearsals finish, or at 10.30 when it's curtain-down. Painting was location-based too. Sure, you could wrestle with a composition in your head, but you still had to go back to one room, one place, one source for the hit. But with writing – here was a drug without end. Portable and self-generating. All in the mind. Puzzles and solutions. Ah – I know how to make that sentence work! Yes – that's the word I need! Quick, where's a piece of paper? Any piece of paper will do. My pockets fill with scraps and notes, my dressing room too, my bedside table. Sleep becomes difficult: a tedious interruption to the ecstasy. Sometimes I work through the night. Feel tired the next day, but no hangover, no coke-over, and then there's a new rush as soon as the first good idea kicks in. Or even a bad one. You can always make it better later. You can endlessly revise and rethink and redraft, that's the wonderful thing about writing a book. And it's so big a task it feels like you'll never finish it, never have to cope with the come down. It starts to fill every corner of the brain. Mine has only one other compartment operating now: a programmed set of lines which begin 'Now is the winter' and end 'A horse, a horse'. Even this gets invaded. There are performances when I'm speaking Shakespeare's words while composing my own. I have to fight to concentrate. Like with sleep, like with mealtimes, the show feels as if it's getting in the way of what I really want to do.

Oh yes, I took to writing.

What a year! Jim was in the Stratford company too, playing roles in several shows, including a splendidly seedy Tyrrel in *Richard*, and we were living half an hour's drive away in Chipping Campden. Julia's Cottage. Double-storeyed, with low ceilings, thick beams, a conservatory–lounge at the back (which I nabbed as my study) and a marvellous banked garden. Chipping itself is a beautiful Cotswold town dating from medieval times (Pasolini used it as the location for his *Canterbury Tales* movie). Its buildings are made of that lovely, honey-coloured local stone, which holds the light on summer mornings and evenings in a way that can stop you in your tracks and induce a curiously tender sensation, a kind of nostalgia maybe, for the stone is truly ancient. Look closely and you'll see it's studded with tiny seashells and fossils from when Albion still lay on the ocean floor. Even the winter is bearable in this part of the world. Freed of all the tourists, Chipping and Stratford reclaim their identities as small old country towns, smelling of woodsmoke, crisp air and open land. There's so much sky here! In London, the months of December and January are personified by tall, damp-stained walls leaning over you, but here, whether the day's bright or cloudy, your eye and spirit go up, up. But then we probably see places in relation to how we feel and boy, was I feeling good. Over in Stratford I'd hit the jackpot and here in Chipping I had a new drug of choice – writing.

When *Richard* moved to London, to the Barbican, in 1985, the RSC found a second project for me. *Red Noses* by Peter Barnes – a rich, savage, comic epic, typically Barnesian, about a troupe of third-rate travelling players trying to cheer up people as they die of the Black Death in fourteenth-century France. I played the troupe's leader, a gentle monk called Father Flote. Jim had a major role too, as Sonnerie, a silent man draped with bells, half-fool, half-spirit, a kind of Ariel to Flote, the most innocent of

Prosperos. Our real-life love was a bonus for the on-stage relationship.

Although *Red Noses* was a special play, Flote was not a particularly special part. Mind you, would any be again, after Richard? Yes. That same year, while both shows were still running, I went into rehearsals for a show which became one of the most personally satisfying I've ever done: Harvey Fierstein's *Torch Song Trilogy*.

Like *Cloud Nine* before it, *Torch Song* manages jointly to address our individual and collective lives, but in a totally non-intellectual way. Both plays rely on an emotional response, they're plays from the heart to the heart – which can leave critics tongue-tied or sneering. They're not for critics, actually – they're audience plays. Say what you like about their literary merit, they *work*. I think Harvey Fierstein's great achievement in *Torch Song* is to take the most exotic of creatures, a Jewish New York drag queen, and turn him into Everyman. Arnold begins the trilogy backstage at a tacky little dive, already in drag, putting the final touches to his make-up as Virginia Hamm. A gaudy if somewhat raddled peacock, he buttonholes the audiences with a stream of outrageous wisecracks and private confidences. This is hilarious but shocking and worse is to come. In the next scene, he's fucked in a back room – still chatting away to the audience. But by the last act he's just a man at home, trying to bring up an adopted child while battling his own formidable Jewish mother. The play has moved from very gay topics of promiscuity and tragi-sweet love affairs (given voice by a torch singer at the side of the stage) to themes of parenthood and responsibility. Bridging them is a middle act about friendship. It's a remarkable journey.

And Arnold is a remarkable part, on stage throughout the marathon play; it's about four hours, Shakespeare length.

I began by visiting London's drag clubs – a milieu with which I wasn't familiar – but quickly abandoned this, or any other research, as a route to Arnold. Like the play itself, the performance has to come from the heart. It's one of those roles. Cyrano is another. The actor either has to be ready to reveal his visible soul, or don't bother. This wasn't natural to me at the time, but I had an excellent new teacher in the director, Robert Ackerman, a gentle, wise New Yorker with a mighty smile. Although he never named it as such, he used the American Method; you had to tap into yourself, into your private experience of love, of fear, of pain – of Jewish mothers! – and you had to do this straight away. 'Yeah, that's fine, but it's got no feeling,' he said about a scene I was doing in the first week of rehearsals. 'Well, no,' I replied. 'I'm just mapping it out technically for now.' He looked puzzled, then gave the big, watermelon smile: 'OK, sure, but we can't really start working properly till we're dealing with real feelings.' It was the perfect way of approaching Arnold, who could otherwise just become a garish but empty tour de force. Bob was rigorous about the relationships in the play; these interested him far more than Arnold's solo turns.

The cast was strong, dominated by Miriam Karlin as the mother. She was like Monty: a figure both intensely familiar to me and not. Frank, funny, over-exaggerating, overdramatising, she could've stepped straight out of a supper scene back in Montagu House – except that she was highly politicised, passionate about our responsibility in society. A veteran campaigner and tireless yet beloved troublemaker for both the actors' union, Equity – I called her 'our Equity guerilla' – and the Labour Party. We quickly became good friends and developed one of the best on-stage chemistries I'd ever known; our mother–son rows felt very close to the real thing and 'feelings' flowed. Among the others was Rupert Graves, playing Arnold's young love, Alan. Here again I needed to do no emotional digging. From the moment I met Rupert – the ultimate soft-eyed boy-man – I became hopelessly infatuated. Over the next half-year, and in a way that Arnold would understand, I suffered terribly and exquisitely.

The play ignites like a bomb in front of an audience. On Broadway it had drawn a naturally sympathetic crowd – gay or Jewish or both – but the West End doesn't work like that. Its audiences are made up of an unpredictable mix of tourists, middle-class Londoners, charabancs from the provinces and, in this case, some RSC supporters. All in all, a fairly straight crowd. They didn't know what hit them. There I was, 'that actor who's just played Richard the Third', in full drag one minute, being fucked the next. (My sexual partner was just imaginary, just fresh air, but all the same – !) The first act was tough going for this audience and some walked out, sometimes noisily. When the Kinnocks came – they're great Mim Karlin mates – Neil said afterwards, 'Ooh hell, Tony, some of that early stuff, I didn't think I was going to make it, boy!' But in the second act the play starts opening its arms wide – this is about straight as well as gay, this is about friendship, about parents and children, about us all. By the end, whatever their initial prejudices, the audience was moved, uplifted and

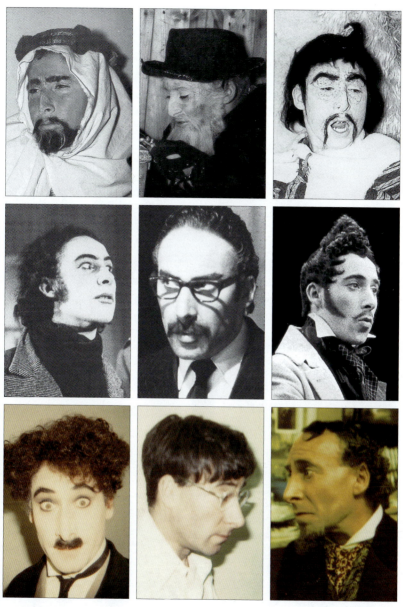

9. DISGUISES. *Top*: The Stroud Make-up Studio; various make-ups on self aged 15 devised by Cecil Bloch. *Middle*: Early roles, in *Love of Four Colonels* at Webber D. (1971), in *Ambassador Extraordinary* at Frinton-on-Sea (1972); in *Government Inspector* at Edinburgh Lyceum (1976). *Bottom*: Make-up tests as Charlie Chaplin (1993), Stanley Spencer (1996), Benjamin Disraeli (1997).

10. PLAYING THE FOOL.
Top: With Jonathan Pryce as Edgar and Brian Young as Lear, Liverpool Everyman (1972).
Below left: With Michael Gambon as Lear, Stratford RSC (1982).
Below right: Self-portrait, oils. 1982.

11. EVERYMAN.
Left: Enoch Powell in
Tarzan's Last Stand (photo
taken during May Day
publicity stunt at Liverpool
Docks in 1973).
Bottom: Ringo in *John*, *Paul*,
George, Ringo and Bert (with
Bernard Hill as John, Trevor
Eve as Paul, Phillip Joseph as
George).

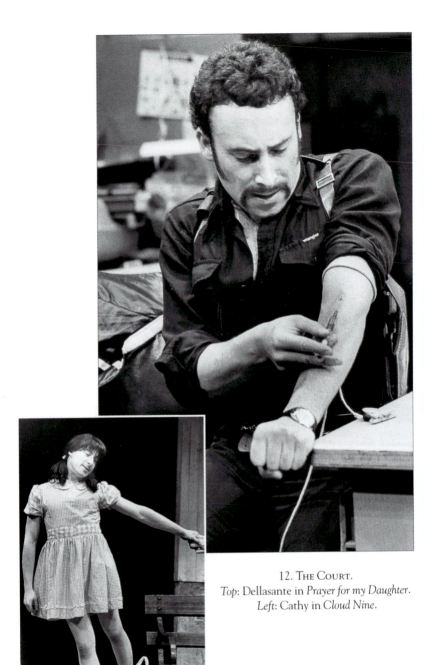

12. THE COURT.
Top: Dellasante in *Prayer for my Daughter*.
Left: Cathy in *Cloud Nine*.

13. HOWARD & MUHAMMAD.
Right: As Howard Kirk in
The History Man, with (l.to.r.)
Geraldine James, Isla Blair,
Laura Davenport, Maggie
Steed and Veronica
Quilligan. *Bottom*: As
Muhammad in *Goose-pimples*,
with Jim Broadbent, Jill Baker
and Marion Bailey.

14. King & Queen.
Top: *Richard III*.
Left: *Torch Song Trilogy*; a photo in my dressing
room at the Albery Theatre.

15. Giant Shadows.
Top: drawings of Olivier as Richard III, and McKellen as Iago.
Bottom: Harvey Fierstein and self at Joe Allen's, 1985.

16. PERSECUTED-PERSECUTOR.
Top: Shylock. *Bottom*: Singer.

cheering. Exhilarating to hear, to see, to feel. Although I was in a long West End run again, it was never an endurance test. I couldn't wait for curtain-up each night, couldn't wait to go on that journey again – with the audience changing, drawing near, returning the play's embrace.

Bob Ackerman hadn't directed the show on Broadway, thank God, but during our previews someone from that original production flew over to see us. Its star. And author. Harvey Fierstein. He'd won two Tonys for it (Best Play, Best Actor); this was his baby. Bob had kept him away from rehearsals, wisely, but now the time had come. I was very apprehensive. Harvey saw the show first; saw me before I saw him. Just as well. The figure who came into my dressing room afterwards *was* Arnold. An extraordinary character, overwhelming, huge. Built like a truck driver yet with a pussy-cat face. One of those incredibly husky New York accents; the voice sounds totally ruined yet crackles with all the ultra-sharp energy of that city, where the streets criss-cross like blades. To say that Harvey is camp doesn't paint an adequate picture. British camp is a light-footed John Inman dance, or a flared Kenneth Williams nostril, or a vinegary Julian Clary aside; it's essentially a friendly, even fawning, tail-wagging thing. Harvey is more sumo-wrestler camp, road-digger camp, ball-breaker camp. He's Elaine Stritch in drag. (And I witnessed them together in my dressing room when *Stanley* was on Broadway, so I know what I'm saying.) 'Ohhh babee,' he purred in those gravelly tones as we met now, batting surprisingly doe-like eyelashes – 'ohhh honee' – taking me in his arms now, those wrestler's arms – 'ohhh darlinnng, you were so . . . ohhhhhhh!'

He couldn't find words. It gradually occurred to me, as he continued to gush without saying anything, that he hadn't liked it. Me. When I finally saw him play it (he took over after I left) I understood why. His was a massive, stage-eating, audience-eating, Broadway-sized performance (later perfectly scaled down for the movie), against which my own work, with Bob's careful layering of inner life and restraint, must've seemed very quiet and rather English. Somehow it didn't matter that he found my work tame in the show – he'd written Arnold, played Arnold, *lived* Arnold, who was I to argue? – the show itself was tame next to its author. He was irresistible. He'd come over not to interfere, but to give his blessing, to wine and dine us, to party. Harvey was in town! It should've been on the weather reports. He lit up the West End long after its stage lights had dimmed. During the show, I never stopped talking. Afterwards, in Joe Allen's, I never said a word. I listened, I gasped, I laughed. It shook with laughter every night – our *Torch Song* table at Joe Allen's.

Harvey returned to London at the end of the year, for the Olivier awards. He was nominated for Best Play, though in the event it went to *Red Noses*, which tested my loyalties. I'd also been nominated and struck lucky. And I'd already won the *Evening Standard* Best Actor too, so I was, to put it mildly, on top of the world. Harvey seemed quite unperturbed by not winning, or already had compensation prizes in mind, when at the end of the Olivier Award dinner, he growled to the group surrounding him, 'OK honeys, it's back to the Savoy for one of Harvey's famous shower parties!' Back in his suite at the Savoy an event ensued which has since reappeared as a chapter in my book *The Indoor Boy* (pages 76–80, for students of the fact-to-fiction process) and a scene in the play *Madhouse at Goa* by Martin Sherman, who was also present that night. Jim was there too, Miriam Karlin, Bob Ackerman and his partner, the beautiful, sweet-spirited Franco Zavani, and two young (straight) actors who'd come along from the dinner. They were the only ones to take up the shower party idea and went into the bathroom, leaving the door ajar. The rest of us sat working our way through Harvey's mini-bar, taking turns to stroll to the door and glance in. Yup they were certainly showering, and yup, fairly innocently. Then, on one of her visits, Miriam Karlin suddenly said, 'Oh my God!' She spun round, intending to return to her seat, but was trampled in the rush to the door. This closed in our faces. Later, when we were leaving, Harvey invited the two young (straight) actors to stay. They agreed. Harvey has that effect on people.

If 1984 was a good year, 1985 was even better. My run of luck was at its height. Not only two extremely popular shows and two major awards, but the publication of my first book, *Year of the King*, to a terrific reception. It was thrilling. I mean, even Simon Callow gave it a rave review.

I was surprised he'd been asked to review it. One or two other actors, too, like Peter Barkworth. All were enthusiastic, so I shouldn't complain, but were these really the most objective of critics?

I was still very innocent about the publishing world. It's a shameless one. Authors frequently review one another's work; friends or enemies, back-slapping or back-stabbing. If actors were sent along with pen and pad to their colleagues' first night, there'd be an outcry. Imagine me reviewing

McKellen's Richard III or him my Macbeth. If our comments were complimentary, the cry of 'Luvvies!' would rend the air and if we weren't, there'd be a flurry of smirks and winks. Yet book reviewing sanctions incest without the hint of a blush. Strange, as I say, this new world I was venturing into. A very restless one, too. The changing of jobs! Editors and agents move about like they're playing musical chairs. Whole publishing houses join the dance. To view it from a theatrical perspective again, it'd be like the RSC and National swopping artistic directors every year, then the two companies amalgamating, then being bought up by Cameron MacIntosh, then him swallowed up by the Shuberts in New York and the whirligig ending with British theatre being run from an office in Manhattan.

By the time *Year of the King* came out, my editor at Chatto, Antony Harwood, was gone – to become a literary agent – and a new man took me out to lunch. A tall, blond Englishman, young yet using a stick, modestly spoken, a gentle, generous spirit. Andrew Motion – now Poet Laureate. He said, 'You know, there's something in the style of *Year of the King* that suggests you could write fiction. Is that something you'd like to do?'

'Never thought about it,' I replied truthfully.

'Well, have a think, then,' he urged, 'because we'd be very interested to see what you came up with.'

I was flattered. I knew and admired Andrew's own writing. And he thought I could write a novel. In fact, was inviting me to do so – for Chatto & Windus, Virginia and Leonard Woolf's publishing house. At that time, in 1985, Chatto was still in its original premises, a dark, marvellously eccentric warren of offices and corridors at 40 William IV Street, off Charing Cross Road. I loved going there. The boss was small, young and female. Carmen Callil. Australian, feminist. Everyone was terrified of her, but she seemed to like me, seemed to be a fan: 'Darling, I'd publish your laundry list,' she told me. Later, when I came to leave Chatto, I'd see the other side of Carmen, but for now all was rosy, all was well.

A novel? – what a novel idea – it had honestly never occurred. Yet a subject immediately came to mind. My family's journey from Lithuania to South Africa, from persecuted to persecutor. Dad's father. A *smous*. I'd often heard this word in childhood, without ever being sure what it meant. I rang home.

'What's a *smous*?'

'I'll ask your father,' said Mom, then reported back: 'A pedlar.'

'And it's a Yiddish word?'

'Hang on.' I heard them conferring again. 'No – Afrikaans.'

'Funny. Sounds Yiddish. *Smous*.'

We took *Richard III* to Australia in April–May 1986. I had a difficult time. Endlessly playing the exhausting man on crutches. Now *was* the winter. And I think it's perhaps difficult for an African to thrill to Australia. It's like his homeland, but without the drama. Its wild animals are smallish, bouncing, climbing herbivores and its people say 'No worries' all the time. This seemed generally true. To them – the whites, anyway – they inhabit a world without worries. So far from the rest of it. So far from any trouble. It's too calm for me. I need more tension in the air.

But as we trekked round the country – Adelaide, Melbourne, Brisbane – I whiled away the long hours in coaches, planes and hotel rooms, thinking about another travelling figure. A pedlar, a *smous*, a sleepy little man – like Muhammad in *Goose-pimples* – arriving in South Africa at the turn of the century. There'd need to be at least two other major characters. An Englishman and a Boer . . .

Back in England, I wrote a synopsis. Both Andrew and Carmen approved it enthusiastically. They commissioned the book. Mic did a deal. I signed a contract. All rather dreamlike. Was I really going to write a novel? How do you do those?

'Just start,' advised Andrew. 'You'll find your own way.'

I tried. It was like driving a car without any lessons. I just kept crashing. Talk about art or shit – which was this? But by November I'd roughed out a draft. Richard Wilson and I were going on holiday to Egypt. I handed over the manuscript to Andrew, saying, 'I honestly don't know what this is like. I want you to tell me the truth. I really don't mind if you say it's rubbish. I'll give you the money back. Happily! Just tell me the truth.'

When we returned there was a letter from Andrew. It began with encouragement – 'There are a couple of things that I want and ought to say, which will, I hope, make you blush a bit' – and then, over the next four pages, gave me a crash course in creative writing; 'free it up,' he urged, 'you get bound up, a bit constipated, you sometimes sound rather formal. Like, for example . . .'

It was these, the detailed examples, which were so illuminating. I could see exactly what he meant. And I realised what had been going on. I'd been compensating. I'm from a non-intellectual, non-reading family; I'm not much of a reader myself, I haven't been to university. So I was determined to write properly, to write poshly, to write Literature. This was the rather formal and constipated sound which Andrew identified. There was another way. Instead of 'And then Smous pondered over the question of how he should proceed', you could just put 'What to do?' It gave instant vitality. These and other basic lessons were all in Andrew's four pages. His letter is one of the best presents anyone's ever given me.

Suddenly it was much easier to write. I had both approval and guidance. Until then the task had been uncomfortable – none of the druggy-druggy rush of *Year of the King* – and lonely. Now there was someone else in the room with me. Another eye. A director.

A new draft came tumbling out: a gushing, ecstatic torrent that didn't smell at all like shit. This wasn't just a new drug, this was a new love affair. Couldn't sleep, couldn't eat, couldn't focus on anything else.

But then – suddenly – a serious interruption loomed into view. The RSC wanted me to come back for the 1987 Stratford season. They would assemble a big line of parts – Shylock, Malvolio and Vindice in *Revenger's Tragedy* – Bill Alexander would direct the first two, Jim would be in the company too, Julia's Cottage in Chipping Campden was free. Was I interested?

Oh, dear. Yes, of course, but . . . aw fuck.

We started rehearsing *The Merchant of Venice* in February 1987 at St John's Church in Waterloo. I remember the first day clearly. A young actor was sitting opposite me during Bill's opening chat. I felt him looking my way, yet every time I glanced across he wouldn't meet my eyes.

'I'm confused by all the new names,' I whispered to Bill during the coffee break. 'What's that guy called?'

'That's, um – oh, one of the Salads – I get them muddled,' giggled Bill, checking a cast list. 'Oh yes, that's Solanio – that's Greg – Greg Doran.'

18

Two Dogs and Freedom

'It is the most impenetrable cur
That ever kept with men.'

– shouts Solanio as Shylock exits in Act Three, Scene Two. But in
one performance Greg yelled after me:

'It is the most impenetrable cur
That ever slept with men.'

I froze in the wings mid-stride, then slowly turned. Greg was standing on
stage, blinking, mouth open, even more stunned than I was.
It was happening, it was definitely happening. And 'allowed' by Jim –
currently next door in the Swan playing Saturninus in Deborah Warner's
Titus – Jim was allowing an affair, not just a one-night stand; affection not
just sex, affection turning into love. Later, Jim found someone else for
himself too. Yet he and I remained devoted to one another; we still
believed we were creating a legitimate, new, non-straight way of leading a
permanent relationship.

Greg didn't fit the usual model. He didn't look like Jim, or indeed any of
the soft-eyed boy-men stretching all the way back to my first love in

kindergarten. He was handsome rather than beautiful. His eyes were big, luminous, certain. A striking feature was his hair, a great mane of glossy brown locks. This large head of his – the wardrobe people actually found it difficult to fit him with hats – held a large mind too. He was ten years my junior, yet much wiser. This drew me powerfully. He was extremely well read and well informed, a sometimes magpie, lifting titbits of this subject or that. Not with Shakespeare, though: his first love, his main passion. Brought up in Preston, in a thoroughly middle-class family, yet with a controversial touch – his father, now retired, was General Manager at Sellafield – and devoutly Catholic. Although Greg had left the faith (partially because of its intolerance towards his sexuality), he'd retained something of Christianity's essential spirit; the best of it, I thought. As I talked about *Middlepost* and apartheid, and my family's involvement, he said, 'You keep saying "them" – but isn't it "you" also? – Isn't it "us"? Your family, or the Afrikaners, they're not some strange, different breed of humanity. They're you, me, us. Surely the only way of ever understanding what's happening is to put ourselves in the middle of it?'

When I began work on the third draft of *Middlepost* the most brutal character, the Boer Breedt, developed an entirely new dimension, of vulnerability, of loneliness, of deep, deep love for the land. This transformed him, not just making him more human, but more convincing as a fanatic. It's what makes those men so dangerous – the Hitlers, the Terre' Blanches, the Enoch Powells – they start from a position of love.

Love. Change. Love and change. These words feel linked. Apart and together, they ruled my life for a while. Neither is a stable thing. Both can terrify. Both can thrill.

South Africa – in the eighties this seemed like a place without love, a place where change was impossible – South Africa influenced everything I touched during those days. Beginning with Shylock . . .

I didn't have much first-hand experience of anti-Semitism. The cry of *Jood! Jood!* which followed me round the army was a routine noise, almost an affectionate one, born of that curious relationship between the Dutch Reformed and Jewish people of the Old South Africa. The Jews were aristocracy there, at the court of Uncle Nat; some of our parents and grandparents had known anti-Semitism in its wildest form, in Europe, but they'd fled and outdistanced it. In our new world we were never a despised population; the boot was on the other foot. So the more Bill and I talked about *Merchant* the more I heard myself using the word racism rather than anti-Semitism. I found this more inspiring as an explanation for who Shylock is, why he behaves the way he does – 'racism' – this rang bells in my head, quickened the blood, brought back sense memories. Grown men grinning and nodding like children, their status nil, eager to please, nervous, fawning, harmless. Yet they're suffering inside, they're profoundly insulted. When their anger breaks out it's ugly, brutal, unreasonable, unstoppable; their eyes are bloodshot, they're not seeing where they're going, not seeing clearly at all. This was on display in every news bulletin coming from South Africa in 1987, as well as in the harrowing documentary which Michael Buerk assembled about his time as BBC correspondent there. What the Soweto children had started the adults were continuing, with adult violence, sometimes in the craziest way imaginable: black on black. When they gained real status, real power, these hurt, furious people – what would they be capable of then?

I've just described Shylock's journey. The Christians go to him for help because, although they need his skills as a usurer, he's essentially powerless. But then the tables turn and a terrible force is unleashed. The intended violence is nonsensical – a pound of flesh? – but the instigator is unreasonable, unstoppable.

As I prepared the role, I didn't feel haunted by Olivier's performance as I had before (though I'm glad I hadn't yet seen Henry Goodman's Shylock, quite simply the best). Together with his director, Jonathan Miller, Olivier had devised a Disraeli-type figure, thoroughly integrated in his society, immaculately dressed and accented. At the time this struck me as perversely inventive – virtually a non-Jewish Shylock – though I admired the master's instinct for avoiding a cod Petticoat Lane voice for the part. It isn't only the actor who needs to wake up every time he comes to the great roles, it's the audience too. *No, the part doesn't necessarily sound like you think; you can't just say the lines with me, can't say it in your sleep – wake up!*

Researching the ghetto in seventeenth-century Venice (our setting for the play), I discovered there was a sizeable population of Turkish Jews. This seemed good. Shylock could be very foreign, very alien. The Christians could be very racist. Especially Gratiano and the Salads. Together with the costume designer, Andreane Neofitou, I devised a

Turkish look – huge beard, long hair, vibrant purple robe – and with dialect coach Joan Washington I began practising a Turkish accent. Meanwhile, the Christians practised hitting, kicking and spitting at me. The latter for real. It's referred to in the text. And it's among the most abusive things one human being can do to another – which is odd, because it's also the juice in a kiss. During the run of *Merchant* I got to know Greg's spit rather well.

The Shylock that I was finding became an angry, violent man, not just the helpless victim. There were cries of anti-Semitism when we opened, but then there always are when you do *Merchant* (it's as guaranteed as letters of complaint from the Richard III Society), along with the customary missive from Arnold Wesker, berating Shakespeare's play, explaining why it's inferior to his own *Shylock*, and asking if you'd like to read this.

Protest of a different kind occurred during the early part of the run. On Shakespeare's birthday, 23 April, it's traditional for all the nations of the world to send a representative to Stratford, usually the cultural attaché, for the day's celebrations. There's a procession through town, a reception in a tent in the Bancroft Gardens and they see that night's show at the theatre. The 1987 Stratford company was very strong, in every sense – the other leading players were Fiona Shaw, Harriet Walter, Deborah Findlay, Brian Cox, Alun Armstrong – we were an articulate, committed and quite hot-headed group. We liked debating RSC policy and we liked calling company meetings. One of these had Shakespeare's birthday at the top of its agenda. Apartheid South Africa had seldom looked uglier than it did that year and feeling ran high about its official representative attending the theatre, our theatre, especially since the play scheduled that night was *Merchant*. It seemed absurd for a symbol of repression to come and pay homage to a writer whose trademark was compassion. We asked the RSC if the South African man could be stopped from coming, whether he could be, not to mince words, banned. The RSC management, in the form of Jenny McIntosh (Administrator) and David Brierly (General Manager), took a deep breath. They'd had trouble on this front before.

Just one season earlier Jonathan Pryce discovered that his *Macbeth* was being sponsored by Barclays Bank, who had huge South African connections, and threatened to withdraw unless the Barclays sponsorship was cancelled. It was. Now the RSC went to Stratford town hall on our behalf. The good burghers on the council, who tend to be quite conservative, were outraged. 'But we even let von Ribbentrop come!' they boasted as ultimate proof that this particular birthday party was seriously non-political. And if you stopped South Africa from attending, what about other unpopular regimes, they argued, what about China and Russia, where would it stop? The company held meetings late into the night, the mood getting angrier and angrier, a strike being considered. I volunteered to write to the South African embassy, explain our reasons and ask them, in the interests of keeping the peace, to stay away. I got a letter back from the cultural attaché, saying that he wouldn't contemplate cancelling, but that he'd be happy to meet with us while in Stratford for an exchange of views. Huh! said the company when I read out the letter, their temperature rising several degrees. The big day was getting close. All right, we said to the RSC, if we can't stop the man from coming, can we at least make a speech from the stage before the performance, registering our objections? Oh dear no, said the RSC, if you did a speech from the stage over this issue what about other ones, where would it stop? No, no, if we wanted to make a speech it would have to be during the procession through town as the South African representative passed; nobody could stop us from doing that. We could make a speech with a loud hailer from the pavement, but no speech from the stage.

Oh, really? I thought privately – even as I joined the majority voting to compromise on a pavement protest – was there really not a way? Was there not something in Shakespeare, something in the play itself? 'Hath not a Jew eyes' was too specific – any child of Uncle Nat would just take that literally, just think it was about anti-Semitism – but was there anything else?

I found out where the man was sitting. Stalls, middle of row B. Good.

When we got to the trial scene and Shylock's speech to the court –

> You have among you many a purchas'd slave
> Which like your asses, and your dogs and mules
> You use in abject and in slavish parts . . .

– I took hold of one of the court attendants, played by the Coloured actor Akim Mogaji, led him to the front of the stage, pointed directly at the South African and unleashed Shylock's venom, and ours, the company's, straight at him. I'll never forget his look of fright as he flattened himself against the seat. Theatre's magical fourth wall had suddenly shattered and someone was talking to *him*. And that someone was the man whose birthday he was here to celebrate.

Shylock was a success for me, as was Vindice in its own strange way (dear God, Tourneur's play is weird, his verse like mouthfuls of barbed wire), but Malvolio wasn't. Malvolio was a disaster. I'd played it before at Nottingham and somehow got away with it then. Not now. I made the simplest, stupidest mistake. Malvolio is the most serious of men and therein lies the comedy. Don't try to make him funny. I did.

It's not a great feeling – stuck in a role that hasn't worked. You've ended up with shit instead of art and, instead of flushing it down the pan, you endlessly present it for inspection. Blessed with fortune is the writer or painter, all hail the invention of scissors, shredder, waste basket and Microsoft invitation to EMPTY TRASH, but woe alas, the actor obeying theatre's dumbest rule: the show must go on. Why? Don't know. All your instincts are to turn and run – very, very far away – but some nonsensical code of good behaviour compels you to keep turning up for work.

Death by slow crucifixion, this was my sentence as *Twelfth Night* popped up on the schedule again and again – God, that fucking play is popular! – death by slow crucifixion, half a year long. Made worse by the excellence of the work around me: Harriet Walter as Viola, David Bradley as Aguecheek. When the season moved to London in 1988, I was finally able to part company with Malvolio. I can't say his name now without a little shiver and don't normally list him on my CV.

'I hope you don't mind but we're entering you for the Booker,' Andrew Motion said over the phone, his low, wise tone strangely apologetic today. 'Can't say I'd fancy the pressure myself, but there we are. Entering you along with our other new author, Alan Hollinghurst. His book, *The Swimming Pool Library*, will be too rude for them, though. But they might like yours.'

Chatto was feeling pleased by the reception of *Middlepost*. As was I. None of my other novels would be as welcomed by the literary establishment. Either because they're not very good, which others must judge, or because of something in the British character that disapproves of people having more than one career (this is surely the only country where you can insult someone by calling them too clever by half). But I was allowed in the first time round. I was widely reviewed. This may sound like the natural right of any book, yet isn't; most fiction is ignored, which is effectively death at birth. *Middlepost* was long-listed for the Booker, its paperback rights were sold to Sceptre for a record £115,000 (record for a first novel at the time), sold also to Knopf in America, and translated into French, German, Italian and Greek. Even the South Africans liked it. Well, the press did – not the family. 'I found it hard going,' commented one Sher. 'Not a book I'd've taken out at the library,' remarked another. 'We thought it would be about the *real* Middlepost,' a third said plaintively.

South Africa continued to dominate my life in 1988. Shylock at the Barbican was joined by Johnnie at the Almeida – my chance at last to do the play that so affected me as an eighteen-year-old: *Hello and Goodbye*, Fugard's two-hander about a poor white brother and sister. Fellow South African RSC player Estelle Kohler was Hester and we were powerfully directed by Janice Honeyman (from the Civic Theatre, Joburg), whom I'd known as a kid. Johnnie is semi-illiterate, defenceless, a recluse. I based him on Alfonso, the *blougat* at Walvis camp who was so viciously persecuted by the *oumanne* that he ended up wandering around senseless in the desert and had to be discharged from the army. A lot of stuff in *Hello and Goodbye* overlapped with my own life. I felt raw, in a good way. But this was just the beginning. Then came *Two Dogs and Freedom*.

The title is taken from a remark by a six-year-old boy in Soweto: 'When I am old I would like to have a wife and two children, a boy and a girl, and a big house, and two dogs and freedom.'

It was just a charity show, just a fund-raiser, just one of those Sunday night events at Sadler's Wells, with dozens of celebs doing their turns to an enthusiastic, partisan and very rich audience. But it had a profound effect on me. It was the first time I got to meet the group of South African exiles in London, white and black. In fact, it was the first time I was properly meeting any black South Africans.

The poet Mongane Serote, the writer Mandla Langa, the musician Jonas Gwangwa, his manager Dali Tambo, the singer Ndonda Khuze. For one reason or another they'd fled South Africa; Mandla's brother had been murdered by the police, Dali was the son of Oliver Tambo, President of the ANC, forced to operate in exile. All were living in London now, yet aching for home – aching for the soil but not the system – aching constantly – it was like a pulse coming off them. They were tired, their skin quite grey from too many British winters; they smoked, they drank, some very heavily. When they came along to the organising committee meetings – and they didn't always; we were sometimes embarrassingly white – they had a strange, distant look in their eyes, almost of amusement. Here they were, joining in discussions about costumes and lighting, programmes and dressing rooms; they really were very far away from home. They saw the humour in it. I liked that in them; it surprised me.

'Them.'

I'm talking like my family. 'Them.' An arm's-length word. Well, yes. Apartheid – separate development – was a very effective form of brain-washing. The alphabet goes ABC, two and two makes four, white and black are different. Us and 'them'.

No question, it was strange sitting round a table with 'them' at last. I felt relief.

Two Dogs was the brainchild of Ethel de Keyser, who ran BDAF – the British Defence and Aid Fund, set up to provide education and legal fees for people in need back home. Ethel was herself an exile, sister of the freedom fighter Jack Tarshish. Short, round, with black hair and wide, smiling, almost Oriental features, Ethel was a tireless campaigner. From morning till night – smoking, clutching a mug of coffee, moving round the BDAF offices with her punchy little walk – she found ways of raising funds for her cause. People mostly said no to her. This was not a word she knew. Eventually they said yes. It was Ethel who approached me to help organise the show. I said no. And then yes.

Greg came on board as director (before joining the RSC as an actor, he'd already been associate director at Nottingham Playhouse) and my (then) agent Sally Hope acted as casting director. The rest of the committee were South African: among them, Mandla, Ndonda, the publicist Joy Sapieka who handled the media, and the documentary film maker Jon Blair who persuaded Channel 4 to film the event. The cast that assembled to do scenes, poems, musical numbers, or speeches was an eclectic mix; as well as the black performers already named, the others included Pieter Dirk-Uys, Bob Hoskins, Trevor Huddleston, the Kinnocks, Harold Pinter, Rudolph Walker, Janet Suzman, Stephen Fry and Spitting Image. We played Sadler's Wells on 23 October and raised £45,000 for BDAF.

I have four abiding memories of the evening. Mandla Langa introducing his poem about the death of his brother; he has a strange humble smile as he talks. Albie Sachs walking on stage at the end of the scene from David Edgar's *Jail Diary of Albie Sachs*, to hug the actor who's just played him, Roger Rees; Albie can do neither thing easily, walk or hug; this is just seven months after the South African Secret Service car bomb in Maputo which tore off one arm, blinded one eye and damaged his balance – yet he's smiling too, lifting his good arm in celebration. The huge figure of Albertina Sisulu (wife of Walter, still in prison) seeking out Greg backstage, kissing him, lifting him off the ground. Myself at the curtain call, the final chorus of '*NKosi Sikelel'i* – I'm towards the back of the huge crowd, hoping that the Channel 4 cameras can't find me; I'm crying; partly because of the show and partly because I don't yet know the words of this song, 'their' song.

I have an impression of being on the sidelines, in the wings, as major events occur, just catching glimpses, a Rosencrantz–Guildenstern impression – I'm Rosenstern perhaps, the Jewish cousin.

Driving up to Scotland after Christmas, I see the crater of the Lockerbie crash; a sight shockingly familiar from the TV news, now a passing view from a car window, going, going, gone. I'm in Scotland to devise a film with Richard Wilson, him directing, me writing. Eventually it'll be called *Changing Step*. Taking a WWI VAD hospital as its theme, it's a Joint Stock-type project; we begin with a long workshop, then I write the script, then we shoot the film. In all, Richard and I spend about three months living and working with a large group of disabled people – for the injured soldiers are being played by real amputees. Some of the guys have lost limbs through motorbike accidents, or cancer, or were born that way. They nickname us 'People with more than the average number of limbs'. The experience is unique and humbling. I think back to my research for *Richard III* and blush – just a Rosenstern glimpse from the sidelines. A double-leg amputee gets pissed one night and tells me he thought the show was an insult – not to the real king, but to the disabled – but now that he's got to know me he's coming round to the idea that I'm OK.

1989. I turn forty. The whole world feels like its changing. Students slaughtered in Tiananmen Square, the Berlin Wall comes down, Poland, Hungary and Czechoslovakia ditch Communism, Ceaucescu is executed, Khomeini slams the fatwa on Rushdie, Olivier dies . . .

You watch television thinking, can all this be happening at the same time, just in one year, my fortieth, am I really living through this? Well, no, not quite – I'm just sitting in front of the telly.

In South Africa, Botha resigns, de Klerk takes over, an election is called. Uncle Nat wins outright – surprise, surprise – and on the same day the police kill twenty-three people in the Cape townships. This is followed by a massive anti-apartheid march through Cape Town city centre, the biggest in thirty years. There are rumours of secret government meetings with Mandela.

And I'm in Stratford, doing a play about England. *Singer* by Peter Flannery. A searing epic play about post-war Britain – the best modern play I've ever done. Directed by Terry Hands. My character, Peter Singer, is based on a notorious 1950s figure, Peter Rachman. Jewish, born in Poland, a concentration camp survivor, Rachman turned into a pitiless slum landlord in Notting Hill, exploiting the new West Indian immigrants, then was marginally involved in the Profumo scandal – just marginally, a Rosenstern too – and died youngish, of a sudden heart attack. Or did he? There were rumours of 'a disappearance'. Peter Flannery takes this option. Singer lives on into the sixties and seventies, confronts his past – specifically a guard from the concentration camp – and ends up in the eighties, reformed, working among the homeless (now like Profumo himself), but wooed by Thatcher's far-right brigade. It's the ultimate persecuted-to-persecutor story, except that it goes in a sort of circle and there is redemption at the end. Right up my street. I shave my head to the bone for the concentration camp scene and then keep it like that: he is prisoner turned skinhead. I put on weight: he has survived and now he is Walking Appetite – women and wealth mostly. He is victim turned monster turned avenging angel turned lost old man. It's the part of a lifetime and I go for it with arms outstretched. Like several recent projects, *Merchant* and *Hello and Goodbye*, this isn't just theatre any more, this is very personal.

I'm not living in Chipping this time, but Stratford, on Welcombe Road, in the house that's to become home from home. The living room has a huge window with a huge view: a beautiful, untidy meadow, sloping down to a vista of Warwickshire trees and fields. I rearrange the furniture and set up my desk here, working on a new novel. Jim comes for some weekends, Greg for others. Sometimes we're all in the house together, Jim and his new lover, a beautiful young Turk, myself and Greg. It all feels very grown-up, very sensible.

(Well, to me it did. I think – no, I *know* – the situation was sometimes less comfortable, more painful for everyone else. It's about status again. We all entered into this complicated arrangement together, yet for reasons of status, professional status, I ended up in the strongest position, the one calling the tune, the one feeling secure. The others were sometimes frustrated or even frightened by our wobbly structure of incomplete relationships. We were like a team of acrobats balancing one another. If the heap tumbled, I could be fairly sure of ending up with a partner. Not everyone could say the same. I feel uncomfortable with this now, but at the time I was simply enjoying myself too much. Having my cake and eating it.)

I was alone in Welcombe Road, can't remember why (maybe both Jim and Greg just got pissed off and left me to it), when the big day finally came:

11/2/90. Spoke to Mom on the phone this morning. She said, 'Our fears are that they'll want everything.' I kept shtum. It was OK for them, the whites, to have everything; still no question about that, no apology, no connections made. Anyway, I then settled down in front of the TV. A clear, cold winter day here, baking summer weather there, that lovely dustiness. He was late, by several hours. We all sat and watched and waited, right round the world. The last time we all sat down to do this together was the first moon landing in 1969: waiting for one man to walk across a pale, unremarkable stretch of dirt. I remember me and Maggie in our little Notting Hill flat, hunched in front of the telly through the night. I remember thinking, the whole world's doing this – except South Africa, where TV wasn't allowed. Now it's South Africa we're all watching. When he finally appeared it was quite confusing – a muddle of cars, bodyguards and ANC people – and at first disappointing. We weren't going to get the solitary figure coming down the road, walking free. But then it was his walk itself that started to intrigue. An American commentator said he walked like he didn't trust the ground. And that's exactly right. Slow, stiff-legged, a slight bounce on each step. I thought of Neil Armstrong again. This was a giant leap for mankind too. Who'd've thought it possible? A remarkably calm expression on his face – first at the gates of Victor Verster Prison, later making a speech in glowing yellow light outside Cape Town's City Hall (where the Eisteddfod was held) – a strangely calm expression. I suppose in prison you see less people, react to less, the muscles of your face grow stiller. The whole world was moved by what was happening, but he wasn't. After three decades in prison this was peanuts.

Later, rang home again. Wasn't sure if they would've watched. They had. And Mom had changed her tune: 'He has great dignity. Someone said he looks reborn. There's actually a feeling of hope – for the first time in years.' Meanwhile Dad had his own distinctive take on it – 'You know why he was so late coming out? He was tipping the staff.'

Still the Rosenstern feeling persists. Even with *Singer*. I'm at the very heart of *Singer*, I'm never off stage in *Singer*, I am *Singer*! And yet . . .

22/3/90. A bizarre night. First performance of *Singer* in the Pit. Vaclav Havel is on a quick official visit to London, and through two RSC connections – Roger Michell who directed Havel's play *Temptations*, and our production photographer, Ivan Kyncl, who was in prison with him – has been persuaded to stay on an extra night to see us. The house was sold out, but Terry H. has managed to reclaim, call back, forty tickets! Now it's a big RSC-promotion night. As well as Havel in the audience, there's Dame Peg, B. Levin, M. Bragg, J. Bakewell, Arts Council man P. Palumbo, Tory Arts Minister Richard Luce and the Kinnocks. Ordinary members of the public are here too, expecting just to see *Singer*'s first London preview, but instead they find themselves at Madame Tussaud's. Things are fine to start with. Auschwitz and Immigration are dark scenes – even darker tonight since the *Newsnight* cameraman leapt on stage during Havel's arrival, dislodging one of our footlights – but then we reach Bayswater, 'a sunny street in London' and all concentration is lost. The audience can see one another in the Pit and we're no match. Every mention of imprisonment is checked with a little glance to Havel, while all the Thatcher stuff is checked with Kinnock.

Afterwards there's a big reception upstairs in the Barbican Conservatory, for all Britain's playwrights to meet the playwright who became president. They're everywhere you look – Pinter,

Wesker, Hampton, Brenton, N. Wright, D. Lan, Ronnie Harwood too, several more. I feel hopelessly upstaged. We've just given our first performance and I've yet to meet a single person who saw it. Wesker says to me, 'So what happened here tonight – did Havel see a performance of *Temptation?*'

RSC Chairman, Sir Geoffrey Cass, takes me across to meet Havel. He's been up since dawn on official engagements and looks it. His tiredness gives him a slightly shifty air. He glances over my shoulder as we talk, and chain-smokes. Small hands, heavy head. Afterwards I kick myself for my actor's hubris. Instead of saying something like, 'Congratulations on what's happened in Czechoslovakia!' I said, 'So what did you think of the show?' He admits he was too tired to enjoy it and the strain of listening to a foreign language didn't help. He speaks of his frustration, as a writer, of only being able to speak basic English, 'like a child!'. When Ivan Kyncl talks to him in Czech, he changes, becoming bright, humorous, energised. But for the rest of the time the playwright has to play president. And it's boring hard work, meeting endless strangers, trying to make conversation in a language you don't properly speak.

The next month Mandela came to London.

A concert was held at Wembley Stadium, a follow-up to the Mandela Seventieth Birthday Concert of 1988. This time the Man Himself was guest of honour. Ethel de Keyser offered tickets, so Greg and I went along. Neither of us had been to Wembley before. Going up the ramp, we felt part of a pilgrimage; the multitudes, the incline, the stadium against the sky – it all induced a sensation of participating in something heroic and exalted. I guess this is the buzz football fans get every week. But once inside, the scale started to overwhelm me. It felt more Nuremberg-like. Although in VIP seats, we were still several continents away from the stage and couldn't see a thing. Except on the TV screen. Which we could've watched at home. Retreating to the VIP lounge, we bumped into the Kinnocks. Neil said, 'Ooh Christ, look here now, they're letting in all minorities!' He was in very twinkly mood: 'Best quote of the day so far is from Trevor Huddleston. Jesse Jackson has been driving him nuts. The good Reverend keeps looking for "photo opportunities", keeps leaning in to Nelson and Winnie every time someone lifts a camera in their direction. Finally Trevor could stand it no more, turned to us and said, "Oh will no one rid me of this troublesome priest?"'

There was, disappointingly, no sign of Mandela himself in the VIP room, but during that same 1990 visit a reception was held for him in Mayfair, and I went along again:

17/4/90. Early evening do at the home of Commonwealth Secretary-General, Sir Shridath Ramphal. Guests all wearing badges, colour-coded, relating to different rooms. I was Ethel de Keyser's guest. Wonderful image of her badgering Robert Maxwell for a BDAF donation. Her diminutive figure barely reached up to his belt. He was peering down with a strained expression: a fat man trying to see his toes. I spent much of the evening with Donald Woods, he of Biko friendship and *Cry Freedom* fame. A humorous, charming man, a listener. After a while he got fed up with the colour coding of this party. 'It's apartheid!' he said, laughing. 'Shall we try and find the Man Himself, try and say hello?' I was amazed. Donald hadn't yet shaken him by the hand. We wandered up and down stairs, through different rooms. Famous opponents of apartheid everywhere. Over there Jesse Jackson again, with bodyguards – a team of black giants – and over here, yes, the equally tall yet infinitely more discreet figure of Archbishop Huddleston. As we squeezed through one crowd, Winnie Mandela's face suddenly loomed into view. She smiled at us in a way that was both automatic (directed at two more strangers in the room) and very piercing. By which I mean that her natural look – her beauty, the clarity in her skin and eyes, no hint of the wild drinker or the torturer of Stompie Seipei – this is phenomenal. Maybe intensifed by our tabloid knowledge of her other lives. Finally we saw another head towering above those round him – the Man Himself. We pushed close. Donald stepped forward and addressed him in Xhosa. Mandela's face lit up, then he replied in Xhosa and embraced Donald. I heard Mandela say in English, 'Oh my friend, thank you for all you've done.' I felt a pleasurable surge of Rosensternitis, witnessing the first meeting between these two famous South Africans, and was so moved that I can't remember how Donald then introduced me. Anyway, I shook hands with Mandela. What can I say? It was better than meeting Olivier.

THE LITTLE FELLA

OVIES? I'VE NOT been too lucky there yet. It remains another world, an Overseas I can't reach. There was *Alive and Kicking*, scripted by Martin Sherman, directed by Nancy Meckler, with Jason Flemyng as a beautiful young dancer who has AIDS and me as a plump, boozy AIDS counsellor; a love story with the oddest of couples and trickiest of themes. It was intensely satisfying to work on, one of the best jobs of my life yet its reception was disappointing. My other leading role on celluloid was also scripted by a playwright – Snoo Wilson's *Shadey* – and here again the film was deemed to have not quite made it. There's been a semi-lead as Disraeli in *Mrs Brown*, which very definitely did make it, for all concerned, including myself – winning the *Evening Standard* Peter Sellers award. There's been a cameo in a mega-hit, *Shakespeare in Love*, a strong supporting role in a good low-budget movie, *Young Poisoner's Handbook*, and fun parts in two Terry Jones movies, *Erik the Viking* and *Wind in the Willows*. But what of the ones that got away?

A life is made up of some highlights – I wrote *Year of the King* about one – and some other times that are sent to test us. Here is *Month of the Tramp*.

Saturday, 3 November 1990. Susie Figgis [casting director] phoned Sally [my agent] yesterday to say Richard Attenborough wants to see me for his Chaplin film, and would I go and see him this morning? Impossible, with two shows today: the last *Singers*. So then

Attenborough offered to come to me. We meet at the Barbican at twelve. He arrives in a lime-green Rolls, dressed in thick jumper and anorak-waistcoat as though on location. He is, as people always say, very decent, very warm, very old-school theatrical. When I mention meeting Donald Woods (the subject of *Cry Freedom*) and witnessing his first encounter with Mandela, Attenborough's eyes start to fill. So that's true about him too. We get down to business. He tells me that all Hollywood wants to play Chaplin. Robin Williams, Billy Crystal; '. . . Dustin too, of course, and one might be tempted if he was ten years younger'. He produces a photo album, with shots of Chaplin alongside contemporary stars. Tom Cruise bears a striking resemblance to the young Charlie. The photo of Robin Williams has been doctored, adding Tramp make-up. 'Doesn't really work, does it?' says Attenborough. 'I'm testing him anyway, next week. But what d'you think of this –?' Billy Crystal as the Tramp; an excellent resemblance. But why am I being shown this and invited to comment? Has Susie Figgis been fired – is he looking for a new casting director? I gradually work it out. Susie has warned him that I don't like auditioning and he's trying to whet my appetite. The budget of the film has just gone up to $30 million, he says, and he's not sure if Universal will back an unknown. 'But I'd like, my dear, if I may, to mention your name to the head of Universal when I'm in LA next week – he's a great theatregoer, he'll know who you are – and then when I get back, I'd like, if you wouldn't find this too presumptuous, to put some slap on your face and turn a camera on you.' A *test*? With all the connotations of that word. I hum and haw, and start talking availability. I'm well into negotiations with the National – to do Brecht's *Arturo Ui* there. 'I thought Mick wanted you too,' says Attenborough, referring to his son. Yes, Michael Attenborough and Adrian Noble keep trying to talk about me coming back to Stratford instead. Laughing, Attenborough suggests that maybe he could lead me on with Chaplin, cause me to lose the National and then let his son pick up the pieces. Ah, an Attenborough conspiracy. At this rate I could end up on a lush green mountainside whispering to some gorillas.

Tuesday, 6 November. In between writing, writing, writing, racing to finish *Indoor Boy*, I catch myself glancing in mirrors, examining my wrinkles, pulling my face taut like some ageing starlet. Apparently the film requires Chaplin to go from twenty to eighty. Could I do twenty? I find a documentary on our video shelves, *Unknown Chaplin*, which has previously unseen footage of out-takes, home movies, etc. Jesus, it's not his age that's the problem. It's his dinkiness. He's a mere sliver of a man, a little scribble, a doodle. And ugh, all that weight I put on for *Singer*!

Unexpectedly, Richard Eyre rings from the National. They want to add to my *Arturo* season. Berkoff is directing his version of Kafka's *Trial*. Would I play K?

Um . . .?

Monday, 12 November. Susie Figgis phones. Attenborough's producer has just rung her from the States to report that they haven't found a Chaplin and that Attenborough is on his way home. Susie winds up with: 'Just wanted you to know that.'

'What are you telling me?'

'Nothing.'

Wednesday, 14 November. Berkoff's dockland flat. Strange to see him again. He's aged. Thicker round the middle (like someone else I know) and the skinhead cut is silvery, catching the light and reminding me of broken glass topping a wall. What are the status readings here? Ex-teacher with ex-pupil. Famous–notorious performer–director–writer with leading RSC actor and sometimes novelist. Today we both play very low numbers, constantly deferring to one another. I like his adaptation of *The Trial* – a nightmare stream of consciousness that's very close to the heart of the book – but what will he be like as a director? Trouble is, he keeps getting up to demonstrate sections – playing everybody – and is so bloody brilliant I just sit there gawping. The phone rings. It's Sally. *How did she track me down?* I ask Berkoff to say I'll ring back. Later, when he goes to the loo, I do. Sally says, 'Are you still at Steven's?' When I whisper yes, she says, 'It'd be better if you weren't.' I make my excuses and leave. Back at home the news is that Attenborough wants me to read the Chaplin script as quickly as possible – his chauffeur's bringing it round in the morning. Do we tell the National anything yet? I ask. There's nothing to tell them, replies Sally breezily (but excited) – 'You may hate it.' Yes, that's it – I'll hate it. Attenborough's films are sometimes a bit heroic for my taste and anyway Chaplin was never that interesting a character. Never a Garland or a Clift. Just endlessly successful.

Thursday, 15 November. Oh dear. The script's good, very good. Hardly surprising – it's by William Boyd. Chaplin *is* interesting. And complicated (his thing for young girls) and dark (his ruthlessness with ditched girls) and, above all, moving (his return to London, and later to Hollywood, after exile in Switzerland). A man divorced from his past, a man 'going back, going home' – all rather familiar, rather enticing. And let's face it, Chaplin was one of my childhood heroes. In adult life I've grown to prefer Keaton, but Chaplin still has a powerful hold on my heart. Oh fuck. I ring Attenborough and ask him to square with me. Before Sally can say anything to the National, I have to know where I stand in the running. With surprising candour he tells me. There are currently four of us, and he takes me through the pros and cons of each.

Tom Hulce. Star of *Amadeus*. Perhaps the favourite, but hasn't been able to do a test yet. Stuck in Moscow, filming.

Andy Garcia. Star of *Godfather III*. A stunning actor, but very broad-built and very Italian.

Matthew Broderick. Best lookalike for the young Chaplin, but can he play the old man?

Antony Sher. 'Very good full-face, but the profile isn't ideal. While Chaplin had a "strong nose" it's not as strong as yours, my dear. Your shoulders and chest are a bit of a worry too. On the other hand, you have an authority the others can't match. Well, Andy Garcia maybe, he is . . . very, very good.'

We decide to go for a test.

Attenborough promises to try and arrange this within a week. 'And then my dear, if you and I are both certain, I won't test the others – and the part is yours.'

So. Dear God. I'm going to try for it. Feel a terrible sense of struggle over this. The risk of *rejection*. But strangely enough, I feel inspired by something Berkoff writes in his introduction to *The Trial*: 'What is K's alias Kafka's guilt? Nothing so complex as world guilt . . . but the guilt of betraying *his* inner spirit to the safety of mediocrity. For every action that is not expressed through fear . . . for every venture not ventured on.'

Friday, 16 November. 'We can't possibly tell Berkoff – he'll blow,' says Jenny McIntosh (National Executive Director) when she and I finally get to speak personally. 'And anyway, maybe by next week there'll be nothing to tell him.' Jenny isn't as pissed off as I expected. Says: 'After what I've just done in my life' – suddenly leaving the RSC to join the National – 'how can I condemn you? There are times when you have to grab chances. As a director of the National I hope you don't get Chaplin. As Jenny McIntosh I hope you do.' Then Richard Eyre rings. He's calm too. 'Let's save recriminations till next week.' Reckons I'm favourite in Attenborough's list of four and adds, 'If it was just a BBC film I'd be furious, but this . . . this is irresistible, isn't it?'

Saturday, 17 November. Very, very edgy. *Chaplin*'s costume designer, John Mollo, rings. We'll go to Angels on Monday, knock together a Tramp outfit. He asks for my measurements. Oh, the humiliation of saying these aloud. I've been dieting for the last few days, but it's pointless. Another actor would've dieted since Attenborough first came to the Barbican. Another actor would've spent the time preparing some breathtaking Chaplinesque routine. But something in me stops me from really going for it. Fear of rejection? Maybe. I also have a real desire to do the National season. Because it's safe? Well, it isn't really. Working with Berkoff is going to be, well, a challenge. And I have an appointment to play Arturo – it's never easy when you come to those.

Jim's away on the RSC tour of *Shrew*, Greg assistant-directing in Stratford – so I'm here on my own. Haven't told the family about Tuesday's test. I dare not. It'll add to the pressure. When I mentioned the initial Attenborough meeting to Mom, I hadn't even finished the story when she said, 'I knew it – I always knew you'd play Chaplin!'

'But I'm not,' I protested. 'He just showed me this photo album of–'

'It's incredible, I *always* knew you'd play Chaplin!'

I told her to shut up eventually.

By a strange coincidence she rings today. With shocking news. Dad was mugged yesterday. Quite badly. Fourteen stitches in his head. They'd popped into 'a slightly rough part of town' where her dressmaker lives. While Mom went in, Dad strolled along the pavement window-shopping. Two young Coloured guys attacked him from behind – an easy target, the shrunken body, the thin neck and arms – and grabbed his wallet. He tried to resist. Ended up falling backwards, smashing his head on the kerb. By the time Mom returned, his shirt was red with blood. She's not squeamish, but this got to her. In the ambulance they had to change places so that she could lie down. When they got home after the hospital, Katie wept – 'Why must this happen to Master?' Hearing the story, I start to get upset too. Dad – that strong angry man – felled. (And I can hear them thinking: it's started, they let that man walk free and now it's started.) Mom hands the phone over. Dad sounds very listless. None of the old humour. I ask what the police reckon. He says they haven't bothered to report it: 'There's no point.' I'm tempted to tell him about the screen test. It would cheer him up – he loves Chaplin – but I can't risk it, can't risk her excitement.

Sunday, 18 November. Don't know if it's what happened to Dad, but I'm feeling very bleak. Keep watching *Unknown Chaplin* (quite an apt title currently) and keep thinking this is just stupid, there is just no way I can achieve his fucking dinkiness. And Attenborough is determined to use real Chaplin footage alongside the actor. Must cancel the test. Or else the only Charlie that's going to get made is me of myself. (And talking of Charlie, what a pity I'm being 'good' at the moment.) Heading to the phone when it rings. Attenborough. 'How are you?' he asks. Nothing for it but to tell the truth. I'm cancelling. 'Ohhh,' he goes. He agrees my physical resemblance to the real man is a problem, but is hoping my acting will compensate, 'My son Mick says you're quite a chameleon.' He urges me to reconsider, think about it overnight. But the test will cost quite a lot – it needs a crew of about thirty – and if we're cancelling, he needs to know tomorrow morning. He's on a reccy in the East End first thing, will ring from the car at about eight.

Monday, 19 November. Haven't slept. Stuck in my mind: *Guilt. For every action that is not expressed through fear, for every venture not ventured on.* When Attenborough rings, I say, 'Look, I've tried thinking about it overnight, but there's nothing to think about. It's a purely physical thing. I'll either look like him when I get into the gear or not. So let's go for it.' He's pleased. I add: 'In fact, I'll probably know at the costume fitting this afternoon.' He says he'll be at William Boyd's. Asks me to ring there and report. He could still pay off the crew and cancel the test.

Now Terry Clegg (co-producer) phones to finalise arrangements for tomorrow. 'By the way, do you have any actors in mind for the scene?'

'The scene?'

'Scene 94. Hasn't Dickie told you?'

'No! He said you'd just get me into the gear and turn the cameras on me.'

'Oh, no. We'll have to hear you talk.'

(TALK? How the fuck does Chaplin talk?)

I ring Sally and ask her to find two friendly clients, preferably ones I know.

At 2.30 I go to Angels, Shaftesbury Avenue. John Mollo is a kind, rosy-cheeked man. We're in one of those little fitting rooms with mirrors all around. No escaping a dozen images of flab as I undress. On the floor are neat piles of Little Fella kit, including bowlers and canes. I put on one of the waistcoats. The deep-cut armholes reduce my shoulders – an optical illusion – and then a miraculous little jacket seems to dispense with them altogether. Things are looking up. Add a bowler and cane, and suddenly the mirror returns the first good news. As I talk, I hear my voice catch with excitement. John says, 'Well, we're clearly going ahead with tomorrow, aren't we?' Someone pops in and asks him for a word. Left alone, I dare to do the walk, the shrugs, the twitches. Encouraging.

At home, I ring Attenborough. He says, 'I hear you're thin as a rake.' (Oh of course – when John was called out of the fitting room at Angels – it was Dickie on the phone.) He tells me to sleep well.

Tuesday, 20 November. Wake surprisingly calm. The feeling persists when the car picks me up at 10.30. But then, halfway to Shepperton,

I start to experience a strange, quiet panic. It's like going back to square one. Like going to school for the first time, or into the army, or a drama school audition. Like you've got no experience to help you through the ordeal ahead. Mind you, every first performance in the theatre feels like that too. This thought provides comfort. Yes, I'm frightened, but it's a bracing kind of feeling. How many people in other jobs get challenged like this again and again? I stare out at the crowds in the streets. I'm going to try and be Charlie Chaplin in a few hours' time, I think. It's a scary, risky, possibly dumb thing to do, but it might make me a film star. That's what's happening to me today. What's happening to you?

At Shepperton I'm taken through the sound stage we'll be using (cold, vast, dark, emptier than an empty theatre) and into a make-up room. The wig lady is Steph, the make-up man is Wally. He's a real old hand, yet there's a moment after Steph has put on the wig, and he adds the moustache – just briefly, just to measure it – a moment when I see his face light up. Like at Angels yesterday a palpable excitement goes through the air. This *is* possible. We start at 11.30 and work straight through, munching at sandwiches, till about 2. We're just finishing, when I hear Wally say, 'Hello, sir!' I spin the chair round. Attenborough is standing in the door. He claps his hands and roars with pleasure. 'I think he likes it,' I say to Wally and Steph. Behind Attenborough are a clutch of colleagues, all peering in, all looking pleased.

Now a long wait while they light the studio. I climb into the costume and toddle up and down the corridor, Chaplin-style. I've brought along my Polaroid camera and someone takes a batch of shots. I sit staring at them. They're good. From some angles, very good.

Arrival of the two actors who're doing the scene: Ian Gelder and Chris Burgess. They come into my dressing room and make encouraging noises about 'the look'. But when we try doing the scene I'm so nervous I can't remember a line. They stare at me wide-eyed, knowing, as only actors can, what I'm going through. They're terrifically patient and helpful. We go through the scene again and again, me starting to relax – or at any rate, *using* my fear. The scene is one where Syd and Rollie try and persuade Chaplin to go into talkies.

He's terrified of talkies. 'It's not about talking,' he says, 'it's about feeling.'

At last the moment has come. Attenborough fetches me personally and walks me, arm in arm, on to the sound stage. Instead of people stopping to stare, nobody interrupts their work. But they all sneak glances (it's like doing a nude scene) and the glances are warm.

We work for about three hours. At one point, Attenborough asks me just to clown around in long shot, while he cranks the camera up or down, whichever it is, and this feels terrible – I knew I should've prepared a routine – but the big scene itself goes well. Chaplin is talking about feeling and the real thing is flowing. Attenborough is very meticulous and keen to teach. A lot of advice about eyes, not blasting with the eyes. Brings over a mirror and photos of Chaplin: 'See – there's never white showing above the pupils. Ben had the same problem when we did *Gandhi*. Too much with the eyes at first.'

'Well, he'd just come from trying to reach the back of the same theatres as me.'

'Exactly.'

At last it's over. Huge warmth, huge support from everyone around. I guess they were all nervous too. Attenborough is beaming and kisses me. He invites me to see the rushes tomorrow. He wants me to be part of the decision making. I tell him I'll have to see if I've got any courage left for that.

But this isn't a good enough excuse for Sally when I talk it through with her. She challenges me, as always (it's why she's such a good agent): 'You're forever saying actors should be treated as grown-ups. Well, that's what this invitation is about.'

Wednesday, 21 November. Shepperton's little viewing theatre is packed. Key figures from the production, William Boyd too. Attenborough makes me sit next to him and occasionally gives an encouraging squeeze of the hand. My reactions as I watch the rushes are directly opposite to when I filmed them. The big scene embarrasses me – I look horribly stout, and the emotional stuff, although for real, seems OTT, one eyebrow jerking about like a dying black worm – whereas the clowning in long shot, with camera speeded up, is surprisingly convincing. The rushes end, rather cruelly, with a clip from *The Gold Rush*. Then the lights come back on. Everyone sits in silence. Attenborough leans close: 'Come, let's go and have a chat.'

We pace round the car park. To my surprise he's buzzing with excitement. He's particularly pleased with the vulnerability I showed. He knows I can do the other stuff and he wants it ('Charlie must have balls'), but wasn't sure if I could move him. Says I did. Feels that with a bit of weight loss, with some special teeth (to create that simian Chaplin smile), and with careful shooting, 'You're a runner.'

He wants to assemble the scene properly, send it out to LA, and promises an answer by Friday. In the meantime he offers to ring Richard Eyre personally and ask him to wait till then.

Says he's going up to Scotland – they have a house there – and will ring me at seven.

I drive back from Shepperton with Susie Figgis. She confesses that, like me, her heart sank in some shots. But reports that Diana Hawkins (associate producer) and William Boyd were both thrilled. Says her biggest worry is the Friday deadline. Thinks Universal will say, yes, promising, but you must test some others too.

Attenborough doesn't ring this evening. Which is funny.

Thursday, 22 November. Damn them. They've made me *want* it now. A long day. Rain on the roof of my conservatory study. Keep waiting for the phone to ring. Distract myself sketching the *Indoor Boy* cover. The phone goes! Greg: 'Sorry, only me, but have you heard the news? Thatcher's resigned.' For the rest of the day I keep the TV on, half watching as events unfold: her going to Buckingham Palace, then doing PM's Question Time. I warm to her for the first time. Moments of spontaneity and vulnerability, and neither are normally in her range when she plays that strange automaton character. It always amazed me that the public fell for it, but they often fall for bad acting. Talking of which, no word all day on the test. Or whether Attenborough has spoken to Eyre. How do Sally and I proceed without knowing? In the evening I ring Susie. She says she doesn't think there's anything sinister in Attenborough not phoning from Scotland, but no, she can't give me his number there; she's not sure if they have a phone. Oh, is that really likely?

Friday, 23 November. Nobody rings. By midday Sally and I are getting very jumpy. There are perhaps good reasons for this odd new silence from Attenborough (he was phoning five times a day before the test), but I can smell it, the silence, smell it turning bad. Fed up, I ring Attenborough's secretary in London and she says *of course* they have a phone in Scotland. Within fifteen minutes Attenborough rings me. At first he's slightly defensive – 'My dear, didn't we agree there'd be nothing to report till 6.30 today after Universal see the test?' – but then he comes clean. He's had second thoughts. It's my profile. It's just not Chaplin's. And he can't see how he'll shoot a two-and-a-half-hour movie without showing it. It's controllable in close-ups but not in group scenes. He says anyway let's wait to see what Universal think. I say but if *you're* not sure it doesn't matter what they think. Taking a deep breath, I tell him that Sally has to speak to the National today; she'll tell them that there'll be a definite answer by 6.30 and that it's probably going to be in their favour. Taking a deep breath too, Attenborough says, 'Yes.'

I feel odd. Calm. Not upset. Just a bit shocked that he's done quite a U-turn since Wednesday. Maybe he was so excited to have found *a* Chaplin rather than *the* Chaplin, he overreacted. Maybe also, as Susie keeps saying, he hungers to repeat the *Gandhi* experience: moulding a theatre actor into a film star.

He rings back at 6.30 prompt. The Universal chiefs watched the test first thing their time. He reports: 'They said, "Shit what an actor!" – which I assume means they think you're good – but couldn't go with you till I've tested some others. By which time it'll be too late for you, won't it?'

'Yes.'

He says he's devastated, yet sounds relieved. I understand this. Universal have confirmed his reservations, like everyone has confirmed mine. We thank one another for the week and wish well for our separate projects.

Later Greg points out that Thatcher and I are both Geminians, and have both had similar weeks: a mini-triumph halfway through (she won the first round of the leadership ballot, I did the test rather well), but ditched by the end. 'And you've both taken it rather well.'

Sunday, 25 November. Ring home. Dad sounds chirpier. The humour's back ('I hear you're feeling better,' I say – 'So they tell me,' he replies), but he gets confused when now, at last, I tell him about the screen test: 'You're playing Charlie Chaplin – hell's bells!'

'No, I'm not.'

'Hang on, I'll hand you over to your mother.'

She has difficulty understanding as well, or refuses to. I'm reporting a failure and this isn't something she can ever let me be. I try to explain: 'It was my nose. My nose was too big.'

'There are false noses,' she cries. 'Why not wear a false nose?'

'How can a false nose make a big nose smaller?'

'Oh, tsk,' she replies impatiently. 'In films they can do anything!'

'Mom!'

'Anyway,' she says, calmer now, 'I always knew you'd play Charlie Chaplin.'

'But I'm not!'

'Hm,' she comments in that way of hers, as though she still knows best. And of course, as always, she's right. I *did* play Charlie Chaplin. For about two minutes. Attenborough has the footage and I have the Polaroids – tucked deeply into my 1990 diary.

Postscript. 11/4/91. Bumped into Ben Kingsley in the Green Room at the National. Told him the story. As I was describing Attenborough's excitement after the rushes Ben said, 'That's interesting. You see, when he saw mine he just went very, very quiet.'

Ah.

JOSEPH K., ADOLF H. AND UNCLE V.

BERKOFF'S BACK!
   I somehow have a picture of this scrawled over the next few months, like graffiti, bold, lawless, intrusive.

Berkoff's back! In my life, in my sights, in my hair.

The man who taught me at Webber-D. and influenced me strongly – fuelling a love of physical acting – this man had changed. The teacher had turned into a superstar. He dressed like one: very fashionably, all in black, ready and quite keen for any passing paparazzi. Back in 1969 his main lesson to this particular student was about energy. He didn't need to articulate this – he radiated it, he was aglow, he shone. It was a very positive force, then. But something had happened. The outer man wore black with an amused, preening swagger; the inner one had gone dark in a different way. I'd already noticed this in the pieces he kept writing in the press, lashing out at any passing target in a brutish, unfocused way. OK, he was making rudeness part of his style too, part of his image. But how serious was he? Always a little difficult to tell with Berkoff. Is he seeing the funny side? On the one hand, he's an innovator, a leading player in modern theatre, while on the other his manner is quite antique, with more than a hint of the old actor-manager. Donald Wolfit in bovver boots. Does he perceive this himself?

As we went into rehearsals for *The Trial*, I found the question even harder to answer. The displays of rudeness were startling. Was this an act, a bit of a larf, or were things getting a teensy bit out of control? There were public floggings daily. Invariably of people least able to defend themselves: younger actors, stage management, the musician – oh, the poor musician – never of high-status people present, like the leading actor. No, I stood by, a rather timid Fletcher Christian, I'm afraid, to this ferocious Bligh, as the day's victim was positioned in the centre of the rehearsal room and the cat-o'-nine-tails unsheathed. This came from between Berkoff's lips and looked like a tongue but, as anyone familiar with his plays will know, it's a formidable, flesh-flaying instrument.

It's traditional for directors and designers to hold private meetings together, both before and during rehearsals, to discuss the set and costumes. In our case there wasn't really a set (we were using an imaginative device from the original 1970 production, where a set of portable door frames become corridors, windows, mirrors, paintings), but costumes were required and our designer, David Blight, had duly sketched them. Trouble was, Berkoff never found time to see him, or the sketches. Since sewing and stitching couldn't start until the designs were approved, David took to standing outside the rehearsal room, portfolio under one arm, hoping to waylay the main man as he came and went. This went on for days. We'd arrive and there'd be David, like a doorman, nodding politely as we went through. Then there'd be the sound of Berkoff coming down the corridor, a fast, stealthy sound, the sound of black wings – actually just the latest Issey Miyake coat – and he'd come into view, with that twist to the mouth – a sneer? a smile? – and that sightless look in the half-hooded grey eyes. David would raise a forefinger and say, 'Ah, morning, Ste . . . !' But already it was too late, Berkoff was gone and the rehearsal room door was slamming shut in David's face.

It puzzled me. Out of politeness, I'd asked David if *I* might see the sketches. They were very good: early century, middle European, a palette of black, white and silver. Quite straightforward. Why was this becoming a problem?

Then one day – who knows why? – Berkoff suddenly gestured David to follow him into the room. This time when the door slammed shut, David was inside. He looked pleased, relieved. Unaware that Berkoff was leading him to the centre of the room. Oh dear. Berkoff invited him to spread the drawings on the floor. The rest of us carried on with our usual morning routines, pulling off outer coats, sipping at coffee, some limbering up for the physical ardours of a Berkoff production; generally making space for the director and designer to have their long-overdue meeting. Then it started, quietly at first, quickly growing louder, *seeking* an audience: that familiar nasal, rasping tone with its hybrid accent of streetwise White-chapel and clipped Theatre Posh. I may not be quoting accurately, but it sounded like something from one of his plays.

'Wass this? . . . wha' a pile a shit . . . this is shit, innit? . . . this is complete fucking bollocks . . . this is a pile of wank, right? . . . this is dog-sick, slime-bag, jam-rag crap! . . . this is . . .' Et cetera.

I mustn't give the wrong impression. I admire the man. Well, I admire the work. No, the man *is* the work. He's mesmeric. Watch him muscle his way into the action. This is a director who can't sit still. He's a compulsive scene crasher. 'Naa, thass fucking bollocks – wotch *this*!' The voice is rough, it snarls and barks, the body is eloquent, swaying and prancing; a drill sergeant played by Nureyev. He shows the cast how to do their parts – a seamstress, a landlady, a police inspector – how to mime typewriters, telephones and strap-hanging on the metro. Not with me though. He never shows me anything. He defers constantly. 'Just say what you want, Tone, we'll build it round you.' It's not the way I like to work, but he can't comprehend this; it's part of his olde worlde view – the others are the Chorus, I am the Leading Man. With me he drops his status and becomes strangely coy. We have a scene together. He's playing a cameo in the show – yes, he's actually contracted to come on stage at one point – as the painter Titorelli and, whenever we do it, there's a new Steven Berkoff in the room; a shy, nervous actor terrified that anyone might think he's no good.

'K's guilt is the guilt of mediocrity.'

He's written that in the introduction to the play and reiterates it constantly in rehearsals. Mediocrity. The ultimate sin.

And I end up being guilty of it. The role calls for it in a way. Joseph K is mediocre – a bank clerk, meticulous and petty, bound in red tape, eventually strangled by it – but is there an interesting way of playing him? No. Well, not for me, anyway. I'm probably not best cast as Mr Ordinary. I thought it would be a challenge. It isn't. 'The Chorus is actually Joseph K,' Steven says. 'Leave all the hard work to them.' I do.

There's only one moment in the part that really touches me. It's at the end of the first half, when the ghost of K's father appears to him. They have a short scene, then K says: 'In front of you, Father, I lose all self-confidence and exchange it for an infinite sense of guilt.'

When I tell Steven I like this line, he reveals he was thinking of cutting it: it's not Kafka, it's him. 'Leave it in,' I urge. We smile gently, both understanding something about the other, our experience linked for a moment.

We move from the rehearsal room into the theatre, the Lyttelton, for the Tech. The first cue involves moving from the wings on to the stage in total blackout. I have to reach the central position. 'How will I find the centre in the dark?' I whisper to the group standing round me.

One of the stage staff, a veteran of the National, whispers back: 'There's a groove. It's called the Michael Bryant groove. Feel for it with your foot.'

The next few days are chaotic, mainly because Berkoff's method of working is a sort of non-method, mainly concerned with shouting at everyone: the lighting man, the musician – oh, the poor musician – and, of course, David the costume designer. When we get to the dress rehearsal it's less pressured than usual because no one's paying the least attention to the stage. The star is in the stalls. He may be unlit, but he still has that tongue, that voice. It grows in volume and viciousness during the laundress scene. A row about her costume. Oh, good, David's answering back. Eventually Berkoff yells, 'But I can see her fucking fanny!' I'm forced to stop and peer out into the auditorium, shading my eyes against the lights. Berkoff immediately checks himself – 'Yeah, sorry, Tone, sorry' – and addresses the actress: 'Just let down that drape on your skirt, will yer.' And then we continue. Couldn't he just've written a note – 'Don't like her skirt' – like other directors do?

We open. The critics are underwhelmed. Berkoff fans flock.

Right, one down, one to go. And it's the biggy now.

I'd missed the chance of playing one little man with a black postage-stamp moustache (Attenborough has cast Robert Downey Jnr), but now I'm about to do the other one . . .

The Resistible Rise of Arturo Ui is Brecht's play about Hitler's climb to power, covering the events of 1929–38 in Germany; telling them as a kind of comic strip, the Nazi figures turned into Chicago gangsters fighting over the city's greengrocery trade. It's essentially satirical in tone, which can't really be said of its subject.

Adolf Hitler.

How to explain the fascination?

I wasn't born during Hitler's lifetime, yet feel a quite personal relationship with him. At the mere sight of him – suddenly on my television screen or in the pages of a magazine – I grow alert and pay special attention. I will read any book on him, watch any documentary. When I do I'm aware of his physical details as though he were someone I fancied. There's a flutter in my belly. A strange, almost excited fear. This man wanted to kill me. I'm looking at someone I know; he's part of my history. He can't be ignored. He mustn't be. *Arturo Ui* ends with the line: 'The bitch that bore him is on heat again.' Well, yes, and I don't have to look far. Eugene Terre'Blanche, South Africa's Mister White Earth, is often on the news these days. Mandela's out of prison and everyone's out of the closet; extremists have stopped mincing their words; there might be civil war. I feel a familiar prickle of horrified interest when I watch Terre'Blanche. The family are watching him too. In fact, he's politicising them. The Shers haven't always made the connection between their own history and the apartheid system, but here's something they recognise: the swastika above his head. When Hitler was a child, the Boer War was raging. He didn't play Cowboys and Indians – little Adolf played at being a Boer. Now, almost a century later, a Boer is playing at being little Adolf. And playing it well. As demagogues, they share two crucial pieces of equipment: pale eyes that burn and the gift of oratory. Their voices may be different – Terre'Blanche's sounds like it's coming from the very soil of his beloved homeland, rich, deep, baked at the edges, while Hitler's is high, shrill and airborne, a bomber on a mission – but in spirit they are remarkably similar. Their audiences don't get a politician's structured performance (Thatcher's strange automaton character has been succeeded by an even stranger creation by John Major), they get a man shaking with rage and grief, pouring with sweat, ready to spill his blood too – anything, anything for the Fatherland.

I plunge into the research for *Arturo* with more fervour than ever before, with real, visceral appetite. This is going to be glorious. Climbing into the skin of the enemy, feeling his power, all the thrill of that, yet positioned to poison him, weaken him, show him for what he is. A bizarre revenge. You become him, you destroy him. I watch the films again and again, re-winding, freeze-framing, scribbling notes, sketching the famous gestures (we think we know them, yet the actual details are surprising, like the little pinkie held away from the others during the *heil* salute, the same little pinkie that's daintily raised when he drinks a cup of tea). I read two biographies, Bullock's and Toller's. The second is much better. Biography is like acting: you have to get inside the character. Hitler's biographers have the ultimate arch-villain to play. Toller does it with relish, gets right to the stinking soul of the man, rubs noses with it, while Bullock is like the actor who holds his character at arm's length, signalling 'I want you to know I disapprove of this chap'. Much useful material in both, though. Vivid descriptions of people meeting Hitler. Someone reports how he looked straight through you, someone else how there seemed to be no bones in his own face. (Both are encounters not with a man but an X-ray machine.) And suicide . . . suicide is never far from Hitler's mind . . . kept there reassuringly, a hipflask in a back pocket. Jung is good on Hitler too: 'His secret was that he allowed himself to be moved by his own un-conscious . . . In our case, even if occasionally our unconscious does reach us through dreams, we have too much rationality, too much cerebrum to obey it – but Hitler listens and obeys. The true leader is always led.' A good illustration occurs in the row when Field Marshal von Rundstedt resigns from Hitler's army. 'It's all very well for you,' shouts the Führer, 'but I can't go to my superior, God Almighty, and say, "I'm not carrying on with this!"'

Right, I'm ready, I'm raring to go. Only one problem.

The play.

The play's not very good.

Only discovered this recently. Got quite a shock. Thought I knew it well.

I never saw Simon Callow's Arturo at the Half Moon (too jealous after reading the reviews), nor Ekkehard Schall in the Berliner Ensemble production which visited the World Theatre Season at the Aldwych (Terry Hands is fond of describing Schall's death-defying flip from an upper level into a throne-like chair below), but I did see the 1968 Blakemore–Rossiter production. About half a dozen times. Rossiter's performance is still among my top ten: a walking cartoon, his limbs like rubber, his beaked face sunk between his shoulders like a vulture's; brilliant clowning (he backs into a sun umbrella, feels one spoke, throws up his arms in surrender), but chilling, too. I remember the script being fast, funny and savage, crackling with gangster-movie dialogue. How could it be the same play I'm reading now, in the Ralph Manheim translation, as plans proceed with the National?

It isn't. The Blakemore–Rossiter production used a 'version' of Brecht's play, by George Tabori – a translation plus adaptation – which *is* fast, funny and savage. Manheim's more faithful translation is awkward and plodding, revealing the play itself to be severely flawed. Brecht never saw it performed in his lifetime; maybe he would've worked on it if he had. But the script he left us is like a brilliant idea for a play rather than the thing itself. The comic-strip structure is there, but the scenes are too ponderous for lift-off. There's one remarkable exception: the scene where the Old Actor tutors Ui in gesture and stance, and there before your eyes the saluting, goose-stepping dictator is born. All the scenes need the same kind of bravura. And Tabori comes close to achieving this; in a way he does the next draft.

Fine, then let's just use the Tabori version too.

Except we can't. With just five weeks to go before rehearsals, the Brecht Estate forbid us to use it. It isn't faithful enough to the Master's work. They would rather have the defective original than the brilliant copy. They somehow permitted Blakemore and Rossiter to use the Tabori version back in the sixties, but aren't prepared to do so again, or at any rate not in a high-profile National Theatre production.

The Brecht Estate, the Beckett Estate – ah, these estates, these guardians of commas and semicolons, of stage directions and speech inflections, these authorities of 'the author's intentions'. If Shakespeare saw half of what we do with his plays he wouldn't just turn in his grave, he'd drill through to Australia. But he might be pleased by the other half. Good writers are thrilled not threatened by imaginative interpretation of their work. The alternative is what Kabuki Theatre presents: plays performed exactly as they were 400 years ago, gesture by gesture handed down over generations of actors; interesting to watch, perhaps, but dead, actually, museum theatre.

Ui's director was Di Trevis, with whom I'd worked well on *Revenger's Tragedy*. Of the Peter Gill school – attention to detail and truth – but with a fine sense of spectacle as well. Di came up with a good solution to the textual stalemate. We'd commission a new translation. Faithful to the original, but with added spin from a new young writer. Ranjit Bolt fitted the bill perfectly. And produced a very witty, very lively piece of work. But – but – but – it was still Brecht's play. We were still flawed at our very centre. The onus moves firmly on to the director and leading actor in these cases. With a great play you have only to try to match its quality. With a non-great play the challenge is different and not nearly as satisfying. The writing doesn't take care of itself, it isn't supporting you fully. In fact, it's the other way round. You have to cover for it, compensate, employ all your skills to keep the thing going. In *Ui*'s case you have to be as inventive as a Chaplin or Keaton, finding business to do with props and furniture (Rossiter and the sun umbrella), or creating slapstick falls and flips (Schall's into the chair). I'm not a natural clown. I just wanted to play Hitler. After years of planning to do *Arturo Ui*, I suddenly wasn't looking forward to it at all.

As rehearsals started Di encouraged me to trust the material, or at least trust Ranjit Bolt's version, which really was very sprightly. Also, who says this play has to be hilarious, she asked, that's how it's been done before, but who says that's how we have to do it now? Let's approach it seriously. That made sense. You can't *try* to be funny. I'd learned my lesson with Malvolio.

So now I went on a different route with the role, studying de Niro and Pacino performances as models of an American gangster rather than the old, less realistic Cagney–Bogart films which Brecht had in mind when he was writing. I worked hard with dialect coach Joan Washington to perfect an Italian-American accent and devised a make-up to match: a wig of jet-black hair, slicked back to start with, later falling into the Hitler fringe, and a big broken nose.

Ah, the nose.

There's this new, wonderfully light latex they're using for film prosthetics now, said the National make-up people, we're having the nose made of that. Fine, I said, as long as it'll stand up to the rigours of the job. My stage energy is quite high and Hitler's is even higher. My costumes have been known to pop and shred, my wigs to fly from their moorings and I sweat like a pig. Let's see, they said, we'll try it at the Tech and Dress.

Well, of course, I didn't sweat like a pig at the Tech and Dress – the pressure isn't on – and the nose was fine. But then we came to the first preview . . .

We'd done the Actor scene. Michael Bryant was playing the old trouper, superbly, of course, and I knew I was good in that scene as well. It works. You only have to *do* it. You can, must, play it absolutely straight and leave the comedy to take care of itself. For it surely will. The audience have been at a kind of Brechtian lecture so far, but now they're suddenly at the theatre, watching an explosive piece of comic drama – the birth of Hitler – and they reward it with gales of laughter and rounds of applause.

You go straight from that scene to the first big Ui–Hitler speech, full-blown Führer stuff, and it was during this that I tasted something odd. Something was trickling into my mouth. What, where, how? With the rant in mid-flow I redirected one of my wildly gesticulating arms to my face, touched finger to lips and glanced at it. A kind of white goo, like pigeon shit. I peered up into the flies. *What on earth was going on?* I got through to the end of the scene, which was our interval, and galloped to the dressing room. There, I stood in front of the mirror, blinking.

My nose had melted.

Half of it was missing, or rather fallen: a little white avalanche over my nostrils, across the black postage-stamp moustache and into my mouth.

We held the interval. We stuck on a new nose. We did the rest of the play.

By the end I was very dispirited. It wasn't just the nose. That was easily solved – by using the old, heavier latex – no, it was the show. When you first put a show in front of an audience you learn a lot about it very fast. About the production, which can be changed and improved, and about the play, which can't. Over the last few weeks my reservations about the play had lessened, vanished even. There was palpable excitement in the rehearsal room and a buzz round the building, but both things can be misleading: everyone *wants* the show to work. Tonight's audience was sympathetic too, as preview audiences tend to be. They'd given me a round early on, when the Narrator mentions Richard III and I tripped, catching myself on two tommy guns, using them as crutches, and they continued to enthuse whenever they could. But it's an uphill struggle and by the end you could feel it. The thing wasn't really firing.

Richard Eyre came to the dressing room. He's not a bullshitter. His comments were restrained. Noting my disappointment, he went into a different gear: 'But the Actor scene – you and Bryant together – I don't think I'll ever forget that.'

The Actor scene. Fifteen minutes in a three-hour show. Hmm. But then comic strips shouldn't last three hours.

Ian McKellen was at the National too, during June, July, August that year, playing his Richard III. We'd often bump into one another in the corridors, me dressed as an Italian-American Hitler, him as a Mosley-like Crookback.

'Oh, damn . . . what's my first line again?' he'd ask with a smile.

'Now is the summer of Arturo Ui.'

But it wasn't. Although well received, Arturo simply wasn't the coming together of actor and role that I'd dreamed of. Both my shows at the National had turned out rather disappointingly. But the next one wouldn't . . .

Ian and the director Sean Mathias (they're former partners) wanted to do Chekhov's *Uncle Vanya* in the Cottesloe, and asked if I'd play the other male lead, the doctor, Astrov. Sean was unknown then, and Richard Eyre was at first reluctant. 'If you two want to do *Vanya*,' he confided to Ian and me, 'I'll line up any director in the land for you.' But Ian stuck out for Sean – wisely, as it turned out. The rest of the cast fell into place excitingly: Janet McTeer as Yelena, Lesley Sharp as Sonya, Eric Porter as Serebryakov. Having read several terrific translations of the play (Christopher Hampton's for the Royal Court with Paul Scofield and Colin Blakely, Michael Frayn's for the West End, with Michael Gambon and Jonathan Pryce), we settled on the version which Pam Gems wrote for Hampstead Theatre, with Nigel Hawthorne and Ian Holm. There's no Chekhov Estate, thank God, so Pam offered to do a further draft for us. This involved workshopping the play at the National Theatre Studio, with a Russian expert present, so that Pam could constantly refer to the original, while tailoring the dialogue to fit us perfectly. This might sound odd; it's not the job of a play to adapt to its actors, it should be the other way round. But there's something about Chekhov . . .

He doesn't write dialogue, in a way, he writes the unspoken; he writes moods, feelings, passing moments, missed chances. He seems to achieve the impossible: unstructured life within a highly structured plot. This double energy, pulling in different directions, creating comedy and tragedy out of the tension, as well as an almost accidental revelation of human behaviour, this had always made his writing very nourishing for me as an audience and now became even more so from the inside. For the duration of the play you have a curious sense of time passing at its normal speed yet filled with all those little incidents that shake us to the core. Life is both intense and boring. We feel this every day. It's a solid, clumsy, earthy substance, and it's air – most wonderfully it's air. Chekhov manages to put this down on paper and you get to breathe it through the character. As with Shakespeare's people, Chekhov's are huge, untidy portraits. Tie the loose ends together at your peril. We're constantly drawn to doing this as actors, to understand who it is we're playing and to try to explain him to the audience: *My character is like this*. Well, you can't with Shakespeare and Chekhov. Their writing is too realistic. We humans are endlessly contradictory and that's how we're portrayed in their plays.

In *Vanya*, Astrov is at first sight a rather heroic character, a tireless doctor riding from one distant estate to another, ministering to his patients, an early environmentalist, dreaming of saving Russia's forests from destruction; a man of compassion and wisdom. But he's also a drunk, a womaniser, he betrays and disappoints his friends. What is he – the good guy or the bad guy? No such distinction exists, answers Chekhov. Astrov has to be attractive. Both women in the play fall in love with him. He's sometimes played as a rural Casanova, a rather dandyish figure touring the countryside in pony and trap. Since this romantic option wasn't available to me, I went for someone rougher, sweatier, a horse rider, undoing stirrups, dusting himself down, more cowboy than Casanova, burning himself out with work and booze maybe, but alight with passion and humour too, the kind of man who'd easily persuade you to stay up through the night drinking with him, and with whom you might as easily fall in love.

There were many reasons why *Vanya* became especially good to do. For some time, now, I'd been playing a series of big, show-carrying parts – *Richard III, Torch Song, Singer, Arturo* – where, for better or worse, the onus is on you, but *Vanya* doesn't have a part like this. It's an ensemble piece built round a central quartet (Vanya, Astrov, Yelena, Sonya), and this was a relief to do now. Share the responsibility, learn from the others.

Eric Porter intrigued me. I'd seen him on my first ever visit to Stratford in 1968, on my first ever weekend in this country, playing Lear. I remembered this as a strong, sinewy, raw-boned performance and told him so early on in rehearsals. He replied, quite curtly, that he'd been very unhappy in it. Well, all Lears seem to say this, but it struck me that Eric was probably unhappy in most of his projects. He radiated severity and gloom. We all started giving him a wide berth. But then one day he and I got into conversation again, and he told me a story that made me view him in a different light. A story about his father. They were a London working-class family and the father worked as a bus driver. He was appalled when his son said he wanted to become an actor – this was no job for someone from their background, this was no job for a *man*. Eric persisted. He left home, went into the profession and subsequently had very little contact with his father, who died before the huge success of *Forsyte Saga* and the honour that brought to the Porter name. After he died, Eric's mother revealed a startling thing. While Eric was at the Old Vic in the fifties, playing a string of leading roles, the bus driver used his shifts off work to come and watch his son. He'd sit up in the gods, never telling Eric he was there. He was too embarrassed – by this strange world of the theatre and by the mistake he'd made about it. So he sat there in the dark, marvelling, but keeping it secret.

I find this story very depressing and very familiar. Fathers, fathers. Dear God, aren't they queer?

I'm always excited to see the working methods of other actors from close to and *Vanya*'s cast was led by one of my heroes:

18/1/92. McKellen begins at a gallop. I'm self-conscious about acting to start with; a cautious creeper-up, a sitter-at-tables for as long as possible, a nose-in-script man. But he's an actor to his fingertips, he lives, breathes and loves it; he says yes it's about showing off, yes I can do that, and then some. From day one, he's there performing, needing to entertain the director, the other actors, stage management, anyone who's watching. He'll interrupt a scene to invent some comic business, people will laugh and applaud. I found some of this irritating at first, yet was quickly won over; his charisma is irresistible. And *Vanya* was somehow there right from the start – gangly, shabby, whispy goatee, specs. He brings character clothes and props into rehearsals straight away. With a minimum of accoutrements and gesture he's suddenly someone new. Like his Richard III (one dead arm, the other belonging to superman), or his Iago (the constant, obsessive checking of military belts and buckles; a man so dangerous he has to keep himself fastened in, tied up). Someone wrote of Olivier that part of his success lay in always giving critics something to describe. Maybe that's cynical about critics (can you be cynical about critics?), but it's true too. Because it also gives audiences something to describe and remember. McKellen certainly does this. He carves in the air. His body carves fascinating shapes, and of course his voice (thick, muscular, smoky) – that's carving away too. You're left with indelible images.

It's interesting to see how much Sean is directing him. They know one another so well. What may seem impressive to us is just a familiar old trick to Sean, a bad habit that needs ironing out. McKellen sometimes finds it hard to dig into himself, to touch real emotions. This might not matter (to audiences, to critics), but it matters to Sean, and they're both working hard to make the work *grow*. Sometimes Sean gets impatient: 'Oh, for God's sake, just do the same thing twice in a row!' McKellen likes to keep changing it all. It's a work method learned from Mike Alfreds (on *Cherry Orchard*) and although an excellent one, it can sometimes make it hard for the rest of us. We're fumbling to find the essence of a scene and he's so busy being *different* the material just keeps slipping through the fingers. He encourages you constantly to reinvent too, but if you do something that doesn't suit him, he'll somehow restrain you. (That's OK – things are on his terms, but he's worth learning from.) His grip – his physical grip – is very strong. His hands are large. Workman's hands. Sculptor's hands. Built for carving in the air.

Vanya was a success, a big success – you couldn't get a ticket – and all the acting was much praised, with special enthusiasm for the central quartet. My year at the National finally ended well. Yet with a little sting in its tail. Upsetting at the time, but comic too. Suitably Chekhovian.

The sequence of events began during a *Vanya* performance, just after Astrov's Act Two drunk scene. In the scene dock, I bumped into Karl Johnson (playing Waffles), who said, 'Have you heard? Sean's been nominated for an Olivier for this.'

'No, I hadn't,' I said. 'How splendid.'

A little later, bumping into McKellen, I said excitedly, 'Did you know? Sean's been nominated for an Olivier.'

'Yes,' he replied, looking uneasy, then quickly confessed, 'so have I.'

'Oh. That's terrific. Congratulations.'

Later still I bumped into Janet McTeer (Yelena) waiting for an entrance backstage and whispered, 'Sean and Ian have both been nominated for Oliviers.'

'I know,' she whispered back. 'I have too.'

'Wow, that's . . . that's wonderful. Great stuff.'

Now nearing the end of the performance, I bumped into Lesley Sharp (Sonya) on the stairs: 'Sean, Ian and Janet have all been nominated for Oliviers. Isn't that just –?'

'And me,' she said. 'Me as well.'

'Goodness. But that's, I mean, that's . . .' Aware that my smile might be looking a bit numb, I said 'Well done' and hurried on.

After the show, in the bar, I saw our director. 'Sean!' I cried. 'You, Ian, Janet, Lesley, all nominated. How tremendous. Four nominations, that's really –'

'Five.'

'Five,' I repeated, my eyebrows raised in a last flicker of hope. 'Why, what's the . . . uhm . . . fifth for?'

'Best revival.'

'Best revival, of course – congrats, *mazeltov*, what can I say?'

Dazed, I wandered over to where my guests for the evening were waiting. The Bermans: Myrtle and her husband, my trusty therapist, Monty.

'That was terrific,' he said. 'That was just the best thing we've seen in ages. I'm so glad you managed to get us in this evening.'

'So am I,' I answered, 'because I've got bad news for you. You're on duty.'

THE LAST JEW
IN PLUNGE

THE CUSTOMS OFFICIAL glances up at me and touches his face. It's an odd moment. He's only commenting on how different I look in my passport (the photo was taken when I was playing Singer, head shorn to the bone), but he could be saying, 'You Shers have certainly changed since we saw you last.'

I'm in the Arrivals hall of Vilnius airport, Lithuania. It's Friday, 24 April 1992. Roughly a hundred years since my family left this country. I'm the first one back.

When I got off the plane a few minutes ago, a feeling came up through the ground that I've never known before. It was only in my mind yet felt like an earth tremor. It's left me very shaken. I keep crying; the tears flow even when I think I'm all right, chatting about other things; it's like having a running nose. I feel completely defenceless. Like a child. No, even younger. Maybe this is what's called racial memory. The Shers and Abramowitzes never thought they'd be coming back. The ground felt hateful under their feet. They said goodbye to it with relief. Yet full of upset too. Second-class citizens, despised since birth, frightened of where they were from, bewildered by where they were going. Which happened to be South Africa, dear God.

Would they have believed anyone who told them: you will return, one of you will, and he'll be an actor. Would they have believed that?

An actor. With the Royal National Theatre of Great Britain. A cultural visit from the Studio. Its boss, Sue Higginson, came to Lithuania last year after independence and promised to return in force. And here we are, our luggage gathering on the airport floor: a slide projector for Alison Chitty's design talks, cane sticks for Annabel Arden's movement sessions, boxes of play texts for John Burgess's seminars on modern British drama. The voice coach Patsy Rodenburg will be arriving in a few days' time, along with playwright Nicky Wright and actress Juliet Stevenson. I'm taking some acting workshops too, together with Jim.

Jim's done a lot of teaching, at Central, LAMDA, the British-American Drama Academy. I haven't. When Sue asked me, I said it wasn't really my thing, but I'd do it if she could help me achieve a long-held dream: to visit the place where three of my grandparents were born (or was it two?): a small town in the north-west called Plunge. In Yiddish, Plungyan.

It's the first weekend. Sue has certainly kept her part of the bargain: a car for Jim and myself, with a driver and a translator, Vladimir. He's a young Russian journalist who, although he's never been to the States, speaks a twangy American brand of English – it's learned from the movies. As we speed out of Vilnius, we pass a large stretch of wasteland heavily parked with vehicles, people crowded round them. It looks like the biggest ever car boot sale. 'Aw no.' Vladimir laughs. 'That's the goddam black market!'

Our journey takes us across most of Lithuania. Flattish countryside, forests of silver birch, old Russian churches, grey Soviet towns, farmers with horse-drawn ploughs, English graffiti on a bridge – PUNK ISN'T DEAD – and suddenly, on open land somewhere in the centre of the country, a giant memorial to the Holocaust. You have to stop. The sculpture is overwhelming. Colossal jagged blocks, their edges soaring above you, their bases crashed into the ground; pillars fallen from heaven.

Three hours later we see a turn-off marked PLUNGE 33KM. I feel emotional again and strangely nervous. Plunge isn't just where my family tree is rooted, but a section of *Middlepost* too. At the time of writing I wanted to visit, but it was complicated then, locked behind the Iron Curtain. Neil Kinnock was in the process of trying to help me gain a visa when Chernobyl suddenly happened. Everyone thought it might be wisest to keep away from this part of the world. I ended up inventing my own Plunge for the novel. Will the real place bear any resemblance?

We pass villages that look promising – *shtetls* straight from *Fiddler on the Roof* – old wooden houses painted a mustard colour, a stork nesting on top of a dead tree. But as Plunge comes into view I start frowning. It's much bigger than I expected and more urban. Although there are some wooden houses, most of the buildings are those ugly, stained concrete blocks that blight the streets of Eastern Europe.

We navigate our way to one battered high-rise estate. We have a contact here. Jakovas Bunka. He's seventy-ish, small, leathery; a sculptor and Jewish activist. His small flat is crammed with files, scrapbooks and artefacts; a meagre, dilapidated museum of local Jewish life. I ask him about my family. He reveals that Sher was a common name. I'm surprised. I take a deep breath before the next question: 'Is there any way we can trace where these Shers, my Shers, lived?' Vladimir translates, then reports back to me in his odd American way: 'OK, Mister Bunka here, he's saying no way, man, absolutely no way!'

'Why?' I ask, shocked by his emphatic tone.

Mr Bunka keeps talking urgently, gesturing to the small, dusty piles of photos around us.

Vladimir translates: 'He's saying . . . none of this goes back to the turn of the century . . . Jewish life from back then is completely wiped out in Plunge . . . Jewish history stopped here in June 1941.'

Jewish history stopped here in June 1941.

That's when the Germans arrived. There was no ghetto in Plunge so the Jews were herded into the synagogue. They were kept there for two weeks, starving, forbidden to throw out their dead. Then they were taken to the forest outside town and in one long day, with the soldiers working shifts and drinking heavily, they were murdered – 1800 of them.

The Jewish population of Plunge was fifty per cent in my grandparents' time, but now the only survivors were soldiers like Mr Bunka, serving in the Lithuanian division of the Russian army and away at the time. 'How many Jews are left here currently?' I ask. Mr Bunka doesn't need to wait for Vladimir's translation. He holds up four fingers. Then he says something in a strange, flat voice.

Vladimir explains: 'OK so, Mr Bunka, he's saying that the other three have just got their Israeli visas. Very soon, Mister Bunka, he's gonna be the last Jew in Plunge.'

Mr Bunka takes us on a walking tour through town. The synagogue is now a makeshift general store. Rock music blasts across the prayer hall, where trestle tables are laid out with everything from children's clothes to hardware. Mr Bunka says he wants to reclaim a corner for his Jewish museum. From there we proceed to the 'Jewish cemetery', a creation of Mr Bunka's again; there are no actual graves, just a dozen or so headstones which he salvaged from the original cemetery (blown up by the Nazis) and arranged on a piece of waste ground, in a strange semicircle.

We drive out to the forest where the massacre took place. Here Mr Bunka has carved tree trunks into human images. There are several mass graves, all overgrown. But on one lies a bunch of fresh flowers. Mr Bunka explains that seventy-five Jewish schoolgirls are buried here. The local priest baptised them at the last moment – a frantic attempt to save them, a futile one. But it nevertheless became a Christian grave and so a few locals from town still honour it. Who will honour the rest when Mr Bunka's no longer here?

The Jewish tour is over. We do a brief *Middlepost* one, visiting the Orginski Palace, on the outskirts of town. Former summer home to a family of White Russians, now a language school. Yes, this is pretty much as I imagined it – I did have some reference photos – the dove-grey mansion, the large grounds, the ornate railings, where I pictured Smous peering through. A stream flows through the estate; a tributary of the Babrungas river – that marvellous name. I climb down the bank and sit on the edge, hand in the water. What a funny day.

I kept trying to imagine my people here. Only two moments came close.

One when we were in the middle of town, and I suddenly heard roosters and realised that several of the older homes had yards with poultry. The place felt familiar for an instant ... a country place, like Montagu or Middlepost ... where some of Plunge's children would eventually end up.

The other was when we were walking through the main square. Mr Bunka was chatting casually to Vladimir, who turned to Jim and me: 'Yeah so, Mr Bunka, he's telling me that when he was a kid there was an old water pump standing right here.'

I stopped in my tracks. Granny was still alive when I was researching *Middlepost*, and I asked her to try and recall Plunge. At first she couldn't – she was aged three when they left – but then she said, 'The only thing I remember is one corner of the big market square – there was an old water pump.'

A memory tugged from her childhood at the turn of the century . . . corresponding to Mr Bunka's from the twenties . . . and here we are in 1992, in a grim Soviet square . . . no water pump . . . but look, there's its ghost for a moment.

The feeling came up from the ground again, shaking me. Jim put his arm round my shoulders. People turned and stared.

But the terrible thing is that, after what we've learned today, the details of my own family history seem almost irrelevant.

We spend the night in a workers' hostel. I feel huge relief as we prepare to leave Plunge on Sunday morning. The massacre seems to haunt the whole place. The synagogue is right in the centre, so everyone must've seen what happened. You find yourself staring at anyone aged fifty or over with a kind of anger. Then you think, what could they have done? You think about South Africa, where the atrocities of apartheid happened under our noses and we never even saw – because we didn't *want* to see. And then you feel sick.

We pay a final visit to Mr Bunka. What a remarkable man, conducting a one-man campaign to keep the Jewish memory alive here, with the dusty little museum in his cramped flat and that semicircle of chipped headstones in his 'Jewish cemetery'. I tell him that I hope he succeeds in reclaiming a corner of the synagogue for a more substantial museum – but even as I speak I picture this as a clutter of faded, shabby items spread across a trestle table, thrown out as junk the moment he dies. As we're saying goodbye, he suddenly breaks down and kisses us all, even Vladimir, even our driver.

We drive to the coast at Klaipeda. I gulp at the fresh ocean air. We paddle in the freezing Baltic, clamber over the ruins of Nazi beach defences, join the locals searching the seaweed for amber. Vladimir has friends here, a family whom he proudly introduces as '*Professional* black marketeers and smugglers'. Great characters. Their mouths glitter with gold teeth and their seaside cottage is stuffed with goodies: video machines, ghetto blasters, a sideboard stacked with coffee, and an endless flow of Russian champagne and vodka. After the last twenty-four hours, it's good to get drunk.

Next thing I know we're back in Vilnius, at the official reception for the Studio visit.

*

The workshops start in earnest the following morning, Monday. They're immediately stimulating. Lithuanian actors are very passionate, very raw. There's a no-nonsense approach to the work. Like in any country which has endured repression, theatre becomes completely unprecious; it's about life not art.

Jim and I are exhausted by the time we join Sue and a few others for supper at the family of Dalia Ibelhauptaite, the Lithuanian director whom we know from London. Halfway through, the phone rings. Dalia answers it and then turns to me: 'It's for you.'

'What?'

'It's your family here.'

'What?!'

'They saw the interview you did on TV last night and want to meet.'

What interview?

It turns out that when we got back to the reception last night I was interviewed by Lithuanian TV. I have no recollection of this. (So it's true what they say about Stolichnaya.) Embarrassed, confused and sceptical, I agree to meet the woman in two days' time.

During the lunch break on Wednesday, she comes to Meno Darbuotoju Rumai, the Artists' Palace, the grand setting for our workshops (Napoleon stayed here en route for Moscow) and we meet in the basement canteen.

Liuba Zingerman. A doctor. Aged about forty-five, a large, warm-hearted woman. She's brought along flowers and old family photos. As I look at them my initial feeling of scepticism remains – one man only resembles me because of the Astrov beard – but when Liuba relates her family history (from Plunge, called Sher, several emigrating to South Africa) and when she shows more photos, I start to take it more seriously. There's a look in some of these faces that runs through my own family. She notices the moment when I change. I think also she understands something that I'm feeling: even if we're *not* related, this is important – this attempt to make contact, to transcend what happened to the Jews of Plunge. We both become emotional, we try and talk about it – all through an impassive interpreter – we try and work out what to do. She says she'll get copies made of the photos. I say I'll check them with my parents. The lunch hour is over too quickly. Now Liuba says she'll personally bring the copies of the photos to the airport on Saturday, when we leave. Changing into halting English, she says, 'The Shers must not leave Lithuania again . . . without someone there . . . to say goodbye.'

The rest of the week passes in a blur, yet heightened – each moment very intense, very clear at the time, but travelling fast – the workshops, the visits to Lithuanian theatres, the suppers, the vodkas. Now already it's Saturday, we're travelling back to the airport and I'm trembling again. Liuba *is* family, I've decided, she *is* part of my history. How wonderful she should be coming to say goodbye.

But she isn't there.

I don't know why. She could've had second thoughts, she could've been knocked over just after she left me. It was a strange, dreamlike meeting. All the Jews of Plunge were wiped out, said Mr Bunka one moment and in the next there was Liuba saying, no I'm your family from Plunge, look, here's proof.

The photos. If only I had copies of those photos. I don't even have Liuba's address or number. I keep looking around, scanning the crowd, hoping she'll still turn up. We go through Customs. We're heading across the tarmac. Suddenly Jim says, 'Oh – look!' I swing round.

My Jewish family hasn't come to say goodbye, but my theatre family has. A group of actors from the workshop, arriving at the airport at the last minute – having stayed up all night no doubt, as actors can – rushing into the departure hall, waving goodbye. Among them is Kestutis. He can't be more than twenty. At the party last night he tried to tell us how much this visit meant. Now he's leaning on the window, hands clamped to his head as if it might burst. Juliet Stevenson goes back and kisses him through the glass. Jim and I start crying again, and smiling.

'What a week!' he says.

'Was it just a week?' I say. 'Not several lifetimes?'

MIGHTY LINES

*T*HIS MAN IS *going to teach me acrobatics?*
  Wearing check suit and little bow tie. Short. Bald. Aged eighty.
We cross the floor of the gym and shake hands. I say, 'How are you?'
'Yes, all right, ta,' he answers in a thick Yorkshire accent. 'Bit of trouble with the wrists these days. Arthritis, I think. Like to begin the day with a little walk on me hands. Just round the bedroom, y'know. But it's tricky at the moment.'
I frown. This man is the same age as Dad. Who can barely walk on his feet any more. And he's worried about walking on his *hands*.
Johnnie Hutch MBE.
Left home aged fourteen to join the circus. Part of a troupe of Moroccan acrobats, The Seven Hindustans. Later moved to the music halls. Later formed his own group, The Half Wits, playing variety theatres – Las Vegas, Monte Carlo, the Paris Lido, the Royal Palladium. At the age of sixty-four, he won the Circus World Championships in tumbling, performing a full-twisting-back-somersault. Later, was the little old man on the *Benny Hill Show*, having his head patted. Later still, worked with the modern-dance company, the Kosh, teaching them acrobatics.
  Which is where, while directing one of their shows, Richard Wilson met him. And recommended him for this job: training me for *Tamburlaine*. Richard said, 'But be warned, he's merciless' – chuckling as he spoke. This was familiar. One of Richard's chuckling warnings. About a formidable old

man. The last one was Monty Berman. Who taxed my brain cells to the limits. This time it's to be my muscles. Help.

Why acrobatics for Tamburlaine?

Because we need some Mighty Action to provide relief from all those Mighty Lines.

Marlowe's two-part play, *Tamburlaine the Great*, manages to be both magnificent and monotonous at the same time. Whereas Shakespeare uses the iambic pentameter like a master jazz musician, constantly improvising round the heartbeat pulse, Marlowe obeys it more like a soldier; he simply falls in and marches alongside, adding the thump-boom of his own spectacular poetic imagination. It's awesome stuff, yet people can seldom quote a single line. It's too much. A meal made up of too many rich courses. It stuffs and sickens you – the bloodthirsty Scythian warrior conquering the world, never losing a battle, till the end when he takes on God. There's little dramatic tension, just splendour and gore, thump-boom, all in the words, hundreds of them, thousands, thump-boom, thump-boom. Played uncut (as in the Peter Hall production with Albert Finney, which opened the new National Theatre), it lasts about eight hours. People reel away, bludgeoned senseless. Thump-boom.

When Terry Hands suggested we do *Tamburlaine* I said no. The play doesn't work – I've been through this with *Arturo* – it's thankless doing these big plays that don't work. Let me show you something, said Terry, and handed over a hardback playscript – small, old, surprisingly slim – Marlowe's *Tamburlaine* adapted by Tyrone Guthrie and Donald Wolfit. They'd done the play famously in 1951 and this is how. By cutting, reshaping, sometimes rewriting the text – there's no Marlowe Estate, thank God – and then by mounting a spectacular production. We could do the same. In the Swan Theatre, where we'd done *Singer*. Which had proved two things to me. One, that it's the best theatre in the world. Two, that it's particularly good for epic drama. It has a camera's flexibility. It somehow offers both the intimacy of a close-up and the range of a long shot.

We started talking about the battle scenes. As written, these are action-less. Again and again Tamburlaine and his latest adversary face one another, strutting and bragging, then they exit to fight, then Tamburlaine re-enters as the victor – yet again. BOR-ING. Tamburlaine starts life as a shepherd. The word has a cosy, one-man-and-his-dog sound to us, but I found a photo book about shepherds in his part of the world, now Afghanistan. They tend to be horsemen. Wiry, moustachioed, fiercely aggressive. The horses look even crazier than they do: mad-eyed, wet-maned, skeletal creatures, snapping and snarling like wolves. The book shows wild races and sport, one of which seems to involve tearing a lamb apart limb by limb. Obviously we couldn't play Tamburlaine as a horseman, yet we could give him some of their insane athleticism. He needed to be a kind of superman, capable of feats beyond the expectation of what's normally seen on stage and his opponents needed to be equally remarkable. Each time the audience should think, the little guy just can't win this one! Mal Storry would play Bajazeth, the Turkish emperor, Tamburlaine's main rival. Mal is already about six foot six. Terry would raise him even higher, on cothurni, and the designer Johan Engels would give him a helmet with tusks. The Turks as elephants, the Scythians as wild dogs. No contest – surely?

Our mistake with *Arturo*, bullied by the Brecht Estate, was to trust the play. With *Tamburlaine* we began by saying it's got some fantastic stuff but it doesn't altogether work. We will do anything, everything, to rectify that. Marlowe isn't very interested in character (again unlike Shakespeare); we'd have to create more of a journey for Tamburlaine. The plan was for me to transform from the superman-athlete of Part One into a bloated godfather-figure in Part Two, inspired as much by the real-life metamorphosis of Marlon Brando as his great performance in the Coppola film. Another of the problems, I said to Terry, was that an English company simply can't do this material with enough balls. They have to play Scythians, Turks and Babylonians, earthy people, in a play written by a head-banging Elizabethan hedonist, the rock star of his day, a popularist who absorbed the bloodlust of the times – the bear baiting, the public executions – and poured it into his verse. You can't do it with polite, neck-upwards, honey-voiced English acting. Terry and I had a bracingly combative relationship – from *Red Noses* as well as *Singer* – and had learned to meet one another's challenges. I was being rude about English classical acting, the bedrock of Terry's company, the RSC, leaving unsaid: unlike me, an African actor! Right, said Terry, did you ever see *Umabatha*, the Zulu *Macbeth*, in the World Theatre Season? No, I didn't. Well, never mind, you're going to be *in* it now. We'll fly over Welcome Msomi, who devised it, and he'll train the company in war dances, in feast celebrations, in chanting and battle cries, in stamping and running. Now then – won't you need to get a bit fitter too?

I started getting into shape about six months before rehearsals began – while still playing *Uncle Vanya*. Astrov needed to be sweaty and breathless for his first entrance (having galloped across the countryside to Serebryakov's summons), so I used to do a workout in the back dock, killing two birds with one stone. Ian McKellen would stroll past, en route for the stage, and sigh: 'Oh, darling, you're such a Method actor, there is an easier way, y'know' – dabbing spit from tongue to forehead – 'Like so!'

But the main training was with Johnnie Hutch, in the small gym at the Guildhall School of Drama, next door to the Barbican, three times a week, one-and-a-half-hour sessions. I hated every minute and loved it too. (Geminians are allowed to say things like that.) Hated it because I'm such a physical wimp, loved it because of Johnnie. He wasn't nearly as merciless as Richard had warned – well, he simply couldn't push and punish me like the acrobats and dancers he was used to training. I was too much of a nance, I'd most likely just disintegrate into tears. He had to coax and charm and encourage instead. I was completely won over. In his check suit and bow tie, here was a little gentleman-entertainer from another world, a world foreign to me, the world of circus, music hall and variety. With a twinkle in his eye, a tale on his lips ('When I was on the bill with Judy Garland . . .') and with feet constantly breaking into a soft-shoe shuffle, Johnnie led me down the yellow-brick road into his world and taught me some of its skills.

Our sessions involved: general fitness, tumbling and ropes. Oich, the ropes. Entirely my fault. I was very taken with one of Tamburlaine's speeches after Bajazeth's defeat ('Now clear the triple region of the air . . . For I, the chiefest lamp of all the earth . . . Will cause the sun to borrow light of you!') and thought it needed a display of physical and vocal virtuosity that you simply wouldn't expect of an actor – it could earn Tamburlaine superman status for the rest of the show. Since the speech sounds like the man is taking off into orbit, we decided he should climb a rope while saying it, reach a point about twenty-five feet above the stage, turn upside down and then, still spouting the mighty lines, slide elegantly back to earth. Oich. Being on a free-hanging rope is a horribly unstable sensation – your hands and feet gripping at something that keeps moving – and being upside down on it is a hundred times worse. But it was a matter of pride to try and master it.

My boasts about physical prowess were already being sorely tested by Welcome Msomi's daily sessions in Zulu war dancing. Our cast wasn't quite the bunch of wimpy English thesps I'd so derided. Greg had recruited a strong team of black actors for his first RSC production – of Derek Walcott's *Odyssey* – and Terry, having nabbed them all for *Tamburlaine* too, was now thoroughly enjoying the spectacle of me at the back of the class, red-faced and breathless, my little legs paddling feebly in imitation of Welcome's great stamping Zulu lunges. Despite its effect on my pride, the ethnicity of our company became one of the show's great strengths. Marlowe wrote his female lead Zenocrate as a rather bland pin-up girl, but we had Claire Benedict playing her, a fantastically fiery match for Tamburlaine and introducing a completely new tone – of real emotion, real grief – to all those booming war scenes. The acting challenges became exciting. The rope climb never did. We played the show for about nine months, first in the Swan at Stratford, then in a hugely magnified production at the Barbican, and I never stopped dreading that bloody rope. Each night as the scene approached I felt I had an appointment with fear coming up. When it was over, Tamburlaine was imbued with new ease for the rest of the evening.

There was added danger to what I was doing. On the one hand my body had never been fitter, on the other never more polluted. It wasn't only Marlowe's mighty lines I was consuming. Charlie was back in my life. What had been an occasional treat, maybe two or three times a year, slowly became a monthly one, then fortnightly, then every weekend. Cocaine's special trick – the removal of self-criticism from the brain – this was irresistible. Me in love with me. Ironically, it's what Monty was trying to teach, what all psychotherapy teaches, except they mean something peaceful – an acceptance of who you are – while cocaine offers the ecstatic version, where you become a violently selfish extension of yourself. *Me, me, me.* You babble at parties. And when alone you're very happy to sit hunched over a mirror. One Geminian half fought against the reflection I was seeing, a man with a growing habit, while the other found ways round any obstacle. I would never phone the dealer sober. I needed to be drunk – not slightly pissed, drunk. Dry white wine, my favourite tipple, wasn't enough. I tried Dad's old poison, whisky. Fairly revolting to start with, but then so are cigarettes and most drugs at first taste – you quickly push past that stage. Whisky would get me warm-aggressive-drunk, in just the right mood to pick up the phone.

I was meeting a strange new breed – the cocaine dealer. Often posh young ladies living in untidy flats, where the curtains were always drawn. I'd visit them with conflicting feelings of excitement and fear. What if the police were staking out this particular dealer? What if that innocently parked van over there was filled with surveillance equipment? In *The Indoor Boy* the wisecracking Leon Lipschitz, a fat, self-abusing, gay Jewish South African slob (a sort of future self-portrait if I maintained my present lifestyle) makes one of these visits:

She passes me the mirror. I'm not very good at juggling it all, mirror and straw, so I put it on the floor and bow like a Muslim. As I take the first snort I get that smell. My God, I'd forgotten. It's sharp, a bit like piss, but piss you wouldn't mind dabbing behind the ear – Monroe's or James Dean's. I sit back on my haunches, smiling at her like a dog, going sniff-sniff. And now, oh that tingle, that numbness. So subtle. And oh, the feeling now, as the first gorgeous glob slips down the throat. 'Perhaps I will take all four,' I say, counting out four times seventy quid.

I'm in her lav, leaking with excitement, when I hear it – a police siren!

I flatten myself against the door, reaching for the lock. There isn't one. I glance at the window. Just one size too small. If only I'd taken the diet more seriously! What to do, what to do? Using a low, ducking run, I return to the lounge. 'It's happening,' I say in a kind'f whispered scream. 'I knew it – oh Jesus, oh God, it's happening!'

'Nothing's happening,' she says tensely, peering round the blind. Down in the street some kids are fighting with a tall man, a tramp. Now the cops get stuck in too. The kids continue to fight like cats, with a kind of high-speed madness, even as they're arrested. Maybe they're high. I glance at Charlotte, wondering if she's responsible, but she's tutting and sighing. 'Oh this area,' she says. 'I'm simply on the wrong side of the borough.'

Leon is one of those South Africans who've left home because paradise is closing down; 'exiled' in London with money to burn and nothing to do. That's where he and I differed, luckily – I had work, hard work, and this helped keep my own indulgence in check. But I'd often go into Johnnie's training sessions with severe hangovers and/or coke-overs. It was crazy, but my body could still cope with the dual rigours of abuse and fitness – it's Geminian too – for the present it could still cope.

Can't you use your eyes more? Can't you develop a drink problem or something?

These two suggestions came from Terry Hands during the early days of our working relationship. The first was excellent advice. The eyes of a theatre actor are vital pieces of equipment. Mine are commented upon, yet off stage they're quite small and sleepy; it's simply a technique I taught myself – to 'use' them – following Terry's recommendation. His second proposal was perhaps not meant seriously – sometimes hard to tell with our Tel – yet addressed an important point too. He felt my acting was sometimes too considered, too placed, too finished off. The best creative work often has a rough edge to it. Shakespeare's plays are good examples. Packed with inconsistencies, ramblings, sometimes just sheer bad writing. Yet the centre is strong. The heart works. We respond to the heart, we rejoice in their strengths and forgive their weaknesses; in fact, we quite like their weaknesses – it's part of their humanity. Their weaknesses are part of the whole: the circular, untidy thing that is life. Terry was arguing that if the artist cleans this up too much, his work becomes unrealistic. Actors especially need to be living, breathing, slightly messy creatures. The American Method School celebrates 'damage' as part of the actor's kit; the hurt side of him or her, there to be tapped into. I don't know if Terry honestly meant that self-destruction was the answer; he was perhaps just noting that it's produced some pretty hot stuff from creative people in the past. By the time we came to do *Tamburlaine*, he didn't know that I had (inadvertently) taken up his challenge.

Whether meant as irony or insight, the remark is typical of Terry. He sails close to the edge. This gives the best of his work an exciting, dangerous sheen – beaming from the darkness, a darkness which he illuminates, as his own lighting designer, with the skill of a chiaroscuro painter. In the past he'd had very intense, very productive working relationships with other actors – Alan Howard (*Henry V*, *Coriolanus*), Derek Jacobi (*Much Ado*, *Cyrano*) – and now it was my turn. I'm indebted to him for what followed. (Actually my debt goes all the way back to 1964, long before I knew him, when he was one of the founders of a scruffy regional theatre called the Liverpool Everyman.) Terry saw potential in me as a classical actor. I couldn't see it myself at first, but he didn't regard this as relevant. It's perhaps one of Terry's faults – the opinions of others aren't always terribly relevant – but in this case I can't complain. Although occasionally I resisted, occasionally was dragged kicking and screaming, he proceeded to claim me for the RSC. He did this by being intensely supportive during my bad times, like the Achilles injury, and by forever enticing me into a deeper and deeper relationship with the company. And it's a very seductive company, especially in Stratford. The great cast of characters backstage, like Black Mac my dresser, surely the least typical of his profession – a squat, toothless army quartermaster with tongue of filth and heart of gold – and all the local families who work in Wardrobe or Boot-making, with successive generations acting as apprentices to their elders. You feel you're stepping into their homes when you join the RSC, and you feel welcomed. Each artistic director becomes honorary head of the household and Terry took his place at the top of the table with pride. Despite his sometime reputation – the Prince of Darkness reputation – he was greatly respected and liked by all his technical staff. The feeling was mutual and very infectious. I'd reach the end of a season, I'd say, well, that's it, I've done my RSC stint, I'm off now – at which point Terry would immediately make me a new offer and I'd start booking my Stratford accommodation again.

Terry has been the patron of my career, half-mentor, half-bully – a touch of Diaghilev, even of Svengali – gradually shaping me into the kind of actor I've become, for better or worse. I feel grateful, as I say, even though our relationship was never a peaceful one. Whereas my other main director–actor partnerships – Max Stafford-Clark, Bill Alexander, later Greg – were typified by two different styles pulling in opposite directions, hopefully stretching both parties in the process, Terry and I shared some of the same tendencies and faults (we can both substitute energy for depth). Rather than this resulting in harmony, it led to a lot of sparring, on our feet in the rehearsal room, by phone and fax outside it. He was much cleverer at this than me. He'd get less upset. The training came from his home life, he'd say; actors were like his infant sons; they crawl over you, they scratch and pummel you, but don't strike back, they mean no harm.

He'd tell you this to your face, smiling, soft-spoken, the hooded eyes unreadable. Always showing most courtesy when being most rude. It's a politician's skill, and he'd have done well in that profession, or as a chess master. It's these qualities – patient, persuasive, foxy – that made him so good as artistic director – possibly the best I've known at either of the big national companies. It's a merciless job and Terry has that tendency. But he was always tougher on himself than his workers; he was tireless; he was available to everyone all of the time in a way which I simply haven't known the other guys be capable of.

I gained a rare insight into Terry during my preparations for *Tamburlaine*. He'd stopped running the RSC by then and was freelancing – currently directing Arthur Kopit's *Indians* in Germany. The play is set in a circus, run by Buffalo Bill, and Terry was doing it in the real thing, a real Big Top, complete with live bears, horses and bare-back riders. I flew out one weekend to see the show – Terry wanted me to consider some of the circus techniques for *Tamburlaine* – and found him living on site, in an old caravan on the edge of the stretch of wasteland where the tent was raised and the animal cages parked. He was half ringmaster, half dogsbody, directing operations yet mucking in too, drinking late into the night with the show's curious mix of theatre and circus folk. He's fluent in German and French. Watching him here, I suddenly remembered that he was a child of the military, born to an officer serving in Europe, brought up on various army bases – so this was familiar to him, this fitted like a second skin, this nomadic life, hard, unglamorous, highly committed. I've never seen him happier.

Tamburlaine marked another time of change.

When I started training with Johnnie Hutch it was the time of the 1992 elections, and I did some work for the Labour Party, touring with Chris Smith round Islington – his constituency, my neighbourhood – attending some rallies and dinners. It was minor work – I must stress this. Actors are often asked to lend their names to causes. It's flattering, but we need to proceed with caution I believe. Unless we're going to immerse ourselves properly in the cause, as Ian McKellen has with gay politics or Miriam Karlin with Equity, we will just end up blabbing foolishly. The 1992 election was a vital one, however, and one that affected everybody. I didn't need to be an expert to comment on this issue. The country that I'd made my home was changing out of all recognition. It had been Thatcher-bashed. It desperately needed a new government, a Labour one. Quite apart from major issues like the Health Service and Education, the Tory Arts policy was virtually non-existent, a disgrace, a joke.

So I became one of the minor celebs in the election sideshow. My proudest achievements was to get Richard Wilson on to the campaign trail – as a telly star he had much more vote-catching clout – and to persuade Ian McKellen to 'come out'. He'd done the same for me when the issue was about sexual identity; now it was about standing up and being named as a Labour man. Although he'd long been a supporter, Ian argued that he needed to appear neutral in party politics in order to have maximum flexibilty as a gay campaigner. I argued this was only like the actor who frets about losing work if he comes out as gay. Which was more important? And anyway, we were going to win, Labour was going to win – every poll proved it – Major simply wasn't a match for Kinnock.

Hmm. Maybe I should just stay out of politics.

It was about 10.30 when Jim and I got to Labour headquarters at Millbank on election night. Although still early on in the vote counting, everyone seemed to know the results already. The man on the door, the PR lady who briefed me in case I was interviewed, they all seemed to know. The atmosphere was awful. We sat with a group of friends – R. Wilson, I. McKellen, M. Karlin – watching the TV as more and more bad news came in. At about 1.30, after another crushing loss, Ian said, 'You watch, any moment now these rooms are going to clear faster than a Broadway party when the notices are bad.'

He was right. And we were among the first to leave – after seeing Kinnock on TV, arriving at his constituency headquarters; the strain on his face, the sense of loss. Not just the election – this was him done as leader. I felt very sad, very grim. The dips in my own career (the Chaplin film that never was, the less than glorious season at the National) seemed to correspond to a country-wide failure now. It seemed self-destructive, what the electorate had done, and this felt familiar too.

Tamburlaine was up and running (and doing flips and climbing ropes), and deemed a big success, by the time Jim's forty-third birthday came round in

September. We had a long happy Sunday with family and friends, making a South African-style *braai* (barbecue) in the garden of our Islington home. The next day was warm and sunny again. As we were clearing up the garden, Jim said, 'We must have a big talk some time.'

It started there and then, the big talk, and ended with him saying, 'I'm going to try living apart.'

Everything stayed very civilised – strangely so. That afternoon Jim and I walked along Islington Upper Street, browsing the windows of estate agents, looking for a flat for him (his new partner, the beautiful young Turk, had returned home, so it was single accommodation he needed). That evening I had dinner with Greg and told him the news. He was surprised, probably relieved, understandably so. Then I went home to Jim. We went to sleep that night holding hands. 'God, all those years,' we said. Eighteen years. We met in our mid-twenties, when our adult characters were yet unformed. We matured together, we influenced one another. He was the calm, wise presence at my side, helping to counter my wilder excesses. We tried to create a new kind of relationship and we failed. It was another failure. The straight world was right, it seemed: you had to just pair off and keep everyone else out, even if this meant becoming another sad, cross couple, occasionally cheating behind one another's backs.

Jim finally moved out in January 1993. He was starting a job at Birmingham Rep and would be living in digs there for the duration, so he took the opportunity to leave the house, our house, for good. I was up in Stratford on the Sunday when it happened. I hated the thought of him walking round the rooms for the last time – rooms that he, much more than me, planned and designed when we first bought and restored the house. And the garden – it was *his* garden, created from scratch, nurtured and cherished over the years. What must it have felt like to leave these things, to close the front door and lock it like we did in ordinary circumstances, on this most unordinary Sunday? The loss of a home. It affected me deeply. I wasn't losing my home but my twin was. Even odder, a new twin would be moving in with me quite soon. I was still having my cake and eating it. Everything was apparently in my favour. I had no reason to grieve. But there we are, I did.

Greg was directing *Twelfth Night* in Philadelphia till March. When he returned he moved into the house. Although we'd already been together for six years, we only started living together now. And I found monogamy far more enjoyable than I thought. Goodbye to the meat markets, goodbye to the endless infatuations with young actors, goodbye to all the rejection, all the restlessness – what a relief. On the other hand there was some amount of mess left over from the strange lifestyle we'd all been sharing. A lot of talking to do. New trust to be established, new security. Helped by the big new family I now inherited: Ma and Pa Doran, brother Mark and his brood, sister Jo, twin Ruth. A *female* twin. An intriguing development in my life as a twinophile. And Ruth is also married to a foreigner, an American, and his name is also Tony.

After his Birmingham season Jim moved into a flat in Waterloo. We've remained the closest of friends.

There was a break before *Tamburlaine* came into the Barbican, during which I made the TV film, *Genghis Cohen*, written by Stanley Price from the novel by Romain Gary. It's about a Jewish nightclub entertainer – a comic-ventriloquist with a Hitler doll – who's killed in a concentration camp and comes back to haunt the commandant. I was the entertainer and Bob Lindsay was the commandant. It's the blackest of comedies, involving the two in a strangely compassionate relationship. Despite coming from very different places as actors, Bob and I cooked together well, and our joint scenes were terrific to do. It was a solo scene that kept troubling me. And this was scheduled for the very last day of the shoot.

The scene is like an epilogue to the film. Genghis has finished haunting his persecutor and his ghost now walks the streets of modern-day Germany. Our location was Munich. A couple of sustained shots were needed: Genghis, with shaved head and emaciated features, wearing the striped-pyjama uniform of the camp, slowly drifting through crowds of pedestrians. We wanted real people, not extras, and they were not to know this was a film – the camera would be hidden, to catch spontaneous reactions if they happened. Munich's in Bavaria, home of old and new Nazis. Bodyguards and plain-clothes policemen would mingle with the crowd, staying close to me.

Our director was Elijah Moshinsky. Best known for his opera productions, Elijah is of Jewish Australian background and has a glittering, merciless sense of humour rather reminiscent of Mike Leigh.

When we arrived on location, he walked me (still in civvies) through the shot. 'There we are,' he said with a giggle. 'Not so bad, is it?'

Mighty lines. The phrase is used about Marlowe, sometimes pejoratively, but applies to all classic drama: great swathes of language which you, the actor, have to find a way of speaking. So that it sounds like you're making it up there and then. There's only one modern playwright who makes similar demands – Tom Stoppard. With *Tamburlaine* running at the Barbican, I went into rehearsals for the revival of Stoppard's 1974 hit, *Travesties*, playing Henry Carr, a minor consular official in Zurich in 1917 who, rather like Rosencrantz and Guildenstern, stands on the sidelines, catching only glimpses of major events occurring around him: Tristan Tzara and the Dada art movement, Joyce writing *Ulysses*, Lenin en route back home to the Russian Revolution. All this, and a pastiche of Wilde's *Importance of Being Earnest* into the bargain. I assumed that Stoppard would just leave us to it. The play was tried and tested, after all. But no, he wanted to revise it. Adrian Noble, directing, was as pleased as I was. We were going to get a close-up view of a master at work:

27/7/93. Arrived at the upstairs rehearsal room at Clapham to find Stoppard pacing around in the corridor, smoking – it's not allowed inside – and pretending to read the noticeboard on which there was nothing but old RSC schedules. He looked quite ill with nerves, which immediately made me warm to him. His play is proven; our work is yet to be. Come to think of it, maybe that's why he was nervous. Adrian, glowing from a three-week holiday in France, was in good form, brimming with infectious enthusiasm. He spoke about the pleasures of Tom's rewrites, especially the fact that Carr and Lenin, ultra conservative and far left, now share a common view of art – a dislike for its poncey practitioners. 'They've met round the back of the world somehow,' says Adrian, then starts laughing and can't stop. We sit, bemused but charmed. Adrian treats theatre like Spielberg treats film; he's a kid with a big new toy, he can't wait to play with it. Richard Hudson's sets are beautiful: all-white or all-red, large, strange, inner-mind spaces. Stoppard says that he's 'dead chuffed' about this revival. The phrase sounds odd on his lips. Like a foreigner speaking English. Which he both is and isn't: born in Czechoslovakia, moved here aged eight. In the tea break, he tells us how the widow of the real Henry Carr came to see the original show, and was so delighted with it, she presented John Wood with Carr's cigarette case.

'I must ask John to pass it on to you,' Stoppard says to me.

'Like Olivier's sword,' says Adrian.

'I think it was Kean's sword,' I say, 'and I think Olivier refused to pass it on.'

Adrian laughs: 'I think you're right – and I think John Wood might feel the same about the ciggy case.'

Stoppard looks surprised. You're struck by the fact that here is a gentleman-playwright, puzzled by any suggestion of bad behaviour, of rivalry!

28/7/93. Wonderful to watch Stoppard worrying at the text. He sits hunched over it, pondering the solutions. On the page, his humour is light and effortless, in life it's serious, almost scientific. 'There are just too many words in this gag,' he'll say solemnly. 'Let me try and think of something else, something wonderful for you.' His humility keeps surprising me too: 'I think I may just have been showing off here, swanking with the research.' (Swanking is one of his words.) Or, after the read-through: 'The first half feels slightly long. We must do some nipping. It's all those duologues. There's only so far two men can carry a rolled-up carpet before the middle touches the floor and starts to drag.' Today we watched the Evans–Redgrave film of *Importance*. Afterwards Adrian said, 'I could've sworn there was a sequence where Margaret Rutherford swotted away a bee. Kept waiting for it, but it never came.'

Stoppard nodded. 'Now that you mention it, yes, Rutherford and a bee.'

Adrian: 'Maybe a different film.'

Stoppard: 'Maybe a B film.'

We all laughed. He looked bored. This was easy stuff.

6/8/93. The week began badly, with me feeling I was just reproducing my old performance (I played Carr at Nottingham seventeen years ago), but today Dave Westhead and I ran the Tzara–Carr duologue, the hard one, the debate on art, and it suddenly took off. Stoppard was sitting forward in his chair – an untypical posture. Afterwards he said it was thrilling, and he was moved – 'which I never expect to be with this play'.

9/8/93. Working on the Stoppardian–Wildean mix, you wake up to language. Its delights and absurdities. Adrian reported overhearing two Americans coming out of the Swan over the weekend. 'I don't understand why that was called a Jacobean Tragedy,' said one. 'I didn't spot Jacobi in it.'

17/8/93. Stoppard back in rehearsals today. He was supposed to stay away for longer, but it seems he can't. He's thoroughly enjoying himself, bringing in more and more rewrites. Takes you aside to show them, with a mixture of pride and modesty. Sometimes there are alternatives – should the line be 'putting a spanner in Lenin's works' or 'putting a spanner in Lenin's Collected Works'? At other times he hands it over glumly: 'Well, it's not going to get into any anthology.' I thought he was joking till I glanced in a Book of Modern Quotations lying on the stage management desk and found several pages devoted to him. I've noticed all the other actors doing what I do: carefully hoarding the handwritten rewrites. Adrian caught me doing this today. Blushing, I said, 'There are American universities that'll pay the earth for these.' He replied: 'Sod American universities – I'm taking mine to Christie's.'

26/8/93. Stoppard away, in the States. Behind his back, we do affectionate impersonations – Amanda Harris (Cecily) is particularly good – the soft 'r', the sideways opening mouth, the flapping hands going up to the great coiff. (It's like an extra head, that hair – another huge brain balanced up there, constantly tossed, rearranged, lifted, stroked.) Stoppard writes language like a composer and Adrian has taken to propping his script on a music stand. When he sits there he's very still, our director, very concentrated. The next moment he's buzzing round the rehearsal floor, his playroom, offering ideas by tugging at your sleeve like a kid, or going on inspirational, off-the-cuff riffs: 'The exhilaration of Tom's language. You get it in Marlowe as well, don't you? You think, gosh that's a good gobful of language! There's air in the lungs. It's heady. It's a circus of ideas, a circus of words!'

2/9/93. Adrian suggested cutting one of Carr's speeches ('Desperate men . . . steady as an alp'). Stoppard summoned out of a *Sunday Times* interview to comment. He said, 'Are you asking whether the section is a masterpiece of subtlety, subtext and wit, or a pile of complete shit?' I thought, hey, that sounds familiar. He watched me do the scene with and without the speech, then said apologetically, 'No, I'm afraid it *is* good.' It's staying in.

9/9/93. Woke in terror at about 3 a.m. First preview today. Eventually fell asleep again, only to wake minutes later, gasping. Not your run-of-the-mill actor's nightmare (What's this show? Never rehearsed it), but a no-nonsense, uncoded one: I come on stage as Old Carr, begin the big speech, get the first laugh, then dry, incapable of going on. Lay in bed doing the lines. But actually it's not these worrying me – it's the laughs. I went through all this at Nottingham. You spend weeks doing that huge opening speech (it's twenty minutes long) to resounding silence in the rehearsal room, until finally you're convinced that it – or you – is the unfunniest thing on earth. But then you get it in front of audience and bingo. Well, that's what happened at Nottingham – but even my Malvolio was funny there – the question is, will it catch fire tonight? (Later the answer is yes.)

10/9/93. Second preview. Even better. A real Stoppard audience. Gales of laughter, tidal waves of it – you're picked up, swept along, set down again, a bit shaken, a bit deafened, but pleased as punch. On the spur of the moment, I tried one of the rewrites we've been discussing: 'Like the man who bet 6d against the *Titanic* making it across the Atlantic.' It got a good laugh. Afterwards, in my dressing room, I swanked at Stoppard, but he continued to worry at it: 'Still too many beats in the sentence. Can you try – "Like the man who bet 6d on the Titanic sinking."' When he's in this mode, pacing round the dressing room, he seems enormous, or at any rate his head does: that explosion of hair, like brains boiling over, or some extra-terrestrial hat. After he left, Kirstin (my dresser) said, 'I can't believe it – a few years ago, I was studying him at school! What's he like?' I was surprised to hear myself answer, 'One of the shyest and most *serious* people I've ever met.'

11/9/93. Two shows. Both good. New *Titanic* line worked even better. But a new problem arising – from a prop. The book that's playing *Lenin on Literature and Art* is, in fact, *Hollywood Husbands* by Jackie Collins – I guess the red cover won it the part. It's truly difficult to concentrate on cues as you get distracted by this astonishing trash, where, either in word or deed, there's a fuck on every page. After the matinée, Stoppard gave me excellent notes, about not overworking the speeches, about letting *him* do the work. Shakespeare would've asked actors the same thing. I've been saying a line like 'rancid little Belgians and incompetent Frogs' with unconcealed disgust, whereas of course Carr's bigotry is second nature and much funnier that way. Delightful moment when Stoppard said, 'In the two and a half hours of the show you only hit one line completely wrong. The "Oh yes" after Joyce has corrected you about who the Prime Minister is. You hit a note that's simply not Carr. It's – how can I put it? – petulant? – not quite – um . . .' The great wordsmith was lost for words.

I helped him out: 'Camp?'

'Thank you,' he said, with a rare smile.

16/9/93. Press night. Went wonderfully. Packed to the rafters and a dream audience for a comedy. I flew. Everyone very high afterwards. At Joe Allen's I presented Stoppard with the original drawing of my first-night card to the others: a cartoon of him as Wilde. He mentioned that he'd bought both my novels and asked which he should read first? I wanted to say, neither – I don't want that big brain levelled at any more of my work. He surprised me by revealing that he hadn't been to university and, like me, wishes he had. (*He wants to be brighter?*) When the waiter came for our order, he ordered duck salad as a starter and Caesar salad as a main course. The waiter was momentarily confused. 'So that's two salads?' Tom replied, 'Yes, sorry, I save my creativity for my work.'

I was in one of my review-reading relapses at the time of *Travesties* and marvelled at how diverse, and healthy, theatre criticism is in this country. In New York, one voice, the *New York Times*, calls the tune. Here there are at least a dozen. We got raves in the *Sunday Times*, *Sunday Independent*, *Observer*, *Daily Telegraph* and *Financial Times*. Both the *Mail* and *Express* found the play too clever by half. The *Guardian* and *The Times* thought I wasn't as good as John Wood. In the *Evening Standard*, de Jongh said what he said about *Tamburlaine* – I was miscast. In *Time Out*, Jane Edwardes said I was perfectly cast, but suffering from first-night nerves. (It must've been something I said in Manchester, Jane.) Anyway, we were enough of a success to transfer to the West End, the Savoy, for a further three months after the Barbican run.

A strange time for me. Dad died that November, while the two shows were running side by side. I flew to Israel, then South Africa, missing two *Tamburlaines*, though no *Travesties*. A few days after returning, Mike Attenborough came into my dressing room to say how sorry he was. Not just about Dad. Terry had won Best Director in the *Standard* awards for *Tamburlaine*, while I hadn't claimed Best Actor for my marathon double. Later, when the Olivier list came out, I wasn't even nominated. This was becoming familiar. Sometimes it was startling (I hadn't been nominated for *Singer* either, the performance I'm probably most proud of) and sometimes it was simply funny (the *Uncle Vanya* nominations), but either way it was becoming familiar. People had different interpretations. Monty wondered if it was anti-Semitic, Greg if it was anti-RSC.

I tried to tell myself it didn't matter. Who cares about the theatre awards anyway? While the annual celebrations of the literary and art worlds – the Booker and Turner Prizes – always generate enormous interest, with much public debate before and after, the Olivier and *Standard* awards go by virtually unnoticed. Why is theatre a poor cousin? It isn't in New York, where the Tonys excite the city for months on end. It's funny. British theatre is hugely valued abroad and hugely productive for the British tourist industry, yet hugely undervalued by the British themselves.

Me too – I decided in maudlin mood – hugely undervalued. I'd worked my bollocks off for *Tamburlaine* and *Travesties* – the physical exertions of the one, the vocals of the other – yet there was no prize at the end, no pat on the head.

You're supposed not to care about these things. I rang for my friend, Charlie. He could make me not care.

Mighty lines.

WOZA SA!

'THIS IS THE ONE.'
  'What one?'
'Oh, Antony – tsk!'
'The one with Mannie's ashes,' prompts Greg.
'Exactly,' says Mom.
'Ah,' say I.
It's March 1994. Five months after Dad's death. We're on the patio at Montagu House, stretching our limbs. Joel is unloading our luggage from the boot of his car. Mom touches the rose in the terracotta pot – it's called a Lincoln rose, she tells us – a single red bud has opened gloriously for our arrival. 'I talk to it when I water it,' she confides.
  'And I bet I know what you say,' remarks Joel, '"Mannie – you're drinking too much again."'
  'Oh, Joel – tsk!'
South Africa's first democratic elections are just four weeks away. The New South Africa, the South Africa that Dad feared, it's happening. And we've just had an extraordinary trip round it, doing research for my new novel, *Cheap Lives*. Set in 1989, during the dangerous months before Mandela was released, the story has two protagonists: a Coloured murderer sitting on Death Row and a white tour guide. It's these two spheres – South Africa's Death Row and South Africa's tourist industry – that we've been exploring.

At first it seemed that Death Row in Pretoria Maximum Security Prison would be a harder world to penetrate than the Saudi Arabian community in London during *Goose-pimples* research. But Ethel de Keyser came to my aid, as always, and put me in touch with LHR (Lawyers for Human Rights) in Joburg. One of their number, a gentle, handsome Afrikaner called Andries Nel, met Greg and me off the London plane and said, 'Look, I've managed to get Robert McBride to speak to you, but it has to be now, this morning – it's now or never – d'you mind if we go there before the hotel?'

'Try and stop me,' I answered, breaking into a light sweat.

Robert McBride. Born in Natal, worked for the military wing of the ANC, Umkhonto we Sizwe. In 1986 was responsible for the Magoo's Bar bombing along the beach front in Durban, the Golden Mile. Three white women were killed and eighty-nine other people injured. McBride was caught, tried and sentenced to death. He sat on Death Row for five years. In 1991, after Mandela's release, an amnesty was agreed for political prisoners. First, McBride's sentence was commuted to life, then he was released altogether. The ANC had to pay a price for this. In exchange for people like McBride, 'Wit Wolf' was set free too. He was the white right-winger, real name Barend Strydom, who went for a stroll round Pretoria in 1988, shooting any black he encountered; killing eight and injuring sixteen. He was also able to claim political immunity for this action.

While on Death Row, McBride met and married a teacher, Paula Leyden. It is their home in a quiet Joburg suburb that we visit on this Saturday morning.

A single-storeyed house, with a sunny overgrown garden, its corners shaded by avocado and granidilla trees, a swing hanging from one. The lawn is littered with toys and two tiny children are playing: the McBrides' eight-month-old twin girls. Their parents are very different characters. Paula is white, blonde, smiling, hospitable. Robert is Coloured, tall, thickly built, baby-faced, guarded. But as he realises I'm not here to talk about the bombing, he relaxes. Death Row? Sure he can tell me about Death Row – every detail, every routine. The rule of silence (twenty-three hours a day), the light in the cells (twenty-four hours). The cells are narrow and tall, he says, like upright coffins – I start jotting notes rapidly – 'Big, bright coffins, white, dead silent, we're already in coffins and we haven't even started up those forty-two steps yet.' The forty-two steps are to the gallows. Andries Nel chips in to mention that it was under this staircase that Tsafendas – Verwoerd's assassin – was incarcerated, so that he could hear the noise of death for the rest of his days (until he found salvation in deafness). Six gallows above him. During the worst times in the eighties, someone was hanged every three days. Your Notice of Execution could arrive at any time. Sometimes, like before Christmas, the warders worked overtime, to clear stock, as McBride puts it, so that they could have a quieter holiday season. He gives me a booklet published illegally during the apartheid years, filled with more first-hand accounts, he sketches the layout of Death Row, he tells everything he can remember.

Finally I've run out of questions. And he's not a man for small talk. There's a return of that aggressive, slightly swaggering air – the air of a man who's seen and done things beyond your wildest dreams – and he wanders away. He spots the twins and lies on the grass with them. We sit chatting to Paula, sipping cool drinks, sunning ourselves, watching a dad play with his kids. It's an ordinary Saturday morning scene. Well, ordinary in South Africa. There's nothing simple here. At the time of the bombing, 1986, apartheid looked immovable. The government was using force to keep things that way – murder and torture by the police were routine – there were persuasive arguments for an armed struggle.

Or so I think at first. As we journey on round South Africa, a curious coincidence will make me think again and fit the McBride meeting into a kind of circle.

Two weeks later Greg and I are in Natal, now exploring the tour-guide side of the story. We're at Isandlwana, site of the famous Zulu–British battle of 1879. The land is beautiful – as Alan Paton put it, 'The hills are green-covered and rolling and they are lovely beyond any singing of it' – but the atmosphere is charged and dangerous. The electric storms of the area, threatening suddenly to darken the countryside, drenching or burning it, these seem to reflect the political chaos locally. Apparently Inkatha favours war rather than elections: there's been terrible bloodshed in the last few months. Our travel agent was nervous about this part of the visit so we had to make private arrangements. A chap called Vic Schultz, large, grizzled, amiable, sometimes jazz musician, sometimes guide/driver for speciality trips. Has he got a sax or a rifle in his boot? Don't know, don't ask. He's brought us to Fugitive's Drift Lodge, a renowned if unusual hotel (every comfort but no electricity; the rooms are cooled by their own shade and draughts), run by David Rattray, an expert on the 1879 war. There's a unique tour here: they walk you round the battle sites at the appropriate times of day, relating the epic tale. I'm not expecting to enjoy this, but David's assistant Chris restores storytelling to an art form, passionately representing both sides equally, Zulu and British. By the time sunset comes and he speaks his final line – 'So the rider reported to Lord Chelmsford that Rorke's Drift had stood' – I feel my eyes filling. Such stories we've heard today; stories of heroism, stupidity, slaughter. So what's changed in South Africa?

Dinner is round an open fire. We're asked about our trip. As I start talking about McBride, our jazz musician driver, Vic Schultz, interrupts instantly: 'I'm sorry – I have to tell you something – I knew one of the girls he killed. Michelle Gerrard. She was a close friend. An artist, a commercial artist. Just twenty-eight. I was going to meet her that night at the Magoo Bar. I got delayed.' Everyone goes silent. We change the subject. Later, when Vic leads us to our room by flashlight – there are poisonous snakes in these hills – I apologise for bringing up the subject. He says gently, 'I don't hate McBride. I just wish he could've seen Michelle's family afterwards. I just wish he could've seen what he did.' I nod slowly, remembering the image of a man lying on a sunny, overgrown lawn, playing with his kids, full of love.

Michelle Gerrard's family could have been my own, if the bomb were in Cape Town. It was us being targeted: the fun-loving, non-thinking whites who partied and sunbathed through the bad old days. When Greg and I reach Cape Town at the end of our trip, we're picked up by Joel and Mom, and driven to Montagu House, where she shows us the Lincoln rose planted with Dad's ashes. Now the other Shers start arriving for a family lunch. Everyone's quite muted. They've had a shock. Older brother Randall was up in the Transvaal with us a few weeks earlier, joining in for the game park section of our trip, and then he went on to Sun City in Bophuthatswana. He left just before their brief civil war broke out, another symptom of pre-election hysteria. Watching it on TV – the wild looting in luxury shopping malls – the Shers saw their worst nightmare. 'You could just imagine it happening here,' says Mom, 'in Adderley Street or the Waterfront.' Joel rattles the ice in his whisky glass and smiles grimly: 'You know what they call looting? Affirmative shopping.'

Terre'Blanche's followers piled into Bophuthatswana to get a bit of the action, sharp-shooting from their cars. This rings a bell. When he was a kid, little Adolf didn't play at Cowboys 'n' Indians, he played at being a Boer . . . the Boers have played at being little Adolf, and now are playing at Cowboys 'n' Indians again. Except the game is a little rougher than they thought: three of them are captured and executed on the spot, in front of the media. The South African Sunday papers carry lurid pictures of the shooting and sentimental stories about the men. It's amazing. In less time than it takes to turn the page of a history book these guys have become victims.

On the last evening of our visit, we go down to Clifton Beach, where Albie Sachs is doing a charity event. In his book, *Jail Diary*, he tells how in solitary confinement he used to fantasise about running along the sands again – he was a keen runner before his arrest – and then, in the last chapter, he describes the moment in March 1964 when he's released from Caledon Square Magistrates' Court:

> I am free. It is quarter to five, the sun is low, and I am running to the sea. I am free! . . . It is six miles to the sea and I am going to run there . . . This is my freedom run . . . I will not stop until I feel the water flowing over me. This is the day of all my days. This is my day.

It's thirty years later – to the day – and Albie's repeating the run. We're part of a small crowd waiting at the finishing line, on Clifton: Greg and myself, Verne and Joan, drinking a bottle or two of wine, lazing in the gorgeous late afternoon light. Eventually a group appear at the other end of the beach: supporters and photographers jogging along with Albie. In that remarkable last chapter to *Jail Diary* he also writes:

> I suppose I look funny as I run. But a man should look funny when he becomes free. It is not every day that a man becomes free.

You could say that Albie looks especially funny today, post-Maputo bomb: only one arm, blind in one eye, his balance still wonky. His run looks a bit drunken. Or maybe that's just my impression as I guzzle on my plastic cup of best South African Chardonnay. I sit watching him: Rosenstern on the sidelines, watching a hero of the story. I feel a strange mix of envy and pride. What if my name had been Sachs not Sher? Albie completes the run and plunges into the waves. The sunshine beams through his red T-shirt, showing the stump of his arm. We join the others surging down to the shoreline as the black saxophonist Basil 'Manenburg' Coetzee adds his own lovely sounds to the noise of seagulls and surf.

I ask Albie to sign my copy of *Jail Diary*, across the last chapter title, 'To the Sea'. He can't yet write easily with his left hand, but slowly inscribes, 'From the older, tireder, but not wiser Albie.'

I'm not sure he needs to be wiser. In that last chapter, he also says: I have won and they have lost.

I'm back in London, playing *Travesties* at the Savoy, when April comes:

25/4/94. Joy Sapieka (publicist on *Two Dogs*) rings to say she's managed to retrieve her SA citizenship at record, red-tape-breaking speed and will be able to vote tomorrow in the Overseas ballot. All thanks to a particular lawyer. Michael Richman. South African, Jewish, friend and colleague of Albie Sachs, currently in charge of the European IEC (Independent Election Committee). 'Bring your old passport,' he says when I ring him. 'Can't,' I reply. 'Burnt it.' Dash down to his Pall Mall office. Together we rush to Trafalgar Square and South Africa House. The atmosphere is chaotic here, reminding me of movies of the last days of Saigon. With a gesture here, a word there, Michael's able to get us past the long queues in the public halls (are all these people hoping to retrieve burnt citizenships?) and into the 'backstage' area: a warren of corridors and offices where the embassy staff, wearing shirtsleeves and determined frowns, are boxing or shredding files. They're packing up, they're leaving, they're finished. The elections haven't begun, yet they seem to know the results. The chief immigration officer is so overworked he's in a kind of daze. Barely checks my forms, my photos, my £37. Says the passport will be ready in the morning. Within ten minutes of our arrival, Michael and I are back in Trafalgar Square. I mention that I'm amazed any bureaucracy can operate so fast. Michael says, 'Think of it as a closing-down sale.'

26/4/94. Here it is, a South African passport again, with my name in it – waiting in a brown envelope at the side entrance, the 'stage door', of South Africa House. Who'd've thought I'd be so bloody proud to hold this thing in my hands again? I'm the citizen of two countries now, two decent democracies. The British public got it wrong last time they voted. South Africans aren't going to get it wrong now. I join the queue. It takes three hours, inching round the embassy, through brilliant South African-type sunshine on one side, cool English spring shade on the other, then the final lap – the famous, or notorious, west side of the building, where demonstrations were always held. 'If this pavement could speak,' says Joy Sapieka at my side, smiling, eyes welling. At last we're through the entrance and into that rather threatening interior, with its old-regime mixture of the grand (marble pillars, teak furniture) and the provincial (dusty dioramas of South African scenes). Downstairs they explain that our votes will be flown out to SA tonight – 'flown home' says the woman – for the elections proper. Finally I'm in a booth. It's small and scruffy, with a feel of having been extensively over-occupied, like a toilet on an aeroplane, and the pencil is blunt with use. I'm trembling with sweet emotion as I make my cross.

27/4/94. Verne and Joan ring from SA first thing. 'We were at a ceremony in town last night . . . they took down the old flag . . . it was the most amazing thing! . . . we drank the champagne you left . . . we really, *really* missed you guys last night.' I watch Breakfast TV. There it is, the flag ceremony. A mixed choir sings 'Die Stem' as the old one comes down, 'NKosi' as the new one goes up. Both tunes move me; one ringing through my childhood, the other through my life here. Later I call Mom. She went early (7.30) to vote. The polling station was at my kindergarten school in King's Road. There was already such a long queue they stood for an hour or so. Eventually the elderly were invited to jump the queue. Mom said this wasn't fair and stayed put. Fifteen minutes later she changed her mind and went to the front. (Wonder how she voted? Probably for Uncle Nat. A lot of Cape people will still vote for him, including the new Coloured middle class. 'I spent my whole life being non-white,' one of them said to us when we were there. 'I'm not going to start being non-black now.') Then Mom went home to lie down and rest her aching feet. It made me smile. This grande dame of the old SA going to vote for the new one, making a token stab at equality in the queue, then jumping it, then coming home to rest from the exhaustion of it all.

10/5/94. Mandela sworn in as the new South African President. A lot of South Africans I know in London have flown out for it. Somewhere in those crowds in front of the podium, hopefully in the VIP ranks, sits Ethel de Keyser. I saw her a few days ago. Stocky, smiling, determined as always. Said she'd had some ill health and couldn't afford the flight: 'But I have to go – my whole life has been for this.' Meanwhile Rosenstern sits in front of the telly, weeping happily like someone watching a soap, clutching not a cup of cocoa but his new passport.

That same new passport was confiscated a few South African trips later, by a dead-eyed customs official at Cape Town airport. It seems that when I secured it in the closing-down sale at South Africa House, the proper procedures weren't followed and I hadn't done everything necessary to hold dual citizenship. I became completely inarticulate as it was taken from me: 'But . . . but . . . this is . . . so important . . . !' My pleas fell on deaf ears. The whole sorry little incident was somehow made worse because the official was female and black.

The confiscation served to raise the old questions again – where is home? who am I? – questions which had come up when I flew to Joburg a few months after the elections. Arriving in South Africa not on a family visit or research trip, but as part of another cultural visit by the Studio of the Royal National Theatre. It was odd. I'd gone with them to Lithuania, now to South Africa – their agenda seemed strangely linked to Sher family history. Our workshops were based at the Market Theatre in Joburg. Greg was on the team this time, as were Ian McKellen, Patsy Rodenburg, Sean Mathias, Richard Eyre and Lady Soames, Chairperson of the National.

I may have been arriving as part of British Theatre Establishment, yet I felt disillusioned with my adopted homeland, with both the larger and smaller pictures: Tory Britain and my career in it. I was supposed to be a leading theatre actor, yet never hit the jackpot any more – my work was never deemed to be among the best of the year. As a film actor I just couldn't make the breakthrough; Mike Newell had fought hard to cast me in a leading role in a film he was making, but the money men just weren't having it. As a TV actor I'd had a fright too. I was offered one of the main parts in Peter Flannery's *Our Friends in the North*. Was about to accept when they said, sorry but we've shown it to someone who's a bigger bums-on-sofas name and he's interested, so piss off, the offer's withdrawn.

So yes, I was feeling fairly disgruntled with England in September 1994 when we flew to South Africa – and this was a place of miracles. One man had walked out of prison and saved his people, saved the land. It was biblical, mythical, heroic. I was sick of watching from the sidelines. I wanted to be part of it now.

So when one night over dinner John Kani said to us, 'Tony, Greg, you just say which play you want to do and we'll schedule it. My brothers, we want you at the Market!' – it was very tempting.

The Market. One of the most famous theatres in the world. Formerly the Indian fruit and vegetable market of old Joburg (they've kept some of the signs round the domed auditorium: 'S. Patel, Vegetables', 'Spitting is Prohibited/*Moenie Hier Spoeg Nie* '). It opened in June 1976, at the time of the Soweto schoolchildren uprising. Like them, the Market became a sort of David to apartheid's Goliath. Forced to do some performances in secret, or with security policemen at the back of the stalls, or with far-right groups issuing death threats. In spite of these pressures it produced classics which condemned the system, first illuminating local audiences and then touring the world: the Fugard–Kani–Ntshona collaborations on *Siswe Banzi is Dead* and *The Island*, and the show Barney Simon devised with Percy Mtwa and Mbongeni Ngema, *Woza Albert!*. The Zulu word *woza* means welcome or arise, and the play ended with a call to the dead heroes of South Africa's past, including Nobel Peace prizewinner Albert Luthuli: '. . . *Woza* Ruth! *Woza* Steve! WOZA ALBERT!'

At the time of the Studio visit the Market was still being run by one of its founders, the guru-like director Barney Simon – white-bearded, baseball-capped – along with the actor John Kani, a dynamic performer, a man with a huge laugh and huge spirit.

John had made Greg and me an offer we couldn't refuse. A dream come true – to work on that renowned stage. And possibly a new career, a new life – back in South Africa? 'Let's just wait and see,' cautioned Greg (wisely, as it turned out). This was the beginning of another of the big adventures in my career, and another that was eventually to be published as a theatre journal, *Woza Shakespeare!*, co-written with Greg. To relate it here, in ten story points, is to tell a hair-raising, tragi-comic tale that is not only typically South African but typical of my relationship with home.

1   October 1994. We want to do a Shakespeare. There's been enormous appetite for Shakespeare in the workshops and he sounds terrific in South African accents – Xhosa, Zulu, Afrikaner, Cape Coloured – earthy accents that release the muscularity and beauty of the text in a fresh way. We settle on *Titus Andronicus*. As Greg says, 'In England it can seem so gratuitous, just a gory melodrama – but not here, somehow – here people know about violence.' It's a perfect Shakespeare for the Market and we'll do it modern dress. I'll play Titus, and a top multi-racial cast assemble in the other roles, led by Sello Maake ka Ncube as Aaron and Dorothy Gould as Tamora.

2   November 1994. The Market can't find money for the project. They get no state subsidy (the new government has to address more urgent needs) and rely entirely on sponsorship. But sponsors are frightened of *Titus*, either because they don't know it or because of its violence. Sue Higginson of the RNT Studio steps in. We'll make it a co-production with them, a follow-up to the Studio visit. Rehearsals will begin with a workshop in London, then we'll open in Joburg, then return for a short run at the National. Richard Eyre says, 'It's a project made in heaven.' This is even better than we thought. The Studio and British Council weigh in with funds, but the Market still have to find their share.

3   December 1994. Barney Simon rings excitedly. They've done it – found big sponsorship! National Panasonic, SA, are giving £100,000. A junior worker in the marketing department made the contact and achieved this fantastic deal.

4   January 1995. The day before the South African actors are due to fly to London, there's worrying news from the Market. They still haven't received the money from Panasonic. In fact, Panasonic seems to know nothing about it. Something weird is going on. Do we stop the South Africans from boarding the flight? No, advises Roger Chapman, Head of Touring at the RNT – let's start and then find a way of finishing.

5 February 1995. With the South African actors now in London and the *Titus* workshop in progress at the Studio, it becomes apparent that the Market have been the victim of a bizarre hoax. That junior worker in their marketing department is a little unstable apparently: she fantasised the Panasonic deal and no one else thought to check it out. A new deadline develops. Will the Market be able to find the funds now, or will *Titus* finish its life as a workshop in Waterloo? Halfway through, on a day trip with the South Africans to Stratford, we hear the news: an American friend of the Market, Michael Kaiser, is bailing us out. We drink toasts on the banks of the Avon.

6 March 1995. We return to Joburg. On the first evening, I write in my diary:

> So here we are, in our home, our South African home. The house in Greenside is very remiscent of houses from my childhood. Single-storeyed, with a green-grey corrugated-iron roof, cool passages inside, one very mannish room which serves as den/bar; and a large, rambling garden, with a rather secretive corner – holding someone else's childhood memories I'm sure – and a decent-sized pool. I feel so strange. It's hard to describe. A peculiar nostalgia which somehow takes me forward as well as back, and what I see in both directions fills me with a muddle of soothing-hurting sensations.
>
> We rehearse and open the show. Stepping out on to the Market stage is an overwhelming moment for me. And Shakespeare, who seems to write all things for all men, allows me to say, '. . . Cometh Andronicus, bound with laurel boughs/To re-salute his country with his tears.' After the curtain call the Minister for Arts, Dr Ngubani, comes on stage to announce that the government is finally giving the Market a state subsidy.

7 April 1995. We've had mixed reviews. Some of the critics raved, some were confused by the South African accents and settings. Surely Shakespeare should be posh, lofty, operatic, *British*? Surely Shakespeare shouldn't sound and look like people here! We're playing to half-empty houses (or half-full, as Greg, ever the optimist, puts it) and not only because of the reviews. It now turns out that serious theatre is in serious trouble here – thanks a

bunch, why did nobody warn us? – and auditoriums all round town are half-empty or half-full. White people don't like coming out at night – Joburg is nicknamed the murder capital of the world – and black people can't afford the ticket prices. Something else, too, something even more crucial. Whether because of censorship within the Old SA or the cultural boycott from outside – probably a combination of both – the Arts are not a vital part of society here. Janet Suzman, who comes to see the show, says, 'People got to the point where they said, what we can't have we won't want. They've lost their sense of curiosity.' I write an article for the *Joburg Star*. They print it on the Leader page. A lively debate starts up. I'm surprised by some of the hostility directed at me – for leaving home, for supporting the cultural boycott. 'It's come back to bite him!' gloats one woman on the letters page. My homecoming isn't quite what I dreamed of.

8   July 1995. We're back in England, waiting for the cast to join us for the UK run. The day before they fly, Barney Simon dies. Unexpectedly, from an undiagnosed heart condition. Once again we go to the airport to meet a group of stunned South African actors.

9   August 1995. You can't get a ticket for *Titus* at the National or at the West Yorkshire Playhouse. We win TMA awards for Best Production and Best Actor, and honourable mentions at the *Evening Standard* awards; Michael Coveney calls mine the Shakesperian performance of the year. (Hey, maybe my career ain't so bad here . . . !) We take the production to the Almagro theatre festival in Spain. We're invited to BAM in New York. Except this involves fund-raising again and our strange luck finally runs out.

10 1996. Greg and I write *Woza Shakespeare!* The book is partly a tribute to the Market and Barney Simon. We print a speech he made while we were there, when the Market won a prestigious American award, the Jujamcyn, given for its demonstration that theatre can change society. Barney was a shy, enigmatic man, not a natural public speaker – in fact, he just read his speech, in a soft, nervous voice. Yet we all ended up on the edge of our seats:

  I believe we live in a place of miracles. I haven't seen a

burning bush, except a veld fire or two. I've never followed a travelling star or even fantasised a flying saucer. But that's not a complaint. The miracles that interest me are not wonderful or delightful, or much to do with the divine. The ones I like best are those that give evidence of the grace that is in all things. There might be miracles in heaven but I suspect they're not nearly as rewarding as miracles in hell. Every adult South African sitting in this auditorium was born into an insane world. Insane because it denied and confused mankind's greatest gift, the equality of our humanity. But here's a miracle. Despite our beginnings, there's our people. Multiple, vivid, absurd, treacherous, generous, adventurous, divinely pragmatic, and always capable of our sound of survival – laughter. We who began the Market, did it out of love for this.

Titus was important to me for many reasons – not least was working with Greg for the first time in an actor–director relationship. And yes, as the pages of *Woza* reveal, plates did fly, glasses did smash. We hadn't yet learned to leave the play in the rehearsal room. Nowadays there's a strict rule: you're not allowed to discuss work at home. It's sometimes allowed in the car to rehearsals, though even this has to start with a formal request: 'May I just discuss a few minor points . . . ?'

The disadvantage of working with your partner is that you lose your best friend. You lose the person you come home to and say, 'That fucking director is driving me nuts!' Or that fucking actor etc. These are normal responses during any rehearsal process and seldom life-threatening.

The advantage is trust, trust, trust. Terry Hands had been trying to mould me into a Shakespearean actor before I even met Greg, but I was a deeply insecure one, haunted by the sense that I was trespassing: surely this was the preserve of honey-voiced English actors, not little Yiddish poofters from Sea Point. Greg has, in a way, given me Shakespeare. He made me feel that Shakespeare can be mine as much as anyone else's. The South African actors in *Titus* had to learn that (as did South African audiences and critics, who tended to resist) – but so did I. And although at that time Greg wasn't yet an associate director of the RSC, he already showed all the qualities which I believe make for a good director of Shakespeare:

- A passion for the language. This needs to go way beyond mere technical understanding of the verse or a philosophical appreciation of it. This has to be something hotter, emotional, boundless, fanatical – stark raving love. When the great Shakespearians (like John Barton or Cis Berry) speak about their subject they could be confessing a lifelong love affair. They're possessed by a special joy; their eyes shine, their voices grow warm and effortlessly eloquent – it's as though, just by talking about him, they're blessed with his gift for words.
- An ability to teach as well as direct. Most Shakespeare productions will involve casts of varying Shakespeare skills: young actors straight from drama school who can barely do it at all, older actors who can do it in their sleep (sometimes the problem), Bard know-it-alls, Bard don't-give-a-shits, traditionalists, modernists and so on. Yet if the production is to have coherence the ensemble must finally share a common approach to the language. At the RSC Cis Berry and the Voice Department conduct both group classes and individual one-to-ones. But some directors, like Greg, prefer to make this work part of the rehearsal process, often running the sessions themselves.
- A strong visual sense. Shakespeare plays have an epic dimension. The director needs the eye of a painter or film maker.
- A compassionate, all-embracing fascination with human nature.

Because we've continued to collaborate professionally (*Cyrano*, *Winter's Tale*, *Macbeth*), the impression might be that work is at the centre of our relationship. Yet it isn't. Work still makes us slightly tense, slightly combative; not really like ourselves. *Ourselves*. I think of this as a single unit. From our earliest days together, Greg talked to me about Plato's *Symposium* and how it helped explain a yearning we both share – Greg as a real twin, me as a Geminian – a yearning for our other self. Plato suggests that the human creature was originally made up of two halves, which got separated, leaving people with 'one side only, like a flat fish'. We spend our whole lives searching for the lost half and if we succeed in finding him, it feels like the expression of a very ancient need: 'And the reason is that human nature was originally one and we were a whole, and the desire and pursuit of the whole is called love.'

I'm completely captivated by this notion – that from opposite sides of the globe we were lost halves destined to find one another – especially since, if I had to choose one thing to stand for the *rightness* of our relationship, the totally loving, peaceful side, it would be travel. Wildlife travel. The addiction which started when I visited the Etosha Pan Game Reserve during my army days had grown – my one healthy addiction – and it was good to discover that my twin shared it: whale watching at Hermanus in the Cape Province or off the Massachusetts coast in North America, animal safaris in Asia and Africa.

Over the years we've returned most frequently to the private game parks in the Eastern Transvaal: Mala Mala, Sabi Sabi and Londolozi. Here you go out in groups of about six, in open jeeps, with a tracker and (armed) ranger on board. You don't have to be back before dark, you don't stay on the roads, you don't keep back from the animals. When you're right alongside it, a lion kill isn't quite as it seems on *Natural World*; film can't quite capture the feeding frenzy, the crack of buck bones, the noise of snouts trying to breathe, eat and fight at the same time. And when a lioness uses your jeep as cover during a stalk you have a close encounter of a very strange kind. She's right there at your foot, she turns to look, you gaze deeply into one another's eyes. Yet somehow she doesn't recognise you as food – a much easier target than the wildebeest in the distance. As long as you don't stand up, don't break the outline, she just sees this beast called Jeep. You kind of understand why. The metal corners of our transport seem to possess the flexibility of muscles as it twists through the densest bush or the deep sand of dry river beds, or up and down their vertical banks.

In Nepal, we exchange these mighty vehicles for the real thing: elephants. It's amazing enough to ride them – on tiger-spotting expeditions – even better to help scrub them down in the river when work's done.

On that same trip, but now in India, we're touring Lake Udaipur in a rowing boat late one afternoon when Greg says, 'Is that an eagle?' A huge winged creature is swooping down from the surrounding forest, then another, then a dozen more, heading for the centre of the water, drifting and dipping, perhaps drinking or feeding on insects near the surface. A few come closer, directly overhead. Fruit bats. Uncanny creatures – at least three in one: bird, dog and dragon – travelling at a sluggish, full-bellied pace, very big, very black, the sunset showing through the membranes of their wings, or just catching the hook-like hands, glinting oddly there, a talon, a spur. You feel both fearful and awestruck. There are hundreds now, thousands, gradually covering the whole lake, possessing it, a strange and wonderful pestilence; flying pieces of darkness showing against the shining body of water, bringing the night, slowly, silently – the silence of so many is astonishing. It's ghastly, it's beautiful.

'How lucky,' Greg and I said that evening, as we had before, 'to see such things *together*.'

These have been the best of our times. And they've been the closest sensation of anything I could call religious or spiritual.

Which perhaps explains why I responded so strongly to the next play I was sent after *Titus*. Its hero is obsessed with paradise on earth and with home. For him these two things are one and located in a small English village, a village called Cookham.

24

STAN

The English painter Stanley Spencer was born in Cookham in 1891, died in Cookham in 1959 and, apart from those times when he was in London (art student at the Slade) or away at war (medical orderly in Macedonia, WWI, war artist in Glasgow, WWII), he lived in Cookham for all the intervening years too.

Cookham is a small village on the Berkshire stretch of the Thames. Stanley saw it not only as his home but his muse. When he painted scenes from the Bible, he set them in the High Street – that's where Christ carries the cross, watched by locals in modern dress – and when he did the notorious nude portraits of his second wife Patricia and himself, these are village scenes too, but behind closed doors; a raw leg of lamb lies on the floor during one sexual encounter, inviting you to contemplate both the nature of human flesh and next Sunday's roast. The majority of the other paintings, figurative or landscapes, are also Cookham-based. Just that small radius, only a few miles across, that little collection of streets and homes, river banks and meadows, it's what he knew best, and could describe best in oils. He didn't need anything else, anything more.

I envy him. Whereas Cape Town was somewhere to blush over and disown – a cultural backwoods – Cookham is celebrated and immortalised. While I flee, he stays on. Life has nothing more to offer. The paintings brim with almost microscopic detail. When the nineteenth-century poet John Clare was going mad, he said, 'Imagine if you could see every flower.'

Well, Stanley Spencer does. And every blade of grass, and every strand in a bun of hair, and every button on a shirt. And yes, it does drive him to a kind of madness – he's certainly hyperactive, unable to stop painting, talking or writing letters round the clock – but it's a benign madness, a fabulous madness, a God-given madness; it produces masterpiece after masterpiece. His world is small, but his canvases are big, both in their dimensions and their themes. He was a visionary. And although selfish and spoilt, childishly naïve and narcissistic, prone to solipsism, male chauvinism and verbal diarrhoea, he had a blessed spirit, a kind of radiance. You can see it in his paintings. They shine with something more than oil and varnish, colour and contrast, more than genius even; they shine with grace.

I'm a fan, yes.

I wasn't always. My heroes of twentieth-century painting were Dali, Bacon and Hockney. I didn't know much about Spencer. I could've probably summoned up vague images of the Cookham Christ or the Leg of Mutton Nude, but my interest, and now love, didn't really grow till the National asked if I'd like to play him in Pam Gems's *Stanley*.

Pam had done the version of *Vanya* we'd used in the Cottesloe and I relished the way she wrote: her stumbling, broken sentences, her sense of humanity, of the comedy and tragedy in everyday things – it all seemed very faithful to the spirit of Chekhov. The first draft I saw of *Stanley* was less impressive, though, very unformed, a bit of a mess, in fact. But its heart was there. And the great last speech, where Stanley talks to his dead wife, that was already intact, word perfect. I was in tears when I put it down. The play didn't read like biopic or bioplay; it felt more autobiographical, as though Pam was writing about her own life in some way (but as I've said before, do writers ever write about anything else?) and it felt Chekhovian too: a group of articulate, indulgent folk, artists and idlers, falling in love with the wrong people, behaving badly, suffering noisily, yet making us care about them. *I've* been in a mess like that, the play makes you think.

Pam said she'd written the part of Stanley for me – she knew about my painting and drawing from *Vanya* days – and I was so flattered that, despite the text still being quite rough, I agreed to it then and there. But a new version was urgently required. Like with *Singer*, when Terry and I worked with Peter Flannery on successive drafts, the director John Caird and I now started working with Pam. It always feels odd this way round. My novels have benefited from strong editors (Andrew Motion, Jonathan Burnham, Philippa Harrison, Alan Samson) and now I'm in their shoes. Luckily Pam, like Peter Flannery, loved the collaboration. A large, hearty lady in her seventies, Pam wasn't remotely precious about her words, and rewrote freely and generously. She continued to do so when the other leading actors came on board: Deborah Findlay as Stanley's first wife Hilda; Anna Chancellor as the second, Patricia; Selina Cadell as Patricia's lesbian lover, Dorothy. Pam also embraced Tim Hatley's brilliant design solution: turning the Cottesloe into a kind of chapel, adorned with Stanley's paintings, the 'church of me' which the real man dreamed of. And finally John Caird created a beautifully fluid, cinematic production, feeding in lashings of Bach, Stanley's favourite composer. In fact, John saw to it that I'll never be able to listen to 'Wachet Auf' again without becoming emotional. This was used as Stanley and Hilda's theme, a celebration of their unique relationship, so strong it survived the messy divorce and even in a way her subsequent death. The tenderness, the delicate jauntiness of 'Wachet Auf' perfectly matched their story: children in adult bodies, clinging to one another, loving unconditionally.

I'd known Debbie Findlay since the 1987 Stratford season – she played Portia in *Merchant* and Olivia in the one I don't mention – and we intensified our friendship now. We learned our lines together. We learned to finish one another's sentences too, swap thoughts, breathe at the same time. Stanley and Hilda had a symbiotic relationship and the actors have to find something similar; you can't fake this kind of chemistry. Also, Debbie's acting has a purity, a truthfulness, which became like a light to aim for, a clue to the way this play could work.

The research during rehearsals was the most enjoyable I'd ever known. Instead of meeting arrogant Saudi princes, sitting through long-winded sociology lectures, immersing myself in the grim worlds of psychopaths or Nazism, all I had to do this time was stare at Stanley Spencer paintings – sometimes for hours on end – and to visit Cookham.

We went as a group, the whole company – actors, stage managers, director and designer – in a charabanc. First to Burghclere Chapel, near Newbury in Berkshire, where his WWI paintings adorn the walls like frescos, dominated by the colossal *Resurrection of the Soldiers* – its broken jumble of white crosses makes an astonishing composition through the centre – and then on to his beloved home village.

I wondered if Cookham would be like Stratford, just another small British town, but it wasn't at all. Stratford half carries sense memories from my youth – it's something about the Avon, that small, brownish, high-smelling river, and its earthy banks, quite dusty in midsummer, with sheep clustered in the shade. But Cookham's more purely English somehow: more foreign, more fascinating. Wetter countryside, greener, darker, heavily forested. And the river's much wider, filled with a deeper, different mystery. It's the Thames, after all, it's washed through half of England, it's headed for London . . . !

We wandered round the town, with little guide maps and big art books spread across our arms. Look, there's the tiled roof from *St Francis and the Birds*, there are those windows from *Christ Carrying the Cross*, there's the church from *The Resurrection, Cookham* and here, at the end of town, is *Cookham Moor*, including Moor Cottage, home of Patricia and Dorothy. Ah, Patricia. Ignorant of her sexuality, Stanley fell in love, abandoned Hilda and married her. She in turn liked his fame and wealth, but nothing more. So he plunged into an agony of unconsummated lust while she just continued to live happily with Dorothy here at Moor Cottage. We knocked on the door and asked if we could look around. Somewhat bemused, the present owners ushered in a small army of National Theatre actors and staff. No, they didn't know much about Patricia and Dorothy. The odd thing is that these two continued to live in Cookham till their deaths despite the scandal – the tabloids called Stanley 'The Man with Two Wives' – and despite their lesbian relationship. I suppose the residents of Cookham just thought of them as two ladies sharing. Only in a polite English village . . .

There's a small Stanley Spencer gallery in Cookham, in the old Methodist chapel. Here I saw the painting that was to become my favourite – probably one of my favourite paintings of all time – *Christ Preaching at Cookham Regatta*. He worked on this vast canvas for the last few years of his life and never finished it. It moves me enormously. Layer after layer of the man and his work are on display. In the centre is a colourful, teeming, typically Stanley scene of local townsfolk and biblical disciples collected on the river banks and in punts; while to either side are large areas of white canvas with pencil divisions, the 'squaring-off' he so favoured, and outlines of the figures yet to be painted – they float like ghosts among the others, the finished ones, the brightly coloured crowd.

Here's a section of lawn, with every flower, every blade of grass painted in. Here's the river – the river he painted again and again, the river that's just down the road from this gallery, just past the churchyard where he and Hilda are buried, just over Kissing Gate. At the top of the canvas, in the middle, he shows the far bank of the river, with a reflection of the sky, lit in rose and golden hues, a heavenly sky. It's where Stanley himself was headed and it looks like he was determined to get that section finished to perfection before his departure. You can imagine him sitting back from it and saying to himself – as Pam has him do at the end of the play – 'Beautifully done.'

There are photos of Stanley working on this painting in his bedroom-studio in Fernlea, the house where he was born, down the road from the gallery. A stretch of the huge canvas covers one whole wall, the surplus rolled into the corner like a scroll. To achieve height, Stanley paints sitting on a chair which is propped on a table.

We decided to re-create this image for the top of the show – except our canvas was even bigger, covering the back wall of the Cottesloe, with scaffolding erected against it; more like when he worked in Burghclere Chapel. (And the painting in progress on our set was not the Cookham *Regatta* but the Cookham *Resurrection*. The latter was one of the few we could reproduce. Stanley's two daughters had taken agin the play and forbidden the use of any of the pictures under their control, which is about ninety-five per cent of his work.) On the first level of the scaffolding was a table, a chair on it and me. As the audience came in I was already there, painting away.

I always feel anxious at the start of a show, but didn't with this one. Sitting there painting was like a relaxation exercise, almost a form of meditation. I can be riven with doubt about my acting, but not my painting. I don't do it as a living, so there's no pressure. I've been doing it since the age of five, it's second nature. I don't care how *good* it is, or not; it's just something I do.

So there I was – painter? actor? – somewhere between the two, vaguely copying Stanley's brush style, while preparing to play the man himself. I sat there for about half an hour each evening, working away on that one area of canvas (we had to keep replacing it every few weeks) and then I'd see the cue light go red – hidden among my pots and rags – and then green, and I'd hear the 'Gloria' from Bach's *Magnificat* swell and soar, and, twisting round in my elevated seat, I'd see Deb Findlay below as Hilda, a raincoat half draped over her naked breasts, eating from a tin of canned fruit, smiling up at me. She was surrounded by darkness. The Cottesloe and the audience had vanished for now. We were in our world, Stan's and Hilda's world, our paradise on earth.

In the first scene Hilda slips off the raincoat and, still munching at the canned fruit, poses for Stanley. He sketches as they chat. Once again it was useful being able to do this without thinking. In other plays, trying to practise a skill while speaking the dialogue – the rope-climbing in *Tamburlaine*, the sword fighting in *Cyrano* – these make for my tensest times in the show. I may have learned to rope climb or sword fight, but these things are not innate and never will be; a part of me keeps screaming help! and ouch!

I suppose it was this happy coincidence – being an actor who could paint – that made the part of Stanley come easily to me. There's film of the man himself, but we chose not to go for impersonation. The real man speaks posh, an RP accent replacing his natural Berkshire brogue. But we gave it back to him, to emphasise his otherness from the London artists. These externals seemed almost irrelevant, however – I knew him, somehow, from deep inside. On paper, there weren't obvious comparisons. With his owlish specs, his neatly knotted necktie, his tweed jacket, his cardy and his corduroys, he was the little Englishman, the chirpy little gent, thoroughly Christian, thoroughly heterosexual, thoroughly at ease with his surroundings and his talent; he needed neither mother nor family doctor to point him towards his destiny, he could scent it in his own nostrils – he always had an inner status of ten. We could not have been more different. And yet he felt close – Stanley Spencer himself – I can't explain it.

I had a vivid dream just before rehearsals started: a patch of long grass, a breeze passing over it, that marvellous effect of rolling silver light. Waking up, I could see it there for a few moments – long grass in the corner of our bedroom – and, just before it vanished, felt a powerful sense of someone crouching within it, smiling at me. Him – Stanley. Unlike my mother, I'm not a believer in spiritualism, yet something quite strange happened again when we did the first make-up test. I don't resemble Stanley at all. He had a beautiful boyish face, with full simian mouth, big teeth, and a great fringe of thick black hair. We decided to go for simplicity, using nothing more than a half-wig for the fringe, and the owlish grey-plastic specs. Yet when I put on these two things, everyone in the room froze. There he was – Stanley Spencer – smiling at me again, not from a dream but a mirror.

I wore the whole look for the first time at the Tech: wig, glasses, jacket, tie and cardy. Pam Gems came in halfway through. She paused, then suddenly sat down, her hand to her mouth, eyes shining with tears. 'Good gracious,' she said, 'it's Stan.'

I could feel the part working well in previews: everything I hoped for, most especially an effortless flow of real feelings for the sections about love and grief – Stanley was a child-man, he had no self-censorship; thoughts and emotions just poured out whenever they occurred. I wanted this to be for real and it was. But now the dreaded press night was approaching. Would I let myself down? This is always the fear – on this one night, when, absurdly, the show goes to judgement – will I blow it by trying too hard? By upsetting that balance between concentration and relaxation, that elusive formula for good acting?

The night before, the actor Vernon Dobtcheff saw the show. Vernon is actually the ubiquitous First-Nighter (there are rumours of clones, for he's sometimes been spotted at different first nights on the same evening), but on this occasion certain circumstances had brought him to the last preview instead. When he came round afterwards he was clearly impressed and moved. 'Yes, but what about tomorrow night?' I fretted. 'How can I be sure of doing it well tomorrow night?'

'Simple,' he replied brightly. 'Just do it for him. Do it for Stanley.'

So I did. And to my astonishment he came into my dressing room beforehand – Stanley – not as a dream or even a trick of the mirror, but as a sketch. An authentic Stanley Spencer sketch. A study for *Up the Rise*. Pam had found and bought it, God knows where or for how much, and was presenting it to me as a first-night gift. It was my turn to cover my mouth, eyes filling, and say, 'Good gracious, it's a real Stan.' Left alone with it, I did a very untypical thing. In the play, Stanley and Hilda kneel like children at their bedside to pray before sleep. This is what I did now. I propped the sketch on a chair, knelt in front of it, clasped my hands in the appropriate manner and whispered a few words to Stanley Spencer, God Almighty, Jesus Christ, or whoever else was listening. And it worked. Or at any rate, I didn't let myself down on that performance. As Richard Eyre said afterwards, 'You went to concert pitch tonight.'

A few days later I spotted Richard again in one of the long dressing-room corridors at the National. He stood at the far end, smiling, watching me walk towards him. It was before a performance and I was in full Stanley gear. 'I've never seen you like this,' he said as I drew close, 'so inside a character. What is it?'

'I don't know,' I replied. 'I just love him.'

'Yes, of course,' said Richard. 'It's always just about love.'

Stanley was greatly loved – the play, the acting, the production, the design – rave reviews across the board and sold-out signs for the entire six-month run. We were a hit, a palpable hit. In November Pam picked up Best Play at the *Evening Standard* awards. I was unlucky again, on this occasion because of formidable competition: Paul Scofield in *John Gabriel Borkman*. No time to dwell on it: Stan, the little Englishman, was Broadway-bound; he was going to the Circle in the Square Theatre on West 50th Street.

I'd never been to New York before, not even to visit. The city had always held a strong mixture of allure and fear for me. During my promiscuous days I'd heard mouth-watering tales about its bath-houses and back rooms, its drugs and drinks, but also about its muggings and murders. That was the seventies. Now it was the nineties. AIDS had perhaps curtailed some of its gay and underground life, and Mayor Giuliani had certainly addressed its reputation for violence. Yet it still felt like a dangerous place. Very dangerous. For me specifically . . .

14/1/97. Touched down at JFK at 4.15 yesterday. The afternoon was cold, with traces of snow, but bright – rapidly going dark during our drive into the city. Took for ever. It was rush hour and the outskirts of any city during rush hour look like there's some kind of refugee crisis. Some of these refugees were in stretch limos. Ours – laid on by the Circle – was more modest. The driver flicked on the radio and a crooner launched into 'Time goes by so slowly, and time can mean so much'. And then New York came into view.

I'd been told how the airport road dipped and rose, and then suddenly offered this view – both Greg and Mic had described it – and reality didn't disappoint. Except it was more sinister than I expected. By now it was dark, and the skyscrapers looked like burnt shells of buildings pock-marked with light. Maybe it was my mood. Maybe if I were just here to holiday I might have said they looked like stacks of jeweller's trays: diamonds on black velvet. But I'm not here to holiday. I'm here to play a starring role on Broadway. My outer status is high, my inner less so. 'You look like a seven-year-old,' Greg observed in the car. Catching my reflection in the window, I saw what he meant. I was sitting forward, frowning in the way children do when they're confronted by a totally new experience. Everything is unknown, there's so much to learn, will they pick it up in time? It felt like I was starting from scratch again, with a big endurance test ahead. Would I survive the army, would I get into a London drama school, would I succeed on Broadway (and *finally* get a movie career)? Here I was, coming Overseas again. Arriving again. For fuck's sake, when would I get there? When would I be arrived, not arriving?

The hotel, Wyndam's, is a curious mix of grandeur and seediness, which Greg says is typically old New York. The lift man sells the *New York Times*. So here it is, the all-powerful, make-or-break *New York Times*. Looks so ordinary. Just a newspaper, tomorrow's litter. But then, opening it, my head jerks back as though punched. Massive, half-page, even full-page adverts for current movies. *Sling Blade* – 'One of the Best Films of the Year!'; *The English Patient* – 'Best Film of the Year!'; *Emma* – 'Undoubtedly Best Film of the Year!' Dear God, the *New York Times* is like the inside of my mother's head. Or mine, on a bad day.

Success, success. This is a dangerous town for me.

I must be careful. As Greg says, I'm developing an attitude.

Can't help it. In *Middlepost* I tried to imagine what a new world would look like to someone coming from an old one and decided he'd feel like an alien fallen to earth. It's how I feel now.

Walked around in a daze this morning. Not just jet lag. Punch-drunk again, head knocked back and lolling. What were New York's architects up to, what were they *on*? Never mind designing an environment that's human-friendly, they said, we'll design one for giants. Humans are small creatures but they dream big. We'll design their dream city. I mean, they are inspiring, the buildings, as you wander through their canyons far below (icy at this time of year), yet in a profoundly different way from natural wonders like, say, Table Mountain, which also rises out of the centre of a city, dwarfing it.

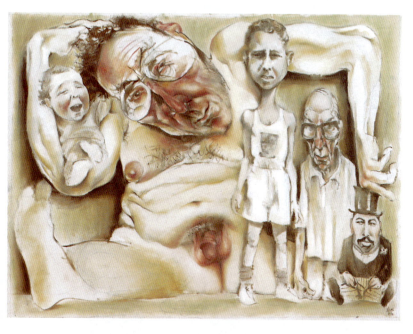

17. 'THE MALE LINE' (1996): self-portraits aged 1, 47 and 9, with Dad
and his father; painted in oils, cocaine and Dad's ashes.

18. LITHUANIA, 1992.
Top: At the Holocaust Memorial
near Kaunus. *Below*: With
Jakovas Bunka,
the last Jew in Plunge.
Right: In Plunge.

19. CORNERING THE MARKET IN MINORITY GROUPS.
Left: Jewish (practising ventriloquism for *Genghis Cohen*). *Below*: White South African (with Estelle Kohler in *Hello and Goodbye*). *Bottom*: Gay (with Jason Flemyng in *Alive and Kicking*).

20. VERY IMPORTANT PERSONS.
Top: With Richard Wilson. *Middle*: Training for *Tamburlaine* with Johnnie Hutch (Mal Storry behind). *Bottom*: First-night cards for *Travesties* (Stoppard as Wilde) and *The Trial* (Berkoff and cast).

21. WARRIOR AND
PAINTER.
Top: *Tamburlaine*.
Bottom: *Stanley*
(with Deb Findlay as
Hilda).

22. The Four Shows
with Greg.
Top: Greg Directing.
Bottom: *Cyrano de
Bergerac*, 1997.
Opposite page:
Top left: *Titus
Andronicus*, 1995
Top right: *The Winter's
Tale*, 1999.
Bottom: *Macbeth* (with
Harriet Walter as Lady
Macbeth), 1999.

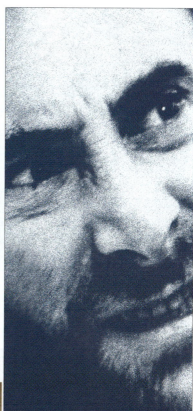

24. THE YEAR 2000.
Top: Mom turns 80 on the 12th January, surrounded by her four children:
self, Verne, Joel, Randall.
Bottom: Knighted by the Queen, 28th November.

These huge man-made rocks are carved to provoke and tease our most urgent desires, for power and spectacle. Now you understand why the *New York Times* has to shriek, 'This film is best – no, this is – no, this one!' It's the only way to be heard in this city of towers. And the newsprint ads are as nothing compared with the billboards. In Times Square, there's one for men's underwear. A fabulous image, with gorgeous, laughing guys under beach showers, the water making their white briefs transparent. This is a size-queen's wet dream. For a moment the whole city makes sense.

We find the Circle in the Square. Nothing like my fantasies about 'playing Broadway'. A dingy plate-glass front on the ground floor of an office block. This is the box office; the theatre's somewhere below. Here at last is a picture of me. As Stanley. A normal-sized poster, looking minuscule in the present context, like a postage stamp. Is someone trying to tell me something? Oh, fuck. How am I going to get through the next few months – without even a drink?

This was the crux. The reason for my bleak, fearful tone. I was arriving in New York squeaky clean and sober. I truly was arriving as a younger version of myself. Only about five months old, in fact.

Five months since I'd left Charter Nightingale Hospital on Lisson Grove. Room 318 on the third floor. The floor for substance abuse.

PART III

And Then Again

25

CHARTER NIGHTINGALE

My first memories are of Sunday evenings and bright rooms. I can see into every corner. I feel calm, peaceful, almost bored. Safe though, like in childhood. Home. Sunday. A quiet place, a gentle time. Not the crash site of another crazed weekend, coke-crazed, whisky-crazed, everything jarring, blurred, greasy; spectacles, mirrors, tumblers . . .

None of that any more. Sunday evenings and bright rooms. Might go to bed early, might read a book. I'm a new man. Reborn, they say. Recovering. Not recovered, you're never recovered, only ever just recovering. Sounds strange. In a permanent state of temporariness. But call it what you like, I'm starting all over again . . .

On a Monday morning three weeks earlier, immediately after the run of *Stanley* finished at the National, Greg drove me and a suitcase across town to Lisson Grove and Charter Nightingale Hospital. We were both upset in the car. The day had finally come. Greg was relieved – no, overjoyed – that it was here, yet anxious for me. His twin was venturing into unknown territory and had to do it alone. I just felt helpless and maudlin, the victim of a savage case of self-battering. I'd been up for two nights. The farewell binge started straight after the Saturday night performance of *Stanley* . . . no, let's tell the truth, it started during it . . . well, it actually started during the matinée . . . just a small line or two in the dressing room, just a little something to keep me ticking over, just a little sampler of the night ahead, oo-la-la, me and the mirror again . . . just a small line, can't do any harm. Oh yes, it can, and it did. I was in a rough state by the second show, separated from my character by a big gulf. Stanley's egotism was a pure, natural state, mine was chemically induced, a very jittery business; I'm half at work, half at play, can anyone notice? – the running nose, the tongue licking the gums – no real Stanley feelings going through me tonight, just Charlie's special brand of paranoia. Mind you, not as bad as a few weeks earlier. Greg was away. I'd been up through the night again. Morning came. A horrible feeling – vampires must know it – fun over for now. All the stuff, too, every last grain licked off every last surface. Unbearable. Have a whisky or two to lessen the comedown. Got a performance tonight, but that's many hours away. I can sleep in between, shower, I'll be fine by then. Fucking hell. The performance that night was the most frightening I've ever known.

So here I am, on Monday, 19 August 1996, travelling to Charter Nightingale. I'm checking in at last. I've booked and cancelled several times, but this is it. I'm doing it this time. Greg and I kiss goodbye in the car. I carry my suitcase into the hospital. I report to the admissions desk. The man says a nurse will come down for me. I wait in the foyer. There's a display case with something about Florence Nightingale – so that's where the name comes from – I stand, reading the information without absorbing a word.

'Mr Sher?'

I turn. Not the kind of nurse I was expecting: small, elderly, no uniform. She says my name again, insistently, checking that it definitely is me.

'Yes,' I say.

'Here for a rest, are you, dear?'

'Yes, yes,' I mumble, 'a rest.'

She nods, wisely, sadly, and starts towards the lift. I follow. The lift arrives and a young woman steps out: a uniformed nurse. 'Mr Sher?' she says brightly.

'Ye-e-es,' I say, starting to frown.

'How are you feeling?'

'He's here for a rest,' the old woman replies before I can. We're all in the lift now. The old woman gets out on the first floor. Then the young nurse explains the layout of Charter Nightingale: 'We're going to the third floor, which is for substance abuse, the second is for eating disorders, the first for depressive illnesses.'

Oh. The old woman wasn't a nurse, she was a patient. She wasn't greeting me, she was recognising me. Odd. I'm hardly ever recognised – theatre actors aren't – how odd it should happen here. How embarrassing.

Mind you, it never happened again. Quite the opposite. 'I'm an actor,' I'd tell the circle in group therapy. They'd sit forward, studying my features intently. Nope, doesn't look familiar from the telly. Claims to be an actor, but so what? Each of them – an assortment of heroin addicts and alcoholics – had professed all sorts of things while under the influence. 'I'm a novelist too,' I'd add. They nodded sympathetically.

Status. It's all to do with status. I was starting one of the most testing times of my life and I had no status. Actors are supposed to be famous. It's a common fallacy that afflicts us as much as the public. We don't go into the business wanting to be just actors, just working actors, we want to be stars. It's mad, but I came to long for the old woman's reaction. That's Antony Sher, he's a well-known actor, a troubled artiste. It'd be a kind of excuse. Instead, I had to introduce myself in the AA manner: 'Hello, I'm Tony, I'm an addict.' (Hated that, hated that.) And of course the others accepted *this* information. It went to a raw place inside me, a place where the coke shit lived, a place of failure. What had happened to Mommie's 'great man'? People recognised him as a coke fiend but not as an actor.

And I don't know why not – I believed what they told me. One of them, a mild-spoken, middle-aged character, revealed he was an airline pilot. We all went very still. He was also a bottle-of-vodka-a-day man.

'Air pilots, heart surgeons, all the high-stress jobs,' confirmed my consultant, Dr Shanahan. 'And actors, of course.' He at least knew I wasn't fantasising.

I'd been seeing him for several months prior to checking in – a replacement for ordinary therapy. My great guru, Monty Berman, had moved back to South Africa, the place where he was born, which he'd fought for and been exiled from; it was the New South Africa, now, and he'd finally gone home. I'd started work with a new therapist, but she suggested that before I could really address the crucial issues I needed to tackle the thing that was acting like a buffer zone between me and myself, the cocaine. She found out about Shanahan. For a while I dubbed him Shenanigans and resisted making the first visit. Then I went. Because of

the Irish name I was expecting some thunderous Ian Paisley figure –
'Repent, repent!' – so was surprised to meet a young, witty character with
delicate tactics. 'Take your time, be sure,' he'd say, with a warm smile –
something of a dare in it too. 'When you want to, you'll check in.'

His diagnosis was cocaine dependency and his recommendation
complete abstention. He said he didn't think I was an alcoholic, yet
wanted me to abstain from booze too, for the foreseeable future. The two
were inextricably linked. Wine leading to whisky leading to the phone
call.

My treatment at Charter Nightingale involved some mild medication –
tranquillisers, sleeping pills and something to discourage coke cravings –
but it was primarily tackled as a mental and emotional problem, with one-
to-one counselling, education (lectures) and group therapy.

I was uncomfortable with the last. The form was familiar; workshops and
even rehearsals are a kind of group therapy: the sharing and solving of
problems. But this was something quite different – and not just because of
lack of status.

The saying goes: cocaine is God's way of telling you you're earning too
much money. Not entirely true in my case. I've never been rich (as an
actor you need to do movies to be rich, as a novelist you need to write best-
sellers), but I have been comfortably off. And with Greg now earning a
good salary as one of the RSC associate directors, we were fairly flush with
the pink pound (while denied the tax and other benefits available to
straight married couples in the same circumstances: dual earning and
childless). We've never been into fancy cars or clothes, but we like our
wildlife travel, we like good hotels and good food. I liked pricey whisky,
too, and cocaine would cost between £60 and £80, depending on whether
you were using the take away or home-delivery service. Money also bought
me BUPA membership (I've often been injured on stage and I'm a wimp
who wants to be cosseted during recovery) and it was as a BUPA member
that I checked into Charter Nightingale. In my first week there were one
or two others of my kind, which means middle class, comfortable, and, let's
face it, spoilt, but the majority of patients, there through the NHS, were a
very different group: streetwise junkies, park-bench alkies, some pretty
hard cases. We were a difficult mix. Quite a shock to me. A bit like being
back in the army. Once again I was emerging from a privileged background
and stepping into the real world. I'm changing their names, but here's Sam

the Can Man, a skinny little figure seriously committed to lager; here's Phil, a friend of Smirnoff's, wild beard, grey skin, suffering such bad withdrawal he tumbles down corridors as though on board a ship; Jez, the handsome dragon chaser, so heavily sedated he sleeps through most sessions; Bobby, another young heroin guy, skinhead cut, Cocteauesque features, very explosive and emotional.

I have to keep reminding myself that I'm not on a research trip, this includes me, this is *about me*; and I'm not in a workshop either, this isn't to make a play, this is make or break. But we're getting nowhere. It's driving me mad. Group therapy is about talking and these blokes are inarticulate. For compelling social reasons, yes I know, but I'm not feeling particularly pc at the moment. And there's nothing like a little stay in hospital, when you're hurting and vulnerable, to bring out some basic tribal instincts. The truth is I just want to get better and get out of here! My panic at finding myself in a room full of fellow addicts is massive. I haven't time for this – their long, rambling monologues made up of just two catchphrases, 'Know whadda mean?' and 'See whaddam saying?' Modern urban speech: all content knocked out of it – leaving only these two little punch-drunk noises, these two numb, dumb questions: 'See whaddam saying? . . . uhh . . . know whadda mean? . . . uhh . . . see whaddam saying? . . . uhh . . . know whadda mean?' No, I don't know what you mean, I want to shout back and the only thing you're saying is see whaddam saying! There's nothing in between! It makes no sense – you make no sense and the system makes no sense! Here we are, trying to use speech as our cure and you can't fucking speak!

25/8/96. End of the first week. 10 a.m. Group session with a visitor from NA (Narcotics Anonymous) to explain how they work and encourage membership. The man invites questions or comment. The young Cocteauesque heroin guy, Bobby, says he needs to tell us something. I brace myself. This'll be another 'See whaddam saying', 'Know whadda mean' monologue.

Not quite.

'. . . I'm HIV positive, just want you all to know, my lady died a few months ago and my lady before her, too, she died too, not of AIDS, though, not sure what it was, her lungs just burst in her chest. So – see whaddam saying? What's the point – what's the point of recovery?

Death is coming, it's definitely coming, man, it's that white light, it keeps coming towards me. Know whadda mean? I've tried doing it, getting it over with, and not with the door open, see whaddam saying, not with come-find-me close at hand. Fourteen hours, man, then I woke and thought, hey I'm dead, this is death. Then I thought, oh no, oh shit, this is life, I'm still here.'

Bobby's face is covered with tears and snot. I can't bear this. I'm in a scene from *Trainspotting*, without the gags, without the sexiness. I want to get up, I want to go out. This is nothing to do with me!

Bobby goes on: 'When you're a kid, you want *this*' – makes a hugging gesture – 'And what do you get? You get *this*' – makes a pushing gesture.

Nothing to do with me?

Later. Greg arrives to take me on a drive into the country. This is a Shanahan treat – trusting me enough to allow freedom so soon. Greg doesn't say where we're going. Turns out it's Cookham. My heart lifts. Greg's also prepared a special picnic, with favourite Kettle crisps, M & S lobster, and fruit juice in the cooler sleeve instead of Chablis. We carry it down to the river, sit under a tree. Cool, blowy, wonderfully English day. The afternoon brightens as we walk across the common and into the village, passing all the familiar Stanley landmarks: Moor Thatch, Fernlea, the churchyard ('Here lies Sir Stanley Spencer and his wife Hilda') and into the gallery. I feast again on the unfinished *Cookham Regatta*. Am recognised by the gallery owner who tells me their attendance has doubled because of the play. He asks why I'm here. I answer: 'Just a little spiritual fill-up.' At Charter Nightingale they're asking us to nominate a Greater Power. It can be anything – God, Science, Art, whatever – anything that helps you stop obsessing about yourself. I've nominated Nature for now. This afternoon in Cookham seems to prove it. (Or is Cookham about Art more than Nature? A perfect union of the two, possibly.) A little panic as we're leaving. I need a loo and the only ones available are in pubs. Feel I can't risk that. Eventually we find a loo in a railway station. Driving back, the weather changes again, turning stormy, and my mood darkens accordingly. The thought of tomorrow morning, and those guys all going see whaddam saying, know whadda mean. I say to Greg, 'I'm not sure I'm going to make this.' We talk it through. Why am I being so pompous and uncompassionate about the other patients? Is it just an elaborate escape plan? And maybe I want Greg, like a sort of parent, to sanction it. But he won't. He *needs* me to get clean – he's never known me clean. 'Let's see what next week brings,' he says as he drops me off in Lisson Grove. I go up to my room. Room 318. I stare out through the Sunday evening drizzle, across the backstreets and roofs of Paddington. This is like being in a bedsit again, newly arrived in London. It's like I know no one, know nothing. I feel terrified, terrible, lonely, lost. How the fuck did I get into this situation?

Art comes to the rescue in week two. Art helps me start to discover why I got into this situation. Art in the form of art therapy.

Marietta Young is the therapist: born in Prague, blonde, strong attractive features. She insists you don't have to possess artistic skills to use the technique – any squiggles, blobs or photo montages will do – but the rest of the group feel intimidated nevertheless. Maybe I'd feel the same if asked to heal myself through singing. But it's painting and drawing, and I'm very comfortable in this world. Even the room itself reminds me of art rooms at school, with its layout of big tables, its childlike sketches stuck round the walls, its long sunny window.

In the first session Marietta invites us to create a picture, anything we want, and then we'll discuss each image as a group. I do a big crayon drawing of a naked man lying on a broken mirror, snorting up a mess of coke, smashed glass and blood. It's a powerful image. The group is impressed. 'Well, yes, I'm a sort of artist,' I mumble. They exchange looks. *Who is this guy – he says he's an actor, an author and now he's an artist too?* I don't make sense in their world of drop-outs and dealers. I don't even make sense to the few middle-class (BUPA) members of the group: an older lady, an expat type, incoherent with alcohol; a businessman from up north, another serious boozer. I'm from the arts community, that mysterious, rarefied thing. Art has been my life, a source of huge pleasure and huge doubt. Art or shit – which am I lifting into the light? As I present my picture to the group and see their expressions of admiration – these people who feel so alien to me, so hostile – it feels strangely familiar, wonderfully, sadly familiar. Art saving my skin again, art being my passport, art winning love, art not *me*. I start to cry. Marietta asks why. I can't explain. 'It's a feeling, not words,' I say. Her face lights up. She says, 'I think this could really work for you.'

It did. Art therapy worked wonders for me. It went to the places other therapy couldn't reach. I picture the spot being deep inside me, in my guts, in my centre, a badly bruised spot, completely vulnerable, yet heavily protected by tough adult muscles and thick adult skin. Other techniques of therapy had tried to reach the spot, but all my defences kept them away. Art therapy went straight there. In the same way that art led me in a straight line to the character of Stanley Spencer, bypassing all the usual humming and hawing about how to play the part and allowing direct access to his uncensored feelings, now art therapy leads me in a straight line to myself.

It's very simple, my 'case history'. The vital factor at my birth wasn't the cowl, but my reigning star, Gemini. A duality in all things. I was brought up with two conflicting messages. One parent said you're a genius, the other said you're not even interesting. Where does that leave me? What do *I* think? The happy individual is the one who's at peace, who likes himself. Cocaine is the short cut. (Never mind liking yourself – you fall in love, bowing to that mirror.) The long way round is therapy. It's very simple, my 'case history', on paper.

The population of Charter Nightingale kept changing, as people started and finished their detoxes. Halfway through week two, I started to feel more at ease in the group. Apart from Bazz, a shell-suited Essex man whose coke habit made mine look like child's play – he was on ten grams per weekend – and who did a runner after two days, the others were mostly alcoholics, gentler than the druggy-druggy guys. There was Sheila, a young housewife who'd taken to drinking all day at home; William, a kind, grey-haired university man who'd stayed sober for twenty years but started hitting the gin again recently; and Jan, a small, warm-hearted Dutch woman, who sometimes went walkabout with vodka. We were talking now, in group therapy, really talking. This, together with Marietta's art therapy, and sessions with another therapist, and consultations with Shanahan, and I started to make progress.

A real breakthrough came with the cracking of my 'Intruder' dream – a recurring nightmare which had plagued me for the last few years. It was the nastiest kind, playing with layers of reality, and would only happen when I was alone in the house. In the dream, I'm asleep in our bed, our real bed, and hear someone coming up the stairs, the real stairs in our Islington home. I wake, very frightened. Then I hear the noise – of feet still coming up the stairs. It's a real intruder. I start to scream. Then, with a gasp, I wake again. Properly. I hadn't before; that was just my mind fooling around. (Who needs enemies when we've got our own imagination?) Monty and I thought we'd decoded the dream one day when I started talking about Dad's insomnia. He used to prowl the house at night. I must've heard him as a child, maybe half asleep, maybe growing scared. He was a threatening, unfriendly figure, after all. I disliked the smell of him: the whisky on his breath, the sharp odour of raw hides and skins on his work clothes. The idea of him wandering, perhaps drunk, into my room as I slept, this would've been awful. But now, in Charter Nightingale, I discovered a much simpler interpretation of the dream and of the intruder figure. Myself. My dark side. My destructive side. The dream only happened when I was alone in the house. So did my coke deals. If Greg was away for the night or weekend, that's when the itch would start, a thrilling, terrible itch. *I'm going to do it again – no, you mustn't – yes – no! – OK, just have some wine, then some whisky, and then we'll discuss it again . . .*

'You must learn to embrace him,' Marietta said in the first art therapy session, pointing to my drawing of the naked man on the broken mirror. She'd say the same of the intruder in my recurring nightmare: 'Learn to embrace him.'

'But to embrace him,' I protested, 'is to accept the man who loves coke.'

'Well, accept him, yes – he's there, he's in you, but he doesn't have to call the tune. You can. You can say no. Let him stop frightening you. Make your peace with him. Embrace him.'

'Sounds very New South Africa,' I said ruefully, 'making peace with your enemies, forgiving them their sins.'

She broke into a big smile. 'And hasn't it given them incredible strength? Incredible strength!'

I'd proved her point. She kept smiling. I gave in and smiled back.

'Embrace him,' she said.

By the end of the third week, Shanahan felt it was safe for me to return home, return to the outside world. Coke was banned for good and booze for the foreseeable future. I would carry on art therapy with Marietta on a one-to-one basis, I would attend meetings of CA (Cocaine Anonymous) in Ladbroke Grove and I'd come to Aftercare, a twice-weekly group session held at Charter for ex-patients.

(I attended both CA and Aftercare for several months afterwards, but then my old inhibitions about group therapy returned and, finding I was contributing little, I stopped going and settled just for Marietta. I still see her for a weekly session, four years after my time in Charter Nightingale.)

And so to Sunday evenings and bright rooms.

The first was my first night home:

8/9/96. The feeling as I move around the house, unpacking, is hard to describe. It's like an evening from childhood . . . something about the light reaching into every corner, no shadows, no darkness . . . memories of the family in Montagu House, the reassuring bump of footsteps on the floor above or on the stairs . . . it's Greg in the house tonight, our Islington house, making dinner in the kitchen (he's cooking my favourite for the homecoming: tomato *bredie*, Katie's recipe), or popping upstairs to check something for his rehearsals tomorrow . . . and me in this room down here, my study, with light in every corner . . . me wide awake, happy, safe. The intruder's gone. I know who he is now and he's gone. Greg and I eat, we watch telly, we go to bed, we make love. Wonderful.

DIZZY AND BIG APPLE

I'm in Recovery.

I don't like the word – it sounds a bit precious, a bit born-again – but I like the experience.

Recovery is its own drug. Everything's very new, very intense.

With any drug you need only a little at first, then gradually more and more. Recovery's no different. On the first night out of Charter Nightingale I could get my hit just from the brightly lit rooms back at home. Later I'd need something more and found it in nature – fairly ordinary weather conditions would feel very heightened, on my skin, in my blood – and then I'd need more again, more variation, more spectacle, please. I think my whole life has been a search for different rushes: the danger of acting – exposure, criticism, success – the huge invasion of book-writing fever, the slow, tingling crystallisation of a painting taking shape; these things provide it constantly and coke did, obviously, and now Recovery.

A couple of months after Charter Nightingale we went to the Mala Mala Game Reserve again. Africa and Recovery, quite a cocktail . . .

2/12/97. First game drive. I'm grinning to myself, my shirt is billowing, I'm singing inside, I yawn with joy, I put back my face and let the blazing light hurt the sunburn already there and it's a pleasing pain; I'm listening with all my might – the noisy jeep, crashing, squeaking, grinding, and the sound of the land, buzzing and ticking, and now we surprise a herd of zebra who break into a gallop and this resonates amazingly in the ground, Africa's natural drumbeat; I'm not actually bothered if we have good game sightings or not, I'm happy gawping at the cloud spectacles, I'm filling my lungs with the baked, almost stale smell of warm air, dust, the earth – it's intoxicating – my imagination is flying, blowing around like a kite; I'm high on my own chemicals; I'm *me*.

Going back to work isn't quite as exciting. Acting feels quite strange in Recovery. Quite difficult, in fact.

The first project is *Mrs Brown*, a film about the ambiguous relationship between Queen Victoria and the Balmoral gamekeeper John Brown during her prolonged mourning (a kind of nervous breakdown) after the death of Prince Albert. I'm playing Prime Minister Disraeli.

The pre-filming work, the research, is a joy. Benjamin Disraeli, 'Dizzy'. A novelist, a Jew – the first, the only, Jew to become British Prime Minister. Except he *wasn't* a Jew by the time he took office – this is the initial surprise discovery. At the age of thirteen, bar mitzvah age, he was converted to Christianity, after his father had a row with the local synagogue. Trouble at bar mitzvah time, that sounds familiar. The more I read about Disraeli, the more I like him. He's a churchgoer now, yet still thought of as a Jew, an outsider. He plays the role elegantly, flaunting it in a way, a peacock–outsider, with outrageous kiss curl and bright waistcoats, yet emanating such wisdom and humour that Victoria comes to rely on him almost as much as on John Brown. My favourite story is when he's on his deathbed. Victoria wants to come and say goodbye. He's asked if he's feeling up to it. 'Oh no,' he groans. 'She'll only want me to take a message to Albert!'

I visit his home: Hughenden Manor in Buckinghamshire. A National Trust property, it's closed on the day that Greg and I go there. Damn – I'm flying to Scotland tomorrow to start filming – this is my last chance. We decide to try to find someone, a caretaker maybe, and throw ourselves at their mercy. We knock on a door. The woman who answers turns out to be the House Steward. Perfect.

I launch in: 'Look, you might find this hard to believe, but I'm about to play Disraeli in a film, you won't know who I am, but –'

She interrupts: 'I know exactly who you are, and you had better know that I'm a member of the Richard III Society!'

The Richard III Society – those people who hate Shakespeare's play.

I squirm. She smiles. A surprisingly warm smile. Then says, 'I think I'm going to show you more generosity than Shakespeare did to poor old Richard. I mean, I don't want you to get Dizzy wrong too. Please come this way . . .'

And so this lady – Ros Lee is her name – whose charm confounds all my prejudices about the Society, takes us on a private tour of the house. I couldn't ask for more. Without crowds of tourists, you feel the atmosphere of the rooms more completely. These are large, shadowy and unexpectedly solemn. I sense a rather quiet, studious man here at home out of the spotlight: more outsider than peacock. In the study, Ros Lee lets me climb over the rope cordon and sit for a moment at Disraeli's desk. I get a good feeling . . .

This continues when we do a make-up test up in Scotland. As with Stanley, I find that with just minimal touches (the kiss curl, the distinctive goatee, a small dental plate to create his underbite) I can achieve quite an impressive resemblance.

All's well. Until I have to start *acting*.

I'll always associate mirrors with addiction but they also came to characterise Recovery for me. Recovery is a world of mirrors – mirrors and echoes. You see yourself very clearly, hear yourself, too. There's always you there, just *you*. Socialising had already become quite tricky for me. What trivial, boring nonsense I'm talking, I'd note – everyone else is, too, but they've got a glass in their hand, a straw up their nose, they don't *realise*.

I started life as a shy, self-hating individual, uncomfortable in his own skin. Acting was an escape from that person. Eventually, because of career pressure, growing older, a hundred and one other excuses, I needed more. More escape. Coke provided it. Escape and reward, but particularly escape. Now coke was gone. Now the shy man was back and the self-hating one, too. Totally alert, totally awake, watching the actor at work.

Bloody hell, you're not going to do it like that, are you?

I'm suddenly seeing my work in the kind of fanatical detail that John Clare described during his madness – 'Imagine if you could see every flower' – I'm aware of every gesture, every inflection. The camera team keep changing lenses, but my performance remains in gruesome close-up to me and in slow motion – *bat-bat* go the eyelashes, *clink-clonk* goes the voice – giving you plenty of time to observe it all and feel crucified.

We shoot the Parliament scenes. This is when I meet George Hall – playing the Speaker of the House – formerly Head of Acting at Central. He turned me down once. He thought my acting was rubbish. Does he think the same today? Because I do.

Apart from the fact that I can't act any more, I'm also working with Judi Dench and Billy Connolly. I'm such a fan of both, I keep getting those flu-like sensations like when I saw British theatre for the first time. I'm playing Dizzy and being dizzy. This will be a disaster.

Others don't seem to think so. Reports from the rushes are good. The director, John Madden, invites me to see some. 'No, no, absolutely not,' I say, unable to reveal that I'm already *seeing* my performance far too clearly.

John is one of those perfect directors, a gentle father figure full of questions not answers, endlessly patient. Even when Scotland's weather tried him to his limit. Day after day our shooting schedule had to be changed or cancelled altogether. I was rather relieved. I much preferred to stay in the hotel than go out and *act*, particularly since there was a free Billy Connolly concert nightly in the lounge. It would happen without him meaning to hog the limelight. We'd be sitting in a group, he'd start talking about something, it would develop into one of those surreal riffs which characterise his stand-up stuff, we'd all shut up and that was it for the next hour or so. I'd sit hugging myself, aching with laughter. Judi Dench fell off her chair once. It was amazing. Billy's gift is this fire, this blaze of vision – an alien seeing how funny we are – and it's completely open and uncensored. Yet he's in Recovery too – this is well known – just from booze, I think. I longed to talk to him about it. I never found the right moment, or the courage, or something.

How am I going to get through the next few months without even a drink?

It's January 1997 and I've arrived in New York to open *Stanley* at the Circle in the Square.

My crisis of confidence over Disraeli was apparently unfounded (John Madden did a rough assembly before I left and phoned to report good news about my contribution), but it now returns a hundredfold to plague poor Stan as we go into rehearsals in New York where, apart from the central quartet, the rest of the cast is new and American. I can't believe what's happening. This is *Stanley*, the show I played for six months at the National, the part I inhabited so effortlessly. It just flowed through me then. What's going on now? The answer is simple and grim. It wasn't just Stanley Spencer flowing through me, but large quantities of cocaine and Chivas Regal too. And somehow the mixture of work, escape and reward led to a kind of buoyancy in the performance, even something of the real man's grace. Let's not be sentimental about this. A lot of good acting is delivered in the same way. It's what Terry Hands meant when he said, 'Can't you develop a drink problem or something?'

What was deft and spontaneous before became clumsy and strained now. 'You're crying too much for Stan,' said John Caird. 'He's suddenly so angst-ridden,' observed Greg after an early preview. These comments helped jolt me out of it. It wasn't just Recovery, it was opening on Broadway. It was all getting too much of a big deal. 'Oh, fuck it,' I said to myself – always the best advice – stopped trying so hard, and immediately felt better in the show. On the last Friday night before opening I gave one of my best ever performances as Stanley. 'I wish there'd been someone special in tonight,' I said to Debbie Findlay afterwards. 'There was,' she replied, 'the *New York Times*.'

(Broadway critics don't come to the opening night, but sneak in unexpectedly during the previews; as a system it's possibly the lesser of two evils.)

By the first night, terror and self-consciousness overcame me again and I gave a dreadful, unfelt performance. I was in shock afterwards and with no line of coke or even glass of champagne to help me through the night. A Broadway opening, a Broadway party, these are meant to be glamorous occasions, the summit of a career. The family back in South Africa were senseless with excitement. Greg couldn't be in New York at the time, but Richard Wilson flew over by Concorde to support me. Kevin Klein was in the audience, I was photographed with Isabella Rossellini. But I just wanted to crawl away.

Luckily, the critics weren't there, so, the next morning the *New York Times* gave me a rave review, likewise all the principals and the production. But not the play. The other papers followed suit. There was a profound difference in this American reaction and it was to do with the man himself, Stanley Spencer, not being known here. (Ironically, his first major US exhibition would happen in Washington just after our Broadway run.) British audiences didn't need to be art lovers to have some sense of Stanley Spencer – the Cookham Christ, the Leg of Mutton Nude – as well as a vague awareness of an early tabloid scandal – 'The Man with Two Wives' – which might be tame by today's standards yet nevertheless went into the collective, the racial memory. Americans knew about neither his private life nor his work. And the reproductions on Tim Hatley's set, the *Cookham Resurrection* and the *Shipbuilding on the Clyde* paintings, these weren't enough. Without more knowledge of the real Stanley Spencer, the events in the play tended to mystify New Yorkers.

Who is this guy, this little jabbering jerk, who leaves his devoted wife for a dyke, a dyke he doesn't even get to screw – what the hell's going on here?

Playing the show in New York it was as if one of the characters had gone missing: Stanley's genius.

I'd been told you were either a hit or a flop on Broadway. Painless either way: standing ovations or the next flight home. Well – not quite. We were in between, somehow. We played our full three-month run, but to half-empty houses (or half-full, sorry Greg) and with the odd celeb popping in: Pacino, Madonna, Elaine Stritch. The last was there the same Sunday matinée as Harvey Fierstein – I've mentioned this – but there was also another important visitor to my dressing room that day. I was sitting there, listening to Fierstein and Stritch wisecracking together, thinking how similar they sounded, when I suddenly noticed a figure in the corridor beyond, a vaguely familiar figure. She stepped forward, more light falling on her face, then came into my arms. Maggie. My girlfriend from Webber-D. I was playing her home town. Sensing something, Harvey signalled Elaine Stritch to follow him out. Maggie and I didn't know what to say to one another. She was married, as I'd heard, with teenage kids. (*God, if we'd stayed together, they could've been mine.*) Since I'd already arranged to have supper with Harvey that evening, we promised to phone one another. She left. As Harvey and I walked to the restaurant, I said, 'You'll never believe who that was.'

He gave his chuckle, that dirty-warm chuckle I remembered from *Torch Song* nights in London's Joe Allen: 'Well, baby, I'd say that was the last lady you bedded!'

'Not quite,' I answered. 'Close, though.'

When Maggie phoned a few days later, I made an excuse and declined to meet her again, I'm not sure why.

*

There was another notable Sunday matinée, early in the run. The Olivier awards were happening at the same time back in London. *Stanley* was nominated for five: Best Play, Best Actor, Best Supporting Actress, twice – Deb Findlay and Anna Chancellor – and Best Designer. I'd been overlooked so often in the past, I was relieved just to be nominated – I knew I couldn't win; I was up against Scofield in *John Gabriel Borkman* and he'd already collected the *Evening Standard* award. I put it out of my mind as the show started. I was never off stage during the play anyway, so I'd only find out if the others had won afterwards.

Our production ended with Hilda, now dead, a ghost, high on the scaffolding, gazing down at Stanley, an old man, still happily painting away. She smiles at him, forgiving him everything, blessing him instead, the Bach swells, the lights fade.

As the curtain call started I always hurried over to help Debbie down the ladder – she isn't keen on heights – and on to stage level. Today, as I reached up to take her hand, she whispered, 'You've won.'

I blinked – this really was like an angel speaking – then I said, 'And you?'

She grinned. 'Yes, me too. And Pam. And Tim Hatley.' Dazed, I turned front to take the curtain call. Our New York Sunday matinée audience applauded politely – none of the standing and cheering of Broadway legend – but I didn't feel any disappointment today. Back in England we'd won. We'd won four of our five nominations. And *I'd* won. You're not supposed to care about these things, but there we go, I do – maybe other people do too. The win was especially significant now. My old reward system was gone. So on this particular Sunday an Olivier statuette was a good substitute for a sprinkle of Charlie.

'Aren't you, in a way, *missing* New York?' Debbie asked me one day. 'I mean, missing actually being here?'

'Don't think so,' I answered, 'I'm just experiencing it in a different way.'

Debbie and the rest of the British contingent were having Manhattan-style fun, sightseeing, shopping, socialising. I was being very reclusive. (A new, growing Recovery habit.) But I was nevertheless enjoying the city in my own way. Using it as a creative stimulus, using its special energy – that breakneck current speeding down the long, straight avenues, criss-crossing at razor-sharp angles – using it to kick-start a new book, a new novel.

I'd moved out of Wyndham's Hotel and found a fourth-floor apartment at 7¼ West 75th Street, just a couple of corners from the Dakota building where Lennon lived and died. A brownstone house, with beautiful, long wooden shutters that folded away into the window frames. Called jalousie shutters, they had adjustable wings and slats. Half closed, they created a marvellously shaded black-and-white atmosphere in the main room, making you feel you were in an old Hollywood movie. This fitted the fantasy. I'm in a brownstone apartment, with a view of other brownstones, some with those distinctive New York water tanks on their roofs, and, if you press your face against the insect screen and peer to the left, a glimpse of Central Park – I'm here, at the window, at my desk, and I'm writing the Great Novel. Well – in my fantasy.

Eventually called *The Feast*, the book is about Africa, about Theatre, and about Recovery. The protagonist, Felix (a sort of Barney Simon director–deviser running a sort of East African Market Theatre) has been an alcoholic, not coke fiend – he's a colonial chap, too old-fashioned for Charlie – who finds himself giving refuge to the dictator of the old regime (a sort of Amin–Bokassa–Banda figure) and fervently engaged in questions of personal and public liberation. It wasn't easy writing about Recovery while it was happening – as someone said, Experience, like Revenge, is a dish best eaten cold – and the book doesn't always make sense to me. I like best the sections where I'm most frank about the reality of Recovery, its comic horror, like when Felix is cowering under the table during an emergency board meeting at the theatre and, unaware of his new abstinence, the chairman slips him a bottle of Chivas Regal:

Felix collected it, feeling the weight, the realness. Oh, so smooth, so elegant, so dangerous, this lump of glass between his fingers. He pulled out the fancy cork, listening to its little flirting pop. It was as if the whisky had been holding its breath and released it now, blowing a kiss, letting Felix smell the smell of a most intimate partner. *This isn't fair*, he thought. As his right hand lifted the bottle to his mouth, his left intercepted it. He arm-wrestled himself, rocking from side to side under the table, trying to conceal his exertions from the people above. Silent tumbles and tugs-of-war now ensued, his movements slowed down and exaggerated like a mime artist, with accompanying grimaces and mouthed expletives. His right hand proved the stronger. The whisky rose joltingly to his face. His left hand clamped itself over his lips. The right unlocked three fingers from the bottle's neck and prised through the fleshy barrier, their nails digging cruelly. At last the bottle's mouth met Felix's own, and levered the lips apart. His teeth were still clamped shut, a last line of defence. The bottle withdrew a fraction and rammed them lightly. His skull rang. In that instant, the bottle was through, home, and tilting. Liquid filled his mouth. His cheeks were bulging, his eyes watering, his tastebuds in chaos. Refusing to swallow, unable to breathe, he started to turn red.

I wrote from about 5 a.m. to 5 p.m. each day, playing *Stanley* or sleeping in the hours left over, and loved it all, my weird, wired New York life. I grew to love the place, too, just glimpsed in my hurried walks to and from the theatre – maybe an appropriate way to see it. New York. City of man-made landscapes, with beautiful orange-red light on the peaks and icy shade in the canyons; city of voyeurs and exhibitionists, in Peepland, the sex shop across from the theatre, and peep land back in West 75th Street where I can look into all the apartments across the road and they into mine; city of coffee, smell it on everyone's breath, *buzz, buzz, buzz*, and of picnics – I mostly eat out of plastic boxes with plastic cutlery – city of food-on-the-hoof, of can't-stop-now, of just-passing-through; city of yellow cabs whose Indian and Arab drivers don't speak English or even American, and never know the address you want. At the end of each journey, a recorded female voice says, 'Please remember to take all your belongings and to ask the driver for a receipt.' Her tone is slow, lifeless, like she's in shock. In New York, city of wannabe stars, here's one actress who's landed the worst voice-over job in the world.

When *Stanley* finished, Greg, I and Debbie Findlay hired a car and drove across the country, playing out some more American fantasies – *Thelma and Louise?* Jack Kerouac? – and halfway through, had an experience to equal any in Africa:

1/5/97. All day spent driving across Colorado, each taking turns at the wheel, Debbie playing her Eagles tapes – 'Tequilla Sunrise', 'Hotel California' – the roads long and straight, the views rocky and forested, reminding me of Saturday mornings at the bioscope; the cowboy serials always took place on pine crags like these. In the afternoon the landscape flattened and the vistas seemed endless. At about 6 p.m. Greg thought we might be close, though this was hard to believe, the surroundings looked so low and dull by now. We parked in a lay-by, walked down a path between trees, then stopped suddenly. A real shock went through us. It was here, right here. We had almost walked off the edge of the world.

Most natural wonders take the eye up. The Grand Canyon makes you peer down, with an accompanying sense of falling, of flying. It's like the negative, the mould, the upside down of a mountain range. Within the one landscape there are whole other worlds. As we arrived, the sunset light was dividing them. To my left, all was thin and translucent – the rocks could have been made of blue air – insubstantial, mystical, dreamy; while to my right everything was weighty, gold and red, a holy land, an ancient, grave presence. Keep gazing down though and you feel you're journeying into the centre of the earth; plane after plane of something else, something deeper; soft grey-green meadows, strange trails, the winding river. Is all this going on below ground? Here, now, where you're standing, where it feels solid, is all this buried underneath you – even the trails?

Back at the hotel, I rang Jim in London. He had news to match what we'd just seen. The British election. An incredible landslide. The Tories were finally out, Labour and Blair in. He said the jubilation in the streets was incredible – as though a dictatorship had been toppled. Said people were shouting 'We've won!' from the rooftops.

'We've got somewhere even better to shout it from,' I told him. 'The top of the world.'

27

VISIBLE SOULS

So we returned to a New Great Britain – like the New South Africa. It really felt like that for a while: a fresh place, a place of hope.

That was the broad picture. In my own, smaller sphere, the New Me was still struggling to find balance.

On the first morning back at home in Islington, there were two moments signifying the struggle.

One was the Olivier award on the mantelpiece. I hadn't seen it till now. A different statuette from the one I got in 1985. That was an abstract shape. This was a literal – no, banal – no, unsuccessful – bust of Olivier. Was this small, ugly thing really worth caring about?

The second, catching me off guard, was the first coke craving in ages. Saturday ahead, with no commitments tonight or tomorrow ... the weather sultry and itchy ... the back door open, the garden overgrown and lush ... just think of a glass or two of wine out there, then some whiskies, then a phone call ...

(In Charter Nightingale I'd had hypnotism to erase the dealer's phone-number from my brain. It hadn't worked. The number was still there. I'd check it now and then, just the first few digits ... yes, still there ... and the rest.)

Awards and addiction. Success and destruction. Approval and dismissal. Mom and Dad.

Did these pairs have to stay linked, have to form an equation? Obviously not. I mean, even Dad was out of the picture. (And his dismissal of me had died long before him, turning to approval.) I was clean. In Recovery. Thinking fairly sensibly.

The coke craving surfaced, excited my flesh and was banished.

The awards craving went the same way.

Stanley got three Tony nominations in New York. Best Play, Best Director, Best Actor. A Tony for Tony? I was delighted when I heard. For about five minutes. Then a man came on the TV (that's how we found out: by chance on a motel TV during the American car trip) and explained that I couldn't win. Well, it wasn't as personal as that. He simply analysed the nominations in that very serious, big-business way with which the Americans treat Oscars and Emmys and Tonys, and worked out who would win. Christopher Plummer for his Barrymore show. Simple as that. I felt rather relieved. You heard the nominations and results in the same moment. Needn't give it a second thought.

When the Tony ceremony was held in June I was invited to fly back to New York for it. I declined. Christopher Plummer won.

But if one part of my brain was cleaned up and thinking clearly – the logical, conscious side – the other was still full of demons. That new horrible self-consciousness which threatened my work on *Mrs Brown* and the Broadway *Stanley* descended with renewed force on the next project: *Cyrano*.

And to make matters worse, I was being filmed throughout. Preparing the role, rehearsing, opening.

The BBC arts programme *Omnibus* had approached the RSC about making a documentary about me, using the new production of *Cyrano* (which Greg would direct) as the hook. I suspected this might not be the best time for any added pressure and was tempted to say no, but the other temptation – to my ego – won hands down.

So now there was a film crew following me around, at work and at home. Led by a classy young director, Rosie Alison. She couldn't have been kinder or more respectful of the boundaries. But she was here to do a job.

'Greg – help – there's a spider in the bath!' I'd yell, only to hear Rosie shout back: 'Hang on, we're coming upstairs with him!'

This was amusing in our Islington house, less so in the Clapham rehearsal rooms . . .

*

The good thing about doing a new play is that nobody has done it before you. The pisser about doing an old one is that everybody has.

With *Cyrano* there were two giants waiting to cast their shadows. The two major Cyranos of recent times are Derek Jacobi on stage and Gerard Depardieu on film.

Jacobi's performance is an RSC legend. I know because I was at the Barbican while it was happening in 1983, playing *Tartuffe* alongside in the Pit. We sometimes went into the wings of the Main House to watch their curtain call: one and a half thousand people rising to their feet, weeping and cheering. We saw the crowds of people outside as well, queueing overnight for returns or waiting for autographs at the stage door, faces alight as though they'd seen a miracle, which is how great theatre can make you feel.

Depardieu's performance is even more famous, though less successful, I think – bluff and soldierly, his soul never takes flight as Jacobi's did. But the film is terrific; as successful an adaptation of a stage play as I've ever seen.

You can ignore your famous predecessors in a role, but others won't, so I've never found it harmful to check them out, to ask whether theirs is the only way, and with some (like Olivier's Richard III) deliberately to find a different solution. The thing that had sometimes puzzled me about Cyranos, even those I've admired, is the element of glamour to them. Jacobi wears glossy Cavalier locks and a magnificent costume, Depardieu is a dishy hunk, Bob Lindsay, Christopher Plummer and even Steve Martin (in *Roxanne*) are handsome men with big noses stuck on; their own attractiveness is always present; never mind the nose, they seem to be saying, I'm beautiful really. Yet reading Anthony Burgess's translation-version of the Rostand original, I first encounter those two great phrases:

The visible soul.

The casual dress of flesh.

Cyrano's beauty lies in his soul. His ugliness lies in his flesh. He believes he is disgustingly ugly. And people who dislike their physical features tend to let their whole look go to seed. I know because I'm one of them. My clothes are well worn, my hair cut to whatever the current role requires, however bizarre (the white bleach for Titus, the bare skull for Singer) and I'm often unshaven. I think I could be described as scruffy. Now Cyrano hates his casual dress of flesh even more than I do mine. In discussion with Greg and the designer, Rob Jones, we decide that he should be a mess, really quite seriously dirty and unkempt. We're going to take a grimly realistic look at him – aware that this might work against the tone of the piece, which is romantic with a capital R. But in a way I've got no choice. The problem's similar to previous roles. With Arturo I'm not a natural clown so I can't do the Rossiter thing. With Astrov I'm not naturally drop-dead gorgeous so I can't do the countryside Casanova. Here I'm not a natural romantic so I'm going to have to approach it as a study of a man who hates himself.

Not hard to do these days. I'm not very pleased with my progress in rehearsals. I can't do the fencing (despite months of fucking training beforehand), I can't join in the Gascony cadet song (because I'm fucking tone-deaf) and I can't act (because of fucking Recovery). I feel watched all the time – watched by the rest of the cast, who look very unimpressed (and include several RSC regulars, veterans of the famous Jacobi production), watched by my increasingly worried director, watched by myself – a strange new enemy, a new *critic* – and watched by a fucking film crew!

(I must say it again: they could not have been kinder people. And the final result is excellent – it has a humour and energy sometimes missing in arts documentaries – but at the time I hated that ever watchful camera.)

I was in a right state by the time we got to the press night in Stratford. I *forgot* to do some of my make-up. Which isn't like me. The applying of the make-up, a painter's hour, is virtually my favourite part of theatre acting. As I was heading on stage I passed a mirror and noticed the omissions. No time to rectify them. I made my entrance feeling unsettled. Cyrano never stops talking in the first scene. My mouth felt dry – with fear – and my lips and gums started to stick together. I heard myself speaking in a kind of slur. I heard and saw everything I was doing – *oh Recovery, oh world of echoes and mirrors, oh shit* – I started writing the reviews myself. In a brief interlude off stage I whispered to Gary Powell, 'Water – please – quick!' He was playing Le Bret, Cyrano's mate, his second in the duel, and had a water bottle round his neck. Not waiting for him to take it off, I began to drink, half strangling him in the process. He swore, unnerved by my panic. *This isn't like me*, I thought as we hurried back on stage, *come on, get a grip*. I did, and acquitted myself fairly well for the rest of it; well, in press night terms. Afterwards, I desperately needed the reward, the escape of old. But – no. Mineral water and a crisp instead. I left the first-night party early, ignoring Greg's pleas – 'This is a big night for me too, *I* need to celebrate, and I need you at my side!' – and slunk home to bed.

The reviews were mostly very good. By now I was definitely not looking at them, but had developed my temperature-reading system, asking others to mark them out of ten. They came out at about a high seven. Deemed a success, a long run now lay ahead: Stratford, a national tour, the West End. I found that the self-consciousness thing vanished very early on, only to be replaced by a more familiar challenge – reminting the marathon role eight times a week for six months.

How to keep revealing Cyrano's visible soul? It surfaces in his love for Roxanne. He can never tell her face to face – he fears she'll laugh at him – but gets his chance when he deputises for the handsome but tongue-tied Christian. Rostand/Burgess gives Cyrano wonderful love speeches here. The actor's feelings have to be very open, very tender, very naked. My inspiration for the required emotional recall came from an unexpected source. Not those hopeless infatuations with beautiful young actors that used to beset me – though these were very close to Cyrano's obsession with Roxanne – but my ultimate case of unrequited love. Dad.

I'd sit in the wings thinking about him before the scene, the Balcony Scene in Act Three, then go on stage and let the emotion come up with the words. When it worked well it was an exquisite feeling – light, free, the text tasting fresh as air. But it didn't always work. The images of Dad (after the Palace visit, say, in dressing gown and bow tie) became too familiar and ceased to trigger a response. I had to dig deeper. Strange pictures came to mind now. Like of him dead. In the hotel room in Herzlia. The security man has been called. He lowers Dad from the bed to the floor and tries artificial respiration. In other words he kisses him. Which I never could.

When the power of this picture fades, I find another.

Now it's Dad in his coffin. Coming home for the last time, coming back to South Africa. He arrives in Cape Town and, surprise, surprise, there's no family to greet him. Just undertakers, apprentice undertakers probably, in T-shirts and shorts; they're not on public show, no one's watching. Chatting and smoking, they take delivery of the box from the plane and drive it to the crematorium.

This has a huge impact on my emotions and they flow freely in the scene once more.

For a while.

When they dry up – *again* – I experience a kind of implosion. Terrible frustration and anger. With the show, with Recovery, with Dad. After a particularly unsatisfactory performance during the tour, the Brighton week, I went back to the hotel – one of those large, dilapidated establishments along the front – and wrote a sort of letter to him:

Dad – you died in a room like this. A shabby, anonymous room, a room casually used by hundreds of strangers every year, a room of one-night stands, a hotel room. That's where you died. A hotel room in Israel. It's like the punch line to some joke about the Wandering Jew. And then, when they sent you back to us, they didn't take care of you. You, Master Mannie, the big *baas* of Cape Produce Export Company, you weren't 'packed' properly. You're scrunched in your box, head twisted in one corner, hands bundled up like a begging dog. Here you are, Mannie, coming home for the last time. I remember you at supper time, sitting at the far end of the table, silent, morose, pissed, hating us, hating your life, the miserable married man – in the bosom of his family, but lonely as hell. Well, here you are now, Mannie, lonelier than you can ever have imagined, making a long, frightening journey all on your own – lonelier than your father when he made his, to start a new life in South Africa. You've finished yours and we've finished with you – you who wouldn't touch us, love us – we're giving you the most terrible, lonely, undignified end. We're ignoring you. We're not going to be there. We'll be somewhere else, eating, drinking, sunbathing, who knows, as you're thrown off the plane, driven across town and burnt.

How could we? How fucking could we? However absent you were as a father, how could we?

I know you were just flesh and bone by then, but so what? Your flesh and bone were important, it was *you* too. Why did we do it like that? Why? What other family would have done what we did? Ignore your last homecoming. It's unbelievable. We're weird – even by white South African standards we're weird. What the fuck happened to us? Our parents – that's what happened to us. Dad – you happened to us. Dad – you just got what you deserved in the end.

I'd been seeking to release Cyrano's visible soul, but it was Dad's out in the open now. Dad's ghost. No – Dad himself. We had never buried him. But we must, we must. I resolved to phone home soon and talk it over with the others . . .

28

ART OR SHIT?

You can't always pinpoint the moment when change happens, but I'm sure it was that night in Brighton, writing the letter to my dead father. It opened a wound, a deep wound. Probably good in the long term. Less so at first.

Things were starting to go awry . . .

I was offered a play at the National. *Camping, Cleo, Emmanuele and Dick* by Terry Johnson, who would also direct. It was about the *Carry On* films and the part was Sid James (alias Solly Cohen of Joburg, SA) in whose film-set winnebago the action takes place. Kenneth Williams and Barbara Windsor were the other main characters.

I thought the play was excellent. The part of Sid reminded me of Archie Rice in *The Entertainer*. Osborne's piece takes an elegiac look at the music hall, and this was about the decline and death of another great British comedy tradition. But how would we do it? I asked Terry Johnson. As impersonations of the *Carry On* stars, or just as people called Sid, Ken and Babs? I favoured the latter. I had quite a lot of experience at this, and didn't fancy the slavish mimicry I'd done for Ringo Starr and Enoch Powell. I preferred the route to Stanley Spencer and Benjamin Disraeli: some token gestures to the physical resemblance, but then a search for the visible soul and, like with any part, the creation of a *character*. Terry argued that, unlike the cases of Spencer and Disraeli, the whole world knows how Sid, Ken and Babs walk, talk, laugh and that we had to serve up the audience's expectations. But it was a problem for rehearsals, he said, a problem for the whole cast to share. Good. I liked the sound of that. We'd start with a blank sheet and all find a way of filling it in.

Terry invited me to attend auditions, to read with the actors. I became worried. People were required to bring in impersonations. Some were so accomplished there'd be nothing left to do in rehearsals. That's the trouble with a good impersonation. You've got your whole performance in a few deft strokes. So have the audience. Now what will you all do for the next few hours?

I was less and less convinced by the impersonation option, Terry more and more so. We should've resolved this. We didn't.

First day of rehearsals and the read-through. As it was about to start, I said, 'We're not going to try reading in the voices, are we?'

Samantha Spiro (Babs) said, 'I don't think I can read *without* the voice.'

Adam Godley (Ken) agreed.

Terry said, 'Well, you two read in the voices, Tony you read in your own, and that's fine for now, it's only a read-through.'

Well, not quite. The read-through is a crucial moment in the process, a tricky one, potentially destructive. People can jump to conclusions – about the play, about fellow actors. I know some directors who don't do read-throughs at all, while others – like Greg – only do them a couple of weeks into rehearsals. Then you're ready to give some kind of rough presentation of the play. If read-throughs are to happen on the first day they need to stay in neutral gear.

The point was proved that day in Rehearsal Room One at the National. Two of the actors gave brilliant, polished performances – Ken and Babs were in the room! – while another sat mumbling his lines, feeling dispirited. He hadn't started rehearsals, the others seemed to have finished.

I went to Terry afterwards. 'I think we need to talk.' He looked apprehensive. I went on: 'We *are* using impersonations, aren't we? We've gone way past the other option. So I'll either have to learn to do a Sid James very, very fast, or . . .' I trailed out. Terry had gone pale. I must've been drained of colour too. '. . . I'll give myself a week.'

I never lasted the week. A few mornings later, I was sitting in my study – at about 5 a.m. – with Sid James everywhere around me: his crumpled face leered up from photographs strewn across the desk and from the TV, played and replayed, his gravelly voice came now from the screen, now from the tape deck – the famous yuck-yuck laugh, the rapid-fire delivery, the Cockney accent immaculately covering his native South African. (Did *he* sit in a room like this once, learning to do Sid James?) Looking around, you'd have thought I was some crazed fan, some Sid James stalker. 'Yuck-yuck,' he'd laugh on the tape. 'Yuck-yuck,' I'd echo, then a quick rewind, and 'Yuck-yuck' we'd go together. I suddenly stopped. *What the fuck was I doing?* Why was I sitting here before dawn, trying to learn a skill I didn't believe in? I didn't want to impersonate Sid James. I wanted to play a character called Sid, a seedy little man hooked on gambling, booze and women, ugly as sin yet attractive too, a clown whose Big Top was collapsing around him. That's what I wanted to play, not Mister Yuck-yuck.

I waited till about seven before ringing Terry. He sounded sleepy at first, then, as I began to talk, very alert. We agreed to meet at the National immediately.

When I drove away from the South Bank a few hours later, I felt a curious mixture of relief and pride. The yuck-yucking was over. And how grown-up we'd all been – Jenny McIntosh had joined Terry and me for the discussion – agreeing that it was best if I left straight away; it was only week one; someone else could take over and the project needn't be damaged at all. (Which proved to be the case – Geoff Hutchings came in, gave an excellent performance and the show was a success.) I'd made a mistake, *we'd* made a mistake – Terry and I – and we'd rectified it, rather than just living with that dumb rule, 'The Show Must Go On'. Sid James would go into my waste-paper basket, where lots of potentially good stuff, book chapters and drawings, had gone before him. Art and shit, work and waste, closely linked substances.

But any feeling of jubilation didn't last long. It was overtaken by a sense of shock.

I'd walked out of a show. A first for me. I felt like I'd been in a car crash. I'd escaped unhurt, yet couldn't stop picking over the events leading up to it. What went wrong? When, how?

Was it anything to do with Recovery?

That would be ironic. Throughout all the years of using coke I maintained a reputation of supreme efficiency and discipline. Even during those coke-fuelled performances of *Stanley* I'd never been rumbled. My private and social lives ran less smoothly – I often had to cancel arrangements because the streaming nose was too obvious this time, or the coke-over depression too crippling – but in the profession I was seen as someone who knew what he was doing, where he was going.

So there was something profoundly untypical in what had happened. Recovery is supposed to bring you closer to yourself – no buffer zone of chemicals any more – but I couldn't help dwelling on a thought which had often occurred since Charter Nightingale: *This isn't like me*.

What to do now? The next few months were supposed to be at the National. But now I was suddenly free. I didn't want to be. Recovery was still too much of a struggle. I needed to work, work, work.

Greg and I went on a long weekend to Wiltshire. At Lucknam Park Hotel, near Bath, we took a walk through a sunny cornfield. There was a subject we were both avoiding. Greg was preparing a production of *The Winter's Tale* for the RSC. He'd offered Leontes to a string of leading actors. Some said no, some were very tempted. A few weeks earlier, I'd sat in a hotel room in Liverpool (there to receive an Honorary Doctorate of Letters from Liverpool University; a surprise gift from a city that's always been good to me) and watched him talking to Henry Goodman on the phone, now and then turning towards me, making a thumbs-up sign. Henry was definitely keen – except he had an arrangement with Trevor Nunn to do *Merchant* and the dates might clash. They did. The part was free again.

'So what d'you think?' Greg said eventually on our strangely quiet walk through the cornfield.

'Well, I don't think I like the play,' I replied. 'And Leontes is just a bit of a puzzle. And not even a very big part.'

'Will you read it again?'

We smiled at one another. 'Sure I'll *read* it.'

We drove into Bath, found their Waterstones, bought a copy, moved on to our next hotel, Manor House, Castle Combe, and I went to sit under a tree and read.

By the time we met up again a couple of hours later, Greg looked excited. (I think he'd jumped the gun and rung the RSC.) His expression crumpled as I started to speak.

'I *really* don't like the play now. Bohemia's just a load of boring, romantic, rural tosh. And as for Leontes, it's not that he's a puzzle, it's just that I could play him standing on my head. He just keeps running round the stage shouting and snarling at people. I've done that so much, the audience will fall asleep whenever I enter. No, no, you must find someone else.'

I don't remember which of us thought up the next idea, but we were back at home in Islington when we started to consider it seriously.

Leontes *and* Autolycus.

Convinced that his wife is having an affair – which she isn't – Leontes, King of Sicilia, thunders through the first three acts like an express train heading for a clifftop. He disappears from the action during Act Four, the Bohemia scene, while the clown, a penniless conman called Autolycus, takes over. And then Leontes returns for Act Five, with its famous statue scene.

The play is often talked about as being broken-backed. The Sicilia and Bohemia sections are so different in tone they could be from separate plays. How to make them live together? Every production has to confront this. Could it be solved if the same actor played both parts: the king and the fool, the king and the tramp? Greg was thinking of staging Leontes's nightmares – festering sexual fantasies where the court would strip off their rigid uniforms and unleash some basic instincts. Could we do the change from Sicilia to Bohemia as one of these sequences, only this time the king strips off too and, now wearing patched and grubby long johns, becomes the dispossessed Autolycus? He proceeds to assume various guises, including that of pedlar. Since our setting was vaguely turn-of-the-century Russia, could I play him as a sort of Smous figure?

It was starting to sound enticing. But then I sat down to look at the text again. Autolycus's speeches – like all Shakespeare's clowns – are virtually incomprehensible; it's like reading a joke book in Eskimo. Greg argued that they weren't meant to be read, but performed. I'd *seen* how well the part could work – Bill McCabe in Adrian Noble's 1992 production (where Bohemia was brilliantly solved, becoming a Stanley Spencer village fête) – surely the proof was in the pudding?

I wasn't convinced. I still felt shaken by that Carry On at the National. I knew that I mustn't just do *Winter's Tale* on the rebound.

As I continued to hum and haw, Greg lost patience. He warned me he was going to offer Leontes out again, now as a double with Autolycus. I said go ahead.

The offer went to Simon Russell Beale. He was very interested. Said he loved the play (what was it that others could see in this piece that eluded me?) and was immensely attracted to the double. I started to get twitchy. Another actor (called *Simon* no less) responding to the idea – *my* idea, partly, by now – and tempted. How would I feel if he did it and had a big success?

(I've spent much of my career arguing that actors aren't just empty-headed little egomaniacs, but on second thoughts . . .)

When Simon finally said no, because of other commitments, Greg gave me one last chance.

'Oh all right,' I said breezily.

'What?' he said. '*What?*'

'Yes, fine – when do we start?'

We started on 14 September 1998, with a luxurious three-month rehearsal period – because Adrian Noble's production of *Lion, Witch and Wardrobe* was rehearsing alongside and sharing much of the company. Our cast was strong and included several people whom I knew well: Estelle Kohler (Paulina) from *Hello and Goodbye* and three from *Cyrano* – Alex Gilbreath (Hermione), Ken Bones (Polixenes) and Geoff Freshwater (Camillo).

I was surrounded by friends. Surely that new syndrome wouldn't happen again, that Recovery thing, that horrible arena of mirrors and echoes.

It didn't with Leontes – I'll talk about him later – but it did with Autolycus, in its most merciless form yet. I could barely be heard when we came to rehearse his scenes, I never lifted my head from the book. It was a little shield behind which I cowered. If I could have crawled into it I would.

Shakespeare's fools are so bloody hard. One solution is to create a character, a sort of Mike Leigh character, whose real-life idiosyncrasies can make the unfunniest lines live. Trouble is, Autolycus only has a couple of short speeches as himself. You can decide he's a Londoner or a Scot or whatever, but you'll have precious little chance to establish this before he starts pretending to be other people – to con his victims. He's essentially an actor, a comic actor, and needs to be played by one.

He also has to *sing*. We thought we'd confronted the obvious obstacle (Tone's tone-deafness) by deciding that he'd mime along to records. Our Edwardian setting allowed the idea of this pedlar using a wind-up gramophone when he's selling the ballads referred to in the text. How we laughed as we contemplated all the karaoke-type gags you could do with gramophones getting stuck, records being juggled and God knows what else. How dull these seemed when we tried them in rehearsals. No, Autolycus really would have to sing, at least some of the time. The composer, Ilona Sekacz, who once taught me to saw the violin for *Lear*, now said: 'There's no such thing as tone-deafness.'

Could this really be happening again?

We began singing classes. I was in a bad dream. Trying to learn something I simply couldn't do. The one-legged man attempting to sprint, the one-armed man to applaud. I could study from now to doomsday and it wouldn't make any difference. When the cue came up for my first song – in three months' time, on the main stage at Stratford – I would open my mouth and . . . oh, dear God.

I couldn't talk to Greg, my partner. He wasn't there. You lose him. I'd discovered that before when we worked together: you lose your closest confidant. I couldn't talk to Greg Doran, the director, either. I'd only agreed to be in the show on condition I did the double. (It was overweening greed worthy of Bottom in the *Dream* who wants to play all the parts.) I could hardly confess to Greg now that I was *unable* to play one of them. You can't tell your director that you're in big trouble. Part of his job, masterminding the whole production, is to disguise his fear. Part of yours, leading the acting company, is to do the same thing. Whenever we do a play we know this fear, we have to ride it through. Most of the time it goes away.

It wouldn't with this, though. I knew that.

Incredibly, for the second time in the last few months I was having to contemplate leaving a production. Except this time it was impossible. It would be like leaving Greg. In fact, what would this do to our relationship?

And to my career?

It was awful. Years as a cokehead – squeaky clean record. But now in Recovery – *he's unreliable*.

'You keep blaming Recovery,' Marietta Young observed in my weekly art therapy sessions. 'Why's that, I wonder?' As we talked I made an unsettling discovery. Yes, maybe this was all to do with Recovery, but not in the way I thought. Not caused by Recovery – more an attempt to abort it. An elaborate route to the other 'r' word: Relapse. I really didn't want that – I'd been clean for over two years – it was my own prized record, a kind of award to myself, yet I could suddenly see exactly what I was doing. Making things worse and worse until I finally picked up the phone and rang that number whose digits I could still remember . . .

I felt stuck. I couldn't go forward, couldn't go back. I started thinking about doing a Stephen Fry. I'd just run away, just secretly disappear. Maybe go to South Africa. Maybe step off Table Mountain.

On the Friday of the third week of rehearsals Greg decided we were finally ready for the read-through. Three weeks of paraphrasing the text (translating Shakespeare into modern English) and of movement sessions, discussion groups, selected rehearsals. Now at last we'd hear the piece as a whole. I was in a shaky state. I'd hardly slept the night before. Yet I was determined to give it my best shot. I had to. Maybe I was wrong about Autolycus – I'd felt uncomfortable in *Mrs Brown* and *Cyrano* too, but I'd have been wrong to leave those projects – maybe the same applied here. We'd find out today.

The read-through started. In the first three acts, I gave a good account of Leontes – the character's angst as nothing compared with the actor's – and in Act Four managed to busk through Autolycus and his different turns without making a complete tit of myself. But then we got to Act Five . . .

Leontes was back. Except now he just sounded like another of Autolycus's funny voices. The famous last scene of the play, the statue scene, the poignant reunion with Hermione, this was strangely flat. The double – the double itself didn't work. It had seemed so simple on paper. I'd be Leontes, then I'd be Autolycus, then Leontes again; the scheme just went A–B–A. But since there's no such person as Autolycus, just his string of disguises, the scheme becomes completely crazy. During the fractured work of the last three weeks we hadn't spotted this.

The problem was worse than I thought.

As the read-through finished, I walked across the rehearsal room, feeling a strange sense of déjà vu.

'I think we need to talk.'

Greg looked up from his script. His expression was odd. Partly excited by the read-through (a lot of it sounded very promising), partly troubled. 'Yes. Let's talk.'

We went for a walk round Clapham Common, down the road from the

RSC rehearsal rooms. This was just a few days after the Ron Davies story broke: he'd been involved in some mysterious misdemeanour here – possibly a gay pick-up (though he was denying this). The Common was busy as a result. Little packs of journalists photographing, filming, interviewing.

Trying to lighten the mood, I said to Greg: 'If we're recognised now, the headlines will say, "Clapham scandal worsens – RSC gay mafia involved!" '

Greg smiled vaguely, his mind elsewhere. We walked on in silence. Then he said quietly: 'It's not going to work – the double – is it?'

'No, I don't think it is.'

'It fucks up Act Five terribly.'

'It does.'

He took a deep breath, and asked: 'If it was just Leontes . . . would you still do it . . . would you stay in the show?'

I turned to him in surprise. The problem had rephrased itself. Not that I *couldn't* play Autolycus, but that I *shouldn't*. Did Greg really not know how much trouble I was in with the part? Of course he did. He must. We stopped walking and turned to face one another. It was the strangest moment. Full of tenderness – yet ambiguity too. Was this him saving me? Or his own production? Both, probably. I mean, there was a major piece of miscasting in this *Winter's Tale*. If we were bold enough to take the next step we'd still be in with a chance. Especially since I'd been quite wrong about Leontes – the part was far more exciting than I realised. While Autolycus made me feel I should give up acting on the spot, Leontes was giving me the special buzz that only comes with certain parts, a buzz that says, *This one's mine*.

'Of course I'm staying in the show,' I said, putting my arm round his shoulder. He looked surprised. I'm normally reticent about touching in public – just an old-fashioned hang-up – and here we were surrounded by zoom lenses. I didn't care. I felt senseless with relief. 'And as for Leontes – you just try taking him away from me!'

29

THE CHASE

'Tony Sher's great to work with,' quips Geoff Freshwater. 'If you can just get him past the read-through.'

It's good to be laughing again – laughing with the company.

We're assembled on Monday morning. The *Winter's Tale* mess has been cleaned up very efficiently over the weekend. Greg rang Adrian Noble first. He gave his blessing to our intended change of plan. Said he wished the creative process could always involve this kind of principle: testing out ideas in practice rather than on paper. Normally the conveyor-belt schedule at both national companies made it impossible, but we were lucky: we still had nine weeks of rehearsal ahead of us. 'Go for it,' said Adrian. Greg was keen to keep the recasting within the existing company. Ian Hughes, presently playing the Young Shepherd, had already revealed himself to be a gifted comic actor and could play Autolycus superbly. (And he was Welsh, so he could sing too!) And Christopher Brand, a gentle giant currently doing assorted walk-ons, would be terrific as the Young Shepherd. Both actors were delighted when Greg phoned them. As are the whole company now, this Monday morning, when they hear the news. I think they all knew we'd made a mistake before. And me? I'm happiest of all. Perfectly content to play only Leontes.

Leontes.

I go for him like a charging animal. When they accelerate, when they go for the kill, neither predator nor prey has any chance to think. It's just down to instinct, win or lose, life or death. That's how acting feels now. It's given me some bad frights recently. But no more, I say to myself, no more. No more time for indecision, for self-doubt or modesty, no time for sneaking up slowly on the part, no cautious tracking, no clever-clever ambushes – I'm going for it on the run now, at full speed, and let's see which one of us tires first.

I've reached that fuck-it point.

The image of a chase isn't fanciful. Leontes has evaded a lot of actors, a lot of productions. The role begins with a brainstorm. He imagines his wife is screwing his best friend. She isn't. Everyone else knows this. Yet scene after scene follows the same pattern – he runs on stage making wild accusations – people try to make him see reason – they fail – he runs off stage. After a while he starts to alienate the other characters almost as much as he does the audience. Why are we sitting here watching this deluded man? they ask. He just needs slapping or shooting. But I feel strongly drawn to him. There's a new fury in me that connects to the raging self-disgust in him.

'Inch-thick, knee-deep, o'er head and ears a forked one!'

An image of flesh, of sewage, of devils and cuckolds, it makes no clear sense; it's his unconscious talking. And that's where I'm starting from too – my bile's just cooking with his. 'Too hot, too hot.' Leontes is talking about despair yet sounds curiously energised ('My heart dances'); he's talking about filth, too, yet his mouth is wet with it (wives are 'sluiced', they're 'slippery'); there's desire in this man's disgust; he's a *Sun* reader, or writer. For me personally the venom of his speeches has a sweet, addictive taste: Shakespeare is inviting me into a very dark place and it's a place I'm happy to go. It excites me. Leontes is a king, a status ten, he has power and responsibility – I know about these things as a leading actor – he's always having to behave himself, to be good, but now suddenly he wants to say fuck it and *destroy* – destroy everyone, destroy the world.

It's strange. The more I unleash Leontes's destructiveness, the more constructive I become towards myself. The more he sickens the more I heal. He's falling apart and I'm pulling myself together. This is drama therapy in a rare form. Not conducted in some safe room in Charter Nightingale, but on the rehearsal floor and eventually the main stage of the Royal Shakespeare Company.

*

It begins with the research. That's when I'm first aware that I need to shift off the psychiatrist's couch myself and put Leontes there instead.

As we work on the text it keeps coming up – the big problem in this problem play, the big question – *why* is Leontes jealous? Why does it start, why does it finish? – both so abruptly. He is often dismissed with crude labels – wicked king, mad tyrant, fairy-tale monster – and I don't like this. From the inside he feels real. The writing is very particular, very personal. It's as if Shakespeare has experienced, or witnessed, some similar brainstorm. He fills the text with references to illness. He's not just describing common-or-garden jealousy, but something much, much sicker. What, though?

If Monty were around, this would be right up his street. But he's back in South Africa (and apparently ill, according to Ethel de Keyser; I make a mental note to get in touch), so I track down other experts in mental disorder and ask them to diagnose Leontes's case.

First off is Greg's older brother, Dr Mark Doran, a consultant neurologist. He doesn't know the play, but from the symptoms I describe, wonders if Leontes is schizophrenic. The man's overwhelming delusions, his tendency to be uncontrollable one moment, almost comatose the next (he's weirdly inactive during Hermione's trial), these fit the schizophrenic.

The next expert offers a radically different view: Leontes as *normal*. Psychoanalyst Helen Taylor Robinson does know the play, having studied English before moving to psychology. As she talks about a sense of loss driving Leontes to his ferocious behaviour, I realise she's not so much analysing Leontes as Shakespeare. *Winter's Tale* is one of the last plays and these are thought to be the most autobiographical. Maybe so, but I'm not keen to play Leontes as a man nearing the end of his life, tired and bitter.

'Is he a manic-depressive perhaps?' muses psychiatrist Dr Antony Bateman. As before, many of Leontes's symptoms seem to fit this new diagnosis: the character's thoughts dance, there's a speediness, almost an exhilaration to his home wrecking: he stops sleeping, he has brief moments of awareness, of sorrow, and then he's off again, prone to extreme unreason.

Schizophrenic? Racked by a sense of loss? Manic-depressive? I can't say which fits.

Then I meet Professor Maria Ronn of the renowned Maudsley Hospital. I'm not sure what I expected of a professor of psychiatry, but Maria Ronn is a surprising character: small, forty-something and Spanish. She tackles Leontes's case with complete certainty: he classically fits a condition known as 'morbid jealousy'. Or 'psychotic jealousy'. Descending out of the blue and mostly affecting men, the dominant symptom is a delusion that the patient's partner is betraying him. It leads to wildly obsessive behaviour (frantically searching for proof, hiring detectives and lawyers) and sometimes extreme violence. It's amazing. Every detail, every symptom is in the play. What may seem like a rather fantastical creation by Shakespeare is actually a completely realistic one.

Max Stafford-Clark's golden rule about research is: never mind if it's interesting, how can you *use* it? Where, specifically – where in the play? All right, so Leontes has morbid jealousy. But how can you demonstrate that particular condition? Well, you can't, actually – other than by playing exactly what's in the text – yet just knowing about it, knowing that Shakespeare didn't make it up, immediately increases my trust in the play. It affects Greg and the other actors too. It feeds a need – something which is perhaps invisible to an audience, but crucial – our own belief in what we're presenting.

The final clue to Leontes comes from a most unexpected source. A visit to Buckingham Palace. For Prince Charles's fiftieth birthday party. In rehearsals, we've been watching documentaries on the royal family to study the etiquette of everyone from princes to footmen, but now – as part of an RSC group invited to our President's birthday – I suddenly get a close-up view of the real thing. Most intriguing is the small army of private secretaries, equerries and aides who, via walkie-talkies, discreet commands or deft body movements, facilitate a route through the crowds of guests, making it possible for the Queen, Prince Charles and the others to perambulate casually, chatting to some as they go. This is when I meet the Queen and she frowns in puzzlement, almost suspicion, as Sir Geoffrey Cass introduces me as 'one of our leading actors, ma'am'. Prince Charles is warmer, more welcoming: 'You're doing *Winter's Tale*? – one of my favourite plays. When d'you open? I'll be there like a shot!' And then they're off again, surrounded by their special scrum, their travelling buffer zone.

How extraordinary it must be to have this amount of support, of protection – of *cushioning* – around you. What would it be like if you were ill, like King Leontes? The illness could have more room to breathe, to fester, to get worse. The pain might become quite dream-like: you're suffering and yet all around people still bow and curtsy, agree with everything you say, laugh readily at your jokes. The royals present tonight have had plenty of traumas in recent years and there must have been times when it felt most peculiar to host events like this, but what's it like if you're *really* in trouble? What was it like for George III as his madness grew, or for Victoria when her anguish after Albert's death became something worse than grief?

What is it like for Leontes?

I began with an instinctive feel for him. Now I have a psychological understanding as well – of the man and his world. Now I can both sense and explain the character. The chase is almost over. And I think I'm winning.

There is no sensation, and I mean *none* – not coke, not sex – nothing like the sensation of a role starting to work, particularly if it's a great role, particularly if it's Shakespeare . . . that thrill, when it starts coming to the boil inside, when its juices start to mingle with yours . . . you get a sense, a tiny sense of what it must've been like to write these words originally . . . you taste them in your mouth and they taste fresh.

They're fresh to Leontes too – these new, terrible thoughts piling into his head. It's important for him to keep surprising himself, I believe. (I'd frequently surprised myself over the last few years, often horribly.) This way he becomes a victim too. Of his illness. And of the reign of terror it unleashes. He's not a natural monster. The court and his family seem to know him as a good man. There's plenty of evidence that he and Hermione have had a happy marriage until now. At the end, at their reunion, she doesn't flinch in revulsion – 'Oh no, not you again!' – she seems to welcome back her decent, sane husband. So if theirs is a loving relationship it would be unbearable if one partner betrayed the other. Which is what he thinks is happening. He's wrong, but he doesn't know that. So it must cause him grief and pain, not just anger. In our production we're finding moments, even in his great rages, to hug her, kiss her, yearn for this *not* to be true. He flies at her, wanting to strike, then embraces instead, weeping, clinging on, then pushes her away again. Alex Gilbreath, playing Hermione, is happy to leave the moves unfixed and changeable in these moments. Leontes is genuinely dangerous here – the actor needs to surprise his colleagues, the audience, himself. As Leontes's 'madness' spirals even more out of control, I sometimes allow him to be as baffled as anyone else. He spews out yet another stream of violent, erotic fantasies, then covers his mouth like a child, shocked and dismayed.

By the time of the trial he's a very ill man. Unable to sleep, unable to hold things together, barely saying anything, or when he does, mumbling his lines, half forgetting them. When we go into previews, I take this as far as possible, encouraging the audience to think that it's me, the actor, losing my way – suddenly stopping mid-speech, for instance, having to find my specs and a scrap of paper before I can continue my address to the court. The overlap between character and performer feels very intense to me. He's ill, I've been ill. He's heading for a car crash, I've just survived two. I'm determined the audience shouldn't dismiss these things. I want them to see the situation from Leontes's point of view.

There's another way I now find – or no, rather learn from the writing – to involve the audience. It's that startling sequence of lines in the middle of the 'Inch-thick, knee-deep' soliloquy; real rule-breaking stuff, which only a great writer would risk. Shakespeare suddenly lets Leontes stick his head through the fourth wall, that invisible barrier at the front of a proscenium stage, protecting the audience from the actors, and vice versa, and lets him say:

> And many a man there is, even at this present,
> Now while I speak this, holds his wife by th' arm
> That little thinks she has been sluic'd in's absence . . .

He's saying *you*, I'm talking about *you*. Stop thinking of this as a play. Start thinking about whom *your* wife might be fucking.

I go right to the front of the stage, toes virtually clawing the edge, select a couple in the front row, point to the man and speak very intimately, very frankly. You can feel a charge go from this poor chap through the whole audience, all 1500 of them sitting behind. The fourth wall has a tear through it now. And I'll return again to it and again throughout the evening, this secret opening, this hotline I have to the audience, and I'll address them with ever increasing urgency: *Listen, this is what's happening to me now – it's very confusing – I know it's frightening the other people here in court, but it's frightening me too. Can you help?*

The audience is seeing a side of Leontes that no one else does – the man in trouble, in pain – a sympathetic side, you could say. Whether they like it or not, they're complicit now, they're involved, they're my friend, my confessor, my therapist; they can't dismiss me as a story-book tyrant any more.

This is helpful for the whole shape of the role. By Act Five, when Leontes reappears, the audience has to care about him. If you don't, you're not going to be moved by the statue scene and the reunion with Hermione. Leontes hasn't just repented during the sixteen years since we saw him last – he's a broken figure, devastated by what he did. I picture him as a man without an outer layer of skin. Nerve ends exposed. Every breeze hurts. I want feelings to burn through him intensely – tears, joy, whatever – an uncensored individual. I have a long time to prepare for these last scenes: all of Bohemia, while Ian Hughes is notching up a triumph as Autolycus (one actor's poison is another actor's meat). I sit in the furthest, darkest corner of the wings, letting my mind dwell on sad things, often Dad again, or my other father figure Monty – I've learned he's seriously ill – or sometimes just gruesome items in the news, and then, when the cue comes, carry this stuff into the light.

Winter's Tale opened in Stratford on 6 January 1999. The first batch of reviews, the weeklies, were tremendous. We held our breath for the Sundays. The week before, John Peter – *Sunday Times* critic – had written a long, vicious attack on the RSC. Surely he couldn't retract his words so swiftly and praise us? He did. The others too. Our final score was about nine out of ten.

11/1/99. Have to report the most delicious, baffling, unfamiliar sense of sheer bloody happiness! Kept asking myself why all day and the answer kept coming: We've had a success. Greg's back in London, so I can only celebrate on my own. Went for a long lovely ramble across the Welcombe Hills up from the house. Bright, windy afternoon. Gulping at the fresh country air. Staring up at mountainous cloud formations with great shafts of sunlight – pictures from a kid's Bible or a Hollywood film – and saying to myself again and again: We've had a success! Eventually walked down to the river. It was a milky brown colour and possessed with beautiful strangeness. The current was pushing one way, the wind another, so the water seemed both rough and calm at the same time, suspended on its journey. My current loo-reading book is one which Greg found in that second-hand bookshop near the Shakespeare Hotel – inspirational stuff when he was a schoolboy, apparently, it's called *Great Acting*. In the section on Olivier there's his great quote about success smelling like the ocean, like seaweed, like Brighton. Sorry to differ, but I think it smells like Stratford and its river. The scent is of summer – you can just catch it even now, in between these sharp January draughts – and of past RSC seasons. They come at me like small, unformed, yet reassuring memories . . . good times I've known here, good times. As I stood on the banks today, the wind dropped and some swans decided to grab their chance and take off. Always an impressive sight and sound. They run along the surface of the river, their giant wings clipping the water. The other day Greg described it as 'an applause of swans'.

YEAR OF THE
TWO KINGS

During 1999 I fell in love again. I've never told Greg. It was in Stratford and he was a local man. Luckily he'd been dead for 400 years. And he'd just been named Man of the Millennium – so my attraction was clearly shared. 1999 was also the year I turned fifty. And the year when I came to a different understanding of myself and of Recovery, which involved, yes, a kind of relapse. But, most important, it was a year that began with Leontes and ended with Macbeth. It began and ended with Shakespeare.

Something snapped on *Winter's Tale*. Snapped in anger and snapped into place. The two were linked. Both about playing Shakespeare.

'There's always violence in Shakespeare,' said Cis Berry during a company voice session in *Winter's Tale* rehearsals. The statement stopped me in my tracks. I liked it – it suited my current dark-happy mood – but seemed at odds with both the speaker and the subject.

Cis Berry on violence? Cis Berry, voice guru, RSC mother figure, a small, white-crested sparrow of a lady, tough in her own way (she's in Recovery too, from alcoholism, many years on), yet an essentially, infinitely peaceful presence.

Violence?

In Shakespeare?

The noble Bard, the lofty poet, the all-embracing humanist. Violent? In the tragedies, well, yes, obviously, and often cruelly so (the eye-gouging in *Lear*, the amputations in *Titus*); and yes, the histories are packed with war and grief (the *Henry VIs* and *Richard III*); and yes, the comedies are often quite savage (the lovers' mayhem in *Dream* or Malvolio's humiliation in *Twelfth Night*) and, actually, it's quite hard even to call some of them comedies (*Merchant* or *Measure*); and yes, clearly the sonnets are filled with personal pain (*The expense of spirit in a waste of shame*) – but violence? In all of it? In all Shakespeare? Really?

I like the sound of it, as I say. It lets me in.

A couple of decades before I arrived in this country, the two giants of twentieth-century classical acting did battle over the 'modern' way to speak Shakespeare, and although Olivier probably won the popular vote, Gielgud's sound was still highly cherished and so quintessentially English it felt very threatening to me – it's that honey-voiced sound I keep being rude about. The territory seemed out of bounds; I feared approaching it. And when I did, I was so disheartened by the sound of my voice, my colonial voice, in a great Shakespeare role – Richard III – that I shrank from doing more of them. I had a go at some of the character ones – like Shylock, where you can hide behind an accent – then gave up and tried to find a different way of being a classical actor. I sensed there was something right about me and the classics – they need a bold touch – but not me and Shakespeare.

Oddly enough, it was this route – doing other verse dramatists – that eventually made Shakespeare available to me again.

Tourneur's mouthfuls of barbed wire in *Revenger's Tragedy*, Marlowe's thumping mighty lines in *Tamburlaine*, Rostand/Burgess's elegant tum-ti-tum tunes in *Cyrano* and even early Shakespeare himself in *Titus* – his genius still unformed, quite clumsy, quite vulgar – all of these helped something snap into place when I came to *Winter's Tale*, while something else snapped in anger at the same instant.

I don't care what my voice is like. Let Shakespeare be un-Gielgudian, unmelodious, imperfect, jagged, rough, *violent*. It's what the South African accents did for *Titus* and precisely why that sounded so good: muscular and fresh. Well, let's hear it at the Royal Shakespeare Company now. Not a South African accent exactly, but I don't care if a few ol' Capie vowels slip through. I don't care how I sound. I just want to do it. Do Shakespeare. Do something that meets what he's written. And what he's written is about the *souls* of men not the *sound* of them!

And it was just when I reached this point – another fuck-it point – that I suddenly heard myself *sounding* better in the verse.

'You just have to breathe it.' This is another of Cis's catchphrases. Patsy Rodenburg, the other great voice guru (at the National) says it too. What on earth do they mean? you think when you're starting out. How can you breathe text? You've got to speak it.

Well, yes.

That's all they're saying. When we speak in normal life it's second nature. Like breathing. We don't think about that either. We can make short, polite conversation or conduct long screaming rows without stopping to think or breathe. Shakespeare needs to sound the same. As natural. As though this is how you talk every day. You think up these images just as a matter of course, these astonishing images. They're part of your imagination – not Leontes's, Macbeth's, or even Shakespeare's – they're *yours*. That's when it starts to sound right. When you're just breathing the stuff – air, words, images – all at the same time. That's when you start to fly on it. Your voice takes off and flies.

Leontes is the heaviest of men, sick, stubborn, stuck within himself, enclosed, entrapped, a turgid weight. Yet he only works when I'm flying with the text, when I'm light, deft, even humorous. When I dance with him.

Something about this is absolutely crucial to the playing of Shakespeare. I can't explain it. Cis comes close with those two phrases of hers: 'There's always violence in Shakespeare' and 'You just have to breathe it'.

We have to breathe it in . . . what we are . . . what Shakespeare writes about so frankly, so lucidly . . . our violence, our animal instincts . . . just pant, just breathe, just *be*.

It's difficult, though.

To play Shakespeare you need a variety of resources. You need enormous technical ease: to phrase, shape and finally *breathe* the language like normal speech. You need great curiosity about human beings. You need to become so fascinated by our strange behaviour that you believe you're perceiving it for the first time – like Shakespeare did, I think – and feel compelled to tell the truth about us. The best Method actors feel this compulsion. So – you have to be raw as hell and supremely skilled. You must be able both to grunt and echo, murmur and sing. You must be Marlon Brando and Placido Domingo in the same body.

It's difficult.

'So what are you doing now – *Macbeth*?'

'No, that's coming up later in the year. No – *Winter's Tale*.'

'Gone well?'

'Terrifically. I mean really terrifically.'

'*Mazeltov*. I'd like to see the reviews.'

'I'll send them to you.'

'Do. I'd like that.'

That was my last phone call with Monty. He died in April – at home in Cape Town. And the last thing I did was fax him a load of reviews, averting my eyes from the pages as I fed them into the machine. How odd. Monty and I did so much work on my need to bring prizes home to Mommie and here I was doing something similar with him. Offering my work, not me. What I really wanted to say was, 'Thank you, Monty, thanks for everything you gave me.' But that would've been like saying, 'I know you're dying.' So you talk about other things.

We held a memorial service in London at Ethel de Keyser's offices – formerly BDAF now Canon Collins Trust – for his friends here: a curious mixture of veteran South African freedom fighters, his 'comrades', and us, his 'client list' – Mike Leigh, Richard Wilson, Roger Allam, Jim, myself and others.

I made a little speech remembering Monty the therapist. Another man spoke about Monty the comrade. Yet another about Monty the man. It was in this last speech that we learned a strange thing. Before he trained in psychotherapy, Monty's profession was not that of doctor, which we all thought, but that of dry-cleaner. Dry-cleaner? Stuck in a corner among the speakers, I could only look across to my fellow 'clients' in bewilderment. They were all frowning too.

Afterwards I hurried over: 'It's not just me, is it? I put it in *Year of the King* – that he's a GP turned therapist – I must've got that from him, I wouldn't've just made it up.'

'No, no, I remember him telling me too,' said Richard, 'and how he delivered his daughters' babies.'

'I got insurance on one of my films,' said Mike Leigh, 'on the basis that my therapist was also a qualified doctor.'

'While actually he was a dry-cleaner,' Roger Allam commented wryly. 'Puts an altogether new meaning on the word shrink.'

We began to laugh.

'You could say he took us to the cleaners,' said Richard.

'If he wasn't so good at the job,' said Mike.

'True, true,' we all agreed, then broke into laughter again. I could hear Monty laughing loudest of all; he had a great, full, hearty bark of a laugh: 'All you big-shot actors and directors hey – all you fantasists – ja well, I could do that too!'

People tell you that turning fifty is a tough one. I never believed them. I don't mind ageing. I have no desire to be young again – God forbid – I was so confused then. As I've exited from various closets over the years and worked first with Monty (my shrink the dry-cleaner – how I love saying that) and now with Marietta, I've become fractionally less confused. So why should I mind turning fifty?

Oh, where did it come from, this weight on my shoulders, this growing weight, as 14 June drew closer? *Oich*. I'm a flop, I'm a failure. A theatre actor. Who cares about theatre actors? I can't get into films, I'm not offered television any more. I'm losing ground, losing strength – I used to be the breadwinner in the relationship, now I'm supported by Greg, his career's on a fantastic ascendancy, mine's going nowhere – I'm becoming just another whingeing, disillusioned actor. And as a novelist – don't even talk to me about being a novelist – the last one, *The Feast*, was published, but totally ignored, hardly a single review, death at birth. And as for the new one, just recently finished, Mic can't sell that for love nor money. No, the time has come to face up to it. My career as a novelist is going nowhere. Maybe I should start painting again – maybe Mac was right – maybe I should've been an artist.

We went to Florence first, Greg and I. As part of a three-week Italian holiday and birthday present, we went to Florence to look at my childhood hero, Michelangelo. 'Och, Sher, you've gone and put a man's chest on that woman,' Mac used to grumble. 'Your male and female anatomy is a complete bloody shambles, lad.' I always wanted to point out that Michelangelo had the same problem, but never had the *chutzpah*. To be in

Florence at last, viewing the real sculptures, is overwhelming. The tiny chisel marks on the four unfinished *Slaves* show like goose bumps. That's how I'm feeling too. From Florence to Canalicchio, a small hilltop village in Umbria. One night after dinner we stroll out of the glare of Cannalichio's two street lamps and see a miracle. There are stars in the sky and stars on the land: great drifts of uncanny, dancing light everywhere you look, on the road and in the olive groves, across whole hillsides, whole valleys. Fireflies. *Lucciola*. You blink, you steady yourself, for it's very like seeing spots before falling over – then you look again, you gasp, you laugh. 'It's a real midsummer night's dream,' says Greg. On to Rome for the weekend – more Michelangelos, the Colosseum, a Versace birthday suit – and already we're moving on, heading for the coast, for Amalfi, for 14 June. Oh dear, oh shit . . .

14/6/99. Hotel Santa Caterina, Amalfi. Happy fiftieth. Today's not as bad as I thought. Mainly because of what happened yesterday.

We arrived in time for lunch. The hotel has a beautiful terrace restaurant, within a lemon grove, halfway up a vertical cliff face; great sea view, fresh grilled fish arriving on every table, plus chilled bottles of wine. 'I think I'm going to have a glass,' I said. Greg looked anxious. He wasn't sure if I was joking or not. Neither was I. Didn't have wine. Felt very restless, though, very itchy. After lunch suggested a stroll down into town. Thought it might distract me to look at the boys on the beach. Didn't work. Just felt low and listless. Said, 'I think I'll have a G & T, want to join me?' Greg looked shocked this time – no longer questioning my seriousness. 'Oh, for God's sake,' I said. 'I'm hardly going to go running round Amalfi looking for the local dealer! It's only a G & T!' *Only?* Haven't had a drink in two years and ten months. I'm that close to my third anniversary. We went to a bar on a sort of jetty stretching into the sea. Sat right at the end. I ordered two G & Ts: 'Make them doubles.' Then we sat waiting. Time became very strange. It slowed to a sort of pulse. You could hear everything, see everything. A last moment of clarity, of sobriety? I was facing the sea, Greg the buildings. He said, 'The waiter's coming back.' It took an incredibly long time. The man must've been walking in slow motion – playing at being an execu-tioner – slowly approaching my back. 'You don't have to go through with this,' said Greg, seeing something in my face. 'I know,' I said. The waiter finally arrived. He put down the drinks and walked away. I sat staring at mine. 'I don't know if you want me to stop you or not,' said Greg. 'No,' I said. This sounded ambiguous so I added, 'I don't want you to stop me.' I lifted the glass and took a sip. Held it in my mouth. Like Felix in *The Feast*, when he's under the table. He doesn't swallow. I do. Tasted of . . . sort of nothing. Felt strange afterwards, though. Not drunk or sick . . . more dreamlike. Went back to the hotel for a lie-down. When we woke I ordered champagne, then wine with supper. Didn't want to think. About the implications. About tomorrow.

Well, tomorrow's here, tomorrow's today, tomorrow's the fiftieth. And I feel fine. No, I feel good. The hotel has its own private cove, a deep basin of Tyrrhenian Sea, all black and turquoise, and you can't indulge in a mid-life crisis while bobbing around in its great slopping swell – particularly not if, just before plunging in, you've shared some champagne with your loved one in the sun.

Back in London, I hurried to Dr Shanahan, my consultant from Charter Nightingale days. How serious was my misdemeanour in Italy? Not very, he thought. He reminded me that he'd only banned alcohol for 'the foreseeable future'. In fact, checking his notes, he found that he'd actually nominated three years as that foreseeable future – I don't remember this – so we were only having the conversation two months early. What now, though? He said the question was whether I'd be able to have a few glasses of wine without the inevitable progress to whisky and phone call to the dealer. I thought I could. He said, 'Have a go, then – keep seeing Marietta – keep talking.'

So far, touch wood, it hasn't been a problem. I tried whisky again – which I hated – I haven't tried coke. I don't believe I will. I miss it, though – let's not be coy – I miss that quick fix of self-love. But I can't handle it, simply can't, end of story. My drinking is much lighter than it used to be. On the other hand, I'm definitely addictive by nature – whether work, coffee or love – so I'm always going to have to watch it. Things are not all neatly tied up. In the meantime it's been absolutely wonderful being able to have a drink again. After the show in the Dirty Duck. Out in our Islington garden on a summer evening. Reunited with three old friends from the family of Burgundy: Chablis, Mersault and Puligny Montrachet. Absolutely bloody wonderful!

I view my addiction as an experience, not a mistake. I don't believe we make mistakes. No, that's not true – I'm in a funny position, I work in the arts: everything that happens, good or bad, can seem like material. Of course people make mistakes. The play I'm about to do tells the story of a man and his wife who make a bad mistake, a seriously bad mistake . . .

'We're calling it *Macbeth*,' says Greg on the first day of rehearsals. 'Not *Mackers*, not *The Scottish Play*, none of the euphemisms. *Macbeth*, *Macbeth*, *Macbeth* – there, I've said it and haven't been struck down. There's supposed to be a curse on this play. Bollocks! The only curse is that it's so hard to do.'

Nodding emphatically, I sit there, sick with nerves. On the outside, on a purely physical level, I've never been better. I've been dieting for Macbeth and training at the gym; I'm over a stone lighter and the shape I want is taking form. I see Macbeth as trimmer and fitter than Leontes. The Sicilian king is court-bound, desk-bound, quite round, a small bear. The Scottish king is a man of action, a soldier, a murderer, more wolf-like.

But internally it's as though I've put on weight. The great chase after Leontes would be difficult to do again. It was like a rush – almost a drug rush – an anger rush – a great mess of feelings about acting, about addiction, about *me*. But that's faded. I am *me* again. The character I've always found hardest to play. I sometimes say that as a gay Jewish white South African I've cornered the market in minority groups. But when it comes to my relationship with myself I can't afford to be the outsider any more. I have finally to inhabit my own skin. And I feel a bit closer to that goal now, after the fiftieth birthday: a bit older, a bit wiser, a bit more relaxed. I've always believed that the best actors brim with conflict (those opposite energies of male and female, animal and intellect, child and adult), yet the happiest people have none. Rubbish. The happiest people embrace their conflicts. I am made up of strengths and of weaknesses. Take it or leave it. This is *me*. Which means that here I am, starting a new job and full of caution again, full of doubt, full of anxious questions.

Aren't we pushing our luck? We had a big hit with *Winter's Tale* at the beginning of the year. Now we're at the other end, starting *Macbeth*. Shouldn't we have waited? Isn't Macbeth a bit like Leontes – two kings destroying themselves and everyone around them? And isn't Greg doing too much work – *Oronoko* and *Timon* since *Winter's Tale* – and isn't he winning too much praise, isn't he due for a clobbering? If so, *Macbeth* is built for the job. What Greg's just said, about the play being hard to do – well, yes, we've been talking about this for months, years, actually. How the play is dangerous on many levels. The writing is superbly dangerous – fast, lean, urgent, beautiful, it cuts like the sharpest, subtlest blade, it gets under your skin, it's truly disturbing. But how to stage it? That's dangerous in a different way. The themes of witchcraft and murder, of horror and the supernatural, these easily become risible rather than frightening. The play invites you to be excessive and many productions, like the one with O'Toole at the Old Vic in 1980, walk gleefully into the trap, pouring buckets of blood over their heads as they go. Other productions, seeking to avoid the excess, flatten out and just become boring. I saw one on the main stage in Stratford – done in a sparse Brechtian style – and another in the Olivier at the National – done monumentally – and both times one of Shakespeare's shortest plays became one of the longest. It's not a play for a large theatre. Sitting in a big auditorium, with volumes of air above and around you, you automatically feel safe. The Swan, where we're doing it, is much better. Actors and audience share the same space, crowd together, can't hide from one another, or the play.

In 1975 Trevor Nunn did it in a very small theatre, the old tin-hut Other Place in Stratford. In the round, using virtually nothing except darkness and flawless acting. Not only Ian McKellen and Judi Dench, but Bob Peck, Roger Rees, John Woodvine, Ian McDiarmid, a dream cast. By concentrating on the inner terror of the play, on psychological fear instead of Hammer Horror spookiness and gore, Nunn made the play work, perhaps definitively. I feel haunted by this. There are times when something's been done so well you just needn't bother doing it again. As an actor, I'd known this with *Arturo*, and to some extent with *Travesties* and *Cyrano*. The shadows of Rossiter, Wood and Jacobi never went away. It should've happened with *Richard III* too – no shadow threatens more than Olivier's – but it didn't and here lies hope. Shakespeare is bigger than any of us. The plays have lasted 400 years because you can – you must – do them again and again.

So instead of being defeated by Nunn's production let's learn from it. Two things:

Nunn Principle 1   Casting. The play's called *Macbeth* but isn't a one-man show. Cast Judi Dench opposite Ian McKellen and you start cooking, you get value for money, you get two heavyweights slugging it out. Greg and I decide we'll only do the play if we can get a top leading actress to play the Lady. We're lucky, we get our first choice: Harriet Walter. OK, we're in with a chance.

Nunn Principle 2   Simplicity. That's what the 1975 production achieved: inner not outer horror. That's what we must go for too. 'But what Trevor did wasn't just simplicity,' says Greg. 'It was inspired simplicity.' Hmm. He's absolutely right, but 'inspired simplicity' is just code for 'great art'. Aiming to do an inspirationally simple *Macbeth* is as difficult and dangerous – that word again – as setting out to paint a masterpiece.

Fear.

We begin with fear.

'Fear is the word used most often in the play,' observes Greg, 'and the word that's used least is love.'

Fear. It's what every single character feels somewhere during the story, even the witches. Greg wants them played as people who wish they didn't know the end of the story.

Fear. It's what the audience must experience.

Fear. It's what I'm feeling.

Greg asks the company to relate their own ultimate experience of fear. Not just us, the actors, but also stage management, the fight director Terry King, the choreographer Sian Williams, anyone who wants to stay in the room has to contribute to the circle, the confessional. It's rather like that Joint Stock workshop where by pooling our different experiences of sex we enabled *Cloud Nine* to come into being. This'll work in reverse. The play's already there, but we need to haul ourselves to it, inside it, to say this isn't about *them* – some weird Brady–Hindley couple called the Macbeths – this is about *us*. Us all. We may not have committed murder, but we all know what it's like to do something wrong. That's what the play's about. A deed and its consequences. Crime and punishment. Conscience. Fear.

The range of stories amaze me – the range of things that frighten human beings. An A–Z of them. From natural disasters – someone's been in an avalanche, someone else a forest fire – to car crashes, near-drowning accidents, a knife attack in a disco, a bad dope trip, fear of spiders, fear of blindness, fear of madness, right down to deep inner phobias and dreams.

When it comes to my turn, I tell the group about my recurring nightmare – now no more – my intruder nightmare. Nothing has ever frightened me more. Because it was inside me, trapped inside. Me as my own devil.

Interspersed with the fear workshops, other group work is proceeding too. Text work. Paraphrasing the play; every single word of every single speech. Research work. Watching documentaries about violence and warfare. Interviewing two Kosovan refugees. Visiting the Tower of London to see the Crown Jewels. This in order to *value* kingship. Monarchy is often satirised nowadays, but in the play it's sanctified, it's holy. When the Macbeths murder Duncan it's like murdering God. And Greg has helped this by casting Joe O'Conor in the role: eighty-three years old (one of his first jobs was playing Macduff to Wolfit's Macbeth in 1949), tall, gracious, white-bearded, beautiful with age.

Certain rehearsals are private: closed-set rehearsals. Just Greg and the witches (Polly Kemp, Noma Dumezweni, Diane Beck). They're creating their own secret world, Mike Leigh style, in isolation. The rest of us mustn't know what motivates them, what they believe in, how they think, how they live. This will pay off handsomely when we come to rehearse Macbeth's and Banquo's first encounter with them; they are a force unto themselves; they aren't the hunched and croaky hags of cliché, they're young, homeless, junkies maybe, driven by that kind of ferocious introspection, hooked on some gear called Dark God.

And there's my own private research. Which leads to two of the most remarkable encounters of my life.

Two men who've committed murder. Both have served their time and are back in society. The RSC has found them, one through his parole officer, the other through a theatre group of ex-cons. Both agree to come to the Clapham rehearsal rooms – at different times – and talk to me. Both are willing to describe their experiences before, during and after the murder in as much detail as I want, or can take.

Mark and Jimmy. (Not their real names.) By chance, both are Scottish and both committed knife murders. There all similarities end.

Mark first. He's about thirty-five, looks older, quite skeletal, stretched white skin, greyish hair scraped into a ponytail. No criminal past but, prior to the crime, a growing gambling addiction. He ended up killing his best friend rather than confess what he'd done with the £50 meant for an electricity bill. He talks about being in a kind of trance in the hours leading up to the murder and through half of it. 'Tony, y'know it takes so, *so* long to kill somebody,' he says in his soft, hesitant way. Then the victim suddenly cried, 'I don't want to die' and Mark describes 'waking up'. He decided to get an ambulance, walked to the door, stood on the threshold, realised that he couldn't possibly take this option, returned and finished the job. He was caught, he confessed, he served thirteen years.

Today he reminds me of that image I had for Leontes in Act Five: a man with no outer layer of skin. Every breeze hurts. Mark is like that – completely raw. His nerve ends are exposed. Face, hands, voice are all trembling slightly. His thin-boned nerviness puts me in mind of a bird trapped in a room; he's a fallen angel, weirdly beautiful. He talks about the crime as killing himself along with the victim. He says the moment was like tearing something apart, stepping through an impossible barrier, going somewhere we aren't supposed to go. (Macbeth on the dead Duncan: 'His gashed stabs were like a breach in nature, for ruin's wasteful entrance.') When Mark was through this impossible barrier, when the deed was done, he saw a terrible vision: 'And there's me now. Alone. Naked in the world. For always.'

Mark is haunted by the crime, Jimmy by the punishment.

If Jimmy hadn't been caught you sense he wouldn't have given it a second thought. He's a Glaswegian hard man, brought up on crime. He's older than Mark, but similarly emaciated; dark-haired, wearing a dark raincoat – he keeps this on throughout our two-hour meeting – and although he's perfectly civil, he emanates danger. Except occasionally, when a surprising expression lights up his long, sallow face. He'll suddenly widen his eyes and blow his cheeks, looking like a ten-year-old trying to communicate how *awesome* the world is! (He does this whenever he gets to the most gruesome bits of the story.) His victim was a suspected grass.

Jimmy went round to this man's flat – 'just tae gi' 'im a hiding, y'know' – lost control, and by the time he walked home his boots were squelching with blood. The forensic people described the attack as so cruel it was like an act of torture. Jimmy remembers nothing about it. But he remembers every minute of every hour in prison – he fought the system non-stop and ended up adding five years to the fifteen already decreed. The punishment, not the crime, drives him crazy.

It's night-time when we finish talking. I'm suddenly aware of sitting alone with this man in an attic room in Clapham. Downstairs, rehearsals are long over, the others have gone. Except for Greg – he's waited for me.

We offer Jimmy a lift to the tube. He sits in the back of our car, chatting about this and that. Turns out he's from Greenock not Glasgow proper. 'Oh – my best friend's from Greenock,' I say, then check myself. Richard Wilson and Jimmy probably won't have people in common.

We stop outside Oval tube. Jimmy says thanks, gets out and walks away swiftly without a backward glance or wave, as anyone else would do. Within an instant his tall, hunched, dark figure has vanished. I think of Macbeth's line: 'And withered Murder . . . thus with his stealthy pace . . . moves like a ghost.'

Both these encounters leave me deeply unsettled and upset. Which is good. The play must do that to the audience.

But what did I get from them, specifically, to *use* in the play? Two things:

1   It helped identify Macbeth as Mark rather than Jimmy, a man racked by the crime not the punishment. Like Mark, Macbeth has the imagination to perceive what he's done – he even foresees it in 'If it were done' – and this imagination of his, a beautiful–ugly instrument, tortures him like nothing else. 'O full of scorpions is my mind, dear wife!' he cries later in the play. Lady Macbeth has no such imagination – she doesn't picture the consequences of the deed – she just wants to get away with it. She's more like Jimmy. And when it finally catches up with her – imagination, conscience – it comes in such a terrible, scrambled, nightmarish shape (the sleepwalking scene) that it destroys her.

2   There was a curious moment when both my murderers gave the same answer to a question. 'Do you dream about your victim?' I asked. Each replied, 'Only when I'm awake.' They went on to

describe strange moments of recall during ordinary, waking life: dreamlike appearances of the men they'd killed. Mark's account was characteristically lucid and chilling: 'He looks at me gently, without vengeance – he knows what I've done to *myself* – he just stands there, very calm, no wounds or anything, just looking at me. It's unbearable.' Right – that's how I must imagine Banquo's ghost.

(Both men come to see the show during its run, and their reactions confound my earlier impressions of them. Mark doesn't like what we've done, doesn't like my performance. I meet him afterwards and he finds it difficult to know what to say. Eventually comes out with: 'I thought you'd be more heroic.' Mark, the least heroic of murderers, longs for something more glamorous when he's watching himself in the theatre. Hard man Jimmy doesn't stay after the show he sees. I fear the worst again. Then I get a letter. In stumbling phrases he says repeatedly how *moved* he was.)

After two weeks of paraphrasing the text and researching its themes, we're finally ready for the read-through.

'Well, nice working with you,' I say to Greg as we drive in to Clapham.

He turns, preoccupied, puzzled.

'I tend to leave after read-throughs,' I explain.

'Ha-ha,' he says.

I know I won't be leaving after this one. But it nevertheless comes as a surprise. And disappointment.

Despite all the work on fear, on violence, on the *reality* of these things, rather than their fictional manifestations, the company don't connect with the play. We're a strong group, real RSC thoroughbreds – Ken Bones as Banquo, Nigel Cooke as Macduff, Paul Webster as Ross, Trevor Martin as Old Man/Doctor – yet we sound fairly reppy today, myself included. Boom-boom, blah-blah we go, making that hollow, heroic *Shakespeare* sound. Only Harriet seems in touch with something more real, more disturbing. Later I try to describe her in my diary:

As a person she's posh, as an actress primitive, it's a mesmeric combination . . . that strong face with its startling beauty, a sort of broken beauty . . . her fringe hangs over it today, you can hardly see

anything . . . only her nose . . . it looks bruised, red, hurt . . . this is
how Lady Macbeth sounds too . . . other actresses make her wicked;
this doesn't seem in Harriet's repertoire; simply that she's
wounded, somewhere deep . . . but who is? Lady Macbeth? Harriet?
. . . can't really tell . . . it's very private, very personal, the way she
reads.

Greg and I are subdued returning to Islington at the end of the day. It's
curiously like the drive home after the *Winter's Tale* read-through. Something's wrong, quite badly wrong. If we, the actors, can't identify with the
material, neither will the audience. The play will simply be as it always is:
risible or boring.

'Thank God for alcohol,' I say, as we pour a glass of Chablis.

Greg doesn't comment, his mind elsewhere. After pondering for a long
time, he breaks the house rule – about discussing work – and says, 'We
should be doing this in modern dress, shouldn't we?'

We've both been mentioning this – cautiously – over the last fortnight.
The present plan is to set the play when it was written. But I've been less
and less inspired by the Jacobean reference material we've seen in
rehearsals: contemporary illustrations and portraits. Who are these people?
I can't *read* them – their clothes, their status. I wouldn't be able to tell a
Menteith from a Malcolm, yet one is a minor lord, the other a prince of
the realm. And I have no idea – unusual for me – none whatsoever – what
Macbeth looks like.

'Yes,' I answer Greg. 'Yes, modern dress would help.'

'What about the darkness, though?'

Greg's most passionate instinct about the play centres on this element.
Darkness. The darkness of the story, the darkness inside human beings, the
literal darkness of night, which is when several major scenes occur,
darkness, darkness. In one of our earliest discussions, Greg said, 'This can't
be a world where you just flick a switch to banish the darkness. It can't go
away that easily.' So – no electricity. So – pre-twentieth century.
Nineteenth? Eighteenth? They didn't feel relevant. So then we decided
simply to go back to when it was written.

But as we discuss it again tonight, we remind one another of images
we've seen on the TV recently – the earthquakes in Turkey, the war in
Kosovo – again and again images of modern societies made primitive,

modern societies with the electricity gone, modern societies in deepest darkness.

Greg suddenly goes to the phone. He dials Stephen Brimson-Lewis (the designer). 'I wonder if you could pop round – as soon as possible – no, I mean *now*.'

Stephen arrives within the hour. He welcomes the news. He felt it at the read-through too: a holding back from real fear, artificial posturing taking its place. We need to jolt ourselves, jolt the audience, jolt the play. It's a dramatic step changing the design a third of the way into rehearsals – changing from Jacobean to modern (not unlike changing your Autolycus) but Stephen feels it's possible. We're finding costumes from stock anyway – to get the well-worn feel of real clothes – so it's only a question of swapping locations in the vast storage halls of RSC costumes, from the seventeenth to the twentieth century. Set-wise virtually nothing has to alter at all. Since the Swan is meant to help solve the play, the Swan itself is the set – with a blasted, broken-down look and one or two surprises in a false back wall.

It's exciting sitting in our kitchen tonight, listening to Stephen and Greg cook up a new world for the production: a modern world but one you can't easily identify. Everything and everyone will be coated in soot, oil, grime, dried blood. Uniforms and weaponry will be a hotch-potch – people grab anything to fight – soldiers and witches look the same, and you can't say which war this is either: Flanders, Vietnam, Balkans? Clothes are unwashed, chins unshaven. There's no hot water, no power. Fires and candles burn. The world is impoverished, muddy, scorched, *dark*.

'Harriet next,' says Greg, picking up the phone as Stephen leaves.

She's been part of the initial design discussions. She has to give her blessing to this change of plan or we can't proceed

At first she has reservations. She argues that a woman in a modern world would be less reliant on her husband; Lady Macbeth only seems able to realise her own ambitions through Macbeth's achievements. Greg replies that one can't generalise about these things. There are plenty of examples of Lady Macbeths in recent times – Mrs Milosevic, Mrs Ceaucescu – powerful ladies who prefer to rule from behind the throne. They discuss it through and Harriet is convinced.

On Monday morning, Greg assembles the company and announces our change of plan. As before – with the Autolycus affair – people look pleased, relieved.

My job was made slighty easier by our change from Jacobean to modern. It was something to do with Macbeth as warrior, as soldier. I've played plenty of these – Tamburlaine, Richard, Cyrano – but there were always reasons why they could be small men like myself, overachievers. But something about Macbeth, some received impression, said that he wasn't short and stocky, he was big and butch. It was probably those shaggy, kilted representations of him in the souvenir shops of Stratford (visit these if you ever want to find out how *not* to play your character), but once we changed to modern dress, once I could recognise the world, I also started to recognise him. One of those Nato commanders-in-chief we see on the telly all the time, very hands-on, one of the lads, liked by the troops, matey with fellow officers, happier at work than at home. 'What, a soldier and afear'd?' Lady Macbeth says of him in the sleepwalking scene. It's a masterstroke by Shakespeare. On the battlefield Macbeth's savagery seems to go beyond the call of duty – he's unseaming people from the knaves to the chops, he's trying to memorise another Golgotha – yet this same butcher can't kill one old man in his own house. And when he does kill him, it's rather like you or I would do it (or Mark, the gentle murderer); he panics, he's upset by the sight of blood, he forgets to leave the daggers at the crime scene, he botches the whole thing. It's very human. The audience can identify with him. It's brilliant writing.

Greg and I wanted to emphasise the irony – 'a soldier and afear'd' – by showing him at the height of his powers to start with. Traditionally Macbeth and Banquo enter on their own, wandering across an eerie stretch of wasteland, the blasted heath, and bump into the witches. All very spooky and portentous. We decided to give our war heroes a triumphal entrance, on the shoulders of their troops, everyone very energised, very euphoric, they're battle-crazed, they're Vietnam vets, they've been slicing open gooks in the undergrowth, nailing others to makeshift crosses, drums are thundering, soldiers bellowing, 'All hail, all hail!' As this finishes, the chant is taken up by different voices – lighter, feminine, mocking the heroism: 'All hail . . . all hail . . .' The generals find themselves surrounded by three bizarre soldiers – or scavangers or refugees? – and their first instinct is to laugh. Until one of the strangers tells

Macbeth he'll be king. This wipes the smile off his face. But once the witches have exited, the men resort to bravado again. Did it even happen? 'Have we eaten on the insane root that takes the reason prisoner?' asks Banquo. In one of our paraphrasing sessions someone translated this as: 'Have we done some bad weed, man?' Meanwhile Macbeth is starting to think. What that woman said . . . about me being king . . .. my most secret ambition . . . *how can anyone know?* . . . other than my wife . . .

Although Harriet and I worked together once before, on the show I don't talk about, I'm calling this the first time. (Anyway, Viola and whatsisname hardly ever meet.) As the Macbeths, a genuine chemistry grows between us, thank God – to act a marriage you have to become one in a way, you have to develop that second-nature sense about what the other person is thinking, feeling, needing.

We get some of our relationship for free. Harriet's so naturally aristocratic that it goes without saying this Lady has married beneath her – her swarthy little husband's certainly not of her class, if even of her *race* – and this provides great ammunition for the power struggle between them. Shakespeare's writing of a long-term partnership is very convincing: the mingling of personality. Although it's Macbeth who conjures images of murdering sleep, it's Lady Macbeth who endures the torment of sleep-walking. Most crucial is the baby. 'I have given suck,' says Lady M., 'and know how tender 'tis to love the babe that milks me.' Scholars invent all sorts of nonsense to explain this: a previous marriage, et cetera. Cis Berry is right when she says you mustn't just *read* Shakespeare; it was written to be spoken, to be performed. You can't play a previous marriage (never referred to), but you can play a dead baby (referred to). They're a couple whose baby has died. It's a taboo subject, we decided, never mentioned. And then suddenly it is. At the very moment he's got cold feet about the murder. Macbeth has to do a drastic U-turn in that short scene, resolving to do the deed. I don't know how other Macbeths achieve this, but for me it was solved by the mention of the baby and the upset Harriet brought to it, not a manipulative upset, real upset. I suddenly needed to be on her side whatever the cost.

I found a photo of a dead baby in one of my Boer War books – the Victorians photographed their infant mortalities – gave Harriet a copy and stuck another in my script. Our baby. Frozen, white, wearing an embroidered shift, lying in a tiny plank-and-nail coffin. The Macbeth baby.

From then on their marriage became more and more real for us. A deeply entwined couple, deeply bonded – love, sex, the lot – introspective, interdependent, hooked on one another, for richer or poorer. During the play you only see them in nightmarish situations, so it's vital to suggest the other side, to find moments of normality, of affection, even of humour. An important one came after the banquet. His imagination is taking off into orbit by now. Trying to calm him, she says, 'You lack the season of all natures, sleep.' At one rehearsal, the line suddenly hit me anew, and I turned to her in amazement. *Sleep? Yeah, sleep would be great, but I think we murdered sleep, didn't we?* Harriet saw the absurdity of it too and we began to laugh. For a moment we were an ordinary couple, late at night, after a ghastly dinner party, collapsed in one another's arms, shaking with laughter. As it faded, we rocked together, seeking comfort: 'We are yet but young in deed.' It's the last point in the play when the Macbeths are together; they will both suffer terribly from now on, but apart. So it was good to discover a closeness at that moment.

Something goes wrong after her exit from the play.

I sense Shakespeare writing *Macbeth* in a single surge of inspiration; I see him sitting up for several nights in a row and it coming out in one beautiful dark, poisonous stream. The creative rush reaches its height with Lady Macbeth's sleepwalking scene, but with her gone, Shakespeare suddenly seems to run out of steam. And then the poor Macbeth actor is left to get through Act Five without all the aid formerly supplied by both his co-star and his author. It's just war scenes now, rather Marlowe-ish, the two sides gearing up, boasting and booming, lots of noise, not much depth. The 'Tomorrow and tomorrow' speech in the middle of it, yes, but what's the context?

We're working hard at that. We've nicknamed Macbeth's Act Five scenes the Bunker Scenes. And here our modern-dress production can help enormously. Macbeth has retreated to some hideaway – attic or basement – with the drunken Porter (taking Seyton's lines) and the Doctor, a crumpled establishment figure. Macbeth is dishevelled too, wearing the crown askew, enthroned on an old suitcase. We're suddenly in a scene by Beckett or Jarry, the war stuff just bleakly comic now, absurd.

Here now is a fitting context for 'Tomorrow and tomorrow'. Half-Führer, half-tramp, Macbeth can peer into the future with terrible nihilistic clarity.

So. Progress with one famous soliloquy. Which only leaves about a dozen still to crack.

You don't get there with Shakespeare. He just keeps changing the rules. I was sure I knew how to do soliloquies after *Winter's Tale*. I'd definitely solved it. No dreamy gazing into the middle distance, no introspection. You charge to the front of the stage, you crash through the fourth wall, you eyeball the audience, you *speak* to them.

It worked so well for Leontes. Surely it will for Macbeth?

Wrong.

Ringo Starr isn't Enoch Powell.

Macbeth isn't Leontes.

I thought they were so alike. Brothers? First cousins at least? Wrong again. Barely related at all.

Leontes goes mad – briefly – whereas Macbeth stays alarmingly sane. He never enjoys the wild, almost liberating oblivion that Leontes knows. Instead, Macbeth just keeps watching himself, increasingly appalled by what he sees. He's locked in a wrestling match within his own body; the limbs, the muscles of the man of action grapple constantly with the head, the great visionary brain, that gorgeous damaged imagination. A very different thing from what nests in Leontes's skull. I see Leontes's imagination as something painted by Bosch; it teems with horrid little sticky pink nudes. Macbeth's imagination is by Dali: elegant, epic pictures of lonely figures in empty landscapes – a newborn baby carried on the wind, one bloody hand turning the sea red, a queue of pointless tomorrows shuffling towards oblivion. Time. Time. He's obsessed with time. 'Time – thou anticipates my dread exploits!' he cries, as though he could still win this race. Right, he decides in this same speech, now I'll stop thinking, now I'll just *do* – now – now! The animal body, slowly perishing with every passing second, tries to keep up with the soul, bent on eternity.

The breakthrough with Macbeth's soliloquies came very late on. We were already in preview. I was rushing round the Swan stage, rushing at the audience – like Leontes – eyeballing them, virtually grabbing their lapels, demanding they listen to me. Adrian Noble came to one of those previews and said afterwards, 'You don't have to work so hard at the early speeches, y'know. The Swan is like a movie camera. We can see into your head. We can hear your thoughts.'

Cis Berry had been saying something similar in our one-to-one sessions: 'Macbeth's subconscious keeps floating up through what he's saying.'

And Greg was saying it too: 'Stop trying to *explain* the speeches.'

'I'm not,' I snapped defensively, 'I'm just trying to speak to the audience, actually speak to them. It's what we found in *Winter's*—'

'That was then. This is now. What you did with Leontes was engage us in his problem, urgently, you forced us to be his friend, his confessor. But Macbeth doesn't need that. He's at a much stranger, quieter, darker place inside himself. Inside that head of his, that imagination.'

'All right, so what do I do – tonight – what should I try?'

'Try doing nothing.'

At that night's preview I went very still for the early soliloquies. I let them happen to him, let them surprise him. 'Stars hide your fires,' he says quietly, amazed by what's coming to mind, almost amused. '. . . Let not light see my black and deep desires.' (*These black desires are deep – Jesus!*) He's shocked – and thrilled. It's forbidden territory – it's very private. He can't rush around telling the audience. He's too pole-axed by it himself, too excited, too frightened. He doesn't know what to do. He has to stop and think.

Think.

I've never played a character who thinks so much. That sounds ridiculous – we all think all the time – but Macbeth is on quite another plane. A man with an existential headache. Thinking, thinking. It's the clue to playing him. And why I found it so elusive. Until this show I'd always been better at behaving than thinking.

Macbeth is the most difficult part I've ever played and the most frightening. Maybe an overlap between the character and the actor. In the same way that Leontes's wild destructiveness resonated with something in my own psyche at the time, so both Macbeth and I seem 'cabin'd, cribb'd, confined with saucy doubts and fears'. The sensation which I'll always associate with Macbeth – real, icy fear in my blood as I wait to go on for my first entrance – this started in rehearsals, increased in previews and has never gone away. What is this – stage fright? For the first time in my career? Or is it good, helpful, *right*? We said we had to contact real fear for this play and in a way I've succeeded so well it's threatening to hijack the exercise.

I've always dismissed the idea of the actor taking the role home with him. But that was when I regarded acting as more about the casual dress of flesh than the visible soul. I'm less certain now. Now I'm sometimes aware of strange mind games when I'm on stage, a blurring of me and the role.

In fact, Shakespeare deliberately brings Macbeth and the actor face to face at the end of 'Tomorrow and tomorrow', when he makes you talk about life being like 'a poor player that struts and frets his hour upon the stage, and then is heard no more'. In case the actor minds saying this – maybe Burbage objected in the original production – Shakespeare then turns the spotlight on himself, the inadequate playwright: 'It is a tale told by an idiot, full of sound and fury, signifying nothing.' This is utterly bleak. The violence that Cis talks of – Shakespeare is turning it on himself, and the actor, and the audience. *What are we all doing here? This experience signifies nothing*.

In our production I climb off the stage at this point and for a moment almost abort the play.

I was getting there with Macbeth, but not in time for opening, I feared. There's no sketch of him in my rehearsal script – the first of these without a portrait of the role – I simply didn't know what he looked like. I mean, I had 'the look' we were using in the production – short hair, compact beard, unshaven jaws – but I didn't know who he was. I couldn't describe him. I'd always been able to describe the ones before, to explain, to sum up, to *draw* them: Richard, Shylock, Titus, Leontes. I couldn't this time. And we were about to open . . .

I knew Harriet was there, ready, with a great performance – and I'm not using the term with luvvie-like extravagance – I could see it, feel it when I was on stage with her. And I knew that Greg had done it too. I could see it again, at the Tech and the Dress. He'd achieved exactly what he set out to do. That tough imperative he set himself – 'inspired simplicity' – he'd done it. Brilliantly. You're not supposed to say that about your partner's work. Fuck it – I've got to the fuck-it point – I'll say what I want. Together with Stephen Brimson-Lewis's design, Tim Mitchell's lighting, John Leonard's soundscape and, above all, the music by Adrian Lee and his Japanese drummer Joji Hirota (the soul and pulse of the show), Greg has made an apparently empty black space teem with the world of the play. 'Come, thick night' says Lady Macbeth early on and this is what Greg has done in the Swan. No set changes, no furniture carried on and off (the banquet table is the first you'll see); scenes just created by stirring up the air, thickening the darkness, with smoke, with noise, with tapping, knocking, drumming – drumming above all, growing, growing, till the Swan itself becomes the drum – you're inside it now, you're trapped; you, the audience, are in the house where the murder is taking place; the characters are using the stairways around you, the passages and doors of the Swan auditorium, and you're forced to become a witness. Like it or not, you're accessories to the deed, you're complicit, you're involved, this is about you, about *us*.

In one of our early discussions I said to Greg, 'You're not a natural director for *Macbeth*. Whereas *Winter's Tale* had your name on it, this is like casting an actor against type. You keep talking about the darkness in the play but you haven't got the real stuff yourself, real darkness. It's why I love you. *Macbeth* will either defeat or reinvent you as a director.'

This led to one of our worst rows. It was too frank, Greg said, it was saying the unsayable. *You're not right for this – prove me wrong.* Actually, I don't think I even meant it as a challenge. Nothing as honourable as that. It just stemmed from a private worry – did I have the best director for *my* Macbeth? – built ironically on the idea that I was a natural for the role. He's one of Shakespeare's 'villains' – I can do those standing on my head – and it's a great meat eater of a part: just to my taste. Well, pride comes before a fall and here we are now, about to open: Greg has not only met my challenge but his own – 'inspired simplicity' – and here I am, staring at the blank spaces in my script, where normally there'd be a portrait by now . . .

We're coming to the end of the story and I favour a happy ending. I don't have to invent one luckily. *Macbeth* turned out successfully. For Greg, for Harriet, for everyone involved, including me. It was a good sign, I now believe, not being able to draw Macbeth's portrait. His face isn't important. What lies behind it is. His brain. 'Canst thou not minister to a mind diseas'd?' he asks the doctor towards the end. It's hurting by then, his brain is hurting. That's his journey, from a man whose imagination soars – with ambition – to a man cradling his hurting head. Macbeth is the dark actor's Hamlet. I'm buying into the cliché – Hamlet as a romantic blond figurine in the gift shops of Stratford – but it's what stopped me from ever having a go at the Danish prince. (Nonsense, of course, I see that now –

now that it's too late.) The thinking parts. I pictured these as boring. They're not. The insides of their heads race and leap faster than any show-off on crutches.

We scored nine out of ten in the reviews. We were described as the best production of the play since Trevor Nunn's. We played to sold-out houses in Stratford, Bath, Brighton, London, Tokyo and at the International Festival of Arts and Ideas, New Haven, Connecticut. The *New York Times* gave us the review of our dreams. It was so good we were immediately invited to transfer to Broadway. On that same day we heard news that Channel 4 wanted to film the production too. (We're not doing Broadway, we've done the film.) A cursed play? No – again and again – *no*. Instead I've come to see it as possessing a strange kind of luck – luck laced with danger – and actually this is the kind I know best. Much of my life has been ruled by what I can now call Macbeth Luck: a sense of angels and devils flying close together. The most extraordinary example of this happened on our return to London after the New Haven festival, where we'd just given the last stage performance of the play.

Sue Powell – an invaluable research assistant on my books – offered to come round and help sort the neglected mail. Passing through the dining room while we were working, Greg suddenly picked up one envelope. 'Shouldn't you look at this immediately?' he said. 'Surely this is important?' It was from the Foreign and Commonwealth Office. I opened it. As my eyes scanned the first few lines, I turned pale – according to Sue – then read it aloud to them:

Dear Mr Sher – It is with great pleasure that I write to inform you that, on the advice of the Secretary of State for Foreign and Commonwealth Affairs, Her Majesty the Queen has been pleased to appoint you to be . . .

I faltered here. Greg and Sue shouted as one: '*WHAT?*'

I looked up at them, dazed. 'It's a knighthood.'

I couldn't believe it. This was beyond my wildest dreams. And that's saying something. I am my mother's son, after all. Abandoning all cynicism about bringing prizes home, I rang Montagu House. 'You'd better sit down,' I said to Mom. 'I have extraordinary news.' She was beside herself with excitement. She couldn't eat her lunch. Confused, Katie thought it was bad news and began to cry. But then, even as I started telling the rest of the family, and even as they started raising cheers that I could hear without the aid of the long-distance connection, I felt increasingly puzzled about one thing. Why had this letter come from the Foreign and Commonwealth Office? I rang them to check. Well, it's because you're South African, they said. But I'm not, I said, I gained British citizenship in 1979. Did you? they said. Oh, dear. We've been misinformed, then, red faces all round. But in that case we're afraid . . .

They explained that the FO is empowered to grant a few special awards to resident foreigners – mine was to have been an Honorary Knighthood. But if this was to become the other kind – called, oddly, an Ordinary Knighthood – it was in the gift of a different department. It would have to go back to the committee room, back to the drawing board and the whole process could take a while. For now I should just disregard the letter, pretend it never happened. This news was almost more astonishing than the first. I'd been a knight for about an hour. It was like I'd been played a strange practical joke. Or taught a kind of lesson – about ambition. (As in a certain play, where the promise of unimaginable promotion comes out of the blue to tempt the protagonist.) I had to ring Mom back. 'You'd better sit down again,' I said. 'The knighthood's off.' Poor Mom. Now she and Katie cried together.

But with impressive speed – under a week – another letter arrived, this time from the Cabinet Office. Apologies all round again, but everything was sorted and now the news was unequivocally good. I was definitely to be made a knight. A kosher knight. An Ordinary Knight.

I rang Mom: 'The knighthood's back on!'

'Are you sure?' she said, 'because I don't think I can take much more of this.'

But it was true – Little Ant would be Sir Ant – incredible but true.

'Everyone's saying it's such a pity Dad isn't here for this,' Mom said next time we spoke, 'but I keep telling them that he *is*. Then I went to a "meeting" last night, and, sure enough, I was proved right. There's a party on the other side, I was told, with Dad and Esther and everyone. There's a party in heaven.'

'A party?' I said. 'Well, I just hope Dad found the local off-licence.'

All this lay in the future.

I knew none of it when *Macbeth* opened. I only knew that for the second time in one year Shakespeare had been good to me. And again I could boast in my diary:

Success smells like Stratford-on-Avon.

So when millennium night came round it was good, it was apt, to spend it in Stratford, in our Welcombe Road house. Just myself, Greg and his parents, John and Margaret. We watched TV, watched New Year arrive round the world – the illuminations on Sydney Bridge, the Eiffel Tower erupting with fireworks, an old man lighting a candle on Robben Island – and then finally it was our turn. The pictures were of the Dome, the Thames, Big Ben about to strike midnight. I can often feel like a stranger at times of public holiday in England, for ours were different in my childhood – either Jewish festivals or gruesome Uncle Nat anniversaries like Blood River – but we did do New Year's Eve. Well, we called it Old Year's Eve. And when I say 'we' I didn't actually participate personally. Mom and Dad usually went to a party, Randall and Verne went out with their friends, Joel was already asleep and I used to sit at the open window of my dark-walled bedroom, cradling Tickey (overcome by a shivering attack because of the fireworks), listening to the car horns blaring down the beach front and to choruses of singing coming from the surrounding blocks of flats.

Singing isn't my favourite thing, of course, but I couldn't avoid it on millennium night – there were only four of us in the room. Luckily we'd had a large glass of champagne by then – thank God for alcohol – so I put back my head and caterwauled: 'Should auld acquaintance be forgot . . .'

The next day we went for a walk along the Avon. A sunny afternoon, with yellow light in the long bare branches of the willow trees. Large numbers of people processing along the banks. Not much talking, the atmosphere very calm. A kind of relief. Here we were on the 1st of January in the year 2000 and planes hadn't fallen from the sky, electricity hadn't cut out, looters weren't rampaging through the streets. The only racket came from all the swans and geese. Assuming us New Year promenaders to be those coachloads of tourists who descend in the summer with cameras clicking and bags of yummies, the river-dwellers had given a collective squawk of 'Party time!' and now it was like being in one of the street markets of India, but with a floating army of beggars. The number of the birds has increased a hundredfold since I joined the RSC in 1982, and I suppose they would've been even fewer when I visited Stratford on my first ever weekend in England in 1968 to see a matinée of *King Lear*.

Did I stroll along the river that day, I wonder, pinching myself that I'm here, I'm actually here, I'm in England, I'm going to try auditioning for drama school, I'm going to try becoming an actor. Is my nineteen-year-old ghost walking past today, somewhere among the crowds and almost brushing shoulders? Is that why, gazing across to the theatre now, it still strikes me as incredible that I'm playing Macbeth over there? It turned out well. I glance at Greg. He's looking across the river too, at that big, ugly, magnificent building. Where he most dreamed of working. It turned out well. Him and me too – living and working together – it turned out well. Mustn't be complacent, though . . . oh, fuck it, let's be complacent . . . just for now. (It won't last.) For now I feel good, I feel at peace, imbued with the spirit of this holiday afternoon. We have another holiday coming up soon, in just a week's time, when *Macbeth* has a break from the repertoire. Then Greg and I will climb on to a plane and fly to South Africa – to say happy birthday to Mom and to try and bury Dad again.

INDEX

MOAB IS MY WASHPOT

Stephen Fry

'Stephen Fry is one of the great originals . . . This autobiography of his first twenty years is a pleasure to read,
mixing outrageous acts with sensible opinions in bewildering
confusion . . . That so much outward charm, self-awareness
and intellect should exist alongside behaviour that threatened to ruin the lives of innocent victims, noble parents and
Fry himself, gives the book a tragic grandeur that lifts it to
classic status'
Financial Times

'A remarkable, perhaps even unique, exercise in autobiography . . . that aroma of authenticity that is the point of
all great autobiographies, of which this, I rather think, is one'
Evening Standard

'He writes superbly about his family, about his homosexuality, about the agonies of childhood . . . some of his
bursts of simile take the breath away . . . his most satisfying
and appealing book so far'
Observer

'This is one of the most extraordinary and affecting
biographies I have read . . . Stephen is . . . painfully honest
when trying to grapple with his ever-present demons, and
often, as you might expect, very funny . . . I hope to goodness
they'll be a sequel. I can't wait for more'
Daily Mail

WHAT'S IT ALL ABOUT

Michael Caine

Michael Caine is the best-loved film actor Britain has ever produced. Here, for the first time, he reveals the truth about his childhood, his family and his hard-fought journey from London to Hollywood, bringing to life the lean years and the triumphs with astonishing candour. And with typical charm and humour he talks about the movies, about his relation-ships – on and off the screen – with other actors and directors, and about the memorable screen presence which is his hallmark.

'Written with just the right mix of warmth and candour, and in a prose style that is the literary equivalent of his easy-going, up-front persona, this is hugely enjoyable. A super book that informs as much as it entertains.'
Sunday Express

'It has taken two decades to get a man back on the Moon, and the man is Michael Caine. Niven's influence as a writer runs right through it . . . some genuinely vintage laughs'
Sheridan Morley, *Sunday Times*

'Caine gives his public value for money, covering his whole life with David Nivernish charm'
Sunday Telegraph

DEAR ME

Peter Ustinov

Peter Ustinov had his first acting lessons from a parrot, spent much of his childhood as a motor car, and played his first stage role as a pig (when his performance was deemed 'adequate'). Since then he has become the playwright, actor, author, designer, director, film star and entertainer *par excellence* so familiar to his world-wide public. He is also Sir Peter Ustinov Kt., CBE, Chancellor of Durham University, tireless worker and propagandist for UNICEF, and a thoughtful, philosophical citizen of the world.

Comic, controversial and full of anecdotes about the right and famous, Peter Ustinov's autobiography reveals a courageous and exquisitely funny man, engaged in a lifelong search for truth.

'Hugely enjoyable . . . written as if it were a collaboration between Jean-Jacques Rousseau and Groucho Marx'
Financial Times

'*Dear Me* is hilariously funny but underneath the clowning, which he admits is a method of survival, there is a shrewd and exceptional understanding'
Sunday Telegraph

'He writes both books and plays, he acts, he sings, he paints, he thinks, he cares. And he tells a very amusing story'
Daily Mirror

PARCEL ARRIVED SAFELY:
TIED WITH STRING

Michael Crawford

'Compelling . . . remarkably candid' *Daily Mail*

By turns hilarious, revelatory and desperately sad, here is the autobiography of the man whose successes such as *Hello Dolly!*, *Some Mothers Do 'Ave 'Em* and *The Phantom of the Opera* have made him a national institution.

The story of the true identity of his father, which is behind this book's title, leads into an evocative depiction of his tender childhood years. Whilst all the men were away at war, he was surrounded by loving women. For him this was an idyllic wartime childhood, but the return of the men in peacetime signalled darker times to come. Crawford's infectious enjoyment of stage work illumines his account of his early struggles to make a name for himself in the business, and his early failures with girls are lifted by his abiding sense of the absurd. Both in his private life and his work he begins a lifetime's habit of pratfalls that he would later turn to good use in the character of Frank Spencer in *Some Mothers Do 'Ave 'Em*.

Michael Crawford's talent for mimicry makes the great personalities in his life come alive on the page; people he has worked with, including Benjamin Britten who taught him to sing, John Lennon – with whom he shared a villa – and Oliver Reed, Michael Winner, Barbra Steisand, Gene Kelly and Frank Sinatra.

'A high-class act' Sheridan Morley, *Sunday Times*

'Entertaining . . . Crawford whips up the merriment from the wings' *Mail on Sunday*

'Refreshingly candid' *Express on Sunday*

OTHER TITLES AVAILABLE IN ARROW

☐	What's It All About?	Michael Caine	£6.99
☐	Parcel Arrived Safely	Michael Crawford	£6.99
☐	Natasha	Suzanne Finstad	£6.99
☐	Moab Is My Washpot	Stephen Fry	£6.99
☐	Still Me	Christopher Reeve	£6.99
☐	Clint Eastwood	Richard Schikel	£8.99
☐	Dear Me	Peter Ustinov	£7.99

ALL ARROW BOOKS ARE AVAILABLE THROUGH MAIL ORDER OR FROM YOUR LOCAL BOOKSHOP AND NEWSAGENT.

PLEASE SEND CHEQUE, EUROCHEQUE, POSTAL ORDER (STERLING ONLY), ACCESS, VISA, MASTERCARD, DINERS CARD, SWITCH OR AMEX.

☐☐☐☐☐☐☐☐☐☐☐☐☐☐☐☐

EXPIRY DATE .... SIGNATURE..

PLEASE ALLOW £2.50 PER BOOK FOR POST AND PACKING U.K.

OVERSEAS CUSTOMERS PLEASE ALLOW £1.00 PER COPY FOR POST AND PACKING.

ALL ORDERS TO:

ARROW BOOKS, BOOKS BY POST, TBS LIMITED, THE BOOK SERVICE, COLCHESTER ROAD, FRATING GREEN, COLCHESTER, ESSEX, CO7 7DW, UK

TELEPHONE: (01206) 256 000
FAX: (01206) 255 914

NAME ....

ADDRESS ....

....

Please allow 28 days for delivery. Please tick box if you do not wish to receive any additional information ☐

Prices and availability subject to change without notice.